UNSETTLED PAST, UNSETTLED FUTURE

The Story of Maine Indians

Neil Rolde

Camden, Maine

Down East Books

An imprint of Globe Pequot, the trade division of
The Rowman & Littlefield Publishing Group, Inc.
4501 Forbes Blvd., Ste. 200
Lanham, MD 20706
www.rowman.com

Distributed by NATIONAL BOOK NETWORK

British Library Cataloguing in Publication Information available

Library of Congress Cataloging-in-Publication Data

Names: Rolde, Neil, 1931-
Title: Unsettled past, unsettled future : the story of Maine Indians / Neil
    Rolde.Description Gardiner, Me. : Tilbury House, c2004.
Identifiers: LCCN 2003023041 (pbk) | ISBN 0884482553 (pbk)
Subjects: Indians of North America—Maine—History. | Indians of
    North America—Maine—Social life and customs. | Indians of North
    America—Maine—Land tenure.
Classification: LCC E78.M2 R65 2004 | 974.1004/97
LC record available at https://lccn.loc.gov/2003023041

TABLE OF CONTENTS

INTRODUCTION

$\mathcal{M}$y real-life encounters with bonafide North American Indians had their inception at a Seminole village in the Florida Everglades during a vacation visit to Miami Beach with my parents when I was no more than six years old. A Rolde family album contains a yellowing photograph (taken, no doubt, by a box Kodak Brownie camera, since this was 1937) showing a boy of the tribe and myself posed side by side. He was my size and most likely my age. Round-faced, black-haired, swarthy, shy, he displayed a stoic indifference to the indignity of needing to be a live tourist curio. As for myself, I retain absolutely no memory of the snapshot's occurring, although it obviously did, but I do keep memories of that long-ago trip. The Seminole native dress, blousy and brightly embroidered, has stuck as an image. Also, the incredibly loud racket made by angry captured rattlesnakes displayed in glass cages and, above all, the wrestling of alligators, done in pits, which ended with the giant reptiles tickled by long sticks and somehow lulled to sleep. One particular brawny wrestler was pointed out because he had lost a thumb, bitten off during an exhibition for the paying customers. I still remember my awe when he presented his hand for us to examine, minus its missing digit.

Memorable though the experience had been, it was but a snapshot, after all, a fleeting glimpse of America's exotica, lodged in the mind of a child. It had no more meaning to my life than the Negro shacks and barefoot piccaninnies in Spanish moss-hung settings I had gazed at out our car window on the drive back north. Colorful scenes like these could have been right out of a movie travelogue, yet their reality left me feeling—at age six, no less—that I had seen people in our country who were not merely different but somehow inferior.

After all, they were not living in nice brick or wooden clapboard houses on quiet, tree-lined streets the way my friends and I were growing up outside of Boston, Massachusetts. They were—well, sort of dirty and grubby, yet not like the poor Irish we had in the patches of slums in our town of Brookline. These alien guys seemed somehow permanently underprivileged, through skin color, if nothing else. Among whites, young as I was, I knew *we*, too, had serious cleavages. In our lace-curtain neighborhood, who was what was soon learned by every kid: whether you were Irish and went to the Catholic church or you were Jewish, or, in rare cases, Protestant. Prejudice? Not exactly. We all played together. But anti-Semitism was in the air, wafted from Europe, palpable even to a youngster, so I had my own worries. "Dirty Jew" was an epithet hurled at me on a playground more than once.

Early on movie Indians became part of our universe. I was probably five when I saw a film version of *The Adventures of Tom Sawyer and Huckleberry Finn* in which Injun Joe scared the living hell out of me. Most often, the Indians were the villains; in a few instances, Tonto-like, they helped the *good guys*. That they were fighters gave them a more respectable image than the Black folks who were kinder but mostly funny and silly.

Starting at the age of eleven, I went away to a summer camp in Maine where pageants based on Indian history were produced. Names like Osceola and Tecumseh emerged from these dramas with a halo of tragedy around them—"lost causes." A sense of perfidy by us Americans, even though we won, was tempered also by the memory of one of our counselors, Billy Hacker, wearing a cavalry uniform and burned at the stake in an ingeniously arranged stage production that left him hidden amid enough smoke to slip out of his bonds and disappear as the pole to which he'd been tied flared up in spectacular flames around a burlap dummy soon reduced to ashes.

I was sixteen and had outgrown summer camp when I met John Turner, the first Indian I ever spoke with at length. He was the owner of a lodge where a buddy of mine and I stayed in the Canadian North, on Ontario's Lake Timagami, the gateway to Hudson Bay. The impression I came away with was of a heavyset man, wise and dignified, conveying the quiet sense of leadership that even the movies associated with Indian chiefs.

A few years later, I had a glimpse of actual Indians in Maine.

Our air trip to Princeton, Maine, with my father was accomplished in a privately chartered three-seater plane, flying low over the seemingly interminable forests after leaving Bangor. Dad was taking me fishing at Grand Lake Stream. I was now a college senior, and while my intellectual curiosity was as finely honed as it would ever be, my mind, frankly, remained glued less to the surroundings than focused on the future vision of the resplendent land-locked salmon I dearly hoped to catch. Consequently, the glances I cast about me at the Indian shacks we passed after leaving Princeton's primitive airfield are to this day simply a blur, a vague impression of extreme poverty. I believe I learned on the spot that this rural slum was called "The Strip." Our head fishing guide, George Smith of nearby Springfield, had sent an assistant to pick us up and drive us to the lodge where we were staying. His comments on what we were seeing were laden with local anti-Indian prejudice, and that fact, rather than what he said, did register with me but not enough to overcome my obsession with imagined finny silvery beauties in the depths of deep, blue, lake waters. I had no idea that the tribal people we had driven quickly past were called the Passamaquoddy nor did I ask about them or think about them during those four or five days we were Down East in Washington County. There wasn't the slightest inkling then, in 1953, that I would ever return to Maine, except possibly for more vacations.

The scene cuts to 1966. By then I had learned that one of the Indian tribes in Maine was referred to as the Passamaquoddy, the other, the Penobscot. In fact, I found myself on Indian Island, the Penobscot reservation as a campaign aide to Kenneth M. Curtis, Maine's secretary of state, who was running for governor on the Democratic ticket. We were on a night visit to drum up Indian votes. The reception was friendly, enthusiastic, a carnival atmosphere in the glare of lights, and I can still recall the excited children trailing the candidate, and one in particular, a handsome, dark-eyed boy perhaps seven years old, trustingly putting his hand into mine and gently leading me about in the flow of the crowd. It seemed so different in tone from the welcomes experienced in other milieus during the election.

Ken Curtis won the election, and as one of his assistants, my experiences with Maine Indians began in earnest.

Michael Crawford's name, no doubt, has been lost to Maine history. Yet the record will show that he was the initial Maine Indian appointed (as deputy commissioner) to a position in the state's Department of Indian Affairs. Created in 1965 this agency, in its brief existence (until 1980), was something of another milestone—the first, and to date the only, official *state* body established to deal with the tribes within its jurisdiction. While my duties in the Curtis administration did not specifically enter these areas, I did know Mike Crawford, a bright, young, well-educated Penobscot. I well remember him sharing a frustration with me after he'd been on the job a relatively short time. Because of something he'd done, a petition from the tribe had been sent to Governor Curtis requesting him to fire Mike Crawford, signed by, among others, his own mother. I believe Ken ignored it, although I don't remember how long Mike stayed on the job.

It was, in all events, a time of extreme turmoil at the Department of Indian Affairs. That piece of history will be covered in detail later on, for it is an interesting run-up and background to the Maine Indian Land Claims Settlement, itself. The actual non-Indian commissioner, Ed Hinckley, to whom Mike Crawford was deputy, did not last long in office, due to his well-intentioned habit of overspending his budget in order to help the Indians, despite the dire warnings of a Republican-controlled legislature to curb his unauthorized spending. I have a vivid memory of Ken Curtis's stopping by my office one day to announce jubilantly that the crisis in the Department of Indian Affairs had been solved because Rodney

Scribner—ex-legislator, certified public accountant, and later finance commissioner and state auditor, and a Democrat whom even the most conservative Republicans saw as fiscally responsible—had agreed to replace Hinckley as Indian commissioner. I'm not sure the Indians were as enchanted, although Rod, one of the most decent persons I've ever known, treated them as fairly as he could. I recall equally as vividly when an Indian protest erupted in the statehouse and ended with a crowd of Penobscots and Passamaquoddy, in traditional dress, stuffed into my tiny office, sitting on the floor as we deliberated whatever the issue was.

Once Scribner left the position, he was followed after a short interval by John Stevens, the young Passamaquoddy governor, and another first—the first Indian to hold the post of commissioner of Indian Affairs. John Stevens, as we shall see, played a key role in the Maine Indian Land Claims Settlement activities that soon came to dominate Maine-Indian relations throughout the 1970s.

To me at the time, this seemingly interminable debate over the Maine Indian Land Claims issue was a matter of newspaper headlines, somewhere in my peripheral vision. I was—at least until I had to vote as a state representative on the legislation embodying the final settlement—primarily a bystander. However, in 1975, I was the house majority leader and, in that capacity, led the fight to pass an order introduced by Representative Judy Kany of Waterville to allow the two representatives of the Penobscot and Passamaquoddy tribes to occupy seats within the house chamber, itself. For forty years, they had been banished to stand—with lobbyists and others—behind the glass partition in the rear of the hall. After many previous tries, we finally made a victorious effort to have them seated in the 107th Maine Legislature. It was a ticklish experience for me as party leader since many of the most vociferous opponents to the measure were fellow Democrats. In subsequent legislatures, I again touched upon Indian matters as co-chair of the special Joint Select Committee on Alcoholism Services, where we gave money to groups battling alcoholism on the reservations and among the Micmac and Maliseet Bands in northernmost Maine. I also made friends with some wonderful folks who came to represent the tribes—Jim Sappier and Priscilla Attean of the Penobscots and Joe Nicholas of the Passamaquoddy—and tried to help them wherever I could.

The Maine Indian Land Claims dispute was still a distant, complicated court case, its political impact more on the federal level (for example, Bill Cohen unseated Bill Hathaway in the U.S. Senate race, largely on this issue) and hardly of immediate impact to a southern Maine state legislator until Legislative Document (LD) 2037—An Act to Provide for Implementation of the Settlement of Claims by Indians in the State of Maine and to Create the Passamaquoddy Indian Territory and Penobscot Indian Territory—came before us on April 3, 1980. Even then, since support for the bill was bipartisan and overwhelming, I merely pressed my green button in favor, as did the vast majority of my colleagues, and like them, didn't bother to read the thick legislative document put on my desk or think much about its implications. The problem had been settled, hadn't it?

Has it? It is now more than twenty years later and specific sore spots are occasionally still rubbed raw in relations between the state and the Maine Indians. The latest argument—a question of sovereignty—went not only to the top court in Maine—the state supreme court—but was also sent to the U.S. Supreme Court, which refused to hear it. The exact contention was whether or not private paper companies could under state law have Indian tribal records subpoenaed in a court case to which they were a party. No, said the tribes—that would violate our sovereignty.

Thus, *sovereignty* is often the crux of the matter in these sorts of wrangles, as it is, indeed, in many cases of conflict between Indians and various levels of government in the U.S. Because they were the first Americans, because the land was theirs by possession, the superimposition of a nation on top of their nationhood has fomented all sorts of trouble. The problem has been compounded to an extent by the legalistic heritage from England of the earliest settlers and the—at least voiced—devotion to democratic methods of the founders of our republic. Less fastidious conquerors of Indians abroad, such as in Brazil, simply wiped out the indigenous peoples they encountered. We were ruthless enough, but guilty consciences, no doubt, and lip service to Judeo-Christian ethics kept us from a completely totalitarian "final solution."

Conceivably, then, there is an answer to a puzzlement that some Maine people will express and that can be echoed throughout our country. Why is it that we fuss so much over such a small portion of our population? Why is there a whole body of law pertaining only to Indians when there are so many ethnic groups—many of them far larger—within our boundaries? The Amish, one could argue, are a tribe apart, unassimilated, but they never agitate the rest of us in any vaguely comparable fashion.

At one time, the leaders of the U.S. thought the Indians would go away, dissolve into the melting pot, and they undertook strong measures to accomplish that "civilizing," as they called it. They might have been arrogant enough to think of it as "Americanizing," except there could be argument over how much of "Americanizing" was beholden to "Native Americanizing." How much of our government, our landscape, our culture, our outlook, our literature, owes its special "American" flavor to the contributions, often extremely subtle and unheralded, of the interesting people who were on this continent for millenia before our first European forbears ever set foot here?

Today, the tone at least seems to be: let these people be themselves. As evidenced by the Maine Indian Land Claims Settlement their calls for justice for past wrongs can lead to heroic clashes. That a compromise outcome was reached in Maine does not mean—and never seems to in American politics—an end to the affair. So a look at what has happened since 1980 when the settlement of the largest Indian land claim until then in the continental U.S. was achieved is certainly in order, as is a full history of the tribes in Maine and their relation to the epic story of the Indians and non-Indians in the development of today's United States—and tomorrow's.

UNSETTLED PAST

UNSETTLED FUTURE

INDIAN LAW 101

$\mathcal{A}$s a befuddled paleface venturing forth into little-known territory—the study of Indian matters—with perhaps the same trepidation as that experienced by the hallowed pioneering forefathers of our American history books when they stepped gingerly into the wilds of a new continent (not my forefathers, incidentally, since mine came from Lithuania and Byelorussia in the late-nineteenth century), I had my baptism by fire, my first primer, my introduction to the subject of *Indian law* one evening in August 2001, not in Maine but in Massachusetts. Along with my wife, I attended an "Indian Law and Sovereignty" seminar at the Wampanoag Tribal Multi-Purpose Building on the island of Martha's Vineyard in a town I had always known as Gay Head, but whose name recently had been officially changed to its Indian designation of Aquinnah.

The lecturer was Robert B. Porter, professor of law and director of the Tribal Law and Government Center at the University of Kansas.

Several impressions whirled in my mind as we sat on our metal folding chairs and awaited the speech. of our presenter who stood facing us in the brand-new lecture hall.

Undeniably, this was a pretty spiffy edifice the Wampanoags had recently erected; I hadn't realized it was here, although I'd been visiting Gay Head as a summer resident for nearly fifty years. Since the entrance to the tribal complex was off the main road and the sign for it, chiseled on a large rock, none too visible, I'd initially driven by, having retained a mental image of the ramshackle, shingled building I'd gone to in the past. This thoroughly modern structure in which we were to hear Professor Porter, no doubt, owed its existence to the Wampanoag Settlement Act of 1987, referred to on the title page of the seminar outline, a copy of which had been laid out on each of the seats for the audience members. So here, too, was another *settlement,* like ours in Maine, that had led to new conditions for a tribe. Later, I learned that the Wampanoags and the Maine Indians had had the same lawyers—and the same arguments.

Professor Porter also made an impression on me. Physically tall, thin, gangly, even gawky, he looked every bit like a dressed-up Kansan farmer in his plain black suit, white shirt, and somber tie. Yet we soon learned he was an Iroquois whose hometown was Salamanca, New York, and the Alleghany Indian Reservation, not far from the Pennsylvania border.

Described in the syllabus as "a citizen of the Seneca Nation of Indians (Heron Clan)," he had his B.A. from Syracuse in political science and economics, his J.D. from Harvard, and had spent time in private practice focused on corporate law with a Washington, D.C., law firm. Then, he had become the first *attorney general of the Seneca Nation of Indians,* and his curriculum vitae went on to state that in addition to his present post in Kansas, he was also *chief justice of the Sac and Fox Nations of Missouri's supreme court.* His course listings at the Tribal Law and Government Center included "Sovereignty, Self-Determination and the Indigenous Nations," "Tribal Laws and Process," and "Federal Indian Control Law." He was also the author of publications such as *Strengthening Tribal Sovereignty Through Peacemaking: How the Anglo-American Legal Tradition Destroys Indigenous Societies* and *Legalizing, Decolonizing, and Modernizing New York State's Indian Law.*

In perusing the seminar outline before the talk started, I noted concepts and terms that struck me as unusual, if not alien, to a non-Indian American. *An attorney general of the Senecas!?* States had attorneys general as we called ours in Maine government. The U.S. had an attorney general. And the Senecas did, too! And the Sacs and Foxes in Missouri— they had a supreme court! I was looking at its chief justice! One wanted to blink a few times over this idea. Then, those terms that leapt out of the cold print of the course listings and scholarly publications—*sovereignty*, again and again, and *self-determination* and *decolonizing* and *indigenous nations,* and even *genocidal acts*—made me realize something I never had given any thought to before—that a whole corpus of legal history and precedent could be summed up into a codification entitled "New York State's Indian Law," which presupposed Indian law for every state and the United States federal government, as well.

I noted also that the outwardly bland academic lesson plan of Professor Porter was comprised of a vocabulary that seemed at times to scorch the very pages on which it was written.

Take, for example, Porter's use of "Anglo-American." We consider Indians "Native Americans." Tit for tat, they are looking at us "whites" as also just another entity, with the term Anglo-Americans standing not only for those folks who came on the *Mayflower,* or before and after, denizens of Devonshire, East Anglia, Scotland, Ulster, etc., but also for a guy like me whose roots stretch back to the *stetls* of eastern Europe. German, Greek, French, Portuguese, whatever—if you're Caucasian, you're Anglo-American and no better than anyone else; indeed, maybe worse in the aggregate, as an innate oppressor.

Some other indigenous publications I was to come upon later used the term Euro-American, a tad more accurate but no less pejorative.

We "whites" were certainly taking it on the chin in Professor Porter's course material. Referring to his belief that "indigenous and non-indigenous peoples have different perspectives on Indian law and sovereignty," he declared straight out that each perspective was shaped by colonialism and that the threat of American colonization had "many faces," driven by forces that he named as: greed, fear, hatred, paternalism, assimilation, and (one that really raised eyebrows) equality.

A quote from a famous law case, *U.S. v. Kagama* (1886) was interjected:

Because of local "ill-feeling" against indigenous people, the people of the states where they are found are often their deadliest enemies.

Professor Porter's prose was thick and fast with references to other landmark court decisions studded with names that resonate, no doubt, with legal historians and specialists in this area of law, while no doubt reaching out to more generalist American historians, too. Names such as the unforgettable *Worcester v. Georgia,* a victory for the Cherokees in the U.S. Supreme Court that nevertheless failed to forestall the doom of a southeastern tribe that was once secure and prosperous and *civilized* in its native homeland.

The titles of these bygone dicta from our American legal system were redolent of mystery, making one wonder who such litigants actually were, like *Oliphant* who squared off against *Suquamish,* or *Johnson* who fought *McIntosh,* and what in God's name they were squabbling about. Research into these matters, I found, unearthed stories as fascinating as fictional tales, yet real-life, or as real-life as lawyerese allowed them to be.

But back to Professor Porter's points.

The field of "Indian law," he said, is comprised of three elements: Indian tribal law; federal Indian control law; international law governing the rights of indigenous peoples (another eyebrow raiser).

Indian tribal law included tribal constitutions, tribal statutes and resolutions, tribal judicial decisions, and even unwritten tribal laws, mirroring the vast body of law of the greater U.S. society. Still, he emphasized, more as an unstated gibe, this same greater society, through the United States government and court system, will intervene, insisting on approving some Indians' laws, or not recognizing their assertions of their own laws.

Thus, we have *federal Indian control law,* which Porter described as the "American Constitution, treaties, statutes, regulations, executive orders, judicial decisions, and administrative decisions." For some reason, possibly to avoid complicating the matter, he does not mention state law, often an area of conflict with Indian law that has had dramatic ramifications in Maine.

Following a nod to *international law,* an "emerging area" that tries to define the rights of indigenous people around the world, Porter discussed how federal Indian control law has continually tried to limit the scope of tribal sovereignty."

Porter's question: "What's the source of federal power over Indian affairs?" was answered by two concepts or "invented legal doctrines" which he called the *Plenary Power Doctrine* and the *Discovery Doctrine.* The former says that the U.S. Constitution holds the ultimate power of decision in the United States and the latter states that the United States received its power over Native Americans by virtue of its British predecessor's alleged discovery of the land and the U.S.'s own eventual assumption of Great Britain's power, which it extended across the continent. Porter commented tersely: "It is clear that force, rather than law, is the basis for these doctrines."

Matters of jurisdiction and taxation entered into the seminar outline, too, and finally the more recent phenomenon of Indian gaming and how it is to be regulated under federal law through the Indian Gaming Regulatory Act of 1988.

A blessing, led by a tribal member speaking in both Wampanoag and English while everyone in the audience held hands, had started off the talk. Despite the prickly if not fiery rhetoric in the packet of papers Porter had provided us, his tone of voice had a soft, dispassionate quality I'd heard from other Indian speakers, masking deeply buried feelings of hurt and anger held for generations, or so it seemed to me.

Damning statistics could be delivered in the calmest of voices. For example, at the time of contact with the Europeans, there were 7 to 20 million Indians in North America, but by 1900 there were only 200,000; and 50,000 Indian lives had been lost in warfare. Potentially flammable statements came out minus a note of rancor. For example: *"The history of*

American colonialism vis-à-vis Indians is a history of the loss of Indian land"; or more baldly: *"The United States is a threat to Indians,"* but he also allowed that his own Senecas had not been angels, either, and had wiped out other tribes.

It was in the context of historic patterns of U.S. government attempts to answer the question of, "What do we do with the Indians?" that the concept of sovereignty was analyzed. *Paternalism, assimilation,* and *termination* all related to Bureau of Indian Affairs (BIA) policies in the past which were seen as impinging on that magic word, *sovereignty.* As Porter had written, "Absent sovereignty, indigenous people cannot survive." They become, in his words, "a mere ethnic group within the dominant society." To give non-Indians an understandable analogy, he showed how the North American Free Trade Agreement (NAFTA) had actually chipped away and possibly undermined *U.S. sovereignty* by requiring that we surrender some of our rights in the economic sector.

A more "aggressive" threat to Indian sovereignty, according to Professor Porter, was from the *states* in which tribes were located. In these smaller venues, the feelings were more intense, he argued, and his first example was his own hometown of Salamanca, New York, whose downtown area had been leased from the Seneca tribe by local merchants since 1892. When their leases ran out in 1991 and were re-negotiated from ridiculous sums of $1 to $3 a year to a still low $200 a year, there was a huge outcry and actual murmurs of possible violence against the Native Americans.

Corporations and individuals have always been a threat to Indian sovereignty, Professor Porter continued, citing the settlers and companies who squatted on Indian lands in the old days, never respecting boundaries that had been mutually established by treaty. And finally, Porter saw Indians, themselves, as threats to their own sovereignty, with specific respect to a tendency they have to quarrel among themselves.

In contradiction to a general belief that Indians never had laws—but only myths, legends, folkways, etc. until the white man came—Professor Porter maintained that Indians did have codes of law. "We were smarter. We didn't write them down. We memorized them." This sample of wry Indian humor was then followed by a disquisition on other components of Indian law, including the recent development of international law covering the rights of indigenous peoples, currently comprising 5,000 to 6,000 groups around the world. In the U.S., alone, 700 groups claim to be Indian tribes. Many are not officially recognized by the U.S. and not just because they're small. The Lumbees of North Carolina, 60,000 strong, have never been officially recognized. The Maine tribes, for most of their existence, also were denied official federal recognition, although early on, shortly after the American Revolution, they received financial help from Washington. Until 1924 Indians throughout our country were not U.S. citizens, and in Maine, the right to vote in certain state and local elections was not granted to Indians until 1967. The notorious "termination era" of the late 1940s and early 1950s was an attempt to end recognition of Indians as Indians. More than seventy tribes were cut loose, but since then many of them have had their recognition re-instated, the most famous being the Menominees of Wisconsin.

As I sat listening to this learned gentleman from Kansas by way of Salamanca, New York, I kept searching in my own mind for a means to connect this body of knowledge to what I knew of the history of our own tribes in Maine. For it was through the medium of present-day law that the Indians of Maine had received redress for the loss several centuries ago of their land. I was swimming in facts and buzz words—"trust land," "Indian Country," "IGRA, the Indian Gaming Regulatory Act," "Indian Reorganization Act of 1934," "plenary power," "allotment," "Indian Commerce Clause," and finally, "Settlement Act."

The latter, yes, that had to do with Maine—the Maine Indian Land Claims Settlement Act, decided in 1980, had been an earthquake in our state, with seismic repercussions throughout the land.

Professor Porter was still on his theme of explaining sovereignty, stating boldly that sovereignty could be taken away from tribes because under the setup of rules and regulations that had grown like topsy since 1783, the Congress of the United States had the ultimate sovereignty—in other words, power—to decide Indian fate.

Following which, when he brought up the subject of *settlements* —those acts that subjected tribes to state and local jurisdiction, as well as federal fiat—up jumped one of the audience, a young man who looked more Irish than Indian, and in a loud, strong Boston accent decried the rich summer residents in the town of Aquinnah who were raising a fuss because they objected to the looks of a pump house the tribe intended to install for the shellfish hatchery it was constructing on its own land. That land, I was soon to ascertain, had been won in almost a mirror image, but miniaturized, version of the momentous agreement reached seven years earlier in Maine. Instead of $81 million in federal funds that the two northern tribes in Maine received, the locals in Massachusetts accepted $2,250,000 from the Commonwealth to buy land in what was then still called the town of Gay Head. In return, they dropped all claims that might have clouded titles to property within the affected area.

As Maine goes, so goes the nation. That old political expression, born of the fact that Maine voted two months before the rest of the country in all but presidential elections, was my automatic thought. A trail had been blazed Down East, so to speak, in the torturous area of Indian land claims in the U.S. Tom Tureen, the lawyer for the Penobscots and Passamaquoddy, wrote that this victory was the "greatest for any of the American Indians in the history of the U.S." How did it all happen? The transformation of these poor Wampanoag Indians was patently evident in our cushy surroundings that night, as was a similar phenomenon of change when I'd visited the Penobscots on Indian Island in Old Town, Maine, or the Passamaquoddy at their two reservations in Washington County, Maine, and so the only question left was: How much had *really* improved since their days of utter poverty and near invisibility?

Was the Indian problem "solved"?

I hardly thought so.

Back to Maine, then, back to the early 1960s, to the dawn of an unimaginable turn of events whose origins lay hidden in those dusty tomes of Indian law piled up on library shelves, awaiting the occasional use of legal specialists and academics. Dry words, ancient logic, and unremembered legislation were about to be put to use after the untoward sound of axe blows was heard one winter day on the forest edge of an exceedingly remote corner of the Pine Tree State.

2

PRELUDE

*T*he noise of a white man cutting wood on Indian land was not exactly an unusual event in Washington County, Maine. The perpetrator in this instance, one William Plaisted, had owned tourist cabins located long enough on the Indian Township "strip" at Princeton that they—and he— were a fixture. The State of Maine, decades earlier, had run its Route 1 right through the reservation and, in the process, leased out Passamaquoddy property to non-Indians (999-year contracts) as a way to help finance the thoroughfare. On this particular day, however, Plaisted was far beyond his boundary line, busily felling trees.

His activity drew the attention of a Passamaquoddy named George Stevens who lived nearby. Waiting until his brother John, the elected governor of Indian Township, came home from work at the Georgia-Pacific Paper Company, George brought the tribal leader to Lewey's Lake where the clearing of trees was taking place.

It was the kind of outrage the local Indians had suffered in silence for generations, and it had effectively lopped off 6,000 acres of the 23,000 acres left to them after a treaty with the Commonwealth of Massachusetts in 1794. That it turned out to be a final straw, or at least the beginning of a resistance to having their rights so casually trampled upon, may have been due to Plaisted's arrogance. When challenged by the Stevens brothers, who pointed out he wasn't on his own land, he declared airily that, on the contrary, he had just won this piece of property from another lessee in a poker game.

Satisfied that these passive Indians would have to be content with his pronouncement, he went on chopping, ignoring John Stevens's admonition to stop his work.

Then, laying out stakes to mark his bounds, Plaisted made the mistake of planting a stick in the backyard of a shack in the vicinity. Out rushed an elderly and angry Passamaquoddy woman with a shotgun and ordered him to "Git."

Plaisted did, but his hasty retreat was hardly the end of the affair.[1]

On Plaisted's part, the lucky poker player decided to bulldoze a driveway into the territory he claimed. The Passamaquoddy, led by their tribal governor, John Stevens, and the tribal council, countered by driving to Augusta, the state capital, to vent their grievance to Governor John Reed, who had seemed sympathetic to them since assuming his post in 1959.

Maine is a large state geographically, the largest in New England, but it has often been called "one great big small town." To expect to see the governor on short notice on a matter of considerable urgency is not as unthinkable as it might be elsewhere. The Passamaquoddy delegation had traveled a long way, and Reed eventually did see them—that is, after having them wait for half a day. He then told them there was nothing he could do since it was strictly a local matter. The way home must have seemed even longer to John Stevens and his companions.

Yet there was something in the air, something of that rebellious Zeitgeist of the 1960s, that kept this disappointing performance of the state's highest official from being simply another put-down of Indians, another defeat, another reason for staying sunk in apathy or alcohol. John Stevens had been a U.S. Marine. He had served in Korea. This was 1964. The previous November, Jack Kennedy had been assassinated. The inspiring, charismatic young president's message of hope for the downtrodden had penetrated into the farthest corners of the globe and had certainly reached this lost corner of rural Maine. Lyndon Johnson was already preparing to use the JFK heritage and martyred memory to promote the "Great Society" and its myriad social betterment programs. Martin Luther King's revolution in civil rights was already making its mark in the South. Although the major events of Native-American activism still lay ahead, like the takeover of Alcatraz, the battle at Wounded Knee, and the sit-in at the Bureau of

Indian Affairs, the Maine tribes were feeling the restlessness in the country. A harbinger of those wider future struggles was initiated by a small knot of Passamaquoddy men and women who undertook to stand in front of William Plaisted's hired bulldozer and block his attempt to build a road on land they considered their own.

In short order they were arrested by the Maine State Police—at least eight of them were, four men and four women, who had stayed on picket duty while the others had gone for lunch.

Their need for a lawyer, it could be argued, led to a denouement as starkly unexpected and yet as ineluctable as that in an ancient Greek drama, as if the Fates, looking down at them, directed the show for maximum surprise, stagecraft, and suspense.

Certainly, the lawyer they chose, Don Gellers, an émigré to far-off Maine from Brooklyn and a graduate of Columbia Law School, was right out of Broadway or even Hollywood. But he was the only attorney willing to take their land claims case, and they had been trying for years to find a member of the legal profession who would.

Tom Tureen, who was to succeed Gellers as the Passamaquoddy lawyer, has described to me his first meeting with this eccentric transplant from the Big Apple. It occurred in the thirty-two-room mansion that Gellers acquired in Eastport. Tom describes entering the empty, unlocked dwelling for an appointed meeting after vainly knocking, hearing a voice answer his hellos with a cry of, "I'm in the bath!" and finally looking up to see a grand, bug-eyed figure descending a staircase in a velour robe, fingers stained yellow by tobacco (and marijuana, it seems). By this time, Gellers had fallen into a self-imposed decline. Deep into drugs and sex, his "knockout of a Eurasian wife" having left him, he had become a sort of a Down East "Mistah Kurtz," the fabled personification of evil depicted in Joseph Conrad's *Heart of Darkness*.

Donald Cotesworth Gellers, which he insisted on pronouncing with a J (and the Cotesworth he had simply made up), was, in Tom Tureen's words, "as weird and perverted and demonic as anyone I've ever met."

Nevertheless, when he took on the Passamaquoddy's case in 1964, he became an instant hero to the tribe, even if his hippyish ways struck sparks among the conservative, provincial folks in Washington County. For example, he appeared in Judge John Dudley's court in bedroom slippers. But more importantly, he talked back to the local authorities and fought fiercely for his Indian clients. In dealing with the Plaisted complaint, Gellers went so far as to have the first assigned judge disqualified since he had helped Plaisted draw up deeds to the land in question. Moreover, Gellers also took on Hiram Hall, the local white Indian agent appointed by the state who had become a despot roundly hated by the tribal people. The New Yorker had the temerity to haul the agent into court, alleging he had expropriated money from his charges. Hall, totally unused to being challenged, never mind subpoenaed, suffered a heart attack the same day he was served, and promptly died.

Another happenstance at this time soon moved this dramatic plot along to a higher level of tension. The old widow of a former tribal governor found an ancient document among his effects, thought it was important, and took it to John Stevens, who eventually delivered it to Don Gellers. It was an original copy of the 1794 treaty that had deprived the Passamaquoddy of most of their land, yet clearly had given them the 23,000 acres of Indian Township *in perpetuity.* Not only was Gellers able to use this evidence to have William Plaisted's case thrown out—in blocking him, *the Passamaquoddy really had been on their own land and weren't breaking the law*—but he also saw a way to recover those purloined 6,000 acres that had been deducted from their property one way or another over the years.

In his 1993 book, *Revolution Downeast,* Bates College historian James Leaman indicates that the impetus for the 1794 Massachusetts treaty with the Passamaquoddy came from the tribe, itself. Since they and their close relatives the Maliseets had essentially backed the Americans in the Revolution, the postwar period after 1783 found them in a ticklish position, with lands in Nova Scotia (which then included New Brunswick) falling under the jurisdiction of the British and American Loyalist émigrés who were decidedly hostile to them. Furthermore, the border, itself, had not been adjudicated in this region and settlers from Massachusetts and other New England states were flooding into the area. Wholesale land speculators like Henry Knox and William Bingham were buying up literally millions of acres in northern and eastern Maine. Consequently, as Leamon writes, the Indians "petitioned the General Court [the Massachusetts Legislature] for a grant of land in Maine on which to settle in exchange for surrendering their rather shadowy claims to other lands in the District [of Maine]."[2]

Their go-between in this effort was their wartime commander, Colonel John Allan, a seminal figure in Revolutionary War fighting and politicking Down East, a Yankee patriot who wasn't a Yankee, but Scottish-born of a distinguished military family, and a refugee driven out of Nova Scotia with a price on his head because of his pro-American views. As federal superintendent of the eastern Indians, appointed by George Washington himself, and the Continental Congress, Allan had kept the tribes on the side of the rebels and helped prevent the British from conquering all of Down East Maine. One way he had kept their allegiance was to promise them the supplies they needed for themselves and their families, but once the war was over, Congress decided not to continue this expense. Unable to find succor from the feds for the desperately poor Passamaquoddy, Allan turned to Massachusetts. Since the Commonwealth was selling its lands in the District of Maine and anxious to acquire more to sell, the Scotsman persuaded the general court to appoint him to a three-person commission to negotiate a sale.

The other two men with Allan had been comrades-in-arms in the Down East fighting: General Alexander Campbell, head of the Washington County Militia, and Militia General

George Stillman, an early resident of Machias.

A final settlement between Massachusetts and the Passa-maquoddy Tribe was signed on September 29, 1794, by the three one-time military men and seven Indian leaders, includ-ing "Governor" Francis Joseph Neptune, a hero of the Battle of Machias.

According to the wording on the treaty document: "said Indians relinquishing all their rights, title, interest, claim, or demand on any land, or lands, lying and being within the Commonwealth of Massachusetts..." would receive in return "the following tracts of land, lying and being within the Commonwealth of Massachusetts, viz...."

Whereupon, a detailed description was laid out of the property the Indians were safely to call their own, primarily Township 2, Range 1, "containing 23,000 acres more or less," as surveyed by Samuel Titcomb in 1794, plus ten acres at Pleasant Point, which the "committee," (i.e., Allan, Campbell, and Stillman) had bought from a certain John Frost. In addi-tion, the Passamaquoddy were to have all the islands in the Schoodic River between the falls at head tide and the falls where the river branched, fifteen in all, several other islands in the vicinity of Nemcass Point, plus fifty acres for a setting-down place at a portage in Lubec, and hunting, fishing, and fowling privileges.

Massachusetts solely reserved the rights in these donated lands to all pine trees suitable as masts (generally 24 inches in diameter or more) for which they would nevertheless pay the Indians compensation, and also stipulated that 100 acres was to be set off for John Baptiste la Cote, "a French gentleman now settled among said Indians," an arrangement to which the Passamaquoddy presumably agreed. Otherwise, all "the said islands, tracts of land, and privileges were to be confirmed to said Indians and their heirs forever."

That familiar-sounding last paragraph of Indian treaties, honored so often in the breach, was now the subject of Don Gellers's litigation. His target, however, was not the State of Maine, the entity that had assumed the Commonwealth's obligations when breaking away to become a separate state in 1820, but Massachusetts, itself, the original party to the deal. Speaking of this strategy long afterward, Tom Tureen saw the decision as a big mistake, in fact almost an instance of legal malpractice. Be that as it may, Gellers, hired by the tribe in May 1964, then sub-hired John S. Bottomley of Boston, a Massachusetts attorney, to try the case in a Bay State court. Yet four years lapsed before the case was actually entered in Suffolk County superior court as *Equity v. the Commonwealth of Masssachusetts*. Much research had been gathered in the interim, and twenty-four separate wrongs were cited, and a substantial amount of restitution, $150 million, demanded.

Among the complaints were:

"That Massachusetts shouldn't have set up the State of Maine as a way of getting out of the treaty."

"That the Passamaquoddy never gave their consent to Maine's being made into a separate state."

"That Massachusetts account for what was done with $37,471.03 that Massachusetts agreed it owed the Indians at the time, together with interest, and that Massachusetts be ordered to pay back accrued interest."

"That Massachusetts be asked for damages for all the trees cut over the years on Passamaquoddy Treaty Lands [except, presumably, the reserved mast trees]."

By the late 1960s the re-awakened spirit of Indian activism in the United States, having made its way into Maine, resulted in, among other things, a *Maine Indian Newsletter*, published in mimeograph form by a Penobscot woman named Eugenia Thompson, who preferred to be known by her Indian name of ssipsis ganesahoway (*ssipsis*=little bird; *ganesahoway*=she carries a big rock). Volume 2, Part 1, issued in February 1968, devoted a good deal of its issue to Gellers's litigation. In reply to a previously printed attack on Gellers by a non-Indian, the point was made: "Some people disapprove of Don Gellers, but even they must admit until he came along, no one has been as involved as he has with the problems of the Passamaquoddy Indians. It is time someone got this involved."[3]

John Stevens was quoted that he felt "damned good" about the lawsuit. "A long time ago, we sold Massachusetts a whole lot of real estate and they never paid us. We think they're going to have to now.... This is the first real claim we've had and we're thankful for it."

A set of dates now becomes important to this part of the story. On Friday, March 8, 1968, Bottomley, once an assistant attorney general under Edward Brooke, the African-American who went on to become a U.S. senator, filed his claim. Brooke's successor, another famed Massachusetts Republican, Elliot Richardson, had until May 27 to file his answers.

On Monday, March 12, 1968, four days after the filing, Donald Cotesworth Gellers and a companion, Alfred Cox, were arrested in the Eastport mansion by the Maine State Police for possession of marijuana. Calling his arrest "an obvious frame-up," Gellers proclaimed his innocence and posted bond. Tom Tureen, in a later sardonic turn of phrase, said that Gellers had made it a crusade of his to convert Indians (and others) to marijuana to help out with the problem of alcoholism, but there appeared to be some truth to that glib, lawyerly protestation of police manipulation. Allegedly, Gellers was first approached in his home by a tough Passamaquoddy named Danny Bassett who brought with him an even tougher-looking gent, obviously armed, whom he introduced as a hit man from the Patriarca mafia mob in Rhode Island. Since Gellers had been dallying with Bassett's wife, he was understandably nervous, but the Indian declared he was willing to forgive Gellers all his sins for $200 and some marijuana joints. Such was provided and more marijuana delivered by Gellers the next day, when the trap was sprung and the "hit man" was revealed to be a Maine State Police detective.

Eventually, Gellers was convicted, as was "Al" Cox, described as the "only black man in Washington County at the time." Cox did time at the state prison in Thomaston. Gellers, on the other hand, skipped bail, leaving his former secretary,

Charley Lewis, who'd pledged his house for him, in danger of almost losing his home. This Columbia Law School graduate, known for his drug use, his involvement with hippies and other people's wives, and who, it has been claimed, insisted on the J pronounciation of his surname and a fictitious Cotesworth middle name in order to appear less Jewish, fled to Israel to escape imprisonment.

The Passamaquoddy land claim, lingering in a Massachusetts court, was assuredly among the least of his worries.

NOTES

[1] My old prep school classmate, Paul Brodeur, in his book *Restitution,* taken from his *New Yorker* stories, has a slightly different version, the first contact being with a Passamaquoddy hired by Plaisted, and wielding a chain saw. The present version of the confrontation follows *Tribal Assets* by Robert H. White, New York: Henry Holt and Co., 1990.

[2] James S. Leamon, *Revolution Downeast,* Amherst, MA: The University of Massachusetts Press, 1993. Page 219.

[3] *Maine Indian Newsletter,* Volume 2, Part I, page 11.

3

The Real Land Claims Case Develops

$\mathcal{E}$d Hinckley, Maine's commissioner of Indian Affairs, apparently had no use for Don Gellers. John Stevens was to accuse Hinckley, who was generally considered very pro-Indian, of wanting to discredit Gellers and have him replaced. Indeed, half a year before the famous marijuana bust, Hinckley had written to the American Indian Rights Association, a Washington, D.C., public interest law firm which then employed Gellers, with complaints against the Eastport lawyer. Any Passamaquoddy defender, the commissioner made it known, in his opinion should not be someone from "Away," but someone from state government.

In the final analysis, the "white knight" who eventually surfaced after Gellers's disappearance and turned the orphaned case in Suffolk County superior court into a genuine tour de force was young Tom Tureen, originally a student intern for Don Gellers, paid $40 a week to do research on the Massachusetts litigation and to serve as an emissary to the outside world for his boss, who'd become almost a total recluse.

Two years later, following his senior year at George Washington Law School, Tom Tureen came back to Eastport. Through John Stevens he learned that a position had opened in Pine Tree Legal Services, the Maine version of the federal Great Society program of free legal help to the poor.

At first the youthful pro-bono lawyer was enmeshed primarily in typical cases that pro-bono poverty lawyers usually handle. He helped close down the local Eastport jail since it had no individual cells allowing privacy but only a holding tank where females (sometimes Indian females) were lumped in with males. Another case he won was to gain back 100 acres of private land owned by a Passamaquoddy named Christie Altvater, from whom it had been taken by the town of Perry for non-payment of taxes in a sloppy legal action easily overturned. Meanwhile, the Gellers land claims suit remained in limbo in Massachusetts.

After about a year of cogitating upon it, Tom found himself assailed by a number of vexing questions. Primary among them was a query also being asked at the time by Maine public officials, including Governor Kenneth M. Curtis: Why weren't the Passamaquoddy and Penobscot tribes receiving any federal benefits? In his quest for answers, Tom came to the conclusion that the Passamaquoddy (his clients) were eligible. They were clearly an Indian tribe; they were living on Indian land; and federal services were being given to tribes who were living on Indian land or land held in trust for them by the federal government or land that was restricted by the feds from being "alienated" (i.e., sold).

This concept of "restricted" land then led Tom to a piece of legislation passed by Congress soon after the national government re-organized itself under the U.S. Constitution. This was the Indian Trade and Intercourse Act of 1790.

What this statute succinctly said was: *Any land transaction by any Indian or Indian tribe after 1790 had to be ratified by Congress or it would not be valid.* Tom knew that 1794 was the date of the Passamaquoddy–Massachusetts treaty, and that it hadn't been okayed in D.C. Therefore, the next puzzler in his mind was not so much vexing as startling: "Wasn't the Passamaquoddy claim in Suffolk County superior court based on a treaty that was inconsistent with federal law, having occurred after 1790 and never having been ratified by Congress!?"

In legalese, this made the document null and void *ab initio,* meaning it had "no value at law or equity." This meant, too, that the Passamaquoddy had a claim—generating a truly startling thought—they still owned the land and could evict anyone who now lived on it and collect damages and rent for all those years.

What land was in contention? Not just the 6,000 acres being claimed in the Massachusetts court, Tom soon figured. No, it would be for everything they had given up in the 1794 treaty. When, soon afterward, it was realized that the Penobscot treaties with Massachusetts and later Maine had all come after 1790 and these, too, had never been ratified by the U.S. Congress, the sum total acreage being contested amounted to two-thirds of the land area of the State of Maine!

We seldom appreciate or study what a task it was to create the United States of America and its government from scratch. The Articles of Confederation held us together for awhile, after John Adams, John Jay, and Benjamin Franklin, the negotiators for the thirteen American states speaking as one, signed a treaty of peace with the United Kingdom in Paris, France, on September 3, 1783. Not present, however, was another warring party—those Indian tribes, like the Iroquois or the Wyandot or the Cherokee, who had allied themselves with the British and, in actuality, were at least technically still engaged in hostilities with the fledgling United States.

Their potential belligerency, and the certainty of pressure from Americans to move into their territories, worried George Washington greatly and prompted the first Congress under the Articles of Confederation to create a committee to examine the problems of dealing with Indians and to report back recommendations.

The congressman chosen to head this Indian committee was a New Yorker named James Duane, a conservative lawyer once judged almost dangerously pro-British by his colleagues in the Continental Congress but also highly respected for his intellect and probity. We find Washington writing to Duane on September 7, 1783, only four days after the peace treaty was signed overseas.

> Sir, I have carefully perused the Papers which you put into my hands relative to Indian Affairs....
>
> To suffer a wide extended Country to be over run with Land Jobbers, Speculators, and Monopolisers or even with scattered settlers is, in my opinion, inconsistent with that wisdom and policy which our true interest dictates, or that an enlightened People ought to adopt and, besides, is pregnant of disputes both with the [Indians], and among ourselves...and for what? But to aggrandize

a few avaricious Men to the prejudice of many, and the embarassment of Government....

As a big-time land speculator in Virginia and the Ohio country himself, the father of our country may have sounded a tad hypocritical, but he certainly knew this breed of entrepreneur and their effect on Indians. Therefore, among further thoughts for Duane to consider, he included the idea of a proclamation forbidding white settlement beyond a specified line in the West without congressional approval. Some three weeks later, such a proclamation was issued, even before Duane's report was completed. The effect of the proclamation as it stated was to "prohibit and forbid all persons from making settlements on lands inhabited by Indians...and from purchasing or receiving any gift or cession of such lands and claims without the express authority of the United States in Congress assembled." Yet, since only the Articles of Confederation were in place at the time, and they heavily favored states' rights, there was an added kicker: these regulations only pertained *beyond* "the limits or jurisdictions of any particular state."

Had such a proviso been on the books in the 1970s, the Maine Indian Land Claims case against either Massachusetts or Maine never, in all likelihood, could have gone anywhere.

The adoption of the United States Constitution in 1787 made the difference. Egged on by James Madison, the ultra Federalist, Congress changed the language of its power to "regulate affairs with Indians" so that it could be exercised "as well within as without the limits of the United States...," i.e., no state involvement.

The 1790 statute, familiarly known as the Non-Intercourse Act, has been attributed to a Maine man—Henry Knox—who was Washington's secretary of war from 1785 to 1794. Like his boss, Knox was also a big-time land speculator. His property in Maine, through his wife's Waldo family, reached into the Penobscot tribe's territory, and his subsequent purchase of 2 million more acres from Massachusetts brought him into the Passamaquoddy realm; consequently, Knox's silence on whether or not the 1790 law applied to Maine was later to become an argument that it didn't.

The only hint in his correspondence with Washington, as the two of them planned the legislation, was his regret that "so many tribes on the eastern seaboard...had become extinct." As secretary of war, Knox might have had his eyes solely on the powerful tribes in the American West (mostly today's Midwest) whose hostility, if it blossomed into war, could cost the fledgling U.S. republic $200,000 to defeat them.

Knox's philosophy, expressed to the president and Congress, was: "The Indians, being the prior occupants, possess the right of soil. It cannot be taken from them unless by their free consent, or by the rights of conquest in case of a just war. To dispossess them on any other principle would be a great violation of the fundamental laws of nature, and of that distributive justice which is the glory of a nation."

Treaties had been signed in 1784 and 1785 with some of these warlike tribes—the Iroquois, Wyandot, Delaware, Chippewa, Ottawa, and Cherokee. Still, friction continued. By July 1789 Knox was being blunt with Washington: "No state should be free to deal with Indian tribes over land matters since any dispute between the states and the tribes involved could plunge the nation into a war not of its own making." Furthermore, "the Indian tribes ought to be dealt with as foreign nations, not as the subjects of any particular state."

His suggestion was: "a declarative law" that Indians "possess the right of soil..." and are "not to be divested thereof" except for "fair and bonafide purchase" made under the authority and "express approbation of the United States."

Washington concurred.

On August 17, 1789, a month later, Congress created the Department of War pursuant to the Constitution, and the act passed to do so assigned Indian affairs to it exclusively. Knox, who was secretary *at* war under the Articles of Confederation, became secretary *of* war.

Almost a year later, Congress finally responded to Knox

and Washington, passing the bill they wanted, the so-called Non-Intercourse Act, in which the all-important Section 4 read:

> That no sale of land made by any Indians, or any nation or tribe of Indians within the United States, shall be valid to any person or persons, or to any state, whether having the right of pre-emption to such lands or not, unless the same shall be made and duly executed at some public treaty, held under the authority of the United States.

The effective date of the law was July 22, 1790.

Where Indians were concerned, a Knox biographer has written: "In Henry Knox, the Indians had one of their best friends. He had toward them the kind and considerate attitude of a John Eliot, and in his counsels to the heads of the government, especially to Washington, Knox continually urged friendly moderation toward the tribes.... If our nation had followed the advice of Henry Knox in regard to the Indians, its relations with them would have been a different story."[1]

How much then did Knox think about his vast holdings in Maine while dealing with the Indian problems out West? Was there a total disconnect in his mind? As a military man from Massachusetts (he had been a Boston bookseller before the Revolution), he had to have been aware of the role played by Maine's Indian tribes in the fighting Down East. All throughout his land dealings in Maine, there was talk in the Commonwealth of acquiring more land from the "eastern Indian tribes," and actual committees set up by the Massachusetts General Court to negotiate with them—one of which included Knox's predecessor as secretary of war, General Benjamin Lincoln. Knox even had to face the onslaught on the surveyors of his properties by squatters who dressed themselves up in war paint and feathers and were called "white Indians." When he had once said he thought most of the eastern seaboard tribes were extinct, did he really mean the Penobscots and Passamaquoddy?

More to the point, did he intend that the Indian Trade and Intercourse Act should *not* apply to them?

No one knew, nor could extensive historical research help find an answer. Everyone, pro-Indian claim or anti-Indian claim, was in uncharted territory.

"We were fundamentally upsetting the apple cart," Tom Tureen has said. Until 1946 Indians could sue in a court of claims and receive only token relief for the value of land taken from them. Even after Congress created a special Indian Land Claims Commission, the results were little better. Damages were limited to land values at the time their property was expropriated, plus simple interest. "Symbolic relief," Tom said. The implications of suing under the 1790 law were not merely novel; they immediately posed the question, How on earth could this be done, if it could be done at all?

Delineating the original land area to be claimed proved the easiest part: the Passamaquoddy and the Penobscots were *riverine* peoples; therefore, the entire watersheds of the Penobscot and St. Croix Rivers, plus tributaries and other nearby flowages, had made up their hunting grounds, which stretched from the Atlantic Ocean to the mountains of Western Maine.

The extent was breathtaking and it was not the sort of claim that could be brought before the federal Indian Land Claims Commission.

But still, Tom and some fellow lawyers he'd recruited decided, it would have to go before a federal court. A State of Maine court was bound to be too hostile.

For almost a whole year, they pondered strategy. In the end, they hit upon a brilliant stroke.

They would not take their "ejectment action" directly to a federal court. To do so would be to risk having their case sent back to a state court.

Instead—and this was the completely novel maneuver they'd hit upon—they would go into federal court and ask the judge *to order the federal government to sue the State of Maine on behalf of the Indian tribes!*

Then, in January 1972, Tom discovered a peril he hadn't counted on—the clock was ticking. Congress, almost six years earlier, had established a statute of limitations on any further Indian land claims. The Maine Indian plaintiffs had only until July 1972, six months away, to have their wild idea accepted for adjudication.

To start the process, a letter was signed and sent by the tribal governors on February 22 to Louis R. Bruce, the commissioner of the Bureau of Indian Affairs in the U.S. Department of the Interior, asking him to make a formal request to the U.S. Justice Department to institute a lawsuit against the State of Maine prior to July 18, 1972, the statute of limitations deadline. From Bruce—himself a Mohawk Indian—the request went to higher-ups at Interior, where it landed in the hands of William Gershuny, the department's associate solicitor for Indian matters. There it rested for months without a reply.

A plea from Tom Tureen to Governor Ken Curtis elicited a public statement that a case of such importance shouldn't go by default because of a statute of limitations. In D.C., Tom also appealed to the Maine congressional delegation of Senators Edmund Muskie and Margaret Chase Smith and Congressmen Peter Kyros and William Hathaway. All sent letters supporting timely action on the Indians' request.

The federal district court judge before whom Tom Tureen and company hoped to bring their case was Edward Thaxter Gignoux, Maine-bred, Harvard cum laude, Harvard Law School magna cum laude, a patrician, and a Republican, who had been seriously considered by President Richard Nixon in 1970 for a position on the U.S. Supreme Court. Despite Gignoux's reputation for scrupulous fairness, Tom had no idea how he would respond in a situation that had no parallel in legal history. Judges, Tom knew, were notoriously loathe to interfere with a prosecutor's discretion about which cases to bring. Would Gignoux tell the federal government they had to sue the State of Maine? The argument Tom used was based on the fact that the Department of the Interior, in refusing even to respond to the tribes' request to be represented by Justice, was, in fact, denying them justice, particularly if the statute of limitations was allowed to run out because of their continued stalling. In his initial plea to Judge Gignoux, Tom maintained that Interior was hesitating because it was confused as to whether or not the Trade and Intercourse Act applied to these two eastern tribes. That question, he argued, was a "live justiciable controversy," which could be settled by Judge Gignoux, and he pointed out it could be done under a federal statute, the Administrative Procedures Act.

On June 2, 1972, the case *was* allowed into Judge Gignoux's court and entitled *Passamaquoddy v. Morton* (Rogers Morton was the secretary of the interior at the time). Two weeks later, Gignoux held the first of two hearings, after which he determined that the Department of the Interior was delaying unreasonably and ordered the feds to report within a week if they would voluntarily file the request to the Department of Justice on behalf of the tribes.

On June 23 a lawyer for the Department of Justice named Dennis Whitman answered the court, saying No, the department could only act on behalf of federally recognized Indians. When Judge Gignoux pointed out that Governor Curtis and the entire Maine congressional delegation wanted action, the Nixon-appointed U.S. attorney in Maine, Peter Mills, jumped up and added his voice that he did, too. Gignoux then issued an order to the two departments that essentially told them to stop stalling. In late June, Justice filed a $150 million damage suit on behalf of the Passamaquoddy. In July, one day before the statute of limitations was scheduled to apply, they filed an identical suit for the Penobscots.

With the statute of limitations problem out of the way, a more leisurely procedure could be followed to litigate the next important bone of contention. Throughout 1973 and 1974, the question of whether or not the 1790 Act applied to Maine Indians was debated, with the State of Maine taking the position that the law created by Knox and Washington had only western Indians in mind and excluded any tribes in the origi-

*At the dawning of Maine Indian activism in 1972, the Wabanaki delegation
to the First Eastern Indian Conference in Washington, D.C. poses.
Tom Tureen, who was to be the lawyer for the Lands Claims Settlement is to
the right in shirtsleeves and tie. In the back row, from the far left, we've been
able to identify Wayne Newell, Allen Sockabasin, Tom Batiste, Andy Atkins,
and John Stevens. Just behind Tom Tureen is Jim Sappier, and in front at the
far right, Gene Francis, with Terry Polchies to his left.* MAINE STATE MUSEUM

nal thirteen states. Their contention was significantly undermined, however, when the U.S. Supreme Court ruled in a case
involving the Oneida tribe of Iroquois in New York State that
the act did apply to the original colonies, which, of course,
would include Massachusetts.

On January 20, 1975, Judge Gignoux declared that the
Non-Intercourse Act did indeed apply to the Passamaquoddy
and Penobscots. A subsequent order was to the Justice Department to bring an action against Maine as the heir to
Massachusetts's responsibility.

An interesting phenomenon was the relative lack of attention being paid to this effort up to this time. Even before filing the case in 1972, Tom Tureen had teamed up with a third-
year student at the University of Maine Law School, Frank
O'Toole, to write an article for the *Maine Law Review* outlin-

ing the unusual concept under which the tribes would make their case, and it received minimal attention. The press paid no real attention, either, since landowners weren't being sued directly. Even Judge Gignoux's unprecedented ruling did not immediately elicit much reaction.

But such relative calm was soon to end. The previous November, Maine had gone to the polls to elect a new governor; incumbent Ken Curtis, having served two consecutive terms, could not succeed himself. Of all Maine governors, Curtis had shown himself the most friendly to the Indians. His unexpected replacement, James B. Longley, turned out to be their most implacable foe.

"Jim" Longley was a political phenomenon. An insurance salesman from the industrial mill city of Lewiston, he had entered the statewide scene after supporting Ken Curtis for re-election and then was appointed, as a "businessman," to head up a special commission to recommend "business practices" to be introduced into state government. Thwarted in trying to impose all of his ideas, he decided to run for governor as an Independent. His two opponents were Democrat George Mitchell (later to be the distinguished U.S. Senate majority leader) and Republican James Erwin, Maine's attorney general at the time. Almost in stunned disbelief, Mainers awoke the day after the election to find that Longley, the unknown, the long shot, the man without a party, was their next governor.

Charismatic, tireless in pushing himself and his ideas, imperious, scathing to those who opposed or questioned him, totally uncompromising, Governor Longley was a formidable opponent. Once it dawned on him and the people of Maine what the true import of the Indian Land Claims issue could be, the stage was set for a titanic, protracted battle.

NOTES

[1] North Callahan, *Henry Knox, George Washington's General.* South Brunswick, and New York: A. S. Barnes Co. Pages 315-16.

4

INTO THE THICK OF THE LANDS CLAIMS ISSUE

*I*t was said that Jim Longley never slept. He was famous for
his late-night letters, penned to adversaries or to those
who had merely contradicted him, written with an almost
Faulknerian prolixity in which you could seemingly detect his
voice thundering and piercing blue eyes flashing in a rage of
feigned disappointment. Yet on his first visit to Washington
County after becoming governor, while listening to a briefing
by Tom Tureen on the Indian Land Claims issue, he fell
asleep. His—and Maine's—awakening was not to come for
some time.

To be sure, the state and federal governments appealed
Judge Gignoux's decision. First, though, Longley had a phone
discussion with him that did not change anything. Nor did
the First Circuit Court of Appeals help, since it upheld
Gignoux's ruling on December 23, 1975. Yet Maine, as if still
unable to take the unbelievable Indian Land Claims issue too
seriously, did not even seek to pursue the matter before the
U.S. Supreme Court.

In D.C. the commissioner of the Bureau of Indian Affairs
announced the two Maine tribes could receive some $5 mil-
lion a year in federal benefits for housing, education, and
health care. Perhaps a quiescent mood in Maine was based on
the thought that the Indians might settle for this nice piece of
change.

"Settlement" was definitely in Tom Tureen's thoughts. As
reported by Paul Brodeur in his book *Restitution*, Tom told
him that in court a settlement was "always...a major part of
our game plan" because he was aware that "no tribe had ever
obtained the return of any significant amount of land."[1]

What Tom and the Indians had in mind for a settlement,
however, was far from what Governor Longley and Maine's
new attorney general, Democrat Joseph Brennan, were think-

30

ing. One way to look at it from the Indians' viewpoint was that the $150 million the Justice Department had been ordered to sue for was just for rent owed by Maine to the tribes. A full indemnification would run to $25 billion.

The blow that finally focused Maine's attention was delivered in September 1976 by the Boston Brahmin law firm of Ropes and Gray through its senior municipal bond lawyer Henry Hall. No clean bond rating could be given to any municipalities in the affected area of Maine since all land titles were now under a cloud and tax liens were no longer enforceable. When Millinocket went to borrow money through a $1 million bond and the Maine Municipal Bond Bank wished to float a $27 million bond, neither entity could do it.

The full ramifications began to appear in the following days. Ellsworth discovered its $3.4-million sewer project had been derailed, Calais developed utility project problems, too, Hampden couldn't raise a bank loan to pay off a contractor—and in the latter case, ironically, it was the Merrill Bank that turned them down. Its president, William Bullock, had been hurriedly chosen by Longley to head up an emergency financial task force to deal with the bonding crisis.

Rodney Scribner, the one-time interim Indian commissioner, now state treasurer, declared it would take one to three weeks to arrange another bond sale—but only if the title obstacles were removed. The town manager of Millinocket, Michael T. Lachance, ruefully admitted: "We treated (the suit) with too much levity.... If they [the two tribes] are successful, we will no longer exist."[2]

On October 1 a 4:00 A.M. phone call woke up Tom Tureen, then living in Eastport. Governor Jim Longley was on the line, furious as only he could be, announcing he planned to embark on the state plane for Washington, D.C., to take action against the Indians' land claims. Tom, the holder of a pilot's license, scrambled to obtain an aircraft, himself, and arrive about the same time.

The *Portland Press Herald*, in its front page story the next day about the bond sale cancellation, mentioned that Longley "met briefly" with Tureen in D.C. and then issued a statement that "the State must make certain that the Indians are not denied their right to proceed in the courts." But the Maine chief executive was also quoted as characteristically lashing out with, "We must not allow any suit, by any group of individuals, to bring government to its knees."

Longley next persuaded the Maine congressional delegation to introduce a resolution directing the federal courts to refuse to hear the tribes' claims for the return of aboriginal land and restricting any awards to the Indians to cash payments—and in the time-honored manner of the Indian Claims Commission, restricting the sums to their eighteenth- and nineteenth-century values.

This hastily offered resolution was not acted upon, since Congress was about to adjourn. Meanwhile, the theme raised by the resolution was hammered home.

"SEEK MONEY NOT LAND" was a headline in the *Portland Press Herald* on October 21. The response, issued through Tom Tureen, was that tribes could not totally reject any attempts to regain land. It would destroy their case because, under the law, they could not claim a fair market value for land unless their right of possession was established, and he cited a New York case in which this had almost happened to the Oneidas.

At the meeting between Longley and the Maine congressional delegation, Tom Tureen had vigorously protested that their resolution would be "disgraceful," if not unconstitutional. "An outrage of historical importance" was another way he put it.

A somewhat contradictory version of this hectic gathering in D.C. has been told to me by a former Muskie staff person, who heard it from a Maine journalist, the late Don Larrabee. In this account, Senator Muskie reportedly met Governor Longley's demand to extinguish the Indians' land claims with the retort that doing so would constitute a taking under the Fifth Amendment to the Constitution, and the state would

32

have to pay compensation. Longley refused to believe him and these two strong-willed men ended up in a screaming match, according to the ex-staffer. At another meeting on the same issue, Muskie was alleged to have declared that "Longley is no lawyer." When Tom Tureen, who was again present, pointed out that Longley had gone to law school, Ed Muskie, at his most stentorian, pronounced: "I stand by my statement!"

More fireworks erupted in the month of January 1977, but not because of the delegation's resolution. On January 11 the Interior Department at last sent its recommendation to the Justice Department and it was a shocker. It was nothing less than for "ejectment actions" against 350,000 persons living in the 12.5-million-acre region claimed by the tribes and simultaneously against the large paper company and timber company landholders.

Two days later, Maine Attorney General Joseph Brennan fired off a proposal to Congress, seeking to remove the tribe's case from the federal courts and place it before the Indian Claims Commission. Brennan was promptly accused of "trying to change the rules once the game had started."

A war of words ensued. The Indians had earlier agreed not to seek the return of 2 million acres of populated land, but they were angry enough now to reverse their decision. Their offer, they said, had been to show they were flexible. Instead, they charged, the attorney general, the state governor, and the congressional delegation had unilaterally rejected "any effort to minimize damage to the people and small businesses in the claim area."

Governor Longley, for his part, came up with the argument it would be unfair to the other states in the union if the Maine case set a precedent. Then, he announced he was hiring Edward Bennett Williams, the famed Washington attorney, to represent Maine. Not to be outdone, Tom Tureen flew to Cambridge, Massachusetts, and was able to enlist the voluntary services of Harvard Law Professor Archibald Cox of Watergate fame and a former solicitor general of the U.S. Cox had only one caveat: he wanted to be sure his ownership of a summerhouse in Brooksville, Maine, in the contended area, didn't constitute a conflict of interest for him. Tom's answer was: "That's no problem. We're not paying you anything."

Cox's involvement in the next phase of the drama turned out to be quite extensive.

National politics also played a role. Jimmy Carter won the 1976 presidential election. His arrival on the scene in January 1977 was to have a significant influence on the simmering Maine Indian Land Claims controversy.

Although the new administration began replacing Republican holdovers from the Nixon and Ford years, one upper echelon G.O.P-connected official left at the Justice Department was Peter Taft, a grandson of President William Howard Taft. As head of the Land and Natural Resources Division, he was soon facing pressure from Senator Ed Muskie, on behalf of the Maine congressional delegation, to back away from initiating the "ejectment action" recommended by the Interior Department. However, Taft refused. Dubbing the case "potentially the most complex litigation ever brought in the federal courts," he said that the Maine Indians had valid claims to between 5 and 8 million acres and— here was the real kicker—*unless a settlement could be reached by June 1, he would begin filing TEST LAWSUITS against a number of major Maine landholders,* beginning with the paper companies and large-scale timber growers!

Implicit in this open threat was the previous promise of the tribes not to press for land in the heavily populated sections within the region, nor to take the property of any homeowner or small landowner. Targets would be restricted to the big private guys and also the State of Maine, itself, which owned 600,000 acres.

On March 1, the Maine congressional delegation formally introduced legislation to extinguish the tribes' aboriginal claims.

Perhaps predictably, the move was a non-starter. The chairman of the Senate Select Committee on Indian Affairs was a Democratic liberal from South Dakota, of Lebanese descent, named James Abouresk. Besides having a large Native-American constituency, he was at the time chairman of the American Indian Policy Review Commission, a congressionally ordered study, which in May 1977 was to issue a strongly pro-Indian report. Senator Abouresk not only denounced the legislation; he refused to hold hearings on it.

Enter the president. Jimmy Carter had campaigned heavily in Maine during his hard-fought primary, and his good showing in the Pine Tree State had helped his cause immensely. Moreover, Ken Curtis had been the first Democratic governor to endorse him publicly, and in Ed Muskie and Bill Hathaway, Maine had two Democratic U.S. senators to whom Carter would have to pay attention. Given the utter impossibility of a bill that would strip the Passamaquoddy and Penobscots of their claims, the new President sought a compromise and appointed an old friend from Georgia, a courtly judge named William Gunter, as a special referee to listen to both sides and propose a just solution.

Tom Tureen does not have happy memories of Judge Gunter, although he admits he was a nice, paternal, Southern gentleman. His actual words to me in an interview were: "Gunter was a complete skunk." This acidic retrospective tone may well be laid up to the nature of the "solution" the judge finally offered. It clearly had more stick than carrot to it. To begin with, Judge Gunter decreed that the matter should not go to trial. As an incentive to settle, he offered the tribes $25 million to be paid by the federal government, plus federal recognition and Bureau of Indian Affairs benefits. Maine was to give them 100,000 acres and the secretary of the interior was to find them 400,000 more to buy. If the tribes refused the offer—and here was the threat that outraged Tom Tureen and his clients—all of their claims to *private land* would be extinguished (but not to *state-owned land*). Gunter's ham-handed inducement to the Maine government to go along was that they (not the feds) would have to pay $25 million out of their coffers and *still be open to suit for their 500,000 acres.*

The best face the Indians could put on this "compromise" was through a statement by Tom Tureen that they were at least pleased by the admission that a settlement would have to include significant land for them. Paul Brodeur, writing from hindsight in *Restitution,* quotes a pithier interpretation from the tribes' lawyer. "The Penobscots and Passamaquoddy," Tureen allegedly said, "were now being warned, in effect, that if they pushed the federal government further, it would resort to the tactics of frontier days."[3]

Probably it was no consolation that the consternation was as great, if not greater, on the other side. Attorney General Brennan was primarily upset over the requirement that *state* land would have to be surrendered. Governor Longley, on the other hand, said he was pleased that *private* lands had been exempted while objecting to the fact that state aid to the Indian tribes would have to continue. The *Portland Press Herald* reported him as saying that the state was already more generous to its Indian than to its non-Indian citizens. "Maine will serve all people in need, whether they be Indians or non-Indians and we don't have to be told by Congress to do so."

Less than two weeks later, the state leaders announced they were meeting with Judge Gunter and presenting new evidence that Longley called "fresh and substantive." The compiler of the documentation was a young history professor at the University of Maine at Orono, Ronald F. Banks, regarded by all who knew him as a rising star in Maine academia. Shockingly and tragically, his career was to be cut short several years later in front of a New Orleans hotel while he was attending a history conference. There, Banks found himself confronted by a fourteen-year-old gunman who demanded money and then shot him because Banks thought the young man was kidding and didn't comply immediately.

The work Ron Banks did, after being hired by Brennan, was indeed "fresh and substantive." It was based on the premise that the Non-Intercourse Act of 1790 and its subsequent versions meant only Indians in "Indian Country" and that the term Indian Country could not, should not, and never had applied to Maine. In a detailed document, Banks emphasized that the federal government saw the Maine Indians in a totally different light from the warriors on the western frontier, i.e., in *Indian Country*. The Maine tribes had long since lost their land, warfare ability, and power and had acknowledged themselves dependent subjects of Massachusetts. Henry Knox, the originator of the first Non-Intercourse Act, did so as secretary of war in order to keep peace on the western borders. At the same time, Banks showed Knox to have purchased land in Maine currently now claimed by the tribes and to be aware of other parcels he couldn't buy "on the grounds that they belonged to the [Penobscot] tribe"; the point being that Secretary Knox knew they weren't in *Indian Country*, and thus not subject to his concern about federal control.

Special weight was also put on a pre-Revolution 1760 treaty with the *Province* of Massachusetts in which the Penobscots had conceded they had already given up most of their land because they'd been conquered by the British. American independence made them subjects of the *Commonwealth* (or *State*) of Massachusetts, and Banks seized upon a letter signed by George Washington responding to the Passamaquoddy that he could not grant them federal funds for a priest, not because of any religious reason but because the responsibility for such assistance devolved upon Massachusetts, alone.

Meticulously Banks brought his study down to the time of Andrew Jackson, who actually met with a delegation of Passamaquoddy in 1829 and heard about their land status when they asked him to help them buy more land in Maine (the implication: they were not telling Old Hickory they wanted to recover lost land). A few days later, the superintendent of the Bureau of Indian Affairs, Thomas L. McKenney, reported to Congress about the meeting and the Passamaquoddy land situation. Banks's point, in his own words: "the [Non-Intercourse] Acts were never even suggested to be applicable."

Historians writing briefs for politicians can also be as supple as the latter, if this piece of work is an indication. In denying a contradiction of sorts—the fact that between 1824 and 1831, the War Department (which contained the Bureau of Indian Affairs) granted money to the Passamaquoddy for a school and various agricultural subsidies, the following spin was used, alleging it was not: "federal recognition of those tribes but rather a humane and considerate gesture of a secretary of war who had a surplus in an account."[4]

In any event, armed with his voluminous arguments from America's past, Professor Banks held a meeting with President Carter's special counsel Robert Lipschutz. Edward Bennett Williams, the Washington superstar lawyer Longley had hired, was also briefed on the new arguments. But Jimmy Carter wasn't ready to give up on his attempt to broker a settlement between the two parties.

His next idea was to appoint a three-member negotiating team to hammer out an agreement with the tribes. The trio he chose consisted of Eliot Cutler, a Bangor native and ex-aide to Senator Edmund Muskie, Leo M. Krulitz, a Department of Interior lawyer, and A. Stephens Clay, a Washington attorney in Judge Gunter's law firm. The tribes were to be represented by their three tribal governors and eight other elected tribal members.

Note the absence of any representatives of the State of Maine. Augusta, no doubt, would ignore whatever decision came from this group. Yet there were rumors that Edward Bennett Williams had advised his clients, Attorney General Brennan and Governor Longley, they might have to settle.

The headline in the February 10, 1978, edition of the *Portland Press Herald* was eloquent in and of itself as to the negotiating team's final results:
"WONDER, RAGE, MEETS CLAIMS PLAN"
The subhead merely reinforced the near apoplexy in Augusta:
"State Officials Were Initially Speechless
and Then Became Outraged"
Attorney General Brennan publicly called the negotiators

"irresponsible and indefensible." Governor Longley blasted the White House, saying he felt Maine had been treated "very shabbily."

Much of the rest of the news story resembled a call to arms. Inflammatory statements from legislators, quite unusual in normally polite and placid Maine political quarters, were freely if not gleefully quoted by the reporter doing the piece, including: "Someone should get a gun and shoot those bastards" from one state representative when he learned the negotiating team was actually in the statehouse; and "I'm going to invest heavily in Winchesters and Remingtons" was a contribution by a state senator who represented a district in the affected area. "State lawmakers could only whistle, mutter profanities, and ask not to be quoted by name when they heard of the White House plan," the story went on.

Politics, too, entered the picture, both intra- and inter-party. Joe Brennan had already announced his candidacy for the seat occupied by Governor Longley, who had promised to serve only one four-year term and was living up to his word, despite his strong popularity. One of the attorney general's declared Democratic primary opponents, a sometimes waspish-tongued state senator, Richard "Spike" Carey, said *he* would risk fighting the case in court and "to Hell with that recommendation"; then, mischievously tweaking Brennan, he called on Governor Longley to name a blue ribbon panel to get a second opinion on the state's legal case and not rely on the attorney general, whose ambitions might be clouding his judgment, even unintentionally.

A Republican candidate for governor, House Minority Leader Linwood Palmer, chimed in that the White House proposal was "appalling...too much to swallow at one time."

What this bi-partisan condemnation had fixed upon so heatedly was a proposal not so significantly different from Judge Gunter's offering.

The feds were to pay $30 million to the tribes to extinguish all of their claims to 9.2 million acres held by small private landowners and help the Indians secure 500,000 acres.

The tribes were also to receive $1.7 million a year from the state. Fourteen large landowners, mostly paper companies, had to sell 300,000 acres of land valued at $112.50 per acre for $5 an acre, but could receive full market value for another 200,000 acres on which the tribes would hold options.

Muted in the uproar was the information that the tribes had already voted to accept the negotiating team's plan and Elliot Cutler's rather plaintive justification that there could be "economic chaos" if Maine rejected these terms and went to court.

A crescendo of fury was being reached in Maine. Pouring gasoline on the fire were subsequent comments of the governor, who likened the proposed settlement to "something that would come out of Red China." In a letter to President Carter made public on February 15, Jim Longley charged that the federal government was using "divide and conquer tactics," treating Maine people like "second-class citizens" and all "to satisfy the demands of small groups and to satisfy the conscience of a nation."

Knowing Carter was slated to visit Maine within the next few days, Longley warned that "many, many people of the

Opposite: Dissenting Indians speak during the Indian Land Claims hearing on March 28, 1980 at the Augusta Civic Center.

Above, Tom Tureen speaks at the March hearing.

Below, Maine Attorney General Richard Cohen addresses the audience.
MARC JOHNSON

State of Maine are bitter and disappointed at this point," and then, as if trying to give the president cover for disavowing his negotiating team, said he found it hard to believe that he (Carter) knew how his task force had handled the case.

However, Carter didn't bite. In fact, in a show of political bravery, at a town meeting in Bangor on February 17, the president openly vowed to veto any legislation not the product of negotiations or that attempted to extinguish the Indians' rights.

The climate of potential violence, fueled, some people felt, by Governor Longley's fiery rhetoric, continued. Gunshops were emptied of weapons, hastily bought by panicked property owners fearful of losing their land and homes. Brenda Commander, the present-day (2003) chief of the Maine Maliseets, remembers as a little girl in Houlton how shocked and horrified she was when her non-Indian best friend asked her, "You're not going to take our home away from us, are you?"—and this at a period when the Maliseets were not even connected to the case. Tom Tureen has said that he had to point out to Longley that his attacks might be responsible for bloodshed if he kept them up and they were used by hotheads in the area as an excuse to take physical action against the Indians.

The political ramifications, while not as dire, soon became evident. The Maine congressional delegation split—the two Republican congressmen, Bill Cohen and David Emery, vehemently opposed the settlement; the two Democratic U.S. senators, Ed Muskie and Bill Hathaway, argued it should at least be considered.

For Bill Hathaway, the issue was critical. In 1972, after several terms as Maine's Second District congressman (the area in which the disputed land was located), he had sprung a stunning upset by defeating the venerable, much beloved and allegedly unbeatable senior senator, Margaret Chase Smith. That same year, young Bill Cohen, then mayor of Bangor, had unexpectedly won the vacated House seat for the G.O.P. and gone on to make a name for himself on the committee impeaching Richard Nixon. Now he was ready to challenge Hathaway for the U.S. Senate. It has been claimed ever since that Jimmy Carter did everything he could to solve the Land Claims problem in order to help Bill Hathaway hang on to his seat—vainly, as it turned out, after a campaign in which Cohen ran television ads showing a map of Maine torn in half and a voice-over charging that Bill Hathaway was giving away one of those halves to the Indians.

Open (non-political) warfare never did break out in northern and north-central Maine. Somewhat miraculously two months later in April 1978, the two previous intransigents, Governor Longley and Attorney General Brennan, announced they would enter into negotiations with the tribes. Despite the fact that Longley subsequently walked out, saying the Indians wanted to be "a nation within a nation," which he wouldn't tolerate, the discussions went on, haggling over such questions of sovereignty as exemptions from state taxes and jurisdiction over criminal and civil laws.

In the middle of October 1978, not long before election day, Senator Bill Hathaway released his plan to end the crisis. The price tag for paying the tribes to extinguish their claims would now be $37 million and they could receive only 100,000 acres, not 300,000 to 500,000. The sweetener was that absolutely *no state money* would be paid out and, on this basis the three principal opponents, Longley, Brennan, and Cohen said they would accept the deal. Alas for Bill Hathaway, it was too little, too late. On November 7 he was unseated by Bill Cohen and, on the same day, Joe Brennan was elected governor of Maine.

From then until December 12, 1980, when President Carter signed an appropriations bill to pay for the ultimately agreed-upon settlement sum, which had somehow mysteriously ballooned to $81 million, more than two years of additional wrangling took place. Several factors—stated and unstated—drove the process. After the presidential campaign of 1980 began, it was fear—on the Indians' part—that Ronald

Reagan could come into office and have no compunction about wiping out their claims; on the State of Maine's part, it was the ever more certain possibility they might lose in court, "lose Baxter State Park," as it was always claimed. The advice offered by a new attorney general, Republican Richard Cohen (no relation to Senator Bill Cohen), was that they ought to settle. Indeed, when Carter signed the very last bill providing the money, he was already a lame duck, awaiting Reagan's inaugural a few weeks later.

But history had been made in United States–Native American relations, a precedent set, and, in some eyes, a Pandora's box sprung wide open.

NOTES

[1] Paul Brodeur, *Restitution: The Land Claims of the Mashpee, Passamaquoddy, and Penobscot Indians of New England.* Boston: Northeastern University Press, 1985.

[2] *Maine Sunday Telegram,* 3 October, 1976, page 36A.

[3] Brodeur, *Restitution,* page 105.

[4] Ronald Banks, et. al., Penobscot and Passamaquoddy Tribunal Land Claims Litigation Documents prepared by the State of Maine, Department of the Attorney General, pending Court Action (1976-77), page 4.

5

The Actual Settlement:
Procedures and Implicationss

*T*o implement the Maine Indian Land Claims agreement, there were three legalistic (albeit political) prerequisites: 1) the enactment of a state law; 2) the enactment of a complementary federal law; and 3) a federal appropriation.

On April 2, 1980, the 109th Maine Legislature took up An Act to Provide for Implementation of the Settlement of Claims by Indians in the State of Maine and to Create the Passamaquoddy Indian Territory and the Penobscot Indian Territory. This was the famous Legislative Document (LD) 2037, and a special Joint Select Committee on Indian Land Claims had been assigned to handle it.

I was a member of the 109th Maine Legislature which sat from 1978 to 1980. We had a Democratic majority in the house and a Republican senate, and a slim G.O.P. majority overall had enabled them to elect an attorney general, Dick Cohen, to replace Democrat Joe Brennan, who was now governor. As we have seen, the new attorney general had strongly urged the state to settle with the Indians and not risk going to court. Governor Brennan, too, had moved in the same direction, away from his former fire-breathing, adamantine opposition to any accommodation.

Thus LD 2037 was in an ideal position to receive bi-partisan support.

This it did from the special Joint Select Committee on Indian Land Claims, although the majority vote by the thirteen members of "Ought to Pass" was not unanimous. When its report was presented for our action, the tally was 11-2. Two members, a senator and a representative, having favored "Ought Not to Pass."

A split report meant floor debate and there were two whole days of it in the house and senate.

No doubt I am telling tales out of school in revealing the reactions of an average legislator to a bill even as titanic as this one. If it's not one of your own bills or one that comes before your particular committee, you are more than apt to give it merely a passing glance. Some 2,000 proposals for laws are handled during each Maine legislative session, and it is humanly impossible to keep track of them all or to delve thoroughly into the minutiae of those that are debated or are otherwise of obvious significance. In other words, the strong tendency is to listen to the members you trust who have sat on the committee of jurisdiction. This, frankly, was my position vis-à-vis the Land Claims bill, but also, I have to admit, I was leaning toward the Indians, partly because of my experiences working with them first as a gubernatorial staffer and then as house majority leader in 1975 when leading the fight to have their tribal representatives seated in our chamber.

As befitted the split partisan nature of the 109th, the Joint Select Committee on Indian Land Claims was headed by a Republican state senator, Sam Collins of Knox County, and a Democratic representative, Bonnie Post of Owl's Head, also in Knox County. (The irony of having the two leaders of this historic effort from the county named for Henry Knox, the man most responsible for this whole affair, was probably unconscious.) Both Collins, a lawyer and later state supreme court justice, and Post, a nurse married to a lobsterman, were highly respected, and my inner voice told me I would listen to the debate and, in the end, "follow Bonnie's light," as we would say, referring to the electronic tote board in the front of the house chamber on which votes for and against were recorded by green or red lit bulbs.

Years later Bonnie Post remembers that the biggest difficulty in composing the final piece of legislation was what had been Governor Longley's chief hang-up—the "nation within a nation" problem—over tribal sovereignty. The state's intent, Bonnie felt, was to project its power as much as possible. The controlling clause, therefore, was language that gave the tribes the same status as municipalities in Maine which are "creatures of the legislature" and can be acted upon by Augusta despite a tradition of allowing them as much "home rule" as possible.

Natural resource issues were a major bone of contention, too, and with an air of slyness, Bonnie told me to look up the section in the law regarding lobsters. While the Indians were given certain rights in regard to fish and game in Maine (like free licenses and certain freedoms to regulate wildlife on their own lands), *state lobster laws* were always to prevail. Unnoticed by many of us who did not read the bill assiduously was the creation of a State–Tribal Commission empowered to deal with conflicts over sovereignty issues and even to change rules and regulations.

On April 2, 1980, the debate opened in the state senate. All legislative committees in Maine, select and standing, are *joint*—that is, having both senators and representatives on them in a ratio of three senators to ten representatives. The three senators voting on LD 2037 split 2-1 with Chairman Collins and the Democratic Minority Leader Senator Gerard Conley voting for the bill and Senator Andrew Redmond against it. This latter gentleman was from Somerset County, an affected North Woods area. Andy Redmond, a fiery Franco-American businessman despite his Irish-sounding surname, was, along with his son Pierre, a statewide leader of the opposition to *any* agreement with the tribes. He and Pierre had already tried to initiate a referendum in which all Maine voters would decide the issue, but had failed to garner more than a third of the needed signatures. A move in the senate by one of his allies to attach a "referendum clause" to the measure failed (yet by three votes only). A 19-9 senate vote accepted the Ought to Pass report.

In the debate in the house, the opposition began with two speakers from my own Democratic party who had been prime opponents to the seating of the Indian representatives five years earlier. One was Ed Kelleher from Bangor, the other Jim Dudley from nearby Enfield, both communities in Penobscot County. After Bonnie Post, as house chair of the Joint Select

Committee moved the Ought to Pass report, Kelleher stood up and asked what the rush was. The fairly tart answer was that there had already been thirteen months of negotiations. Commencing his full-scale attack, Kelleher launched a Populist tirade designed to appeal to Democrats, citing the big-name landowners and paper companies who stood to profit greatly from their sales to the Indians under this proposed law: Dead River, Diamond International, Scott Paper, the Cassidy heirs, and a certain Bertram Tackeff who, alone, would take in $1,210,000 for 5,500 acres.

Dudley sounded a different sort of Populist note: the strong feelings of the folks in his hardscrabble district with their frontier feelings toward Indians.

"Believe me, if this bill passes, you are in for a lot of trouble," he said. "I live in that neck of the woods. I live with some hillbillies. I live with some Ku Klux Klansmen.... I know what goes on in that neck of the woods...." And then he muttered darkly about half a dozen killings that had never been reported in the press and ended by regretting there was no referendum clause attached to the bill.

Republican James Silsby, also from an affected area, Hancock County, likewise intimated potential violence, referring to "poor woodsmen, seeing that the tribes will have more than they ever had, may feel differently, especially when all they have to do is drop a match."

Another Republican, the arch-conservative Reaganite Porter Leighton, used an age-old argument in the nation's struggles over minority rights, one in which he tried to make himself sound almost liberal: "...it would be in the tradition of our melting pot of a society to blend the Indian into our society rather than further ostracizing him from it."

The house vote was 87-51, followed by equally comfortable margins against attempts to attach referendum provisions.

In his opening remarks in the state senate, Sam Collins, ever the jurist, had explained to his colleagues the unusual character of the legislation they were about to debate. "The bill will not be a general statute," he told them. "It will be a unique document that is similar to an agreement between the state and the Indian tribes that has been authorized and ratified by the United States Congress."

So the next chapter was federal approval and the key event took place almost three months later on July 1 and 2, 1980, in the Dirksen Senate Office Building in Washington, D.C. Bonnie Post, who was present for these prolonged hearings of the U.S. Senate Select Committee on Indian Affairs, remembers how excrutiatingly hot it was in the nation's capital.

When the proceedings opened shortly after 10:00 A.M. in Room 1202, three members of this special five-member committee—Chairman John Melcher, Democrat of Montana; Daniel Inouye, Democrat of Hawaii; and William Cohen, Republican of Maine—were joined by a special guest, Maine's new junior senator, George Mitchell, recently appointed by Governor Joseph Brennan to take the place of Ed Muskie, who had resigned to become U.S. secretary of state. The bill up for discussion and decision was S.2829, The Maine Indian Land Claims Settlement Act of 1980, which had been introduced by Senators Cohen and Mitchell.

Included in the federal measure was a new wrinkle not covered during the Maine debate. Another group of *Maine Indians* had been added as interested parties (i.e., beneficiaries) of the proposed law. This was the Houlton Band of Maliseets. In actuality, the band represented the southernmost membership of a much larger Canadian tribe who, since time immemorial, had roamed a large area of Aroostook County while centered in and around the small city of Houlton. The Maliseets have always been closely related in language, history, and family ties with the Passamaquoddy.

Under the provisions of S.2829, the Houlton Band was to become federally recognized and receive from the funds allotted to the other two tribes, with their consent, $900,000, out of which they could buy 5,000 acres in Maine.

An explanation of the bill's purposes began the first hearing. These were: 1) to remove any cloud hanging over land titles in Maine; 2) to clarify the status of any other land that might be sold to the tribes; 3) to ratify the Maine Implementing Act; and 4) —a key point—to affirm that the Indians recognized in Maine "are and shall be subject to all laws of the State of Maine."

Another key point justified a complete federal payment. On the grounds that the State of Maine had taken care of its Indians from 1820 on and the federal government did little or nothing for them, it became the "intent of Congress that the State of Maine not be required further to contribute directly to the claims settlement."

The first scheduled speaker was Senator Bill Cohen. An original opponent of any settlement—indeed, of whom it was said he had ridden his opposition into capturing his Senate seat—he spoke rather circumspectly as a proponent. He made reference to his belief that the early members of Congress from the original thirteen states were presumably aware of the 1790 Non-Intercourse Act and felt it didn't apply to them, so, in not having their states submit their Indian treaties to be ratified, they were not acting in defiance of the law. Then, he heaped blame on the federal government for not observing their trust obligations to the Maine tribes.

Senator George Mitchell followed, noting he approached "this legislation with a fresh perspective as a new senator from Maine..." but was familiar with the issues from his previous position as the U.S. attorney in Maine.

The other "heavy-hitter" proponents who testified were Governor Brennan; Attorney General Richard Cohen; Donald Perkins, Sr., the attorney for the large landowners; Tom Tureen, the tribes' attorney; four members of the tribes; and Cecil Andrus, an ex-governor of Idaho who was now U.S. secretary of the interior.

The latter, who called the sovereignty questions involved "a novel jurisdictional relationship" between the tribes, the state, and the feds, fielded a few "softball" questions. For example:

Senator Inouye: "So it is your contention that the passage of this law would be in the best interests of this country?"

Secretary Andrus: "Yes, sir."

Senator Mitchell: "Do I then take your remarks to mean that in your judgment the effect [of passing the bill] will be favorable?" (Andrus had said it would show other Indian nations of America that they did not have to go to court, but could negotiate a fair settlement.)

Secretary Andrus: "Absolutely. We are starting to keep our word, Senator. We are just 200 years late."

Senator Mitchell: "Better late than never, they say."

Governor Brennan, in his presentation, sounded a similar note, opining that the State Implementing Act, passed in April and signed by him, "represents a positive step in the history of State–Indian relations, not only in Maine, but also nationally...." However, his spin soon became that a new model had been created to avoid the "nation within a nation" difficulty. The Indian territories would be treated as municipalities—and, by the way, the State Department of Indian Affairs had been abolished. "The Indians would be full-fledged citizens, responsible for their own services, taxes, welfare, and destiny, just like the people in every other city and town in our state." And the state's chief executive ended on this hopeful note from his point of view: "I can think of no better way to create in our Indian communities a sense of self-sufficiency and self-respect than through the reform contained in the Maine Implementing Act."

In a statement of opposition to the bill, Pierre Redmond included an editorial from the *Bangor Daily News* that predicted future trouble. If the Maine Indians received money and land, the editorialist rather peevishly asked, "will the Native American Rights Fund and other foundations that have bankrolled the Indians...dispatch an army of well-financed lawyers...to chase down other historic injustices heaped upon the Native Americans by our forefathers?" As if in partial answer, the writer went on to attack the mechanism in the law that was supposed to avoid or resolve conflict—the Maine Indian Tribal–State Commission. The question was asked, "Is its membership makeup realistic or even workable?"—implying it was not.

The opposition wasn't only from white people. Dana Mitchell, a Penobscot, claimed a majority of the Penobscots did not back their leaders, and the referendum vote on the reservation that had approved the Maine bill was an illegal referendum since there had been only four days in which to consider it. His prime objection was to "making the Indian people of Maine come under state and federal laws or, lower yet, a municipality, which isn't much for a sovereign people."

The Penobscot woman Eugenia Thompson, who styled herself *ssipsis*, presented her complaints from an Indian traditionalist's point of view. Calling her own leaders "traitors who have sold our rights," she stated: "We are an ancient people living under the Creator's laws.... If you think you can rewrite your history books or rewrite your holy books, you had better start doing it now, for you stand to read of guilt, deceit, treachery, and fraud and we will always be around to remind you of it.... If this bill gets passed, we will cease to give thanks to the Creator. We will cease to dance in thanksgiving, and we will no longer hold up our corner of the earth."

Sam Sapiel, like the *Bangor Daily News*, pooh-poohed what he called "this nine-man commission thing" and Eunice Crowley seemed to sum up the sentiments of the 124 Penobscots who'd voted No: "I disagree with this package deal because it goes against all our rights as a sovereign nation."

A voluminous appendix of written testimony and related documents was published after the federal hearing, containing a broad range of historical material, as well as contemporary opinion. Combining both was the extraordinary submission of J. Russell Wiggins, a former editor of the *Washington Post* and *New York Times* who had retired to Maine and become publisher of his own newspaper, the *Ellsworth American*. A strong opponent of the settlement, he tried in more than a hundred pages, crammed with facts dating to 1493, to present the argument that if "the [Indian] occupiers of land discovered by Europeans" possessed any rights in that property at all, those in Maine had forfeited them by being beaten in the

*President Jimmy Carter uses a quill pen to sign the Maine Indian Land
Claims Settlement Act. Left to right: Maine Governor Joseph Brennan,
Secretary of State Edmund Muskie, Secretary of the Interior Cecil Andrus,
Maine Senator George Mitchell, and Maliseet Chief Terrance Polchies.*
AP PHOTO/BARRY THUMMA.

French and Indian wars and surrendering and submitting to
the authority of the English king. Massachusetts Bay
Governor Thomas Pownall's treaty of May 23, 1759, with the
Penobscots was enclosed in full in this massive piece of work,
which was dotted with such comments from the erudite journalist as: "The Maine Indians no doubt are fortunate that
their plight was left to the State of Maine from 1832 to 1848
or they probably would have joined the Cherokee and the
other tribes in reservations across the Mississippi."[1]

In contested legislative matters, one can usually see which
side has momentum. In this case, it was absolutely clear. The
settlement, so delicately and tediously worked out, would certainly be accepted via S.2829. The only fuzziness concerned
the funding, without which there was no deal. So Senator
George Mitchell asked Secretary of the Interior Andrus if he
saw any difficulty in getting Congress to approve the final
amount of $81 million. The former Idaho governor said he
could conceive of none.

In the end, though, according to Tom Tureen, had it not been for George Mitchell, as a member of the Senate Budget Committee, this ball could have been dropped.

The photo-op run by many of the nation's newspapers on October 10, 1980, has become the emblematic historic symbol of the entire affair. It shows President Jimmy Carter signing the Maine Indian Land Claims bill with an eagle feather pen, while behind him, watching earnestly and with satisfaction, are some of the principal Maine players, including Governor Brennan, Secretary of State Muskie, and Senator Mitchell. It is a photograph still often in use.

But the real moment of accomplishment was another unpublicized signing some two months later on December 12, 1980, when Jimmy Carter signed the $81-million appropriations bill.

The machinery was then, so to speak, turned on.

NOTES

[1] Hearings before the Select Committee on Indian Affairs, United States Senate, 96th Congress, Second Session, on S.2829: *To Provide for the Settlement of the Maine Indian Land Claims*, Volume 2, Appendix. Washington, D.C.: U.S. Government Printing Office, 1980.

Looking Back, Way Back

*I*n many, if not most, of the discussions regarding the Maine Indian Land Claims controversy, a citing of history was almost always included.

Take for example the testimony offered to the U.S. Senate by a man named Robert Cleaves in favor of the inclusion of the Houlton Band of Maliseets in S.2829. His condensed history of the Houlton Band begins in the 1600s when the Maliseets were using the lands of the St. John River watershed, including 1 million acres in Aroostook County, Maine, giving them aboriginal rights in "vast areas" of the state. It continues through the 1870s when the hunting economy collapsed and they settled in an area known as the "Houlton Reservation." They resided there, to quote Cleaves, in dire poverty in what local whites called "Houlton's ghetto." In 1970 the Association of Aroostook Indians, made up of both Maliseets and Micmacs, was formed and commissioned an account of its own history. Compiled by anthropologist James Wherry, it ran more than a hundred pages and was submitted to the U.S. Department of the Interior, where it helped gain the inclusion of the Maliseets' claim for federal recognition.

It can equally be said that Tom Tureen's entire original case for the Passamaquoddy and Penobscots was built upon history—the discovery of a historical fact, the Non-Intercourse Act of 1790, and its ramifications, and the transformation of that knowledge into the realm of the American legal system, a landscape derived, like sedimentary rock, from layers of precedent, applications of knowledge, argument, and decision, but also an area in which action could be taken and new history created.

On the other side, Joe Brennan, when attorney general of Maine, hired historian Ronald Banks to provide a compendious document employing Maine and U.S. history, trying to prove the Maine tribes had no valid claim to anything. Even speaking for the settlement, Brennan still criticized the federal government for its failure to clamp down on Massachusetts in 1794 (the date of the treaty that took the bulk of the Passamaquoddy's land) and for its silence on the matter when Maine was admitted to the union in 1820.

J. Russell Wiggins, publisher of the *Ellsworth American,* must have worked countless hours and spent a small fortune to assemble his own history, even delving into the European past and fifteenth-century papal pronouncements on "discovery." One Bangor editorialist reached back at least to General Jedediah Preble's acceptance of "the surrender overture of Maine's aboriginal people at Fort Pownall 220 years ago...."

The use of history by both parties in the public debate logically calls for a sharper, more comprehensive study of Maine Indian history, itself. In order to do so, however, it seems to me the approach cannot be left where J. Russell Wiggins and Robert Cleaves and others may have left it—in the seventeenth and eighteenth centuries—but way, way back—well beyond the fifteenth century—and into the very origins of today's tribes in an environment that had eventually emerged in the northeastern corner of North America after eons upon eons of geologic and biologic activity.

The concept of time expressed in terms of millions or billions of years is often hard to grasp. Geologists have found rocks in Maine in Chain of Ponds Township near the Quebec border that are actually 1.2 billion years old. Nothing visible lived then. Nor were Maine nor Chain of Ponds located where they are today.

Maine was once five degrees from the equator. According to the recent theory of plate tectonics, it was shoved northward, then split off from Europe and spun around to end in our present spot on the eastern coast of the Atlantic—a coastline that, by the same reckoning, is imperceptibly inching its way west as the plate beneath us shifts. In 50 million years, it's estimated, Maine will be where Minnesota is.

All of these fantastic, hard-to-believe events occurred, the savants tell us, before there were sentient humans on the scene. Elements of this earlier story have been extrapolated from geological formations, the mineral composition of rocks, plant and animal fossils, bits of animal bones, insects trapped in amber for all eternity, petrified wood, and other artifacts to paint a picture of a Maine–Maritime region characterized by volcanoes, tropic heat, arctic cold, earthquakes, and weird, extinct creatures like the sail-backed Dimetrodon (a mammal-like dinosaur) or the Yvonaspis (an armored, jawless fish). Ice ages alternated with warming trends until the most recent of the great "cold snaps" known to us—which featured a Laurentide ice sheet that once covered all of North America east of the Rockies and extended as far south as modern-day Missouri. Like all glaciers, that monster mass of frozen snow advanced and retreated until its final subset, dubbed the "Wisconsin Ice Sheet," started to leave the northeast about 19,000 years ago. Imagine a mile-high, white covering with a bluish tint slowly peeling away and leaving a bare, rock-strewn, scraped, and scarred plantless landscape. That is how Maine began to look. Then, green things began to grow, arctic grasses formed a boggy tundra, and animals appeared that could live off this minimal flora, some, like caribou, still on the planet today, and others utterly gone—mammoths and mastodons and bear-sized giant beaver and sabre-toothed cats. However, these latter creatures stayed around long enough for the first humans in the area to encounter them and remember them in their oral histories.

Those Paleo-Indian pioneers of perhaps 12,000 years ago left us mere tantalizing fragments of their existence—"artifacts"—painstakingly coaxed from the earth by archaeologists, both professional and amateur, and pondered over by experts. New finds, including petroglyphs dating back 8,000 years, continually add to postulations about generations of shadowy figures for whom it has only been possible to assign patterns of style as a means of identification. No tribal names, no personified histories—not yet.

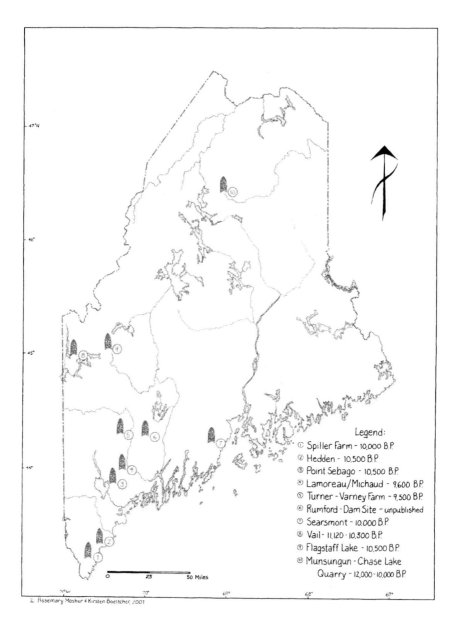

Legend:
① Spiller Farm - 10,000 B.P.
② Hedden - 10,500 B.P.
③ Point Sebago - 10,500 B.P.
④ Lamoreau/Michaud - 9,600 B.P.
⑤ Turner - Varney Farm - 9,500 B.P.
⑥ Rumford - Dam Site - unpublished
⑦ Searsmont - 10,000 B.P.
⑧ Vail - 11,120 - 10,300 B.P.
⑨ Flagstaff Lake - 10,500 B.P.
⑩ Munsungun - Chase Lake
      Quarry - 12,000-10,000 B.P.

Rosemary Mosher & Kirsten Boettcher, 2001

Major Paleo Indian Sites

A group of hunters at a meat cache, shown in a mural by Philip Carlo Paratore at the Maine State Museum. MAINE STATE MUSEUM

For the better part of a week in late June 2002, I participated in a "field school dig" organized by the Friends of the Maine State Museum, poking in the hard-packed dirt of the Goddard Site in Brooklin, Maine. On a breathtakingly scenic headland fronted by two gently sloping beaches in full view of Blue Hill Bay and Mount Desert Island, generations of aboriginal inhabitants had encamped, millennia after millennia in succession, and left evidence of their occupation in the abutting fields. We may well have been dealing with ancestors of the Penobscots but the language of science was unwilling to concede such a modernism. We still had to talk in terms of mere "traditions," like the Laurentian and the Susquehanna, cultural influences from north and south that may, themselves, have represented whole civilizations long since vanished and replaced.

The Goddard Site is (or was, since ours would be the last dig ever there) arguably the most famous of all archaeological repositories in Maine.

"It's the richest site," we were informed right off by Steve

Warren K. Moorehead and his crew during the 1914 "Survey of the Red Paint Indians of New England," at Grand Falls, N.B. Moorehead, considered the leading pioneer of Indian archaeology in the Northeast, is standing to the far left. COLLECTIONS OF MAINE HISTORICAL SOCIETY

Cox, the professional archaeologist contracted to direct our efforts. This plot of ground, he said, had enclosed probably the largest early Indian village in Maine and maybe all of New England and initially had gained its archaeological fame from the numerous graves of the so-called "Red Paint People" unearthed within its boundaries. First popularized as a "lost, ancient Indian tribe" by Warren K. Moorehead, a giant if highly controversial figure in American archaeology, these "Red Paints" are actually now deemed to have been members of a burial cult that interred its dead amid copious amounts of powdered red ochre. They were not, today's scientists insist, an extinct separate ethnicity, although in deference to the man who first publicized the discovery, this red ochre phenomenon, wherever it occurs, is referred to as the "Moorehead Phase," which now extends further back in time than originally thought.

However, the Goddard Site, named for its recent owner, owes its greatest notoriety not to gaudy funereal observances nor the abundance of artifacts gleaned from its excavated meadows since the 1950s; rather, a bit of blackened metal, smaller than a dime, discovered after the fact amid a collection of its findings, caused a worldwide sensation. It was a Norse coin—a Viking relic—of the eleventh century, dug up in Maine and authenticated by the best Norwegian expert on the period. Did this prove, as some people hoped, that Leif Ericson's Vinland had been located Down East? Well, not really. The more likely explanation was that in the dim depths of time it had been traded as a trinket—maybe with the Eskimos up north who had traded it to Indians who had traded it to other Indians, and so forth.

At Goddard itself, we learned, a stone tool of prehistoric Dorset–Eskimo design had been uncovered. The presence of *Ramah chert* there was further evidence of an extensive north–south interchange in the past; it was a type of volcanic rock imported from northern Labrador and used for making arrowheads, scrapers, and other useful handmade Stone–Age gadgetry.

This raw material that Paleo-Indians needed came from all over. *Onandaga chert* traveled via the St. Lawrence to Maine from precursors of those Indians in New York and Canada we now call Iroquois. At Mount Kineo on Moosehead Lake and the Munsungan Lake region in Piscataquis County, whole mines of chert and similarly flakeable rhyolite supplied our own natives. Trading, we know from what has been found at Goddard, went south, as well, to Pennsylvania and New York, and west to the Great Lakes. Was this simply a copying of contemporary styles? Had wanderers from *Away* brought their gear with them? Had ancient Indian Mainers canoed to those distant parts? No one can tell exactly.

The oldest date of any object in the Goddard collection is about 6,000 years ago. Our "dig" would be in a much more recent layer of earth, almost modern times, 1,000 to 600 years ago (A.D. 1000 to A.D. 1400), just before the period of contact with Europeans.

Like a new kid on the block, I began my first morning *in situ* fairly wide-eyed as the opening of a new section of the Goddard Site commenced. At first, all I saw anywhere was a

Our field school archaeological group at work in the last dig ever at the famed Goddard site on Naskeag Point, Brooklin, Maine, June 2002. AUTHOR PHOTO

grassy meadow stretching to the rims of the beaches, totally intact, with no signs of digging, because the turf is always put back at the end. Since we were starting a fresh dig, our first task was to cut through some rather tough turf—"the hardest job," one of our veterans said. Needing to do so with great care, we used sharp-edged spades and followed a pattern of squares laid out for us with stakes and string by the group of pros assisting Steve Cox. We were then divided into pairs, and my partner Robin, a widow from New Jersey who'd done this before, and I began removing our grass cover, mindful not to sever any fingers in the process. At length, we had sliced through enough of the grass roots in order to roll up the whole matted square like a carpet. We deposited it with all the others on the ground nearby, in the correct order in which it would be returned to its earthly home.

Before us then was a square of solid dirt, which we subdivided again with stakes and string, allowing Robin one half and myself the other. A kit had also been prepared for each of us containing a triangular trowel, sharp as a razor, a tape measure, a scoop, a whisk brush—the archaeologist's tools—plastic bags and trays for what we collected of worth,

My partner Robin and I, working on and in our pit during the Goddard dig. Note the many rocks—none artifacts—that had to be delicately removed as we inched our way downward with our trowels. AUTHOR PHOTO

and markers for labelling the bags. Kneeling, crouching, lying stomach down, later sitting in the pit that we created, following precise and periodic instructions from Steve Cox, Robin and I began slicing and scraping away.

First lesson: Which is a "flake" and which is a "JAR," the acronym for "just another rock"? The flake, we were to keep, put in our tray, and later place into one of those little plastic bags with a notation of what level and in what corner of our square it had been plucked from the dirt. A flake, we learned, is a bit of chert or rhyolite or quartz discarded by an Indian ages ago while trying to create an arrowhead or other necessary tool of trade by striking a chunk of rock with a piece of deer or moose antler until it cracked enough to produce a perfect workable template. Finding the first confirmed flake in my territory (Robin knew what they looked like) was a thrill. Eventually, they became a dime a dozen, except when we came upon one that Steve declared to be "utilized"—i.e., maybe big enough and sharp enough to be a knife or scraper—whereupon it was transformed into that prize of prizes—an ARTIFACT—and bagged and catalogued separately.

Oh, yes, we had also been given large, heavy plastic buckets, which we filled with the dirt we were creating, then brought to mounted sieves where we sifted out a million pebbles and a few flakes and occasionally sherds of pottery. These latter were invariably tiny and had the cute pet name of "kibbles," because they resembled dog food. It took some practice to be able to identify them without the help of Steve or one of his assistants. Meanwhile, beneath the sieves, the piles of loam to be replaced grew ever higher and the holes to which they would be returned ever deeper. We were descending in time, lower and lower, alert as eagles to anything that appeared different or interesting.

It crossed my mind finally that this operation was not dissimilar to fishing. I kept waiting for a strike—digging, digging, digging, into earth that only slowly varied in color, patiently, expectantly, until—whamo!—my trowel strikes something that doesn't seem to be "just another rock" and I pry it loose and rush it to Steve or one of his assistants and watch their faces anxiously as they scrutinize the thing.

My own "trophy fish"—the most exciting of my finds—was a sizeable piece of almost 500-million-year-old *Ordovician chert* from Munsungan; it was one of those "utilized flakes," large enough and sharp enough to serve as a knife or scraper. But most of all, it was gorgeous—smooth and sleek and a lovely maroonish color prettily streaked with veins of green. I could easily see where this "sport" of archaeology could become habit-forming. Robin, for example, was back to Goddard for her fifth consecutive year.

There were endless opportunities, digging and digging and surrounded by heavenly scenery, to imagine those "first Americans" who had occupied the same location on a far different mission. They were simply unselfconsciously living, doing what they needed to do in order to stay alive and make use of an environment that millions of years of geology and biology had provided them. No doubt, much of what they did was learned behavior, handed down by elders in each generation, so that they knew how to flake rocks efficiently; how to build pottery coil by coil; how to make clothes from the hides of animals; and how to hunt and fish for their food, plus gather it from plants; and how to form receptacles from birch bark and canoes from it, too, plus coverings for their shelters. Earlier perhaps, before the birches grew big and plentifully enough, they fashioned dugout boats from whole logs. In craft of either type, they ventured onto lakes and rivers, and here at Naskeag into the surrounding ocean where they used hand-held spears as crude harpoons to capture swordfish and seals and porpoise. When summer was over, they had other inland places to go to, other places to visit, to exploit wisely for their sustenance.

There is much the archaeologists can decipher from the small clues so literally sifted out of the dirt. Although what we were collecting—and some of the group found perfectly intact arrowheads and other whole artifacts—had no tribal connotations, a logical deduction, given Goddard's physical location and the timing (up to A.D. 1400), could be that we *were* dealing with the direct ancestors of the Penobscot Nation.

In point of fact, *legally* that was the case, we learned in an evening lecture back at the house where we were staying. Steve Cox told us that under NAGRA (the federal Native American Graves Reclamation Act), all human remains (full skeletons, skulls, or miscellaneous bones) must be repatriated to an appropriate tribe if, as stipulated in the act, they are within 1,000 years old. On the Goddard Site, it had been determined that any such remains belonged to the Penobscots, and a few recovered ones had been returned. It has never been revealed, we were told, where they were re-buried.

Suddenly, in that rented house in Brooklin, we were back in the twenty-first century when attitudes toward what we were doing in trying to gain scientific knowledge and interpret the lives of native cultures of the past had a new dimension—taking into account the sensibilities of their descendants. Steve Cox said that while he agreed with the law as written, he was upset with Massachusetts and other states that gave back everything, well beyond 1,000 years old and where there was absolutely no demonstrable connection to any contemporary tribe.

Another pet peeve of Steve's hit closer to home—that in Maine, there were many other oceanside sites, like Goddard, identified as promising but as yet untouched by archaeologists due to lack of funding, and many would be lost forever before they could be tapped because of rapid shoreline erosion.

Perhaps a final word was given on the subject by a member of our group of "students." Wes was a middle-aged Vietnam veteran from Vermont whose hobby was collecting Indian artifacts. He proudly showed us photos of his mounted collections of arrowheads and was undoubtedly the most enthusiastic among us when anyone found anything of interest. His ethnic origin, he early on made us aware, was part French-Canadian, part Western Abenaki Indian—and the Western Abenakis, he also let us know, were not yet recognized as a tribe by either Vermont or the federal government, although they were trying hard to organize. A component of the New England Algonquian-speaking peoples, they were distant relatives of the very same folk—the Penobscots—whose record in the earth it had been deemed we were examining. Somewhat wistfully, as if envying the modern Penobscots their federally recognized tribal status, Wes spoke of bones of his own ancestors stored away, unburied, in a cellar at Fort Ticonderoga. "That sort of bothers me," he confessed to us in his understated way.

7

THE PEOPLE

*W*ho were the Indians in Maine? Where did they come from? Where, indeed, did any of the Native Americans originate? One theory is so well known it seems like gospel—that they crossed over from Asia to Alaska on the land bridge of the Bering Strait and spread throughout North America and South America.

Yet some other ideas have been raised, roiling the scientific world, including the notion that some Indians in the East were of European Caucasian origin, not Asiatic, and had migrated via northern ice packs from Europe to Nova Scotia and then south. The impetus here is the discoveries in North and South America of Indian relics, bones, skulls, and other artifacts, that precede an arbitrary cut-off date established by a cluster of academics known sardonically as the "Clovis Mafia"—those who have emphatically declared that no Indians were in the New World earlier than 11,000 years ago, the age of the material first found at Clovis, New Mexico. Recently, a confirmed date of 12,500 years ago was established for an Indian find at Monte Verde in Chile, and others, 14,000 and possibly 17,000 years ago, cropped up in Pennsylvania and Virginia. Ties have been made between Clovis culture and the Solutrean culture of France and Iberia, Caucasian features appearing when certain of the skulls found were reconstructed.[1]

And then, again, what do the Indians, themselves, think of such discussions?

That night in Brooklin, Maine, talking about archaeology and the federal law on the disposition of Indian remains, one of the archaeologists present, Laurie Lachance of the Maine State Museum, mentioned a certain Penobscot tribal elder she knew named Arnie Neptune who told her he didn't believe an Ice Age in Maine had ever existed. Yet every book on Maine's geology and pre-history speaks of a line of glaciers that buried the state's land area well beyond its present size under a mile of ice and snow, and only after the last of the glacier had receded 15,000 years ago could the land be populated.

Arnie Neptune's reason for denying the Ice Age, Laurie said, was that in his opinion, Glooskap, the Hero-Creator of his people, would not have put them into such a harsh climate. It had taken all of her powers of persuasion to convince Arnie otherwise and make him understand the geological evidence pointing to a glacier's existence.

Just as there are "Creationists" in the Christian religion who insist on a literal interpretation of the Garden of Eden and maintain that Irish Bishop James Ussher's calculation from the Bible of the earth's beginning on October 23, 4004 B.C., is the absolute truth and that Darwin is dead wrong, etc., there are "Creationists" among Indian believers, as well. They deny the Asian–Bering Strait hypothesis and presumably any other scientific theory that has them coming to America from *Away*. As "First Peoples," the Indians see themselves as *really* "native Americans," established by their Creator on the spot. Where the Wabanaki are concerned, the actual agent for the Supreme Being was Glooskap who, according to some accounts, was sent in a great stone canoe (in effect, an island of granite covered with trees) and fashioned the local Indians from the trunks of ash trees. He shot arrows into those trees and "out stepped men and women. They were strong and graceful people with light brown skin and shining black hair...."[2] Not only did Glooskap populate the land with handsome people whom he called Wabanaki, "People of the Dawn," he provided animals, too. Some, like the beaver and frog, he reduced from giants to normal size and gave names to. He also named outstanding geographical features of the land.

Glooskap has many spellings among the different Wabanaki tribes—from Koluscap among the Micmac to Gluskonba among the Western Abenaki of Vermont. The most authentic pronounciation, I suspect, is one I heard from Arnie Neptune, *Glooskaby*. On several occasions, I have been in the presence of this spiritual Penobscot traditionalist, watching him open a ceremony with a "smudge" of incense from a tobacco offering, diffusing the smoke using a long, sacred feather, or keeping a group of non-Indian children at the Hudson Museum in Orono enthralled with his tales.

Because of the rich panoply of Wabanaki legends, a different kind of archaeology can be practiced—digging up glimpses of what the ancients were like from their myths, in much the same way we use clues provided to later generations through their material cultures. The nameless occupants of sites like Goddard, and some far, far older, obviously had views and beliefs with which they populated their mental world and, by transference, their physical environments.

No one, in my opinion, has done a better job of trying to re-create this atmosphere for a modern audience than the Western Abenaki novelist Joseph Bruchac of Vermont. His setting in a series of books of fiction is the heartland of these neighbors of our Maine Abenaki, namely Lake Champlain and vicinity, and the time period approximates that of the oldest of the Paleo-Indian occupations found in Maine, which is the "caribou-killing grounds" at Aziscohos Lake, around 10,500 years ago. So there is a likelihood that Bruchac in his use of legend has struck close to the cultural roots of our own anonymous, prehistoric Native Americans in Maine.

In *The Waters Between,* the finale of a trilogy, the tribally unnamed denizens of a sort of dreamscape universe are called "The Only People," as befits the tendency of Indian groups to call themselves The People in their own language.[3] Are these ancient Indians alone in their corner of the planet (with as yet no consciousness that they are on a planet orbiting the sun)? No, not exactly alone, because in their world everything inanimate has life and animals are often interchangeable with humans and vice versa. The sun, itself, is called "Day Walker"; darkness is "Night Walker"; the man known as Bear Talker is as much bear as human and speaks with his fellow bruins; Gray Otter moves like an otter; Carries-Snakes is like a snake, himself, and always surrounded by these reptiles, with whom he similarly converses; and Walks-in-a-Hole steps on a solid boulder or hard ground and his feet go right into them. These more-than-human types are accorded in the book the title of "deep-seers"; otherwise in Western Abenaki, *mteowlins*, in Eastern Abenaki, *m'teoulinos*, or shamans.

Some of these Merlin-like wizards, as in Anglo-Saxon mythology, are good; others are evil, like the villain of *The Waters Between* who is called Watches Darkness and travels with a ferocious (because mistreated) white bear. Bruchac's Only People, like all Native Americans, are inveterate story-tellers and he weaves *their* stories—like the tale of Chibai, the cannibal ghost, into the Only People's own creatively imagined existence. Magic is everywhere, but magic often with a moral and a meaning, teaching them, as it did the real first Americans, how to extract a living from their not altogether benign environment. As hunting and fishing folk, dependent on nature, the Only People show a great respect, as their actual descendants do to this day, to the animals they must kill, thanking them ceremonially for volunteering to give up their lives so Indians might eat, and the same with plants, and even with stones that are used for implements. Young Hunter is the hero in Bruchac's trilogy. He is on his way to becoming a "deep-seer," a shaman. Through his narrative of this conceived dawn of Native American life in North America, Bruchac, a sensitive, perceptive writer of the same ancestry, has tried to bring out of anonymity a concept as concrete in its images as the archaeologist does in sifting out his artifacts and extrapolating from them.

In the Summer 2002 issue of the magazine *Parabola*, dedicated to "Myth, Tradition, and the Search for Meaning," Joseph Bruchac beautifully illustrates how this *deep-seeing* into the past of his fellow native people is brought forward into the present. The theme for this particular issue was dying, and Bruchac's contribution was to write of the common American Indian concept of the Milky Way as a path followed by human souls—the Spirits Path of the Great Plains Sioux and others, the Sky Path of the Paiute, the Ghost Road of the northern

Algonquins like the Crees, the Montagnais and Naskapis, and the Sky Trail of the Abenaki and Iroquois. The innumerable stars are the footprints of the dead, not only humans but also animals, and the edges of that heavenly road are lined with a supply of delicious wild strawberries (leading to an Iroquois saying by those who recover from a near-fatal illness, "I almost ate strawberries"). At one point on the way, according to a Lenape (Delaware) legend, a bridge has to be crossed and it is guarded by dogs. The object lesson here is that if you mistreated your own dog in real life, you will not be allowed to cross. Finally, Bruchac writes of a story told in his own family, connected to the grandfather of one of his mother's cousins. When that gentleman, known as Grampa Lewis, was dying in 1918 at the time of the great influenza epidemic, his last words were to ask about his favorite grandson: "How's my little Eddie?" But that same afternoon, Eddie, also stricken with influenza, had died and no one had the heart to tell the old man, who not long afterward died ignorant of the fact. Just before he died, however, the family had looked out the window and noticed a lone little light in the sky, wandering about as if lost. Then, after Grampa Lewis passed away, a bigger light appeared, went to the smaller one, and together the two lights mounted side by side into the darkened heavens until they joined the Milky Way—Grandpa Lewis and Little Eddie, they were sure.

Bruchac refers to such an act of belief as "the ancient and sacred understanding that dying is not a final act, but a link between worlds, part of a great eternal circle."[4]

It is also a token of the "spirituality" that one hears so often spoken of in regard to American Indians. Again, to quote Bruchac: "To the native people of the Americas, that world of the spirit is as everyday as eating and sleeping."[5]

Charles G. Leland's book *The Algonquin Legends of New England* was published in Boston by Houghton Mifflin in 1884. In his introduction, Leland stated: "I sincerely trust that this work may have the effect of stimulating collection." In explaining why this was important to him, there were echoes of a common idea among white Americans of the time that the Native Americans were about to disappear forever. Out West, the U.S. Army was trying to see that they did, and back East the survivors of earlier warfare and a prolonged retreat in the face of settlement had become virtually invisible. Thus, Leland's logical supposition that: "Archaeology is as yet in its very beginning: when the Indians shall have departed it will grow to giant-like proportions; and every scrap of information relative to them will be eagerly investigated."

But beyond simply amassing a bunch of Wabanaki tales for the sake of their potential historical and intellectual value to the reigning Anglo culture of the day, Leland had his own particular theory to promote.

Leland was absolutely convinced that two influences on the myths created by the Indians of Maine and their Algonquin cousins farther north had to be the Norse Vikings and the Eskimos.

The *Edda*, two separate sets of ancient Scandinavian tales, were cited again and again as models for the Wabanaki stories. Take, for example, their almost identical versions of creation. According to the *Edda*, the steps were: 1) Two giants were born from their mother's armpit; 2) Dwarfs were created; 3) Man was made from the trunk of the ash tree. According to the Wabanaki version: 1) Two giants were born, one from his mother's armpit—one of these giants was Glooskap, the good principle; the other was Malsum, the bad, whom Glooskap later trickily eliminates in self-defense; 2) Dwarfs called *Mikumwessuk* were created by Glooskap from the bark of the ash tree; 3) Humans were created by Glooskap from the trunk of the ash tree.

This American mythology of the North, the very last to become known to American readers according to Leland, "is literally so nearly like the *Edda* itself that...there is hardly a song in the Norse collection which does not contain an incident found in the Indian poem legends...."[6]

The Vikings also influenced the Eskimos according to Leland, and they in turn made their own contribution to the

Wabanaki tales—spooky stuff, for the most part, sorcery and other horrific elements. Leland wrote:"I believe it was from the Eskimo that this American shamanism all came." Ghostly cannibals with icy, stony hearts like the *chenoo* (*chibai* in Western Abenaki) seem likely throw-offs from those snow-bound blubber consumers, for "Eskimo" is an Algonquin word meaning "eater of raw fish or flesh." As we all now know, Eskimos call themselves *Inuit* or "The People."

Stressing a possible transatlantic quality, if not origin, for his Wabanaki subjects, Leland makes this startling statement: "Glooskap, who is by far the grandest and most Aryan-like character ever evolved from [an Indian] mind...is more congenial for a reader of Shakespeare and Rabelais than any other deity imagined out of Europe...."[7]

One of his recorded legends, itself, states that Glooskap arrived in "the land of the Wabanaki, next to sunrise" from somewhere else and that "there were no Indians here then [only wild Indians very far to the west]."

Charles G. Leland was an expatriate American journalist who spent considerable time in England and Italy and became known for a book he wrote about an Italian witch fully practicing her arts in the nineteenth century. A devotee of the occult, as well as a dedicated if opinionated folklorist, he has been called "the father of modern witchcraft."

Other claims made for a non-Asiatic connection to the Wabanaki have a decidedly occult ring to them, too, such as a direct tie to the ancient Egyptians. An entire chapter of *America B.C.* by Barry Fell has been given over to the alleged similarity between Egyptian hieroglyphics and a pictorial writing developed by the Micmacs. Originally a certain Abbé Maillard, who published a *Manual Hieroglyphique Micmac* in 1738, claimed he had invented such visual symbols to help his Indian converts to Catholicism learn their catechisms; yet even earlier, in 1677, a Recollect priest, Father Christian Le Clercq, said he had formulated this written sign language.

Barry Fell argues the Micmacs were already using hieroglyphics before the French priests' arrival, and he dogmatically declares that: "New England was either visited or in some cases, settled, by European and Mediterranean peoples who employed the Celtic, Basque, Phoenician, and Egyptian languages."[8]

A "substantial injection of Egyptian vocabulary," Fell continues, also has been observed in Wabanaki languages and he produces a number of examples in his book. Some Norse and Gaelic ones are thrown in, too. His ultimate conviction is therefore boldly stated:

> The voyages and colonizations during the Bronze Age were performed by the European and Mediterranean peoples whose vocabulary has given rise to that of the modern dialects of the eastern Algonquins and the eastern Algonquins themselves are for the greater part descended from these early visitors.[9]

The person who first brought this matter to my attention fifteen years ago was the late Honorable S. Glenn Starbird, a fellow legislator, from tiny Kingman Plantation in Penobscot County. Later, Glenn, a non-Indian, became the "Rights Protection Researcher" (some would call it "genealogist") for the Penobscot Nation. Accompanying a packet of material from him on this subject was the notation: "What really fascinates me is the remarkable resemblance between the Micmac glyphs, Ancient Egyptian, and [referring to another document in the pile] the glyphs on the Mormon plates." The latter refers to the mysterious script of the original *Book of Mormon*, found in upstate New York, which, too, has been deemed to have an Egyptian character.

Where such a tie-in might fit with the Wabanaki, I never had a chance to discuss with Glenn. I might add he was an indefatigable scholar of knowledge pertaining to the Maine tribes. His collection of every document from 1820 on in which Maine's governor and executive council discussed Indian matters can be found in several volumes of original papers in the state srchives and in transcript form in the state library—a fitting memorial to a lifetime spent as a champion of Maine Indians during a period when it was not very fashionable to do so.

The sort of fanciful stretch that sees a link somehow between Mormonism, Egyptology, and the Wabanaki is not hard to come by when speculation turns to the origins of American Indian people. A particularly striking example can be found in the works of Dr. Allen "Chuck" Ross, a Dakota/Lakota (or Sioux) writer from South Dakota. In his tribal heritage, as in many others, the Bering Strait idea has always been rejected in favor of the fact, as he puts it, "that the [Native American] has always been in the Western Hemisphere and in particular in North America."[10]

How did they get there? Ross's idea, which he voiced after reading Barry Fell's book, is: "Maybe the connection for these linguistic similarities came from Atlantis."[11]

The above was not written tongue-in-cheek. Ross's beliefs go well beyond the usual range of North American mythology—or let us say they have been modernized if not scientificized. He is a Jungian in his belief in the "collective unconscious." He takes the arrival on earth of UFO cosmonauts as a reality. As he sees it, Atlantis, that long-ago vanished island continent civilization about which Plato wrote, lying midway between North America and Europe, helped spawn the Native American or at least the eastern tribes, in addition to those who might have spontaneously emerged on the mainland. In regard to the far western tribes, he attaches them to another lost continent in the Pacific—Mu—ancestral home, along with South America—of the brown race. Ross also attributes this odd and unprovable schema to the *collective unconscious* of Edgar Cayce, the noted psychic and another of his gurus.

Although Chuck Ross did articulate the Native American thought that America was their Eden and the Creator placed them in it—that they weren't migrants from anywhere else— he still had to hedge his belief in a sort of Westernized, mysticized, parapsychologized, stylistic mode.

For an unsophisticated Native American interpretation written expressly for a non-Indian audience, there is an extraordinary and fascinating book by a Penobscot elder, possibly the first Wabanaki to appear in print, a feat he accomplished just before the advent of the twentieth century.

The year was 1893 when Joseph Nicolar's *The Life and Traditions of the Red Man* was published by C. H. Glass and Company, Printers, of Bangor. In his preface the author stated he was bringing forth a work that "no studies or researches of the white man have ever penetrated" and that he would "answer the question of where did the red man come from."

Concerning his claims for his book, Nicolar not only succeeded in producing material white scholars hadn't touched, but his tales have an originality, in regard to Indian origins, that I have not found elsewhere in reproduced legends or translated writings which often convey a sense of having been perceived from the outside, looking in; with Nicolar, you are clearly on the inside, looking out—despite the fact, as some Indians feel, that Nicolar unconsciously mixed elements of his Christian faith into the tales he reproduced.

He was writing only three years after what seemed to be the end of the Indian saga in the United States—the last great battle (it was more of a massacre) at Wounded Knee on the next-to-last day of 1890. Earlier that same year, the most famous Indian resistant, Sitting Bull, had been shot to death by Indian police who had come to arrest him for continuing to make trouble. Nicolar wrote about how he was a descendant "of the remnants of that once numerous and most powerful race." He also apologized for his lack of education or at least enough to "make them [the white world presumably] pronounce me as a brilliant and popular writer." His work, he added, was the result of forty years of study.

A lone voice in the year when the U.S., having completed its internal conquest was about to turn outward (1893 was when the Hawaiian monarchy was overthrown by American businessmen bent on its annexation), Nicolar and his work have remained a curious relic on library shelves, a miniscule tidbit of Maine history. Fannie Hardy Eckstorm, a non-Indian who started writing about the Penobscots within that same decade, still speaks to us today. But Joseph Nicolar!? It is as if he is speaking to us in a language and from the depth of a personal Penobscot point of view that we whites can only dimly understand. Even the names he uses, geographical and otherwise, are mostly ones we have never heard, and as he relates his tales, we know in the midst of our puzzlement that he is a *true believer* in that spirituality, not an *observer, coolly calculating* from secondhand material.

Nicolar begins with a name that does sound somewhat familiar—*Klose-kur-beh*—none other than Glooskap—a name he translates as "The Man from Nothing." Sent by the Great Spirit to make the earth "a happy land for people," this Wabanaki Adam opened his eyes and found himself lying on his back in the dust, facing eastward to the rising sun, his feet toward the west, right hand to the north, and left hand to the south. Sprawled there, paralyzed, he saw an inanimate universe, the sun at its highest, the motionless moon next to it, the stars fixed—he had no feeling, no mind. But then, there was brightness. The "Great Being" materialized, raised a hand, caused lightning, and said: "Let us make man in our image," whereupon, the *dust shook* and *heaved* and an image of man, "pale and lifeless," could be seen on the ground. Whether this was Klose-kur-beh, Glooskap's own vision of himself as the "first man" or a "first man" he created, becomes murky at this point.

Note there is nothing about arrows being shot into ash trees and people springing to life. In fact, Nicolar's description is infused with a biblical feeling straight out of Genesis and he writes that when the dust shook and heaved, it did so in the "form of the cross." Yet there is Indian symbolism, too, in his use of the number seven. Klose-kur-beh–Glooskap is told to climb a mountain "seven rainbows high" and it takes him seven tries to do so. The Great Being says he will visit him "Seventy times seven nights...." Dr. Ross also made a big thing out of the number seven, claiming that among his people, the Dakota/Lakota, there was a tradition they had descended to earth from the Pleiades, a group of seven stars, and that it was a sacred number for them and numerous other North American Indian tribes.

Mysteriously, in Nicolar's creation story, a female appears—an old woman, *Nok-ami* (Grandmother) who comes to cook for Klose-kur-beh–Glooskap. She owes her existence not to a male rib but to the dew on the rocks when heated by the sun.

The Eden to which these initial inhabitants adjust has food to offer—lots of animals and plants—and reflecting the respectful relationship to their prey that Indian hunters maintain to this day, Nicolar has his folk-hero god call an animal to come and it obeys and allows itself to be killed as a gift to humanity. And because it is "not good to eat meat and blood together," fire is provided in a streak from the sky.

Other humans arrive in this dawning Arcadia—a young man, telling Klose-kur-beh–Glooskap he is his nephew, born from heated foam on the ocean's waves, and a young maiden, created from the heat of plants, who joins him, bringing love and peace. Before departing with Grandmother "for the north," Klose-kur-beh–Glooskap leaves these inheritors of the world-to-be a set of instructions. The young woman is told she will be the first mother and bear seven sons and seven daughters and they will form seven tribes and from them "many times seven tribes shall come until they cover the land."

The coming problem of diversity is also broached—that there will be many races of man—and Nicolar, no doubt speaking from his own experiences, has Klose-kur-beh–Glooskap cautioning his people about the white man:

"...the white man will feel it as a duty to his children to seek new land for them and that he will not rest until he finds the land the Great Spirit gave unto you."[12]

"Don't get into the white man's fights. The Great Spirit did not make the land for brothers to fight for; He made it for love's sake."[13]

When war does break out, however, it precedes any inter-race conflict—it is Indian against Indian, their weapons the bow and arrow, war club, and stone sling. Nicolar says it was brought on by the "disappointed class" and that no mercy was shown—old people, women, and babies were slain.

A particular incident of real-life intertribal battle involving Micmacs, Penobscots, and Saco Indians most likely is the basis for Nicolar's venture into actual Penobscot history. No dates are offered—the Mohawks are somehow mixed up in it—and the geography is baffling, resulting in a narrative almost as fanciful as a myth, yet reflecting events no doubt handed down orally by Nicolar's forebears.

In this part of the book, southerners from *Go-eh-suk* (afterwards identified strangely enough as Cohasset, Massachusetts), led by *War-har-weh*, attack the north (presumably Penobscot territory). The Maine Indians counterattack and capture War-har-weh's wife and son. He comes to sue for peace and ransom his son. But *Nequ-tar-tar-wet* (Lone Star), the northern general, orders his execution and War-har-weh is beheaded. His son escapes, rallies the "*May-Quay*" (Mohawks), and the war continues until the "white man's big canoe" lands on the north shore of the *Maquozz-bem-to-cook* Lake River, wherever that is.

This internecine warfare ends in the use of spiritual force, causing an earthquake that swallows up the Indian armies, and an agreement with the May-Quays for a lasting peace—"the Great Council Fire"—another historic actuality in which regular meetings at Caughnawaga on the St. Lawrence River near Montreal, Quebec, between the Wabanaki Confederation and various Iroquois tribes, including the Mohawks, were held over a period of two centuries, starting in the 1670s. At one time or another, many of the Maine tribes who have since passed from the scene, like the Sokokis, Androscoggins, Kennebecs, and Wawenocs, belonged to this loosely knit association.

Meanwhile, ominously, according to Nicolar, the white man landed in the north country on a high hill.

"Here the red man received the religion of the white man. The red man was now ready to be converted and resigned himself to wait for the future fate that may come."[14]

Nicolar's peek into the future from 1893 is not a decidedly optimistic one. The Indians, he says, "are these people who are now on the descending slide scale to a point not yet settled."[15]

NOTES

[1] *Newsweek,* April 26, 1999.

[2] From a description of a 1992 animated film, *Koluscap and His People,* on display at the Abbe Museum, Bar Harbor, Maine.

[3] Joseph Bruchac, *The Waters Between.* Hanover, New Hampshire, and London: University Press of New England, 1998.

[4] *Parabola,* Summer 2002, New York, page 68.

[5] Bruchac, *The Waters Between,* page xv.

[6] Charles G. Leland, *The Algonquin Legends of New England.* Boston: Houghton Mifflin, 1884, page 5.

[7] Ibid, page 2.

[8] Barry Fell, *America B.C.,* New York: Quadrangle, New York Times books, 1976, page 282.

[9] Ibid, page 285.

[10] Dr. A. C. Ross, *Mitakuye Oxasin.* Denver: Wicona Waste Publishers, 2001.

[11] Ibid, page 62.

[12] Joseph Nicolar, *The Life and Traditions of the Red Man.* Bangor, Maine: C. H. Glass and Company, Printers, 1893, page 31.

[13] Ibid.

[14] Ibid, page 140.

[15] Ibid, page 141.

8

THE PEOPLE II

*W*ith the exception of the May-Quays, it is impossible in reading Joseph Nicolar to recognize our latter-day names for the Indian tribes of Maine history. The same holds true for his labelling of the landscape, which stretches from *Mik-mark-keag* to *Odur-wur-keag*.

The names we know—Penobscot, Passamaquoddy, Micmac, Maliseet, Kennebec, Saco, Androscoggin, and even less familiar ones like Wawenoc and Pigquacket—are of our own making. They are what we think we heard the Indians call themselves and their surroundings, honed by our continued usage through several centuries.

To compound the confusion, a third language is also encountered—namely, the interpretation the French gave to the Indian sounds they heard. At least one of their labels has stuck—*Iroquois*—for a large grouping that refers to itself as the *Haudenosaunee*. Others—the ones in Maine—*Souriquois, Etchemin, Armouchiquois*, remain vivid only to historians. Translating this French-Indian into English-Indian, we have respectively: Micmac, Maliseet–Passamaquoddy, and Eastern Abenaki (particularly Saco, maybe Penobscot, too).

Trying to categorize the tribes of Maine and the Maritimes just before the contact period becomes, then, a task that incorporates some of the insubstantial fluidity one finds in the Indians' tales and legends, themselves. Though they had territories, these, too, were fluid, as was their semi-nomadic existence. On top of that, they were not necessarily ethnically fixed. Volumes have been written about the tendency of tribes to adopt members to replace those lost in battle or through natural death—whites included. No eugenics here. Whole tribes, if broken up, joined with other tribes. Some disappeared. New ones emerged. As our archaeology seems to suggest, this is a process that went on for thousands of unrecorded years.

One thing is certain. There were once more tribes in Maine than there are today.

Currently the organized Native American population of Maine consists of four entities, all of them recognized by the U.S. government as bonafide Indian tribes. They are, as officially styled, the Penobscot Nation, the Passamaquoddy Tribe, the Houlton Band of Maliseets, and the Aroostook Band of Micmacs. Although the last two are independent groups residing entirely in the United States, they have strong ties to their Canadian relatives in New Brunswick, Nova Scotia, and Quebec. They assert that Jay's Treaty of 1794, which first established a border between Maine and Canada, allows them to cross it at will. All four of these peoples, when acting in concert, as they often do, constitute a *Wabanaki Confederation*.

But let us leave these moderns aside for the moment. At the point we have now reached—starting roughly in the early 1500s—it is important to see how much more tribally populated Maine and its vicinity were at the instant (in 1524) when the earliest known European interloper—Giovanni da Verrazano—an Italian sailing inder the French flag, brought his vessel briefly alongside the Maine Coast. The land this stranger was visiting could not be considered empty, in any fashion. All along the Atlantic Coast, various "peoples" or "nations," to use the Indians' own names for their tribes, had staked out the well-defined sites they occupied, plus long-established claims to exclusive hunting grounds.

That Verrazano received a hostile reception from the locals (the tribe has never been identified), including a version of "mooning"—i.e., lining up on the shore and presenting their bare buttocks to him—may well have been due to a previous undocumented collision of the two cultures that was not a happy one. Or conceivably it might have been the Italian's personality and approach—he was killed a few years later by natives in the Caribbean. This was a misty era of infrequent interaction—ships like Verrazano's were seen, then not seen again for years, although as the 1600s approached, nameless fishermen were coming and staying on certain islands in the Gulf of Maine and doing so with increasing regularity. Inadvertently, they brought European germs with them, and quite deliberately, quite rapaciously, they took huge catches of cod and other toothy fishes which were properly salted on their offshore havens and taken back across the Atlantic.

The *Pennacooks* were the southernmost tribe in Maine, spreading across the Piscataqua River from New Hampshire. In the town of York, where I live, they were wiped out by 1614 due to smallpox or maybe measles that reached them from the English mariners and fishermen who had made a summer headquarters out on the Isles of Shoals. Cleared, deserted fields met the hardy Anglo settlers who ventured into the area around 1630. South of the Saco River it was warm enough for the tribes to practice extensive agriculture. But the Pennacooks had vanished, leaving only the memory of their great chief Passaconaway and his name to grace a famed Victorian tourist hotel at York Beach.

To the west, in the shadow of the White Mountains, lived a branch of the Pennacooks called the *Pigquackets*. Or maybe they weren't Pennacooks and thus not *Eastern Abenaki*, say some experts, but in actuality, *Western Abenaki*, like my friend Wes from Vermont. In any case, they were fierce fighters, both *against* the English and *for* the English, most notably as scouts in the last few of the French and Indian wars.

Two other tribes in this lower part of today's Maine had similar-sounding names and are sometimes confused with each other: the *Sokokis* and the *Sacos*. The former were definitely a Western Abenaki tribe whose heartland lay in western Massachusetts around the Connecticut River, although they wandered a lot. The French called them *les nations errantes des Abenaquis Socoquis* and reported them in New Brunswick and among the Penobscots, with one of their number allegedly becoming a Penobscot chief. The Saco Nation, on the other hand, lived along the river that, to this day, bears its name. Their most famous leader, Squando (or Atecuando) played a major role in the fighting in Maine when King Philip's War broke out there in 1676. The drowning death of his infant son by some drunken English sailors who wantonly upset his wife's canoe led him to seek ferocious revenge before defeat by superior forces drove his people fleeing northward to Canada.

The Saco is one of Maine's five major rivers. Each, in one way or another, also reflects the Indian tribes that peopled its banks.

Moving north, after the Saco, the next great flowage is that of the Androscoggin. The main tribe there, although usually called *Androscoggins,* can trip you up because some historians will refer to them as *Anasagunticooks* and others *Arosaguntacooks.*[1] One reason may be the enormous reach of these people when they were still a viable entity—occupying land all the way west to Lake Umbagog, well into New Hampshire, and east toward the Atlantic, debouching into Merrymeeting Bay where it joins the Kennebec at Topsham—a length of 210 miles and a drainage of 3,430 square miles, with 7 tributaries and 83 lakes and ponds. The Androscoggins have been depicted as a "powerful, warlike, relentless tribe, characterized as the first to make war and the last to conclude peace."

Various subsets of this same group existed under names such as *Rockomekas, Pejepscots, Sabbatis,* and *Amascontees* at particular geographic points along the Androscoggin River. The principal village early on was at Canton Point; others were higher up at Rumford Falls and Bethel, and lower down at Auburn and Brunswick Falls. Salmon ran up as far as Rumford Falls where many were speared, there and at Lewiston Falls, as were sturgeon at the latter site. Agriculture was practiced here, too, and on a large scale. One cornfield, alone, at Canton Point measured 600–700 acres. In a key location, both economically and militarily, the Androscoggins had at least three canoe routes straight to Canada, easy access to the Kennebec Indians at Norridgewock, the Pigquackets at Fryeburg, and a clear, close shot, when war came, to raid English settlements at Casco Bay and in the Bath–Brunswick area.

Depending on which version is told, it was either the Androscoggins or the Kennebecs who had a prolonged

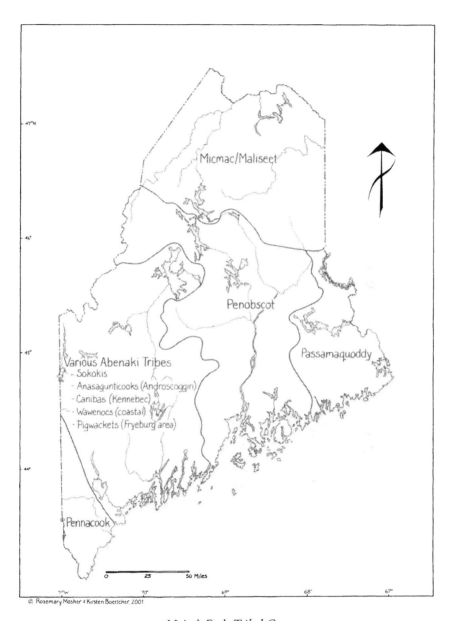

Maine's Early Tribal Groups

encounter with the English in their first major attempt at colonization in the northern part of the eastern U.S. seaboard—the famed 1607 Popham Colony. The confusion no doubt results from the mingling of the waters at Merrymeeting Bay—in other words, up which river did the English, led by their captain Raleigh Gilbert, ascend into a sort of madcap incident with the natives? Were they Sabbatis Indians, as one story has it, or *Sagadahoc*, a generic term for the Kennebec? The plethora of nomenclature as we enter this phase of history can be absolutely maddening. One gem of a misconstrual, however, relates to the very term "Androscoggin." Coincidence would have it that a notorious English governor of the 1670s to 1680s was named Sir Edmund Andros. An equally notorious (for his alleged inaccuracies) chronicler of the times was the French Jesuit Eugene Vetromile, whose book on Maine Indian life was for many years thought to be an impeccable resource until such seeming howlers were discerned as his defining "Androscoggin" to mean "Andros is coming." It supposedly really means something close to "fish arriving in the spring." Then, again, an extremely reputable Maine historian, Dean R. Snow, has said the river's name was changed from Arosaguntacook to its present form precisely to honor Andros.[2]

The *Kennebecs,* too, had subsets and at least one alternative name, the *Canabis*. Norridgewock has always been the most celebrated of their villages due to its pivotal role in the history of Indian–French–English relations once the post-contact world began to develop in earnest. The Kennebecs may or may not have been the Indians Raleigh Gilbert interacted with in 1607. The same holds true for one of the earliest French explorations in October 1611, which actually visited Gilbert's Popham Beach Colony site after its abandonment. The intruding vessel, which held the nobleman Sieur de Biencourt and the Jesuit Pierre Biard, most certainly entered the Kennebec River, sailing past Seguin Island, past the Sabino Peninsula, and upstream about nine miles. Father Biard's description of the people they met was no help—

Armouchiquois—that Gallic catchword for all of the natives south of the Penobscot.

The Kennebecs' territory stretched from Merrymeeting Bay to Moosehead Lake—the source of the actual river, itself. The *Sheepscots* have been listed as one of the most powerful Kennebec sub-tribes, and these may well have been the folks Biencourt and Biard came upon. If so, there is considerable argument from those who consider the Sheepscot River beyond the Kennebec Indians' pale.[3] In geo-political terms, both French and English were entering a "noman's land," where their presumptuous claims to territory in the names of their respective monarchs overlapped. The French said they owned Acadia, whose southern border was the Kennebec River. The English drew their northern line actually at the Penobscot, but halted their penetration initially at the Sagadahoc (the Kennebec's outlet to the sea) and the Pemaquid Peninsula.

Far outstripping the Androscoggin in its drainage, the Kennebec covers 5,800 square miles and encloses 300 ponds and lakes. That early French explorer Samuel de Champlain had already been at its mouth before the English, but was said to have desisted from voyaging inland when his Indian (perhaps Passamaquoddy) guides told him the Kennebec Indians were their enemies. In 1611 Champlain reportedly planted a cross in the Kennebec region. Three years later Captain John Smith, who did as much to promote the Northeast in England as Champlain did in France, sailed up into this river and its adjacent coves, mapping the coast and trading for furs with the locals, many of whom were no doubt Kennebecs. While Smith is credited with coining the name "New England," Champlain is cited as the source for *Quinnibeque*, supposedly an Indian assignation for a narrow "hellgate" passage between Bath and Sheepscot Bay derived from *Kinai-bik*, the water-dragon monster who guarded the foaming, boiling connection.

The final large-scale tribe of Indians once living in Maine before we reach the Penobscot River was the *Wawenoc*.

On a modern-day website created by the Davistown
Museum of Liberty, Maine, an unnamed book reviewer vents
considerable spleen at those authors who would deny the
Wawenocs their space in history. He angrily charges that a particular writer "in one brief paragraph...has eliminated one of
the most important Native American communities of Maine's
late prehistoric past," thus, as is claimed, contradicting "the
huge body of written and oral history of thousands of English
settlers and their descendants." Seeking an answer to this
atrocity, the reviewer asks rhetorically: "Is this because the
Wawenoc Indians had no significant role to play after 1620,
having been decimated both by Micmac (Tarrentine) massacres and the epidemics that followed?"

This part of midcoast Maine likewise received an Indian
name the Wawenoc booster charges has been neglected in
Maine historical writing. *Mawooshen*, a land described by
Samuel Purchas in 1625, was estimated to stretch from Mount
Desert Island to the upper Saco River; its heart, however, lay
in "highly populated areas of the Sheepscot, Medomak, and
St. George Rivers," and especially included Pemaquid.
Arguments have been made there were Wawenoc villages on
the Kennebec River, too, and even on the Penobscot.

Some of the scholarly dithering on this subject is due to
the role in history of a shadowy Indian figure known as the
Bashabas, or alternatively, as *Bessabes*. This fellow was either a
great chief who bore the title, like *emperor*, of the Bashabas or
was an individual named Bessabes, whose force of personality
made him an imperially great chief, with a realm stretching
from Hancock County to York County. Was he a Penobscot,
as Dean R. Snow has stated, locating him in a village at
Kenduskeag Stream near Bangor? Our Wawenoc patriot, in
his review of Snow's book, pounces immediately upon this (to
him or her) bad idea. Kenduskeag is too remote from the areas
where "numerous early writers" have placed the legendary
leader. One thing only is certain: the Bashabas or Bessabes, or
whoever or whatever he was, found his death in combat—
most likely against other Indians—in this dawn-time at the

beginning of the first European beachheads.

Yet the Wawenocs, there is no dispute, were inadvertently involved in one of the most important and far-reaching of the very earliest English–Indian interplays to occur along the New England Coast.

In June 1605 a veteran sea captain named George Waymouth anchored his shsip off the Pemaquid peninsula and made contact with a body of Indians, mostly Wawenocs but including a Wampanoag visitor from Cape Cod. Waymouth was under hire to an English aristocrat, Sir Ferdinando Gorges, and his backers in a commercial venture to explore the New World. His cover story for the famous (or infamous) incident at the mouth of the St. George River, where he kidnapped five Indians and took off with them to England, has the rather hollow quality of a public relations "spin." It was claimed by Waymouth that one of his scouts reported 283 "salvages [*sic*], every one with their bows and arrows, with their dogs and wolves" lurking about and, having no visible signs of trade goods with them, had to be up to no good; therefore, capturing five of them to wring out intelligence of their motives was a perfectly acceptable strategy— except, after enticing that quintet aboard with the promise of bowls of green peas (which the Indians apparently loved), he carried them across the Atlantic. The "spin" hardly meets the straight-face test.

There were, eventually, some fairly momentous consequences due to this dastardly act which was essentially motivated to acquire "intelligence" of America's potential for certain English investors. Three of the tribesmen were boarded with Sir Ferdinando Gorges and two with one of his partners, Sir John Popham, the lord chief justice of England, and they were taught enough English so they could converse. Their tales were exactly what the Englishmen wanted to hear— riches and resources galore awaited them. Fired with new enthusiasm for an enterprise they had already backed with significant money, Gorges and Popham used their influence in high places to persuade King James I to issue charters for two colonizing, joint-stock companies to populate *Virginia*, a catch-all name for the entire Eastern Seaboard. Called the Plymouth Company and the London Company, these two business organizations divided their target zones into North Virginia and South Virginia, then set about planning the expeditions that led, in 1607, to the Popham Beach and Jamestown settlements.

Ironically, about the same time Weymouth was acting so badly, a French ship was also in the same immediate area. Champlain was passing by before heading home to France after his voyage to Maine and Nova Scotia. Off midcoast Maine, he met with a group of Wawenocs at Wiscasset and entered the Kennebec via a back channel. Somewhere along the way, Anasou, a local native, gave him the misinformation that English sailors had killed five natives while pretending to befriend them.

Those Indians, however, were very much alive and soon coming back to New England, although not together and not all at once. One of them—the Cape Codder—was Squanto, who played such an important role in American history by helping the Pilgrims acclimatize themselves. Contact had not only been made; it had, for better or worse, begun to jell.

NOTES

[1] Professor Colin G. Calloway, *The Western Abenaki of Vermont, 1600–1800*. Norman, Oklahoma: University of Oklahoma Press, 1990.

[2] Dean R. Snow, *The Archaeology of New England*, New York: Academic Press, 1980, page 61.

[3] Charles M. Starbird, *The Indians of the Androscoggin Valley*. Lewiston, Maine: Lewiston Journal Printshop, 1928.

9

SETTING THE TONE

*T*hat Indians had more than a touch of paranoia, despite the sylvan environment to which they had adapted so well over many millenia, has been amply illustrated in their myths. From their imaginations, inspired by oral tales handed down by ancestors and the *collective unconscious* memories of animals (like mammoths and mastodons) and events (like earthquakes) long gone, they created monsters who could harm them, magicians of ill will, and supernatural phenomena—all to be propitiated and feared. There was even a Wabanaki oral tradition, the Legend of the Seven Fires, foretelling the arrival of white men on their shores which, in retrospect, later left them open to charges by the western tribes that they had failed as keepers of the Eastern Gate by not stopping the interlopers' invasions. Yet one wonders how much creative imagination would have been needed to anticipate the actual onslaught of the real troubles that would arrive from the other side of the ocean.

To be sure, even before the first European ships hove-to in their waters, theirs was hardly an entirely pacific existence.

Inter-tribal and, for that matter, sometimes intra-tribal conflicts, occurred. Warriors were slain, lightning-like raids from enemies carried off women and children plus stores of precious food, hideous tortures of prisoners had been invented, and starvation and sickness were experienced, but the scale was miniscule. Who could foretell that as early as 1600, hundreds of fishing vessels would be traveling each year from European ports to these shores? Who among the Native Americans, including their best shamans, could understand what invisible germs did? The Europeans, themselves, had no concept of the origins of illness. As for the vagaries of European politics, the growth of nationalism among individual countries, the murderous split in Christianity that had led to a seemingly permanent civil war between Catholics and Protestants, the aftermath of feudalism and the hunger for land ownership, Europe's budding imperialism, the Renaissance—you name it—the "salvages" in America had to be clueless.

The four kidnapped Wawenocs and one unlucky Wampanoag spending their time on the estates of their wealthy hosts, learning English and English ways, were probably not much better informed about Old World conditions than if they'd been left at home.

England was at the tail end of the Elizabethan Age. Good Queen Bess had died in 1603, to be replaced by the Scottish monarch, James Stuart, who became James I in England. Sir Ferdinando Gorges, despite his foreign-sounding name, was pedigreed Norman English with roots back to William the Conqueror. An adventurer and soldier since his youth, he was a cousin to Sir Walter Raleigh and Raleigh's half-brother, Sir Humphrey Gilbert, who, under Elizabeth, had vigorously promoted English overseas activity. Sir Humphrey, himself, had claimed Newfoundland for his queen in 1583, and then drowned when his flagship sank on the way home.

Although James I showed little interest in these ventures, his oldest son Henry, for as long as he lived (he died of fever at age nineteen), kept a coterie of expansionists such as Raleigh and Gorges and their noted scientific advisors and publicists like Thomas Hariot and Richard Hakluyt at his own palace. Sir John Popham joined in later. Alleged to have been an outlaw highwayman in his younger days, he had ended up as lord chief justice, England's top prosecutor. In that capacity, he had condemned Raleigh to prison and ultimate execution on behalf of James I, notwithstanding which, he, himself, showed real interest in English emigration to America—some claimed in order to get rid of the numerous miscreants he was sentencing in his court, many of them vagrants, ex-peasants forced off their lands.

The premise on which the Europeans made their claims in the New World seemed logical enough from their point of view: *first come, first serve.* They landed on a distant shore, planted a cross or a placque, and stated they were taking the land in the name of such and such a king or queen. How much land? They hadn't the foggiest idea of its outlines, so they just considered they were taking all of it.

The Portuguese and Spanish had started the process and given it a certain panache by having the pope bless their efforts at the Treaty of Tordesillas of 1494 whereby those two countries blithely divided the entire world between themselves. Other countries, even devoutly Catholic ones like France, protested. After the Reformation, of course, the pope's writ no longer mattered to Protestant countries, especially England and Holland.

The race was on.

Where it concerned Maine, the French actually won the race. In 1604 the first settlement in our state was made on an island in the St. Croix River. Ironically, this was a period in French history when tolerance between warring Catholics and Protestant Gauls still existed, and the joint effort was led by Sieur de Monts, a Protestant, and Champlain, his Catholic navigator. However, the site they chose was terrible—more than half their people died that winter, mainly of scurvy, until the Passamaquoddy came to their rescue with fresh food and tribal medicine—but inexplicably, although Champlain afterward traveled to Cape Cod and could have picked any of a number of lovely harbors—Portland or Boston or Plymouth—in which to transfer the survivors, he picked Nova Scotia instead, leaving France's claim situated rather far north.

The expedition that Gorges and Popham sent to Maine in 1607 was as evanescent as the French attempt had been Down East.

Raleigh Gilbert, son of Sir Humphrey Gilbert, co-led this expedition with George Popham, Sir John's nephew. Hostility from the natives has been given as the reason for the settlement's abandonment after less than a year. Gilbert's own writings reveal an interaction with local Indians that was more dicey than dire and it seems other factors really sent the Englishmen back home.

Gilbert's logbook reveals that on the 23rd and 24th of September 1607, he and some of his men in a shallop were on the Kennebec, and around 6:00 P.M. found a campsite on a "flat, low island" with rapids on either side of them. In his work, *The Indians of the Kennebec*, Captain Charles E. Nash thinks this happened at Randolph or possibly Augusta.[1] That night, Indians began calling to the whites from one side of the river *in broken English* and a colloquy went on all night.

In the morning they were visited by a sagamore named Sebenoa who declared himself the lord of the entire Sagadahoc (Kennebec) River. A series of comic opera mishaps next transpired. Sebenoa got into Gilbert's shallop, but demanded that an English hostage be placed in one of his canoes, and once this was done, the canoe took off. Gilbert chased after them, his men holding Sebenoa so he couldn't jump overboard. They reached an Indian village. Still pursuing their hostage countryman, the English came face to face with "fifty able men very strong and tall...all newly painted and armed with bows and arrows." After a parley and a few words from Sebenoa, the hostage was handed back.

Trading then began, the Indians producing tobacco and "certain small skins that were of no value." But trouble arose once more when an Indian threw an English firebrand, used for lighting flintlocks, into the water. Gilbert ordered his men to raise their weapons. The Indians held onto the shallop's rope. "Aim muskets!" Gilbert cried. The Indians let go, ran into the bushes, and began notching their arrows. No one shot, however. At length, an Indian in a canoe paddled out to the shallop and tried to apologize. Gilbert "made show as if they were still friends." End of incident.

On September 27, in this same region, Gilbert went ahead and took possession of the land for King James I by erecting a cross.

In such casual fashion was "possession taken" of another unsurveyed body of acreage for the ruler of England to parcel out to his cronies—for a price—and they, too, to make their money back, to divide in a hierarchical, quasi-feudal fashion. The Popham Colony, had it lasted, had a pre-planned pecking order, starting with "Gentlemen of Quality" at the top and descending through various gradations to "Commonalty, Landsmen, and Planters"—those who would presumably do the work and pay rent for the privilege to their "betters." No provision had been made for any rights the "salvages" might have vis a vis the property that was being dispensed. Only later, to nail down claims to the ownership of real estate that fellow Englishmen might dispute, were "Indian deeds" sought. The moral question of taking native land, raised by a few thinkers, received, if anything, mere lip service.

But even this early in the game, the original inhabitants were no longer wholly anonymous. Raleigh Gilbert and company had gotten to meet Sebenoa. They also knew Skidwarroes because they had brought him with them—one of the four abducted Wawenocs—from England. The idea had been to have him serve as their interpreter and go-between, but once back in his own neighborhood (he was from Pemaquid), Skidwarroes had other plans and immediately decamped. Similar difficulties were experienced with yet another member of the Wawenoc quartet—Nahanada—who, a few years before, had been brought home to Pemaquid by Captain Martin Pring, one of Gorges's sea captains. Reinstalled as sachem by his people, Nahanada proved to be no more a puppet for the English than Skidwarroes.

The failure of the colony was due more to a collapse of its leadership than to any overt hostility from the natives. George Popham died during that first winter, but was the only casualty. Resupply ships arrived in the spring. In the summer, another ship brought news that Raleigh Gilbert's older brother had passed away in England and that he needed to go back and fulfill his role as head of the family estate. Bereft of its twin heads, the expedition easily self-destructed.

Whatever the Indians' role in the thwarting of the first English venture in Maine, a pattern had been initiated, a tone

*Archaeological excavations began in 1997 (and continue every summer)
after the site of the Popham Colony's Fort St. George was confirmed
at the tip of Sabino Head near the mouth of the Kennebec River.*
FRIENDS OF THE MAINE STATE MUSEUM

set. It could be categorized as one of "distrust" and "attraction." *Trade* was the attraction, more so possibly for the Indians, since they had seen useful objects—muskets, metal axes, copper pots, etc.—that were so much more efficient than their own Stone Age equipment.

Nevertheless, the English were aware of the value of furs, which they could bring home and sell for prodigious profit. A claim has been made, too, that Popham was abandoned because the fur supply available in that part of midcoast Maine had proved so skimpy.

The real wealth in beaver, the most sought-after species, (especially for men's beaver hats), apparently lay farther north and in the interior. Another of the five kidnappees, the famous Tisquantum, or, as all American schoolchildren know him, Squanto, played an indirect role in its eventual exploitation. By teaching the Pilgrims to fertilize corn with fish, he assured this new, later wave of English settlers in New England of a food crop they could use to trade with the Indians of Maine. A Pilgrim outpost was established at Cushnoc (Augusta) on the Kennebec for gathering furs only five years after the landing at Plymouth. Even though these "saints" were ostensibly strictly a religious community, necessity and the fact they had borrowed money led them into the commercial go-round in these years of pubescent European capitalism—an economic system that ultimately powered all colonization and engulfed the tribes, themselves.

Squanto had taken a long time to return to southern Massachusetts. His adventures could fill a book. En route from England, he'd been, so to speak, "re-kidnapped" by pirates, sold into slavery from which he'd escaped, reached England again, and finally made it home to Cape Cod to discover that all of his family and tribe had died of disease. But at least Squanto made it into the history books. The two remaining Indians taken from Maine—Manida and Assacomoit—were similarly captured at sea on their way back, also sold into slavery, and were never heard from again.

The French experience in the same "Sagadahoc" region mirrored that of the English. On Father Biard's trip in October 1611, he heard that the Popham colonists had been driven away because they had treated the Indians badly, an exaggeration that has survived in various accounts. Then, on the upper Kennebec, the priest and his party faced twenty-four warriors in six canoes and tensions arose. "You would have likened them to a flock of birds that wishes to enter a hemp field, but fears the scarecrow," was how the Jesuit described them. The French readied their arms, which included muskets and a cannon. The Indians, eyeing those guns warily, retreated a cannon shot beyond the French, then all night long created a commotion, "haranguing, singing, dancing, for such is the life of these people when they assemble together," the good Father wrote.

Fearing the Indian songs and dances were invocations to the Devil, the Jesuit had his own people sing church hymns such as "Salve Regina" and "Ave Maria" in competition. Then, the French took to mimicking the—to them—unholy Indian sounds. Biard commented they were "like two choirs answering each other in concert and you would hardly have known the real Armouchiquois from the sham ones."

Down south in *Armouchiquois* country, Father Biard was a long way from his home base in Nova Scotia. The French had been consolidating their bastion in the north among the people they called *Etchemin* and *Souriquois*. Since they had a talented writer to chronicle their efforts, we have, in Marc Lescarbot's three-volume *History of New France*, a good idea of the French colonists' experiences. Lescarbot was a small-town lawyer in northern France who, exasperated when he lost a case he should have won, shipped out to the New World and became a strong proponent of French emigration, lamenting, "I see many people in our France so wretched and so idle...that they had rather die of hunger or live in slavery or at best languish upon their miserable dunghill, than endeavour to get out of the mire and by some generous action change their fortune or die in the attempt."

Lescarbot was on an adventure (possibly only to gather material for a book), rather than merely seeking his fortune overseas, and he let his inquiring mind go where it would. He has praise for the two pioneer Frenchmen, Sieur de Monts and Sieur de Poutrincourt, who singlehandedly, as he puts it, "Want to see the land christianized." He has nothing but scorn for the merchants, some from Normandy, some from St. Malo in Brittany, who had gotten the king to take away de Monts's monopoly. The result, Lescarbot writes, is that the price of a beaver skin had risen in eight years from two biscuits or two knives to fifteen to twenty of the same items for a single pelt. He quotes the Indians as saying that "the Normans and the Malouins only want to make war on beavers."

The Indians with whom Lescarbot is most acquainted seem to be the Souriquois, or Micmacs, although he claims a strong friendship with Chkoudum, a Maliseet chief or one of the Etchemin.

The great Micmac chief of the time was Membertou, and it was during his reign (he died in 1611) that Lescarbot describes the customs of the tribe in detail. Like Father Biard, he is somewhat appalled by their singing and dancing, also seeing it as "in honor of the Devil," but a devil "who guides them to the deer." While complaining, too, that "the dance has served as a pander [*sic*] and broker of unchastity...," he likewise tells of a dance performed to thank Poutrincourt for tendering them a dinner, singing to the French nobleman in Micmac, "We have feasted well and we sing your praises often."

Other Micmac habits mentioned and described are the use of sweat baths (Lescarbot sees them as wholly medicinal rather than including an element of spiritual cleansing), the oiling and greasing of their bodies to ward off black flies and mosquitoes, the love of gambling, even to the extent of wagering their wives, and the employment of shields in battle and horseshoe crab tails for arrows.

Yet when he refers to "*nos sauvages*," which can just as easily be translated as "our natives" as "our savages," Lescarbot concedes that "though naked, they are not void of those virtues that are found in civilized men. For one thing, "they do not bargain..." compared "to our petty merchants who bargain for an hour to beat down the price of a beaver skin." For another thing—and here the disappointed lawyer must have exulted as he wrote: "They have no suits at law...this itch which today devours our France."

The seminal event in the beginning days of French North America occurred on June 24, 1610. It was the baptism into the Roman Catholic religion of Membertou. The ceremony was conducted by Father Jesse Fleché, and Membertou was given his Westernized name of Henri by Sieur de Poutrincourt. The baptismal registry records the recipient's age as 100 years old. The date was that of St. Jean de Baptiste Day.

Membertou was a noted warrior. When discussing Indian warfare, Lescarbot no doubt had this venerable Micmac leader in mind. Stating that "*nos sauvages* do not found their wars upon the possession of the land...," that they have enough property, Lescarbot likens their reasons for fighting to those of Alexander the Great, "that they may say, 'I have beaten you.'" Or, in some cases, he adds, to exact revenge.

The latter seems to be the case in an epic poem written by

Lescarbot (he was also a playwright and furnished the first theater production in the New World). Its lengthy title in translation almost tells the story in itself: *The Defeat of the Armouchiquois Savages by the Sagamore Membertou and His Savage Allies in New France in the Month of July 1607.*

In classic Greco-Roman style, Lescarbot weaves a rhymed, heroic tale based on an incident of Maine–Maritime Indian historical warfare definitely motivated by "revenge." The real-life version began with a not unusual Micmac raid on the Indians in southern Maine, identified in this instance as the Sacos. The leader of the northern warriors, named Iouaniscou, took prisoners, but somewhere around Mount Desert Island, massacred these captured Sacos. The southern Indians then headed north, prowled around Penobscot country, found a Micmac and killed him in retaliation. The victim, Panounias (Lescarbot calls him Panoniac), was a fur trader and the Sacos robbed him, as well. The return of his body by the Passamaquoddy to his Micmac people created a war frenzy and Membertou, asking the French for muskets, assembled all of his subordinate chiefs, including the one the Sacos most feared—Panoniagues, the murdered man's brother. After a rousing speech, which in Lescarbot's poem had reference to Marc Anthony's harangue over Caesar's corpse plus a burial ceremony of Viking proportions, the Micmacs sallied forth to the attack. The Sacos counterattacked. However, technical superiority won out for the Micmacs; steel arrowheads provided by the French proved better than bone arrowheads, and the muskets procured by Membertou won the day. "Let us sing of Membertou," Lescarbot concludes, and well might he laud this legendary figure who not only defeated his Indian enemies but helped firmly establish the New France connection through a religious conversion far more epic than any of these obscure, small-scale battles in the North American wilderness.

Historically, too, Bessabes or the Bashaba was involved. Although this equally prominent chief apologized to Membertou because Panounias's death had happened on his territory, he was never really forgiven nor trusted. Some years after the events celebrated in this poem, he was killed by the Micmacs.

Meanwhile, armed conflict had also erupted between the French and the English. It was only a brief firefight on the coast near present-day Lamoine opposite Mount Desert Island, yet the consequences were long-lasting. A French settlement attempt, led by Jesuit priests (among them Father Biard) and financed by a devout lady-in-waiting to the queen of France, had no sooner landed its people and supplies on shore than it was attacked and demolished by an English warship out of Jamestown, Virginia. In this incident at St. Sauveur in June 1613, the French suffered casualties, including one priest shot dead, and Gallic intentions of moving deeper south into Maine from Nova Scotia were thwarted, quite permanently, as it turned out.

But of revenge Membertou-style—sudden Indian raids, often with French complicity—the future would see plenty of that kind of action!

NOTES

[1] Captain Charles E. Nash, *The Indians of the Kennebec.* Hallowell, Maine: Valley Publishers, 1994.

—

10

ONE HUNDRED YEARS OF WARFARE

*I*t seems a leap of faith to believe that for the first three-quarters of the seventeenth century, Indians and transplanted Europeans lived together peacefully in Maine. Less than half a generation after the settlement at Jamestown, the English in Virginia were embroiled with the natives during the so-called Powhattan Uprising of 1622, and a mere seventeen years after landing on Plymouth Rock, the godly Pilgrims and their Puritan allies expanded outward in southern New England, crushing the neighboring Pequots of Connecticut in a fierce, no-quarter blitzkrieg in 1637. But all was quiet on the northeastern front from 1604 to 1675.

The reasons were various: isolation, wilderness, tiny populations on both sides, beaver and other fur-bearers enough to provide a brisk and satisfying trade between the two disparate cultures, and perhaps some wise leadership. Not that hostility was absent in this vast region. The Abenaki tribes, as we have seen with Membertou and Bessabes, went to war against each other. Some fought the Iroquois, in partnership with the French. Deadly Mohawk raids into Algonquin lands were a constant threat. (There is an old joke that when Mohawks were asked what they called Algonquins, these reputed cannibals answered: "Lunch.") Then, too, the French in New France had their internal differences: the rivalry between two officials, D'Aulnay and La Tour, in Acadia (which included some of Down East Maine) ended in actual battles and casualties and atrocities. When all of England broke into two camps—Parliament versus the king—and a civil war raged for several decades, the bloody conflicts in the home country were reflected in intense political infighting between the settlers brought to Maine by Sir Ferdinando Gorges, who tended to be pro-king, and the Puritans, who were pro-Cromwell and

Parliament. Sheer numbers turned the tide for the Puritans, and English Maine, in these years before any trouble with its Indians, slid inexorably under the control of Massachusetts.

The outbreak of King Philip's War in southeastern Massachusetts in 1675 is seen as the boundary line. That enmity against encroaching whites was brewing in the north and needed only such a spark to set off an explosion there could have been foreseen. It was now more than half a century since the Puritans had begun their diaspora to the New World, time for generations to grow up and need to seek new land. Once installed politically above the Piscataqua River, their settlements grew—always at the expense of the local Indians. Deeds of sale, signed with totem-like marks by some chiefs, were misunderstood on both sides. The natives thought they were sharing hunting and fishing rights; the English thought they were gaining hereditary property. In the area of trade, there was no misunderstanding by the Indians when they thought they were being cheated—only sullen resentment that on occasion burst into brief violence.

Very early during the settlement of Maine, in 1631, Indians killed Walter "Great Walt" Bagnall who had been given a grant of what today is Prout's Neck, in Scarborough. Bagnall, a giant of a rapscallion kicked out of Massachusetts by the Puritans, had been mistreating local tribal people for seven years. The actual accused killer, an Indian named Black Will, was captured, tried, and hanged on Richmond's Island, the site of a bustling settlement underwritten by the lord mayor of Plymouth (England) Robert Trelawney. Run by John Winter, a tough overseer, this plantation had a somewhat nervous relationship with its neighboring Indians, garnering in trade "...but three skins," Winter wrote his boss in England, "and that was two months after I came hither, and was for strong waters...." Later Winter complained that Indians were killing his pigs (so were wolves). "There is no Indians [*sic*] comes near us since they killed our pigs," he wrote in correspondence eventually published in the nineteenth century by Maine historian James Phinney Baxter as *The Trelawney*

Papers. Also, Winter documented the devastating effect of European germs on the natives: "There is a great many of the Indians dead this year [1634] both east and west of us and [a] great many die still to eastward from us."

The "strong waters" were recognized from the start as a real problem, at least by the perspicacious writer John Josselyn, on two transatlantic voyages to visit his brother Henry, the "Squire of Scarborough," in pre-Massachusetts Maine. As early as 1638, John Josselyn observed: "Their (the Indians') drink they fetch from the spring, they were not acquainted with other until the French and English traded with that cussed liquor called Rum, Rum-bullion, or Kill-Devil...." Although Josselyn expressed a typically haughty English attitude toward "lesser" people, likening Indians to the barbaric Irish, he was honest enough to add the insight: "They have no law but nature. They are generally very loving and gentle."

Josselyn, to be sure, had no real insight into Indian laws and culture. Yet he certainly intuited no good could come of the liquor trade. Indians were easily addicted and the merchants were well aware of the effect rum or brandy could produce. Thomas Purchase, who set up a trading post in 1640 at Pejepscot Falls on the Androscoggin River, possibly the earliest deep penetration of midcoast Maine, was notorious for watering his alcoholic beverages, so much so that an Indian is reported to have cried, waving a rum bottle, that he was drinking from "Mr. P., his well."

Despite Purchase's thirty-five years at his location, it seemed no surprise that the very first blow in Maine, once King Philip (a.k.a. Metacom, the son of Massasoit) went on the warpath farther south, was against this conniving exploiter. The tribal warriors who sacked his premises while he was absent and killed his livestock were most certainly Androscoggins. This happened on September 5, 1675, three months after fighting had started at Swansea, Massachusetts. In the week following the Purchase raid, a far more serious incident occurred near present-day Portland. The Wakely family was massacred, all but one young girl, who was carried off a captive. The exact tribe responsible has never been identified; the attack site's closeness to the Presumpscot River may have involved the Pigquackets; equally possible was the Sacos, who were definitely known to have attempted an assault on the settlement of Saco six days later. Revenge, indeed, was a motive in that instance—Squando's revenge for the death of his own child.

The events of King Philip's War and of other wars involving the natives of Maine and the Maritimes have been exhaustively described in many books. Elsewhere, I have used Harvard professor Samuel Huntington's term of *fault-line wars* from his study *The Clash of Civilizations* to characterize these protracted on-again, off-again flareups between different cultures and religions that can last for as long as a century or more.[1] They are struggles not only for power over people but more especially for control of territory, and often lead to examples of the legal definition of genocide, which is "the denial of the right of existence of entire human groups."[2]

That charge, in Maine's Indian wars, can be applied across the board. Each side was out to destroy the other entirely. Women and children were killed, as well as combatants—total war, seventeenth- and eighteenth-century style. Or maybe not so totally genocidal, because captives were taken. The English were apt to sell theirs into slavery; the Indians sold some of theirs, too—to the French or back to the English for ransom—adopted others into their tribes and, indeed, made slaves for themselves out of still others. Religion—and the hatred it spawns against people it labels heretics—fanned the flames of atrocity, Protestant versus Catholic and vice versa, since the majority of the Indians in Maine had been converted to the Church of Rome.

Membertou started the trend. The missionary priests then spread out. Unlike their English counterparts—the frosty Calvinist clerics being graduated from Harvard and Yale—the French didn't mind mingling with the Indians, living among them, sharing their hardships, learning their languages, and winning their trust and awe.

A towering figure here, a pioneer in the conversion of the tribes deep in Maine, was the Jesuit, Father Gabriel Druillettes. At the age of thirty-three, after studying at Toulouse and teaching in southern France, he came to Canada and immediately spent time with one of the northern Algonquin tribes, the Montagnais, mastering their difficult tongue and traveling with them on their hunting expeditions.

His home base of operations, as it was for so many other missionaries, lay on the St. Lawrence River at Sillery, which today is a suburb of the city of Quebec. This early outpost had become a magnet for the Native Americans the Jesuits in Canada were converting to Catholicism. During the spring of 1646, several Abenaki converts brought word to Sillery from Narantsouk, or Norridgewock, the principal village of the Kennebecs, that at least forty local natives wanted to become Catholics and many others were willing to listen to a priest, if one were sent. Father Druillettes elected to make the trip and establish what was to be called the Mission of the Assumption.

In a vast, forty-plus-volume history of the order's work in North America known as *The Jesuit Relations,* the comments about that young priest's choice of duty contain a certain sympathy for the difficulties of his assignment. The trip, alone, "as the only Frenchman with two canoes of [Indians}, whose chief was Claude, a good Christian," would be undertaken at the "most trying time of the year" (they started from Sillery in late August). His sole company would be *celles des Barbares* ("that of Barbarians") and perhaps worst of all from a French standpoint, there would be "neither bread nor wine, nor any food of the kind which are commonly used in Europe." Still, someone who must have known of Father Druillettes's aptitude for hardship also commented: "He will be able to satisfy in full the desire he has for suffering."

He stayed among the Kennebecs for nine months that first time, winning their confidence. He amazed them when he learned their language, which was totally unlike Montagnais, in three months, a feat that fellow Algonquins from other tribes had not been able to do. By tending to the sick and stay-

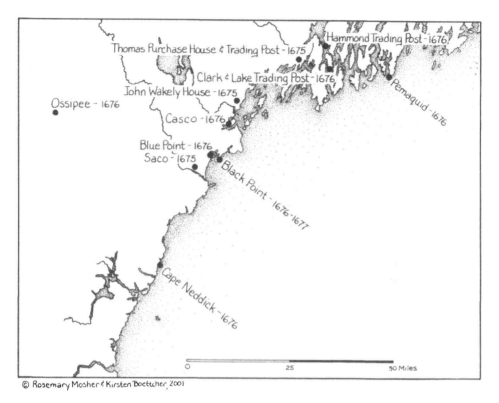

Sites of skirmishes in Maine during King Philip's War

ing well, himself, he re-inforced his prestige as a powerful personality, able to overcome the hostility of the shamans who were losing their hold on the people because they couldn't cure those afflicted by European diseases. Thus, many of the Kennebecs converted to Catholicism, now believing that the white man's "medicine" was stronger. On a subsequent visit in 1647–48, Druillettes traveled the whole length of the Kennebec River and actually visited a number of English settlements, where he was received despite the outspoken anti-Catholicism of these folks from Massachusetts.

In fact, it was his friendship with John Winslow, the Pilgrim leader at Cushnoc (Augusta), not far downriver from Norridgewock, that led to Father Druillettes's most famous trip in 1651, one that took him beyond Maine to Boston and Plymouth. His goal was to enlist the English in both colonies to join with the French and Abenakis in a war against the Mohawks. Rugged as he was in surviving the rigors of his trips (on one of them he went ten days without eating), Gabriel Druillettes must have been a man of great charm, sophistication, and erudition. The crusty Puritans and Pilgrims, whose laws forbade Jesuits specifically to be on their territory, welcomed him into their homes and, during his stay in Massachusetts, he was able to meet with their top officials, such as Governor Thomas Dudley, John Endicott, William Bradford, and Edward Gibbons, head of the Boston Militia. In Roxbury he was the houseguest of Reverend John Eliot, the famed Protestant missionary to the Indians. On Damariscove Island off the coast of Maine, he won over a group of tough Anglo fishermen who initially had accused him of being a French spy.

The Indians at Norridgewock called him "the Patriarch," although he had barely passed forty when he made this last visit to them. Plaintively, they told him when he said he had to return to Sillery: "If thou hast done us much good by thy presence, thou hast done us much evil by thy absence." While he was with them, it was pointed out, he had banished the "Demon of drunkenness," but as soon as he'd left, the English had brought it back, and so he had to go talk to his friend Winslow and tell him the Kennebecs "hated firewater as much as they hated the Iroquois."

"The Patriarch" was also a peacemaker among the Indians, themselves, stopping a quarrel with the Wawenocs that might have led to war. They had another name for him, too: their "Umpire." A shaman named Arambinau, who had once raised a hatchet against the Jesuit and been restrained, now became an out-and-out friend and supporter. The force of Druillettes's personality had won a strong foothold for the Roman Catholic religion and, notwithstanding the fact he left the Kennebecs shortly after his return from Boston and never came back, he paved the way for other Jesuits to follow him, the most famous of which was Father Sebastian Rasle. This latter figure, far better known than Druillettes, was with the Kennebecs during a time of constant war—a war of French and Indians versus English—and his tragic end occurred in the course of a 1724 raid on Norridgewock which essentially destroyed the village and sent its survivors fleeing north to Canada or east to the Maine Coast to merge with their fellow Abenakis.

The modus vivendi that had existed since the 1650s between the French, the Abenakis, and the English, as illustrated by Druillettes's visit to the Puritans and Pilgrims, was shattered by the outbreak of King Philip's War two decades later. From then on, it was war to the death—at least intermittently from 1675 to 1763.

Any sign of tolerance toward other religions and cultures had almost completely vanished following the revolt of the Wampanoags. Writing in 1699 after much fighting had ended, the Reverend Cotton Mather showed no patience with anyone who even dared to breathe an understanding word for the Native Americans. In *Decennium Luctuosum, A History of Remarkable Occurrences in the Long War, Which New England Hath Had with Indian Salvages from the Year 1688 to the Year 1698,* Mather fulminated against "one Tom Maule," an inhabitant of Salem who wrote a "Volume of Nonsensical Blasphemies and Heresies, wherein he sets himself to defend the Indians in their Bloody Villainies and revile the country for defending itself against them."

Cotton Mather, students of American history will remember, was one of the prime apologists for the Salem Witch Trials, which, incidentally, had a direct connection to King Philip's War. The hysterical girls who started it all were evacuees from the border town of York, Maine. To Mather, for whom the Indians were the spawn of the Devil, it was inexcusable that Thomas Maule would write a pamphlet entitled "New England's Persecutors Mauled with Their Own Weapons," which Mather referred to as "Alcoran" (The Koran), probably the harshest insult this Harvard-trained minister of Boston's North Church was able to summon.

Maule wrote: "God hath well regarded the inhabitants of New England for their unrighteous dealings toward the native Indian, whom now the Lord hath suffered to reward the inhabitants with a double measure of blood, by fire and sword, etc...." And those unrighteous dealings, he explains, were the killing of Indians "or Murdering of them by the old planters of these colonies in their First Settlement."

Thomas Maule was no Muslim. He was a Quaker, which in Cotton Mather's prejudiced eyes was just as bad. Consequently, *Decennium Luctuosum* ("*Sorrowful Decade*") contains this concluding passage:

> For the present then, we have done with the Indians...[but there were] molestations of another sort.... If the Indians have chosen to prey upon the frontiers and outskirts of the province, the Quakers have chosen the very same frontiers and outskirts for their more spiritual assaults.

No doubt any threat posed by a handful of Quakers in Massachusetts Bay had to be exaggerated; not so, the Indian hostility, which if anything was to intensify. While speculating that the Indians temporarily "have done murdering," Mather wondered what had become of the "chief murderers among those wretches," and then, trying to be witty and show off his Harvard learning, devised a Latin name for them, a mockery of their own long and complicated Indian names: *Bombardo-gladio-fin-hasti-flammi-loquestes*, meaning *Breathing-bombs-swords-death-spears-flames*.

Thomas Maule is not well remembered in American history as one of the earliest—and most courageous—of those non-Indians who stood up for the Indians. Yet interestingly enough, in the nineteenth century, Nathaniel Hawthorne used the names Thomas Maule and Matthew Maule in his celebrated novel *The House of the Seven Gables*. There is not much about Indians in Hawthorne's classic, but part of the plot hinges on a lost Indian deed to many acres of land in early colonial Maine.

Hawthorne was portraying fictitious Puritans, but implicitly condemning the land greed of their (and his) actual ancestors. His story has the Salem property on which the famous house stood taken from the original owner, Matthew Maule, by the unscrupulous Colonel Pyncheon who contrived to have the humble man condemned and hanged as a witch when he refused to sell—an allegorical foreshadowing, one might say, of techniques used to wrest away Indian land. Although the first generations of Puritans and Pilgrims tried hard to keep their settlements from spreading, their offspring soon broke all bounds—and always at Indian expense, whether by guile, by bullying, or by outright force.

A case in point is the illustrious Winthrop family, starting with John Winthrop, Sr., the leader of the Puritans who founded the Massachusetts Bay Colony. This God-fearing, autocratic squire from East Anglia in England believed the Lord personally had directed them to the Boston area because the Indians within 300 miles had been wiped out by illness. On that site, his group would build their "city upon a hill, and as far as Winthrop was concerned, remain congregated on those three hills (Tremont) forever. Yet within John Sr.'s own lifetime, his son John Jr. had to be sent north to Agawam (Ipswich) to create a new Puritan town as a buffer against the Indians.

Nor did John Winthrop, Jr., stay put. Going south, he went to Connecticut and acquired large tracts of land belonging to the defeated Pequots. To quote the family's biographer, John Jr. was exhibiting "the second generation's increasingly pronounced drive for property, which was supplanting the first settlers' religious impulse."[3]

The third generation, including John Jr.'s sons, Wait and Fitz John, became out and out land speculators, but none more so than his son-in-law Richard Wharton. Despite a lingering distaste in Massachusetts for gigantic landholdings by a single individual, Wharton managed to end up owning more than 250,000 acres in Maine.

It is instructive to look at the "Indian deed" used by

Wharton in 1684 to gain some if not all of that land in mid-coast Maine. Whoever wrote the document had to have been an English lawyer. Although six "sagamores" signed their names to it, it's hardly likely they could understand a word of such convoluted, run-on phrases as:

> And we the said Warumbe, Derumkine, Wihikermet, Weedon-Domhegon, Neonongasset, and Nimbanewet do covenant and grant to and with the said Richard Wharton that we have in our selves good right and full power thus to confirm and convey the premises and that we our heirs and successors shall and will warrant and defend the said Richard Wharton his heirs and assigns for ever in the peaceable enjoyment of the premises and every part thereof against all and every person or persons that may legally claim any right, title, interest, or propriety [sic] in the premises by from or under us the abovenamed Sagamores or any of our ancestors or predecessors....

and so on, for another seven lines of print. The land included some that sixty years before had been acquired from various Indian chiefs by the notorious Thomas Purchase. The Indians may well have understood the clause that said nothing could prevent them from "improving [their] ancient planting ground nor hunting in any of the said land *not inclosed* nor from fishing for [their] own provision so long as no damage shall be done to the English fishery...," but the caveat that they could not "prejudice" any of the existing English settlers may well have escaped them. The transaction took place during a lull in the hostilities, yet the interaction of pioneers clearing woods, raising cattle, and cultivating crops, and Indians competing with them for a dwindling supply of game and fish led to constant friction.

To pay for his "Title and Propriety [sic]" in Maine, Wharton gave the Indians an unspecified "valuable sum...in merchandise." The dependence of the natives on manufactured goods was as destructive to them and their way of life as was their susceptibility to imported germs. To illustrate the problem, an imagined narrative contained in the resource book *The Wabanakis of Maine and the Maritimes* portrays a young Penobscot boy in the year 1685 traveling with his father by canoe to do business with the English at Pemaquid.[4] The boy's father had trapped a nice supply of beaver and he spread the pelts on a table for the English trader to examine. Next, in the boy's own words, as re-created in this fictionalized example of Indian trading needs:

> My father walked over to the place where muskets were hung on the wall and I began to hope this was the year I would get one. He reached for powder and shot, instead. He picked out needles and thread, blankets and cloth, beans, peas, and flour, and he gave me a hard brown cone to suck on.... My father called it by an English word—sugar. Then, my father found a hoe and two knives that he wanted....

The trader also allowed him several measures of corn, but not as much as he thought were due him.

The Indians' dependence played a major role in the fighting that flared periodically and then subsided into fragile periods of peace. The Indians' absolute reliance on shot and powder (the first thing the father reached for) often led to war. When the English tried to disarm them, their pleas they would starve to death without rifles for hunting were ignored, and so they fought to keep their guns.

Throughout the nearly century-long struggle affecting Maine, there were at least six separate outbreaks of open warfare that have merited formal names in history. Over here, they were King William's War, 1689–97, Queen Anne's War, 1703–13, King George's War, 1744–48, and the French and Indian War, 1756–63. Two other lesser, more localized fights were King Philip's War, 1675–78 and the clashes in Maine of 1722–26 that have a number of sobriquets, the most popular being Dummer's War, after Massachusetts Lieutenant Governor William Dummer who presided over the peace treaty signed at Casco Bay.

Aside from the heroics of these military actions, which have been well covered by other authors, there were individual

*Death of Father Rasle of the Society of Jesus, killed by the English
at Norridgewock, August 12, 1724.*
T. W. STRONG/NATIONAL ARCHIVES OF CANADA/C7219.

stories that have echoed down the ages in personal narrative, fiction, and poetry. John Greenleaf Whittier's early work, the epic *Mogg Megone*, takes its title from a real-life Indian leader felled by a marksman's bullet in a raid on Scarborough during King Philip's War. The poet fancies that Mogg lusted for Ruth, the daughter of John Bonython (a real-life personage, a retrobate in Puritan eyes, but a friend to the Indians) and his heroine. After Ruth repulses Mogg and kills him in his drunken sleep, she then, out of remorse "goes Indian" herself and dies in the massacre at Norridgewock fifty years later. That event, in which a ranger unit of militia, led by officers from the town of York, destroyed the main village of the Kennebec tribe, was retribution for the 1692 Indian raid that had leveled their community. Jeremiah Moulton, four years old when he saw his parents slain, took revenge in spades at the head of his troops. It was in this surprise dawn attack that Father Sebastian Rasle was shot dead, but lest the shock of a Catholic clergyman's premeditated death serve as unanswered enemy propaganda, Moulton and his superior, Colonel Johnson Harmon, could cite the cold-blooded fatal shooting of a Protestant minister, the Reverend Shubael Dummer, by those Indians attacking York in the past.

Decades of tit-for-tat massacres made terror possible at any moment, and Maine was never safe for anyone. The career of John Gyles spans much of this period. He started life as a frontier child in Pemaquid and became one of the best known of the English captives carried off to Canada due to his adult skills as an interpreter. He not only experienced firsthand the effects of the Indians' hostility to the English, but also the hostility of the English to the Indians, and he tried to play an intermediary role by participating in many of the parleys and treaties that attended these wars, both declared and undeclared.

Captured one sunny day early in August 1689 at the age of eleven, John Gyles spent six years with the Maliseets at Meductic in New Brunswick and then three more years in Quebec after being sold to a Frenchman. At firsthand he saw, too, the turmoil in Indian ranks due to these wars, the losses they suffered in battle and through disease. He became totally conversant with Wabanaki ways and fluent in two of the Algonquian languages, but unlike some captives, he never became completely "Indianized"—maybe because they killed his father and later his brother James.

As an intrepreter following his redemption, John Gyles had the ability to tone down the harsh words used by either side, but whether he chose to do so is hard to tell. The official statement at the end of a conference where he had done the translating would usually include a disclaimer like the following from a conclave in January 1714:

> Captain John Gyles Interpreter made oath that the aforegoing questions and answers are the substance of the Conference had between his Excellency the Governor and General Nicholson and the Indian messengers truly rendered as spoke on either side allowing only for idioms of speech necessary for the understanding thereof.

In this instance, the "Governor" was Joseph Dudley of Massachusetts and the "General" was Francis Nicholson, military governor of Nova Scotia, and the meeting was held (apparently at Boston) after a peace treaty had ended the formal fighting of Queen Anne's War. At the start of the gathering, General Nicholson gave Querabannit, the Penobscot group's leader, and Abomasein, the Norridgewock spokesman, each a Queen Anne guinea coin to take back to their tribes to show they were kindly received. The next day, the two Indians appeared with their coins suspended by ribbons around their necks and Querabannit told the assembly: "I desire to tell what is in my heart. The present made me yesterday by the General...I wear upon my breast and upon my return shall acquaint the sagamores who sent me thereof."

In reply, General Nicholson showed the Indians a New England shilling with a pine tree emblem, saying the Indians and the English "should be like that tree but one root though several branches...." Afterward, he gave each of the five Indians present one of these shillings and three more apiece to the two leaders to pay for "the ribbons and loops about their necks whereon they had strung the Guineas."[5]

This kind of ceremonial cordiality only somewhat masked the tensions underlying such encounters. Trying to be conciliatory now that the status quo ante was restored, Querabannit said: "We should rejoice that all the English that dwelled in the Eastern parts would return to their former settlements there. And as Captain Gyles's father lived there formerly, so that now Captain Gyles return to his place [Pemaquid], which is the request of our chiefs." Yet he also put in a plea for fair prices. Abomasein was even blunter, stating, "The Indians are very much grieved that the price of beaver is so low...and desire the government to put forth the price what it should be sold at...."

John Gyles was continually busy. If he wasn't translating orally at conferences, he was often translating written messages the Indians wanted sent to the authorities in Boston. His spelling was usually as tell-tale as his signature at the end of a dispatch, such as the one from Fort George in September 1720 with the postscript: "the Indian Wampam Belt I have in closed and sent in a pees of brown peaper."

116

Whether it was Gyles who that same year translated a long and interesting letter and then had someone spell-check and transcribe it for him isn't known, but it brought up a new type of Indian complaint, neither finagled beaver prices nor usurped land, but the incredibly poor workmanship of an English carpenter who was building a church for them. They expressed consumer outrage, such as: "The joists to uphold the ceiling are ill cut and bending under them like rushes.... The belfry is not at all solid.... The covering of shingles is ill-made, it's easy to see the holes that are in it...."

In 1738 John Gyles was still interpreting after more than a quarter of a century, but in a discussion that year between the governor of Massachusetts and some Penobscot and Norridgewock Indians, he, himself, became a subject of concern. The governor, learning Gyles had been criticized by an English official, was upset and said, "I look on J. Gyles to be an honest man and much disposed for peace."

Loron, the Indian spokesman, agreed, noting: "John Gyles reproves us as much for drunkenness as a Minister would...." The man who talked against Gyles lived in Boston, he believed, but owned land in Maine and had been overheard declaring that if it hadn't been for Gyles, he would have gotten all the land in the St. George area. Under eventual prodding from the governor, Gyles's critic was revealed by Loron to be Samuel Waldo, the largest landowner in the District of Maine.

Waldo's landholdings, however, had been challenged by the Penobscots on the grounds that the deed to much of it was from the famous chief Madockawando. They argued that Madockawando had no right to give away the land in question, since he was neither a Penobscot (as history seems to have deemed him) nor a St. George Wawenoc. In their eyes he was either a Machias Passamaquoddy or a St. John Maliseet, with no ties to midcoast Maine property. However, nothing indicates that their objections ever affected Waldo's vast landholdings in Maine.

In 1749, when John Gyles was seventy-one years old, the

Indians were still asking for his services. He lived until 1755, a critical year, since it saw the beginning of new fierce hostilities—the French and Indian War—and in all reality, although no one realized it at the time, the beginning of the end for those selfsame French and Indians.

NOTES

[1] Neil Rolde, *The Interrupted Forest: A History of Maine's Wildlands.* Gardiner, Maine: Tilbury House, Publishers, 2001, page 151.

[2] Samantha Power, *A Problem from Hell: America and the Age of Genocide.* New York: Basic Books, 2002, page 54.

[3] Richard S. Dunn, *Puritans and Yankees: The Winthrop Dynasty of New England.* Princeton, New Jersey: Princeton University Press, 1962, page 107.

[4] "A Penobscot Boy's Thoughts," *The Wabanakis of Maine and the Maritimes.* Published by the Maine Indian Program of the New England Regional Office of the American Friends Service Committee, 1989, page C-35.

[5] *The Baxter Manuscripts: Documentary History of the State of Maine.* Volume XXII. Portland, Maine: Fred L. Tower Company, 1916, pages 52–54. Collections of the Maine Historical Society.

11

The Last Phase

On November 3, 1755, a gubernatorial proclamation was issued in Boston and began with the following sentence: "Whereas the tribe of Penobscot Indians have repeatedly in a perfidious manner acted contrary to their solemn submission unto His Majesty long since made and frequently renewed."

A new paragraph then was used to complete the issuer's intention—to declare war on the Penobscots. The Penobscots were stated to be "enemies, rebels, and traitors to His Majesty King George the Second" and His Majesty's non-Indian subjects in the Province of Massachusetts Bay were invited "to embrace all opportunities of pursuing, captivating [sic], killing, and destroying all and every of the aforesaid Indians."

The signer was not the governor. Lieutenant Governor Spencer Phips was acting in place of William Shirley, the crown-appointed chief executive, who had gone off to command (very badly) His Majesty's main forces in the French and Indian War. Thus the Phips name graced a document that has become infamous through the ages, still displayed and cited today as an ultra-symbolic relic of white cruelty, if not barbarism, toward the indigenous people of North America. This prominently posted edict ended with a ghoulish price list:

> For every male Penobscot Indian above the age of twelve years that shall be taken within the time aforesaid and brought to Boston, £50.
>
> For every scalp of a male Penobscot Indian above the age aforesaid brought in as evidence of their being killed as aforesaid, £40.
>
> For every female Penobscot Indian taken and brought in as aforesaid and for every male Indian prisoner under the age of twelve years taken and brought in as aforesaid, £25.
>
> For every scalp of such female Indian or male Indian under

the age of twelve years that shall be killed and brought in as evidence of their being killed as aforesaid, £20.

A graduate of Harvard, the adopted nephew of the renowned Maine-born governor of Massachusetts, Sir William Phips, Spencer Phips was no doubt just doing his duty, business as usual, in appending his signature to a statement of official policy. Seven months later, it should be noted, the house of representatives in Boston saw fit to increase the scalp bounty to the extraordinary figure of £300 for every Indian killed.

Yet the implementation of a total-war doctrine upon the Penobscots, even unto their women and children, need not have happened, and nearly didn't. The story of how and why it took place is worth telling in detail to illustrate the tragedy, in the Greek sense of foredoomed fate, which underlay so much of the relationship between Indians and whites in America. As one reads the legislative records of the general court in Boston for 1755 and 1756, it is difficult not to keep Aeschylus or Sophocles in mind.

By then there had been peace in Maine, at least formally, ever since the Treaty of Aix-la-Chapelle in 1748 had ended King George's War. As such "fault-line conflicts" are measured, that one was relatively short, lasting only four years, although it raged from India to the Caribbean and from North America to Europe. Not a lot of Indian warfare was involved during those four years; the natives were mostly auxiliaries, such as the Pigquackets who accompanied the colonials under the Kittery squire-turned-general William Pepperrell when they attacked the mighty French fortress at Louisbourg. The Pigquackets had not disappeared after their earlier defeat at Lovewell's Pond in Dummer's War, nor had the Kennebecs after Norridgewock was burned. The Androscoggins were still around, and so were the Wawenocs. Some members of these tribes (no longer extant in Maine) had kept up a transient existence, filtering in and out of French bases in Canada. In time, many of the survivors would merge into the remaining Wabanaki tribes.

By 1754 the English at their advance posts in Maine were growing ever more nervous. Letters sent to Boston by Captain William Lithgow, commander of Fort Richmond on the Kennebec, and Captain Jabez Bradbury of Fort St. George north of Pemaquid bore warnings of the "natives are restless" variety. The house of representatives in Boston was sufficiently alarmed that on April 30, 1754, they voted the considerable sum of £5,300 to fix up Fort Richmond and enlist 500 men. On May 15 Captain Samuel Goodman, writing from Frankfort, close by the mouth of the Penobscot River, injected four pieces of disturbing news into this climate of rising tensions: 1) The French were "building a fort on the back of Mount Desert Hills"; 2) German settlers in Frankfort had been told (by "straggling Indians") that the Canada Indians planned an imminent attack in which "all the old people were to be killed and the young carried to Canada"; 3) News from Fort Richmond was the "Arresigunticook [*sic*] Indians" were planning to attack English settlements on the Saco; and 4) Indians had killed a hog at Frankfort, and when Abram Wyman went to challenge them, one aimed a musket at him and fired, but the gun was knocked aside by another Indian. Since then, the Indians had not come in any numbers to trade, "only now and then, one or two, who are looking on only as spies...."

Nine days later, Captain Lithgow was writing that the "Nerrigewalks [*sic*] and Arssegunticooks [*sic*]" did not seem to be well-disposed toward the English, but that the Penobscots "may be harty [*sic*]."

A deposition by the Boston merchant Thomas Walker received in June 1754 quoted an Indian he met in the French fortress at Louisbourg (which the British had given back to France after Pepperrell's capture of it). Walker claimed the Indian had said he would scalp Walker if he met him in the woods, that he was one of a party that had killed eleven English the year before, and that he swore the French priest, Father De Loutre, paid the Indians 100 *livres* for every English scalp and 150 for the hair of an officer.

One of the most exposed English forts was at Taconic on the Kennebec River (Waterville–Winslow area), and it was attacked by unidentified Indians in November 1754. The Bostonians suspected the Norridgewocks and Penobscots. Hearing of this, Wambewando, the Penobscots' top chief, tried to communicate his tribe's innocence. In a letter dated December 9, 1754, he and his fellow tribal leaders wrote: "We did all we could last year to stop them...." Who the potential war parties were, they did not indicate, but did say they had talked to the St. John Indians (Maliseets) and the St. Johns would speak to the *Mukimuks* (Micmacs) among the potential belligerents. But if they did not receive an answer soon, they were afraid these Canadian forces (mostly made up of Abenaki refugees from Maine) would "not mind us...." A final plea from the Penobscots was: "We would have you strive for peace whilst the Kings (of England and France) are quiet."

Another Penobscot chief, Necterramet, swore that his tribe was trying to live up to the terms of the Treaty of Casco of 1726, which had ended Dummer's War. "We have hindered the Indians from coming against you and you must hinder the English from coming against us, we have done all that's in our power to do...." Also included was a request: Since it was a long way to the trading post, or truck house, at Fort St. George, could not the English load a sloop with provisions and bring it upriver to the main Penobscot village at Panouaske (Old Town)?

These communications were turned over to the legislators of the general court, and the lawmakers, anxious to reward the Penobscots for their peaceable conduct, called for placing the wanted truck house at Panouaske, while assuring them they would still "retain their property in all their lands."

That was in February of 1755. By June the same legislators were voting not to supply the Penobscots with any gunpowder or musket balls for their weapons unless they were joining the English military forces. Distrust of all Indians had set in following the formal declaration of war on June 11,

1755, against "the Arasaguntacook [*sic*] tribe of Indians and all other tribes of Indians eastward and northward of the Piscataqua River." Only the Penobscots had been exempted.

But they were not to be left neutral. On June 17 letters went out to them from Captain Bradbury, but more importantly also from the Massachusetts governor, reminding them that treaties they had signed, like Dummer's, required their warriors to fight side by side with the English against their fellow Abenakis.

The Penobscots hesitated. Talking up peace was one thing; fighting their brethren was another. After a nasty scene at Fort St. George in late July, when nine Indian leaders were almost assaulted by settlers and militiamen who demanded they take up arms against the enemy Abenakis, Chief Wambewando and others sent a letter to Boston. Three of their leading men would travel there, they said, to show their sincerity. They would "go against...those who come against us in a hostile manner." The letter added: "You must not think that we dissemble; if you could see our hearts, you would know that we are true." War would hurt them, any war against the English; they were strongly opposed to it.

At this juncture, a terrible thing happened.

It was a massacre near Owl's Head, in the vicinity of present-day Rockland, and the victims were all Penobscots, a dozen of them, including one woman and an infant. Their ambushers were local militia led by a tough woodsman from Newcastle named James Cargill.

In American literature, if nowhere else, frontier Indian fighters like Cargill have been heavily romanticized. However, the reality was that this offspring of Scots-Irish immigrants, who'd been brought to the Broad Bay region of midcoast Maine in the 1740s, had a long and somewhat checkered military career, but ended as an American colonel and regimental commander during the Revolution. Under the English earlier, he was primarily a dare-devil scout at the head of his rag-tag neighbors, always out front, and so much of an Indian killer that he never asked questions about who the natives he attacked were, and he was always adamant about collecting scalp money.

The incident in 1755 that initially upset Lieutenant Governor Phips's plans to convert the Penobscots to active allies earned Cargill jail-time—at least a year of it—little enough for what was an inexcusable atrocity—"felonious murder," the Crown called it.

The first indication the general court in Boston had of this development was a "Mimarandum [*sic*]" from Cargill, undated but estimated to have been sent between July 1 and July 4, 1755. On July 1, he wrote, he left "home" (Newcastle) with twenty men, soon augmented to thirty-one, and they scouted around the Fort St. George area. On July 2 they "came up with three Indians and killed and found their cannon...," then went on, and about sunset encountered some more Indians, fired at them, and killed nine. On July 3 Cargill went to Fort St. George and with the help of some of Captain Bradbury's men, returned and buried his victims. On July 4 he dispersed his men after dividing "what small plunder we had got," and they all went back to their homes.

What, of course, this matter-of-fact soldier's report did not mention was that the "enemy" Cargill and his men slew weren't enemies at all but putative allies of the English. Nor was there a whisper of a hint that the first three Indians were a peaceable Penobscot man out hunting, his wife Margaret Moxa, well known and well liked at Fort St. George, and their two-month-old infant who was dispatched by a blow on the head along with the declaration—either by one of Cargill's allegedly drunken rangers or possibly by Cargill, himself—that "every nit will make a louse."

The correspondence between Lieutenant Governor Phips and the Penobscots during this period shows a sharp contrast between Phips's tone before he heard the news and after he learned about these tragic incidents. At first he stressed that the Penobscot men must join the British forces, bring their women and children to Fort St. George and that a further delay in their abandoning their villages "must be looked upon as a refusal to join with us and will constrain me to treat you as enemies in common with the other tribes." Then, five days later, the bullying, threatening quality of Phips's language was diminished. The "Commander" (Cargill) and several others, he assured the Penobscots, were now in the process of being arrested and the guilty, he promised, would be brought to trial and punished. He added, "I am at a loss what to say to you. My grief on this occasion is very great.... There is a great God who governs every event. He has permitted this terrible affair and suffered a great cloud to come over us."

The next letter from Phips, two days later, was even more conciliatory. Cargill had been arrested, the lieutenant governor informed the Penobscots, and, moreover, Phips would no longer "insist upon your young men going out with us against the other Indians...." Nor was the tribe going to be required to evacuate its villages and remove en masse to Fort St. George, unless they so desired. Efforts were being made to set up a meeting and see what reparations could be made. Wambemando and Umbewesoo, speaking for the Penobscots, wrote back to Phips: "Brother, we shall say nothing further about what's done to us, but you must make it up, do so, make it up, that's all we can say." The Massachusetts House of Representatives followed up with a vote, confirming Phips's promise that no Penobscot warriors would be forced to fight against their fellow Indians and that "Justice shall be done in the course of the law" in the Cargill case.

Unfortunately, both the house and council (an early version of the senate), while sensitive to the blows the Penobscots had suffered, were impatient for the natives to put themselves under the "care and protection of the English," in other words, to leave their home territory and "come in," *surrender*, to the authorities at Fort St. George. Commissioners would be sent from Boston to treat with them and warnings were given that failure to accept these commissioners could lead to their being treated as enemies.

The last communication back from the Penobscots was dated September 6, 1755. They were specific, in keeping with traditional Indian concepts of justice, that they did not expect an eye-for-an-eye retribution, no one should be put to death, but there must be reparations of a material sort. They also made it plain they didn't intend to abandon their lands and homes and move in with the English. For, they argued, "If we should come to live among you, our dogs will destroy your creatures, and when we are drunk, we might sometimes treat you ill."

This disingenuous response was not long in creating a hostile climate among the Boston lawmakers toward the Penobscots. Its first indication surfaced three weeks later. The house voted to have Phips declare war on what they saw as a recalcitrant tribe. The council, the upper body, refused. Three days later, the council repeated its non-concurrence. The action was dead—temporarily.

By November, the house was back at it. Their argument was that the Penobscots had refused to take up arms and act offensively against the "Arrasagunticooks [sic]" and other tribes as obligated to do by treaty. In this instance the council finally agreed, whereupon Phips issued his notorious proclamation.

Thus did the Penobscots enter a vortex of events that would eventually cost them most of their land and much of their existence as a nation. They did not receive the English justice of seeing James Cargill swing from the end of a rope for his murders nor the Indian justice of reparations to make the victims' families whole again. Within little more than a year, Cargill was out of gaol and leading a party of scouts up the Kennebec River, passing Fort Halifax at Winslow, and inspecting a deserted Norridgewock. So unrepentant and brazen was he that he soon claimed the bounty he argued was due him and his men for the scalps of the twelve slain Penobscots, since they were now official enemies.

He even requested a £300 bounty for yet another Indian he had killed and scalped, but having dropped the scalp while engaged in hand-to-hand combat with a Frenchman, he had only retrieved it some days later, yet swore the gory hairpiece was the "very scalp" of the warrior he'd killed. A committee of the general court, headed by none other than Samuel Waldo, awarded him the £300 he so stubbornly sought.

But lest it be thought all of the cruelty and hardship was a one-sided affair, there is also in the same period a litany of English losses in Maine collected by the Massachusetts government. Here is a sampling:

> Frankfort: William Pomeroy, killed May 12, 1758, at Eastern River near Frankfort; William his son, aged about 14, captured at same time and place; Thaddeus Davis, grandson of Pomeroy, aged about 4, captured at same time and place.
>
> Georgetown: June 9, 1758, Ebenezer Preble and wife Mary, killed [it was highly unusual for a woman to be slain by the Indians; women and children were usually taken captive]. Children—captivated [*sic*]:—Rebekah, aged about 12, Samuel, about 10, Mehetabel, about 8, Ebenezer, about 6, Mary, about 4, William, about 3 months, Sarah Fling, servant maid, about 16, Simeon Gurdy, servant, about 15, small for the age.
>
> Newcastle: [Cargill's own town] John Nickels, aged 34, Murice Joan [*sic*] aged 27, William Cochran, age 18—went to hunt at Sheepscot ponds, taken to Canada in May 1758. John Machear, aged 50, William Hopkins, aged 40, James Kennedy, aged 13, all taken 3rd June, 1758.

By 1759 Cargill was a captain of militia, performing the same bushwhacking services for the new governor of Massachusetts, Thomas Pownall, on the expedition this young, ambitious, rising star of English politics organized to claim once and for all the entire Penobscot country for His Majesty, King George II.

Crowning this effort was the placing of a lead plate at Treat's Falls in the town of Brewer on the east side of the Penobscot River. Its inscription read: "May 23, 1759. Province of Massachusetts Bay. Dominions of Great Britain. Possession confirmed by T. Pownall, Governor." Pownall, himself, buried the plate beneath a large white birch tree, then had a flagstaff erected and the Union Jack run up for his troops to salute.

This push into the wilderness opposite today's Bangor was the northernmost advance of the English in Maine until that time. The French still claimed all of Maine farther south to the Kennebec. Pownall's logic, in requesting funds from the Massachusetts General Court for his expedition, was to end any French title to these disputed northern territories. To do so, he proposed taking these lands from the Indians, arguing the Indians never disputed the loss of their lands if it happened in a war, and that "as long as an Indian has any claims to these lands, the French will maintain a title to them." He likewise made a similar argument to Prime Minister William Pitt, adding it "would effectively drive off the remains of the Norridgewock and Penobscot Indians as it would break their hunting and fishing...."

His primary means of enforcing and maintaining the British claim was to build a fort at the mouth of the Penobscot River. Consequently, once Pownall had his funds, he set forth with 333 men and eventually found an appropriate site on Cape Jellison in Stockton Springs for a strong fortification that would dominate the Penobscot region.

En route, there was a skirmish with the Indians in the vicinity of Fort St. George and here James Cargill was again involved. Encountering an Indian encampment while on a reconnoitering mission, he called out to the natives, "Come in at good quarters," i.e., "surrender peacefully." According to his account, they shouted back: "No quarters!" and fired their guns. In the resulting melee, two Indians were killed, one of whom proved to be an old woman, for whom, presumably, Cargill demanded scalp money.

During a subsequent non-violent meeting with several Penobscot representatives, Governor Pownall told them that as subjects of King George (which they denied ,but he insisted they were), they had "forfeited their lives, their liberties, and their lands." They could be protected if they "came in," but the land—because he was building a fort on it—was now England's. And he further warned them, "When I have built my fort and set down at Penobscot, if ever an

Englishman is killed by your Indians...you must all at that hour fly from the country."

Fort Pownall was built at a place now called Fort Point. While it was being erected, Pownall and other members of his entourage continued upriver to lay their claims by placing that lead plate. They landed on the *east side* of the Penobscot River because one of their number said he owned the land there. This person was the famous Samuel Waldo, now a brigadier general of the militia because of his service at Louisbourg. Waldo epitomized the large-scale proprietors responsible for peopling Maine with English settlers and the ultimate gobbling up of most Indian land within the state's boundaries.

An extraordinary incident occurred about the same time the lead plate was installed at Treat's Falls. Showing off his property line just above the falls, Samuel Waldo took a step toward the riverbank, announced to the group, "Here is my bound," and dropped dead from a heart attack, "notwithstanding all the assistance that could be given him," according to Pownall. Initially, Waldo was brought back and buried on the grounds of Fort Pownall, although the body was later transferred to Boston's King's Chapel Episcopal burying ground.

The fort's command was given over to Brigadier General Jedediah Preble. Governor Pownall, after a short detour with Captain James Cargill and twenty men to Castine, where they found the former French stronghold deserted, returned to Boston. A year later he left Massachusetts to become governor of South Carolina, and then a member of Parliament, where he became a noted friend of the American colonies during the Revolution.

The war was winding down, but Maine continued to be a dangerous place, right up until the epic battle of Quebec when Wolfe defeated Montcalm some four months after Pownall had established that looming English presence at the mouth of the Penobscot. With the smashing British victory, it had to become evident to the Maine tribes that the days of their French allies in North America were numbered.

The Penobscots were most in peril. They had been declared belligerents and, therefore, enemies of the English Crown, and a powerful fortress had been constructed at the entrance to their traditional territories. On March 2, 1760, representatives of the tribe appeared, apparently unannounced, at Fort Pownall.

Their conversation with General Preble has been recorded.

> Preble: From whence came you and how many of you came in company?
> Indians: We came out of the company from up Penobscot River and there is five of us.
> Preble: Did you leave any of your tribe at the place from whence you came?
> Indians: We left seventy men, women, and children.
> Preble: What is your design in coming in now?
> Indians: We are glad God has spared our lives and that we have the pleasure of seeing each other and now we will tell you our business. Our tribe are desirous of peace and we would know whether we can have it and on what terms....[1]

Although they at first said they were there on behalf of their entire tribe, probing by Preble revealed they were really speaking only for themselves and their families and not for all Penobscots. Preble warned them there was to be no more "trifling" with the English, that Forts Niagara, Ticonderoga, Frontenac, and Crown Point, and the city of Quebec were already in English hands, that a formidable army would march early in the spring, and within three months, "the English flag will grace the walls of Mount Royal [Montreal]...as it does now the walls of Quebec...." By the end of the summer, Preble forecast, the whole province of Canada would be English "and then where is all the fine spun cobweb promises of the French by which you have been so often deceived...?" Most threatening of all, from the Penobscot point of view, there would be no supplies for them, since "you will find King George's subjects too loyal to their prince ever to supply you with one farthing so long as you persist in a war with the English."

Opponents of the Maine Indian Land Claims Settlement, harking back more than two centuries, made much of this *"treaty" of 1760* as indicating the Penobscots' final and definitive submission to English authority and their total agreement they had given up all their lands. Actually, it seemed, this was simply a unilateral declaration by the English that they had conquered and absorbed the Penobscots' territories.

Any *stated* submission did not come until 1763. By that year, despite a French counterattack that nearly recaptured Quebec City, it was clear, with the signing of the Treaty of Paris, that the English now had full control of Canada. The Indians, counted as English enemies, or even non-allies, knew they had to make the best peace they could. Thomas Pownall had been succeeded in the governor's chair in Boston by Francis Bernard, a lawyer and career bureaucrat, and it was to the latter in June 1763 that the Passamaquoddy, who had been entirely neutral, addressed an urgent inquiry. The letter was signed by Abowndrawonit on behalf of the "Passamaqoduia [*sic*]" Tribe.

"Governor Bearnnard [*sic*], we think it hard that you settle the lands that God gave to us without making us some consideration," it began. "We hear that it is peace and rejoice that the English command the greatest part of North America." Their other main concern, besides the land question, was that they had heard their "ministers," i.e., French priests, were to be taken away from them and they wanted a substitute cleric, preferably French, but "if not, send us one of yours, for any is better than none."

The response from Bernard stated unequivocably that English interlopers on the "Island of Passimaquida [*sic*]" or vicinity had no authority from Massachusetts. Areas laid out by the province for settlement had been restricted, Bernard wrote, to the east side of the Penobscot River and "about Mount Desert."

What his excellency, the governor, did not reveal was that the general court had already granted *him* one-half of Mount Desert Island as his personal property, plus other lands nearby he claimed to Abowndrawonit had "not been inhabited by Indians for many years." This gift to their chief executive by the usually penurious Yankee legislators was said to be in payment for a lawyer's brief he wrote successfully establishing Massachusetts's title to lands between the Penobscot and St. Croix against a claim by Nova Scotia. This in-kind payment was in lieu of cash Bernard had demanded because his expenses in Massachusetts were greater than they had been in New Jersey, when he'd been governor there.

Not surprisingly, Bernard pushed for a conference with the Indian leaders of a region in which he had a significant pecuniary interest. His action was symptomatic of the ways in which sharp operators were eyeing the vast acreage Down East that could be confiscated from the Indians. General Preble had already bought 2,700 acres for himself in the fall of 1762. A year later, he was replaced as commander of Fort Pownall by Colonel Thomas Goldthwait, and it wasn't long before Goldthwait and Governor Bernard were collaborating in a large-scale real-estate venture near the fort.

In addition to his military duties, Goldthwait had been appointed by Thomas Flucker, Samuel Waldo's son-in-law, as the land agent for the Waldo heirs, and as such was to survey the area and settle the late brigadier general's vast holdings. For £960 Goldthwait and Bernard bought out Preble's 2,700 acres, which had also been Waldo land. Towns like Stockton Springs, Searsport, Prospect, and Frankfort were eventually to emerge out of the activity in this newly opened territory.

The meeting Bernard had sought with the Indians took place in the Council Chamber of the Province House in downtown Boston. The three Indians who appeared were Penobscots.

The Indians were asked if they had been given the power to represent their entire tribe. They said Yes. Then, they were asked if they considered themselves subjects of King George. Their answer, it could be deemed, was instinctively devious enough to leave some wiggle room. "We have no particular king, but acknowledge we are governed by English law." The

English shot back: "Are you willing to submit to King George and this government as your fathers did formerly?" The Indians said Yes. Implicit, though, was that their forefathers had questioned submission as not including the alienation of their lands. They declared themselves desirous of peace and willing to renew ancient treaties. They said they were also appearing on behalf of the Passamaquoddy but made it clear they did not represent the Norridgewocks, Wawenocs, or Arrasegunticooks, the primary English foes, whose remnants were refugees at Becancour in Canada. Most of the rest of the gathering was taken up with complaints of how poorly the truck house at Fort Pownall was being run, how the provisions for which they exchanged their furs were lacking: clothing, flour, bread, corn, peas, pork, tobacco, rum, wine, etc. Prices were too high, as well, and worst of all, soldiers of the garrison and "strangers we do not know" were hunting on Indian land.

Other such conferences were held by Bernard with Indian groups, including members of the Norridgewock, Arrasegunticook, and Wawenoc tribes, throughout the summer and fall of 1763. Rumors of continued Indian restlessness and even planned hostilities reached the Massachusetts capital; another murder of Indians by Englishmen roiled the waters in 1766. However, matters like these had to have paled before the newer problems confronting the authorities in Boston. Those most restless now were the non-native Americans. They were no longer so *submissive* to King George. Almost overnight, it seemed, they had become *Americans*, not *English*. Governor Bernard, thoroughly hated because of his need to enforce the Stamp Act and other draconian, "intolerable" measures voted by Parliament, was hounded out of office, to be replaced by Thomas Hutchinson who, although of ancient Massachusetts lineage, was hated even worse as a traitor. Before long, this arch Tory would be in exile and with him would be Thomas Flucker, whose inheritance through marriage of the vast Waldo lands in Maine would pass to Henry Knox, the son-in-law Flucker had despised for his patriot sentiments. The American Revolution had begun, and the Indian tribes Down

East, on the verge of being overrun by white hunters, "strangers," settlers, and speculators, inadvertently were given a new lease on life by joining the bulk of their neighbors in the battle against King George.

NOTES

[1] *Baxter Manuscripts: Documentary History of the State of Maine,* Second series, Volume XXIV, Portland, Maine: Fred G. Tower Company, 1916, page 98. Collections of the Maine Historical Society.

12

Yet a New War

*I*n 1763 no one in Maine could foresee that within a dozen years, pitched battles Down East would erupt and a new threat would arise to hang over the settlers thronging into its vacated lands worse than that once posed by the local Indian tribes. The enemy for most Mainers-to-be had changed—subtly at first as émigrés from England morphed into a different breed of folks; then, once the French menace was gone and the British government decided to recoup its expenditures on these colonies through added taxation, resentment and rebelliousness flared and soon turned violent.

An intriguing book about this pre-Revolution period was published by Princeton University Press in 1966 and written by Franklin B. Wickwire, described as an Assistant Professor of History at the University of Massachusetts. Its undramatic title, *British Subministers and Colonial America, 1763–1783,* made it seem just another specialized academic tome, but it provides a fascinating look, hitherto unpublicized, at the most important of those unknown men behind the scenes in England's government who wrote the laws and devised the policies that so enraged the thirteen colonies. These were faceless senior bureaucrats, advisors to the high and mighty of the realm, and they played a major role in helping to bring about the American Revolution.

Actually, the first question His Majesty's government faced after the 1763 Treaty of Paris brought peace with France was: *What should be done about the Indians?* While the northeast tribes, like the Penobscots and Passamaquoddy, were pacified, others west of the Appalachians had gone on the warpath. Four months after the British took over Canada and the Midwest, Pontiac, chief of the Ottawas, fomented a full-scale rebellion. The government official in London most responsible for preparing an answer to Indian unrest in America had a familiar surname—that of Pownall. Indeed, he was John Pownall, the older brother of Governor Thomas Pownall, and the person credited with having engineered his sibling's rise to prominence.

The post that John Pownall held for almost a quarter of a century was that of secretary of the Board of Trade. In matters pertaining to the American colonies, it was the Board of Trade, functioning as a foreign office, that issued instructions to governors, who were appointed by the Crown in those days, not elected; examined laws passed by colonial assemblies, which could be vetoed at the Board's recommendation; heard cases that ranged from boundary disputes to land speculation; and listened to colonial lobbyists, including Indian agents. As the key executive of this powerful body, the elder Pownall brother, smart and competent, was an indispensable fixture, plus he was a mover and a shaker.

The ultimate policy he chose—contained in the Proclamation of 1763, which he, primarily, wrote—was to keep settlers out of the Indian country on the other side of the Appalachians. Furthermore, all trading with the Indians was to be regulated by the home government. The "licenses to trade," formerly a lucrative source of patronage for colonial governors, would face Whitehall's strict oversight.

Pownall couldn't have known it then, but the eminently rational edict from George III, which he had written, was the opening gun signaling the first in the series of England's missteps that brought about eventual rebellion across the Atlantic. Americans engaged in land speculation, such as George Washington, were furious at being denied access to Indian lands in the West. Thomas Jefferson denounced the decree's legal basis, claiming vacant lands on the continent were not part of the king's domains. Although the Stamp Act and other later English political follies caused much more of a commotion, the Proclamation of 1763 was certainly a major, if overlooked, factor in riling up the land-hungry colonists. J. P. Kinney, in *A Continent Lost— A Civilization Won*, thinks it significant. He writes: "The extent to which British policy regarding the control of the purchase and settlement of Indian lands played a part in the alienation of the affection of the American colonists for the mother country has probably never been generally recognized."[1]

Since it was outside the juridically confined area, Maine was still a legal wide-open frontier. As early as 1760, the Massachusetts General Court was incorporating the lands north of Pemaquid, claimed for it by Governor Pownall, into a brand-new gigantic county they called Lincoln. Its shiretown was Pownalborough (now Dresden), but the settlers were already on the move much farther Down East.

The peace treaty with France had not yet been signed when the lawmakers in Boston carved thirteen townships out of land east of the Penobscot River, mostly in today's Hancock and Washington Counties. The six David Marsh townships were named for a leading speculator who was from Haverhill, Massachusetts, while David Bean promoted half a dozen others east of the Union River. Boston businessmen Francis Shaw and Robert Gould founded Gouldsborough, and other modern Maine towns having their genesis in this era included Sullivan, Trenton, Sedgwick, Bucksport, Steuben, and Milbridge. Nor was the Penobscot area neglected. Before the Revolution, pockets of settlement had cropped up at Orrington, Brewer, Bangor, and Hampden.

Particularly important to events in this flow of Yankee humanity into lands "conquered" from the Indian tribes was the English re-settlement of Machias after it had been taken back from the French. The return to that harbor on the Washington County coast was first effected by sixteen men from Black Point, Scarborough, who had arrived in a whaleboat to cut salt marsh hay and timber. Just as Shaw and Gould developed Gouldsborough, so, too, did a fellow Boston merchant, Ichabod Jones, spark the re-birth of Machias. Men like Jones, members of the Massachusetts gentry with money to invest in the rich local natural resources, especially the lumber potential, were of a much different social strata from the rough-tough breed of settlers flocking to these new towns way down the coast.

The Revolution, when it broke out—America's very first naval battle and victory took place off Machias on June 12, 1775, less than two months after Concord and Lexington— found Jeremiah O'Brien, a leader of the settlers, on one side and Ichabod Jones on the other, or at least cooperating with the British.

Meanwhile, between the British triumph over the French and the uprising against King George, the situation of the Indians in Maine went from bad to worse. Another major murder of innocent Indians occurred in 1767 when Joseph, an Indian trapper, his wife Molly-Eneus, and two daughters, Hannah, fourteen, and Pasanway, four, were robbed of their beaver skins and a gun with a silver thumb piece and then killed. The record of the Massachusetts General Court is filled with references to this crime, which happened near Sebago Lake, and there are the usual promises—and even a £100 reward offer—to bring the two English hunters accused of the crime, Daniel Austin and Frank Douglas, to justice, but no clear-cut evidence this was ever accomplished.

Such an episode was simply at the pinnacle of cross-cultural friction as it inevitably increased in Maine. Wherever the English came, they, too, hunted, depleting the Indians' food supply and available source of revenue-producing furs. The ecology was changed when settlers cleared the land and continued to cut down trees for timber products. So it was that the Penobscots found themselves on July 26, 1769, with emissaries once more in the council chamber in Boston, soliciting Governor Bernard and his council for economic relief. They could do nothing else. Going on the war path was really not an option now that the French in Canada were gone. What they were asking for primarily, they expressed as follows: "We should be glad of a sufficiency at present for our hunting but as hunting is daily decreasing, we would be glad of a tract of land assigned us for a township settled upon us and our posterity for the purposes of husbandry."[2]

The three Penobscots who engaged in this dialogue with Governor Bernard were Espequeunt, Anson, and Arexes. When asked to name three Indian "judges" (justices of the peace) to work with English counterparts in a system meant to straighten out mutual differences, the first two were named by them, to be joined by Orano [*sic*]. It was the earliest mention of a Penobscot destined to become famous as a leader of his people—Joseph Orono—blond and blue-eyed and rumored to be the illegitimate son of the equally famed Baron de St. Castin.

In the discussions in Boston, the Penobscots, asked how big a tract of land they wanted, simply replied: "Sufficient to support ourselves and our families by husbandry." Offered a township—six miles square—they replied they didn't think it would do, since their numbers had already grown and "we are increasing fast."

Bernard asked: "Would six miles in length on each side of your village of Passadonkey (Passadumkeag) and six miles back in the country do?"

It would, he was told.

Yet these tribal leaders were careful not to acquiese entirely in the loss of all their other lands. "The land which we now possess was in possession of our fathers from the beginning of time," they declared, and while admitting they had been conquered and had become subjects of "that great King George," they never actually said they had given up their land, and emphasized, despite their words about husbandry, that they needed space to hunt in, for without it, "We and our wives and our children must perish."[3]

Both governors, Bernard and Pownall, in written statements, expressed their opposition to all potential Maine Indian land claims.

"In regard to regulations for purchasing lands of the Indians, there is no occasion for them here," Bernard wrote the Board of Trade in 1764. The English had conquered their country from the natives, as well as from the French. Pownall made his views known in a book he published in 1765, *The*

Administration of the Colonies. As he phrased it: "The Indians began an unjust war against Massachusetts and acknowledge that the Massachusetts claim is just." However, neither Englishman addressed the absence of any treaty that irrefutably backed up their opinions.

Thus, the great importance to the Maine Indians of the "Treaty of Watertown," which occurred in July 1776, once the Revolutionary War had started. Whether or not it was a legal reprieve for them from the British insistence they had lost everything previously has become a matter of heated debate, right down to the present. In Maine Indian eyes, their alignment with the Americans at Watertown, Massachusetts, and an even earlier commitment made by George Washington, himself, constituted a whole new situation.

There was at this period a ring of ambiguity to just about everything concerning land in the Down East region. Even the land grants made by the general court in Boston to people such as Francis Shaw and Ichabod Jones and Governor Bernard were not officially final until approved by the Crown government in England, and often the process took several years. Consequently, landowners, in order to hold onto their property, had to think hard about which side to join when the American Revolution broke out. Some tried to play both sides against the middle. So did the Indians to a certain extent, although in political parlance, they generally "leaned" American.

Less than a week after the Declaration of Independence was defiantly proclaimed from Philadelphia, "Eastern Indians" were at Watertown. This crossroads town outside of Boston had become the headquarters for the Massachusetts General Court when sent into exile by the British occupation of the capital. Although the King's troops had evacuated Boston by July 1776, the Massachusetts lawmakers still hadn't moved back yet.

On July 10, 1776, the Watertown group, which used the Congregational Church meetinghouse for its deliberations, received a delegation of St. Johns (Maliseet) and Micmac tribal chiefs. It was a transitional period for the American patriots, who had not received word that the *United Colonies,* which they had been calling themselves, had become the *United States.* While their Indian guests were still with them, the news arrived, and Jefferson's immortal words, transcribed on parchment, were read aloud and translated for the tribal chiefs.

A *treaty* between the two entities was the culmination of this pow-wow at Watertown. Throughout the discussions, the primary Indian spokesperson, the Maliseet leader Ambrose St. Aubin, talked repeatedly of his people's reverence for George Washington and, among the documents he had brought with him was a letter of friendship, dated February 1776, from the American commander-in-chief. Said Ambrose: "We shall have nothing to do with old England and all that we shall worship or obey will be Jesus Christ and General Washington." Finally, he added pointedly, "General Washington advised us to pray to Jesus for aid and assistance and to be thankful for the lands that God has given us."

His last phrase had to be the most significant. The Indians needed to hedge their bets, too, as did Ichabod Jones and Francis Shaw, on how they were going to hang onto their lands. That most of their territory lay beyond the jurisdiction of Massachusetts was of no consequence at this time. The rebelliousness of Massachusetts was equally reflected in those parts of Nova Scotia that today we call New Brunswick. The Yankee settlers flocking Down East were mostly all of the same mind, whether they ended north or south of the St. Croix River. In fact, the first people to re-populate Machias had initially applied to Halifax for support and legitimacy, until told they belonged to Boston.

The Micmacs and Maliseets had also been wooed by the British, Ambrose reported, and he displayed a sword given to him by a man named Anderson, an agent of the Nova Scotia government. "I told him we would give it to General Washington," he said, handing the weapon to the president of the Massachusetts Council, and along with it, a "silver gorget and heart," bearing King George's portrait and arms. When the president tried to return the latter item, the Indians objected and only agreed when he said the piece of jewelry would be refurbished with a bust of George Washington and the insignia of the United Colonies.

A further American response aptly expressed the patriots' justification for their rebellion, but in light of later U.S.–Indian experiences now seems laden with unconscious irony. It was stated that the English "have grown old and covetous...because they cannot obtain in their own country a sufficiency to support their excessive luxury and satiate their avarice they want to take from us our money and our lands for those purposes and at the same time to deprive us of our liberties and make us slaves."[4]

As an end result of this exchange of mutual sentiments, the Micmacs and Maliseets agreed to furnish "600 strong men" for the American cause, have them brought to Boston, and then marched to New York to join the new United States Army under General Washington. They would try to enlist the Passamaquoddy, as well, they promised, and eventually did. Another conference some months later enlisted the "St. Francis Indians," that amalgam of Abenaki refugees, mostly from Maine, who had resettled in Canada during earlier wars. These promised to assist General Schuyler, who was at Crown Point, if he moved against Montreal and Quebec.

There is no indication the Wabanaki warriors ever left their immediate vicinities, although fight they did, many of them, side by side with American forces in the region.

The Penobscots had already met with the Massachusetts Provincial Congress a full year before the other tribes—just two months after Concord and Lexington. Consequently, on June 21, 1775, the Penobscots, led by their blond, blue-eyed chief Joseph Orono, had their territorial claims recognized, presumably to secure their allegiance in the struggles to come. These limits extended from the "Head of the Tide on the Penobscot River" (around Old Town) "extending six miles of each side of said river."

That September a further conference was held in Maine with local Massachusetts military officials at the truck house the Commonwealth had built below Penjajawock Stream in present-day Bangor. A Colonel Jonathan Lowther, detached from Fort Pownall, reported that the Indians present, including both Penobscots and St. Johns (Maliseets) had said they were resolved to stand together "with our brethren of Massachusetts and oppose the people of Old England that are endeavoring to take your and our lands and liberties from us."[5]

A year later, the general court appropriated funds for twenty whites and ten Indians to guard the Penobscot area, sending a load of flints, gunpowder, and three months' provisions to a Lieutenant Gilman and a Mr. Jeremiah Colburn.

The latter was one of the first two settlers in the vicinity of Old Town, where the Penobscots had (and still have) their principal village. He, and the area's other white pioneer, Joshua Eayres, were "squatters," most likely on Waldo property, who in June 1774, had settled on "wild and un-improved lands, where they thought no person could claim to turn them off." But evicted they were, despite having built two "dwelling houses," a saw mill, and a six-mile-long road. Meanwhile, they had become friendly with the Penobscots, who urged them to return, which they did, and so here they were, in the fall of 1775, among the Penobscots as militiamen defending the all-important Penobscot River.

Fort Pownall, from which Colonel Lowther had been sent upriver to confer with the Penobscots and Maliseets, strategically commanded the mouth of the watercourse. A British naval captain, Henry Mowatt, was ordered to dismantle it, an act he accomplished with his usual thoroughness (later he became a major villain in Maine history by bombarding Portland and levelling the city). The few remains of the redoubt he'd destroyed were, themselves, subsequently torched by none other than the equally ruthless James Cargill, ex-Indian fighter turned Revolutionary militia colonel in charge of 500 men operating around Penobscot Bay, who, to quote Bates College professor James S. Leamon in *Revolution*

Downeast, "terrorized Tories, seized vessels suspected of trading with the British at Boston, and burned old Fort Pownall...lest it fall into British hands."[6] Mean as Cargill's Lincoln County irregulars might be, they were really no match for the English, and throughout the Revolutionary War years, that entire section of the Maine Coast was vulnerable to raids by the British navy, often abetted by local Tories who had fled to Canada.

These early years of the conflict witnessed several American attempts to invade our neighbor to the north. In each such effort, the Maine Indians played a role, always on the American side. During the very first attempt, though, which was Benedict Arnold's heroic if quixotic march through Maine to Quebec, there may have been some doubt of the Abenakis' loyalty—that is, if Kenneth Roberts may be believed. Admittedly, the famed novelist was writing fiction in *Arundel,* his epic story of the ill-fated expedition, yet as an ex-journalist, Roberts was noted for underpinning his imagination with exhaustive historical research. In the bibliography of non-fiction titles he includes at the end of *Arundel,* some deal, in his own words, with "the Abenaki Indians of New England, on their relations with the early settlers of Maine and on Indian warfare, magic-making, hunting, folklore, and customs."[7]

Therefore, although a key scene in which George Washington, Benedict Arnold, and the novel's hero, Steven Nason of Arundel (now Kennebunk), discuss the proposed invasion of Canada never took place in actuality, the references to Maine Indians have a ring of verisimilitude.

Nason tells General Washington: "Sir, I can find you enough Indians to take canoes safely wherever we'd have to go."

Whereupon, the American commander-in-chief is allowed to indulge in a diatribe that would have utterly shocked and discouraged those Wabanakis whom we have seen at Watertown likening him to Jesus, so strong was their hero-worship of the man. "Sir, I know Indians," Washington thunders. "They're cowardly, plundering, murdering dogs, contemptuous of treaties, devoid of humanity...." Speaking of "the darkest day" of his life, twenty years earlier when retreating from Fort Necessity, he claims he was "deserted by Indians, threatened by Indians, attacked by Indians, my medicine chest destroyed by Indians, and two of my wounded murdered and scalped by Indians."

Nason is quick to protest that this was done by a different group of Indians. "The Abenakis of the Kennebec and Androscoggin are honest and brave," he insists. "I've lived among 'em and traveled with 'em. They'd be our friends. There's no man could give us more help in reaching Quebec than the Abenaki Natanis and the Abenaki Hobomok and the white man Paul Higgins, a sachem of the Assagunticooks."[8]

Natanis and Hobomok, according to the story, are Swan Island Indians, living on that now uninhabited wildlife refuge in the Kennebec River just opposite Richmond, Maine. Although Washington says he has reports that Natanis is a spy, the plot allows these warriors named by Nason to offer key support, faithful to the patriot cause, in a mission that ends in military failure. To quote historian James Leamon again, "Arnold's expedition made little impact on Maine, which merely represented territory to be crossed en route to the objective."[9]

The real-life challenge for Maine occurred Down East.

No one has better articulated the question of what would happen to this entire area than a fiery American patriot who, until the events of April 1775, had been a clergyman in Nova Scotia. The Reverend James Lyon, having had to take refuge in Machias due to his outspoken pro-American sympathies, became the first chairman of that rebellious town's Committee of Public Safety. As such, writing to the Massachusetts General Court in September 1776, the feisty Presbyterian well expressed the aggressive cockiness of the local settlers, mostly like himself from Massachusetts, living on both sides of a border that had yet to be ultimately defined.

Lyon's somewhat sarcastic words followed upon the recent

local action whereby residents of Machias, on their own, had struck a blow against Britain by capturing a Royal Navy sloop, the HMS *Margaretta,* and killing its captain in the ensuing battle. This daring deed, he felt, had not been sufficiently appreciated in Boston.

> Some members of the Court consider the eastern country as a moth (costs more than it is worth and would be wise to let it suffer and sink). Should your honors believe the east to be a moth, dispose of it, and give us the right of dominion. We shall then become an independent state ourselves and we shall think of Nova Scotia as worth annexing to our domain.

Adding, perhaps, to Lyon's bragadoccio was support rendered to the American cause by the local Indians. The Passamaquoddy not only had helped in the capture of the *Margaretta,* but fifty of them, led by Captain Selmore Soctomah, captured a British schooner and brought it to Machias to add to Colonel Allan's forces.

Although the minister's bravado may have been unrealistic, two invasions of Nova Scotia from Machias did follow. These expeditions were hardly on the semi-epic scale of Benedict Arnold's abortive march against Quebec—in fact, they bordered on the comic-opera, except for the casualties—and both involved Indian auxiliaries. Some of those tribal warriors who never went to join General Washington in New York were willing to accompany Colonels Jonathan Eddy and John Allan, when each separately ventured forth to conquer British territory in Canada.

Colonel Eddy had been a neighbor of the Reverend Lyon in Onslow, Nova Scotia, and, like the cleric, had sought refuge in Machias. A transplant from Massachusetts, he knew the temper of the people in his adopted southern section of Nova Scotia to be no different from that of the folks in and around Boston who had risen in revolt. Why not an uprising in this part of Canada? Sent to Massachusetts by his townspeople, Eddy sought an armed force to liberate them or, failing that, ships to come and evacuate the settlers. But the members of the Provincial Congress, alleging they had no authority to act beyond their borders, told him to take his petition to Philadelphia to the Continental Congress.

A sort of bureaucratic runaround involving George Washington and the Continental Congress went nowhere and finally led, after the Declaration of Independence, to another rather desperate trip by Eddy to Boston. To his surprise, on this occasion, he received permission to attack the British strong point of Fort Cumberland at the Canadian far end of the Bay of Fundy. However, he had to raise and equip his forces, himself.

Upon hearing the news, the Reverend Lyon, in Machias, was exultant, writing to the general court: "I highly approve of the noble spirit and resolution of Captain Eddy and heartily wish him success and all the honor of reducing Nova Scotia."

But it was, at best, a ragtag operation. Eddy's force barely consisted of two hundred men, including sixteen Maliseets and four Micmacs. When reinforcements were rushed to the British commander at Fort Cumberland, the game was over and Eddy had to beat a hasty albeit successful retreat back to Machias. Those pro-patriot ex-Massachusettsans left in Nova Scotia's Sunbury and Cumberland Counties either fled or kept quiet and accepted British rule. The Indians, despite their avowal of love for George Washington, did not come forward to fight for the Americans in large numbers.

With John Allan, the natives had a more drawn-out relationship. It was also to continue for years, since his was a pivotal position, appointed by the Continental Congress to be the overall "superintendent of Eastern Indians." Like Eddy and Lyon, he had fled Nova Scotia, except in his case, he'd had a price on his head and had had to leave his wife and five children behind. As the Scotch-born son of a British army officer, he was conceivably thought more of a "traitor" by the English than those other riffraff rebels from Massachusetts. In any event, when it was Colonel John Allan's time to lead an attack across the border, he had authorization from the Massachusetts General Court to raise three thousand men in order to capture first Fort Cumberland and then Halifax, Nova Scotia's capital city.

Authorization was one thing, but the lawmakers in Boston only provided resources enough for Allan to recruit a single regiment in the District of Maine. Going forth to occupy the lower St. John River Valley in what is today's New Brunswick, Allan had Indian auxiliaries with him. More joined to help cover his retreat, once a superior British force had routed the Americans. Had it not been for Chief Ambrose St. Aubin, the Maliseet leader, Allan and his men might never have found their way back to Machias through a maze of water routes. Twenty-seven canoeloads eventually reached Machias, carrying not only the escaping patriots but many warriors and their families. John Allan was amazed at such loyalty and certainly grateful for it—all the more so when the British under Commodore Sir George Collier attacked Machias before that summer of 1777 ended.

It was on August 13, while Allan was conferring with his Indian allies, who now included Penobscots, Passamaquoddy, and Micmacs, as well as Maliseets, that the British ships were sighted. The actual assault on the town, conducted by British marines aboard a brig that sailed up the Machias River, was finally and definitively repulsed. The opposing commanders quibbled over their respective claims of losses, the Brits acknowledging merely three dead and John Allan maintaining that only at Bunker Hill had the enemy suffered larger casualties.

As the story of this American "victory" has been retold, one fact has remained constant through the ages: the critical participation of the Indians with their expert marksmanship and "hideous yells" that contributed mightily to the undermining of British nerve and morale.

The most famous story to come out of that fight concerns Francis Joseph Neptune, the Passamaquoddy chief, and the *unbelievable* long-range hit he made with his musket on a British officer conducting the vanguard of the invasion fleet. Years later, a non-Indian participant in the battle gave one ver-

Passamaquoddy Chief John Francis Neptune, the son of Chief Francis Joseph Neptune, hero of the Battle of Machias, who was renowned for his extraordinary long-range musket shot that killed a British officer and repulsed the attackers. Some versions of the story say John Francis, then fifteen years old, was the deadly marksman.
MAINE HISTORIC PRESERVATION COMMISSION

sion of the famous incident, stating that a "barge" had left the English flagship lying off Potato Point carrying troops, and that the Americans and Indians, under Captain Stephen Smith, were waiting for them at White's Point, and that "Old Chief Francis Joseph" requested permission from Smith to fire and received it.

"He, the said Francis Joseph, then fired and at the discharge, I saw the coxswain (who was sitting in the stern of the barge) fall and the barge then returned to the vessel."

Other versions speak of Colonel John Allan offering a hatful of money to anyone who could make that distant shot, and even that it wasn't Chief Neptune who accomplished the feat, but his fifteen-year-old son.

The testimony of another veteran of the Battle of Machias, Joseph Drisko, adds that the Indians "did more to expel the enemy than all the white men, that their warm attack took such effect upon the enemy that they made sail and left the town and that every [British] officer the Indian saw he killed."[10]

The war Down East still had another six years to run. Its outcome was never clear. A betting man could certainly have put his money on the British, particularly after they captured Castine in 1779, and then utterly destroyed the American fleet sent to the Penobscot to recapture this important outpost.

Throughout all these daunting times, John Allan had the task of keeping the Indians from changing allegiance, a job made much harder in that, right from the start, the Maliseets had split—a faction under Chief Pierre Thoma having accepted British rule. The Indians, themselves, had immense motivation to gauge who would end up the stronger power controlling their territory and which side could most effectively provide the trade goods they needed.

In the battle for their hearts and minds, Allan had a formidable rival in Michael Francklin, his British counterpart as Indian superintendent, a wealthy merchant and former lieutenant governor of Nova Scotia. Francklin had several advantages for winning over the Indians; more money from his government for trade goods and, if that lessened, his own financial resources to pay for the required supplies. After the Battle of Saratoga, the French-American alliance formed in 1778 helped even the odds for Allan. He was soon addressing his Indian allies as "...the Penobscots, Marisheets [sic], Madewascow, all the rest of the St. Johns, Passamaquoddy,

Michmach [*sic*] and all others friends and Brothers to America and the French Nation," telling them, "You will not allow any of your young men to have any connections whatever with any of the people of Great Britain."[11] The emotional ties of the Down East Indians to the French were revived. They allowed Chief Pierre Thoma of the Maliseets to bring his people over to the American side, telling Allan: "I am now come to obey you in anything for the good of America and the King of France...." Allan was also able to procure a French priest for the Indians, the vast majority of whom were Catholics, and the arrival of Father de la Motte was greeted with considerable joy by the natives.

Yet in June 1779 events abruptly turned against the Americans in this part of Maine. To a degree, "the attack of Penobscot," as the British called it, followed a pattern of aggressive action the Redcoats were likewise pursuing on the coasts of South Carolina and Georgia in capturing Charleston and Savannah. The difference was they had to fight their way into Charleston and Savannah, while Castine was surrendered without a shot fired.

The attempt by Massachusetts to recapture the town, also known by its Indian name of Majabagaduce, which the English had slated to become a haven and magnet for American Tories, has been labeled the worst American naval disaster until Pearl Harbor. Left on the bottom of the Penobscot River was (and still is) an entire American fleet, scuttled when driven inland by a reinforcement of Royal Navy warships. Commodore Dudley Saltonstall, the pusillanimous American naval commander, was later court-martialed for his repeated failure to attack the British positions. The more aggressive army leader, Brigadier General Solomon Lovell, once he had escaped beyond Fort Pownall, quickly went to visit the Penobscots, "which I thought a matter of utmost importance," he wrote the General Court, "as they might from our defeat, be drove to despair...."

He found they had left their "Lower Town" (Old Town) and gone to their "Upper Town" (Passadumkeag). The conference held at the latter site has been recorded. Lovell spoke first. "My brethren, I heartily thank you for your faithful services while with me at Majabigwaduce [*sic*], a true representation of which I will not fail to make to the Grand Council at Boston." The massive American defeat, he called "a little disappointment," but assured the tribal people the Americans would still protect them.... "I am heartily sorry to see you and your little ones drove from your habitations...," he continued, "but fear not, you will be restored to it again shortly...."

In response, the Penobscot chiefs told Lovell they would supply five canoes and eight Indians to take him and his party to the Kennebec and not to worry, "that a little misfortune would not make them change their hearts, they would ever be friends with the Grand Council and open enemies to the Tories and British troops who had hurt their young men...." They also asked for supplies, and the general promised to "get them some necessaries by way of the Kennebec in the future."

Notwithstanding such evidence of loyalty to the United States by the Penobscots, distrust of Indians had never been extinguished in American ranks. Quotes from a letter penned by the Reverend John Murray to a regimental commander who'd escaped the debacle provide a case in point. Apparently this Protestant minister had been at Fort Western in Augusta with some of General Lovell's aides, anxiously awaiting news of him, mindful he was last seen in the company of Indians. "Indians keep no faith unless it appears to be their present advantage to do so," the religious leader dogmatically insisted. "The hope of reconciliation with a victorious enemy [the British] and the prospect of a present (even if it were a gallon of rum) would be a sufficient price for the life of an American...." Agreeing, the regimental commander rejoined: "It is very suspicious that the Indians have either killed the general or delivered him to the enemy." And all the while, General Lovell was safe, saved by the Penobscots.

But even John Allan, probably the closest of all Americans to the tribes, vented feelings against them. The scariest period of the entire war had commenced for him. As he put it, "The unhappy and unparalleled defeat at Penobscot has put this Department in a most critical and dangerous situation, such as requires the most vigilant attention for its preservation."12

Even before the defeat, he had found the Indians at "Passamaquoddy" [Machias] in "a far different temper," partly because of internal disputes, and it had taken several days to win back their promise to go along as reinforcements for Castine.

En route by sea to the battle with forty-seven Indians in canoes and twenty white militiamen in boats, Allan reached Mount Desert only to learn of the Americans' catastrophe. So he returned with his troops to Machias. But the "dishonorable flight," as he called the rout, and "the disgrace brought on the arms of our country on the Penobscot River" had—and his warning could not have been more explicit—"given a wound to our Indian affairs."

His job, difficult at the best of times, was now close to impossible. The Indians, looking out for their own future, were asking: "What assistance can be expected from Americans when so fine a fleet and army were destroyed without opposition?" Some of the natives, Allan reported, had become belligerent, "treating people ill"; others, intimidated by the British, "skulked away" to far-off lakes; others, still, contemplated an apology for fighting on the American side. "I am obliged to let them go often a-hunting for fresh provisions, as they must be in action or drunk," the eastern Indian superintendent continued, and he bemoaned the divisions among his charges, and that "they abuse everybody behind their backs who have had any connection with them," and that "their demands are insatiable and perpetual."

However, Allan ended his rant by declaring he didn't believe the tribes would fight the Americans nor that their attachment to the U.S. and himself would ever diminish.

Time proved him right. His expression of frustration was penned at Machias on September 10, 1779, almost a month after the Penobscot defeat. Two months later, he had gathered 280 native people, including 90 braves, under the formerly pro-British Maliseet chief Pierre Thoma, with whom he had "buried the hatchet." Still a bit wary, he appended a message to the Board of War in Philadelphia that stated: "The virtuous conduct of those [Indians] requires the generosity of the States, to attend to their situation...." The reason was obvious: "for fear of their drawing off from us, [it] commands the exertions of government to give an immediate ear to the care of them."

Suspense in the Down East region remained operative, actually, for five more years. British troops did not evacuate Castine until 1784, a whole year after the peace treaty was signed. The Tory province of New Ireland proposed for Castine already had been torpedoed by internal British politics well before the end, but found its resurrection in the nearby Nova Scotian territory that soon became New Brunswick. John Allan, despite sporadic enemy attemps to abduct him, kept control of Machias and, in turn, preserved de facto the American claim to northeasternmost Maine.

He also remained a steady friend and protector of his Indian allies.

John Howard Ahlin, in *Maine Rubicon: Downeast Settlers During the American Revolution,* grasped what would happen next.[13]

"After the war, they [the Indians] were not important in the consideration of either party [the British and the Americans], although men such as Allan continued to plead for their interests on the basis of their part in the war."[14]

NOTES

[1] J. P. Kinney, *A Continent Lost, A Civilization Won: Indian Land Tenure in America.* Baltimore: Johns Hopkins Press, 1937, page 26.

[2] *Baxter Manuscripts: Documentary History of the State of Maine,* 2nd Series, Vol. XXIV. Portland, Maine: Fred L. Tower Company, 1916, pages 157–58. Collections of the Maine Historical Society.

[3] Ibid, page 159.

[4] Ibid, page 171.

[5] As cited in *The Ancient Penobscot* by the Honorable John E. Godfrey of Bangor. 1st Series, Vol. 7. Bath, Maine: 1876, page 7. Collections of the Maine Historical Society.

[6] James S. Leamon, *Revolution Downeast.* Amherst, Massachusetts: University of Massachusetts Press, 1993, page 85.

[7] Kenneth Roberts, *Arundel.* Camden, Maine: Down East Books, reprint, page 488. Originally published in 1930.

[8] Ibid, page 174.

[9] Leamon, page 87.

[10] Material from the *Wabanaki Collection,* Huntington Free Library, Bronx, New York.

[11] Ibid.

[12] *Baxter Manuscripts,* Second Series, Vol. XVII. Portland, Maine: Fred C. Tower Co., Collections of the Maine Historical Society, page 109.

[13] John Howard Ahlin, *Maine Rubicon: Downeast Settlers During the American Revolution.* Camden, Maine: Picton Press, 1966.

[14] Ibid, page 156.

13

POSTWAR UNDER MASSACHUSETTS

*D*espite the skepticism of Maine settlers who had memories of the French and Indian War raids, their relations with Indians throughout the Revolution had been fairly benign. The tribes up north fought with them against the British or at least stayed neutral and quiescent. Fears, however, never entirely vanished that the Redcoats might somehow incite the "savages" to resume their scorched-earth tactics.

Indeed, elsewhere in America, British military leaders had done precisely that—particularly using the Mohawks and Senecas in and around New York and the Cherokees in the south, with resultant massacres so horrific they actually drew condemnation in Parliament. The illustrious orator Edmund Burke, pro-American in his politics, was said to have given one of his best speeches on the subject (sessions were closed to the public and his attack on the practice of using Indian auxiliaries to spread terror was never published in full). "He attributed Burgoyne's defeat [at Saratoga] to the horror excited in the American mind by the prospect of an Indian invasion," George Otto Trevelyan, the noted English historian, wrote in his classic work, *The American Revolution.*[1] And in a footnote, he quotes a contemporary, Sir Michael le Fleming: "Mr. Burke never displayed the powers of oratory so strongly as the other day when the affair of the contracts with the Indians was agitated. His speech drew tears from the whole House, particularly that part of it where he described the murder of Miss McCreay...."[2]

What part British authorities may have had in the one incident in Maine where Indians, without warning, raided an American community has never been determined. It happened in western Maine in 1781 far from the Down East battlefield, and seemed but a mere flame in the context of a wider conflagration. However, around Bethel, then called Sudbury,

Canada, "Tomhegan's Raid" is still remembered. Three men were killed and three others, including two militia lieutenants, captured and carried off as prisoners of war. The Indian leader Tomhegan was an Arasaguntacook and had lived in the vicinity before ending up as an exile in Canada.

Thus, after the war, the conventional wisdom about this area was that the Indians were gone for good. The same was true in other places where they once had been—that is, outside of the Down East tribal territories. Yet at various locations in the state, small clusters of Indian families or lone individuals either remained in or drifted back from Canada, staying "underground," known possibly to the locals, while some, through special talents—such as Oxford County's Molly Ockett, medicine woman and foreteller of the future, and "Chief" Henry Red Eagle (Henry Perley) of Greenville, writer, showman, and movie actor—achieved recognition beyond their immediate habitats.

These informal enclaves aside, it was the known Indian tribes that primarily concerned the powers in Boston, once the peace treaty of 1783 had been signed. Left on the Bay State's side of the northeast border were two intact confederations—the Penobscots and Passamaquoddy. The Micmacs and Maliseets, since the negotiators in Paris had established commissions to lay out the eastern and northern boundary lines between Canada and the United States, were essentially living for the time being in a no man's land.

The Penobscots, or rather their lands, were the most immediate preoccupation of the Boston lawmakers. The "Treaty of Watertown" in 1775 had protected a vast acreage—six miles on either side of the Penobscot River, as far north as it flowed. But by 1783 various pressures from the District of Maine led to second thoughts. Bangor historian John E. Godfrey put the matter straightforwardly in one of his articles: "After the war, it was found that the Indian claim to this tract was an obstacle to the settlement of the country. The whites encroached upon it and some ill feeling was likely to prevail unless the Indian title could be extinguished."[3]

The Massachusetts General Court thus was obliged to deal with this and a number of other land issues, such as disputed land titles in Massachusetts, itself, including the sale of lands by Indians to private individuals, which while illegal in Massachusetts proper, had been perfectly legal in the District of Maine. In time-honored legislative fashion, a committee was formed to deal with these questions, plus the thorny problem of trespassing or "squatting" on private lands by impecunious settlers, and, most of all, the major reason for the "Committee on the Eastern Lands," the need to sell vacant land to pay off the tremendous debt the Commonwealth had incurred during the Revolution.

Soon the entire task proved too much for one general court committee and the chore was split up geographically. A three-person body was chosen to deal with Lincoln County, alone, since Lincoln County comprised all of Maine outside of York and Cumberland Counties and contained most of its marketable wild land. The initial trio of members were Samuel Phillips of Andover (better known as the founder of Phillips Academy, Andover), Nathaniel Wells of Wells, Maine, and Nathan Dane of Ipswich (a future congressman). Their responsibility was to open up northern Maine to settlement—and the sooner the better. That sense of urgency came from several directions. Massachusetts was losing population—its young people emigrating to more open lands to the west. Then, too, all of that unoccupied territory to the north was an invitation to the British in Canada to intervene. John Allan, Down East in October 1783, was already warning Governor John Hancock that their former enemies, displaced Tories, were settling in areas across the St. Croix and St. John Rivers that could and should become American soil. The Boston lawmakers felt a pressing need to fill up Maine with Massachusetts people as soon as possible.

By March 1784 the committee was recommending that four new townships be laid out on the west side of the Penobscot River, and on the east side, as many townships as could be allowed, taking into consideration the protected Penobscot Indian lands and thirteen townships granted there before the Revolution. They also called for six new townships open to settlement on the western side of the St. Croix River.

An example of how the group worked was their agreement in March 1785 to sell Colonel Jonathan Eddy and his "associates" an entire township on the east side of the Penobscot River above head tide for $18,000. This land later became the town of Eddington. Apparently it lay outside the six-mile-wide band accorded the Penobscots, for the record attested: "And said Eddy further agreed to produce evidence to the General Court that the Penobscot Indians have relinquished their pretensions to the said township." This veteran officer of the campaign Down East and in Nova Scotia had promised to settle thirty families, including his own, on the property.

That same month, the committee chose three men to go north and negotiate a land purchase with the Penobscots. One was Captain William Lithgow, who had commanded Fort St. George, another General Rufus Putnam, a Revolutionary War hero, and the third was Dr. Thomas Rice. They reported they would leave for the Indians' "Old Town" in July, in order to be on hand when the Indians returned from hunting.

In this case, there was a real glitch. Not until December did the general court learn that no meeting with the Penobscots had taken place. Lithgow's explanation was that he and Rice had not been able to make contact with Putnam until November, much too late, since the Indians were leaving for their winter quarters. In the high-flown, wordy language of a military man trained under the English, the captain suggested the lawmakers select "persons for the purpose who, by residing not so distant from each other may from that circumstance, be better able to embrace the most favorable opportunity of obtaining the object of their appointment."

The irony here is that a whole year was lost, thereby pushing up the date when a preliminary treaty with the Penobscots was discussed to 1786. This fact would have meant nothing at the time. The magic year of 1790, when the federal government passed the "Non-Intercourse Act," still was several years away, and neither the Massachusetts negotiators nor Chief Orono and the Penobscots could ever have dreamed of the colossal import of stalling their agreement beyond that date. No one planned what eventually happened. Even the most clairvoyant *m'teoulino* had no idea that the natural reluctance of his fellow tribal people to hand over large chunks of territory would redound to their benefit almost two centuries later.

A new member of a second Massachusetts delegation that was sent to Old Town in 1786 had also been a military man and hero of the Revolution, and later became the commander of the troops who put down Shays's Rebellion and the first U.S. secretary of war under the Articles of Confederation— General Benjamin Lincoln. From Hingham, Massachusetts, the son of a farmer, he had returned to the Bay State from his government service in Philadelphia, and the first job given him was to lead this renewed effort to deal with the Penobscots.

Lincoln has been described as a hulking, genial man who walked with a pronounced limp due to an ankle shattered by a musket ball at the battle of Saratoga. He could be tough, and during the conclave with the Penobscots at Kenduskeag (Bangor), he did not mince words.

The setting was a grassy lawn on the banks of the Penobscot River, on which the four Penobscot chiefs, Joseph Orono, Orsong Neptune, John Neptune, and Neptonboyett sat, with the rest of the tribe standing behind them. The interpreter for this event was John Marsh, known as the "linguister," fluent in several Indian languages, a one-time scout in Arnold's expedition, and a close friend (even alleged blood brother) of Orono's.

The date was August 28, 1786. General Lincoln was disingenuous enough in his opening remarks, never really showing that the intent of his mission was to garner Penobscot land, but instead harping on Massachusetts's "kind intentions" to settle the Indians' land claims to the "mutual satisfaction" of both claimants.

When told the Penobscots' claims went down to "a small stream below Old Town one mile above Colburn's" (home of that earliest settler in the region, William Colburn), and they were planning to keep everything upriver from there, Lincoln took off his verbal gloves. Despite his previous chummy words about fighting the British together, he was suddenly citing a *British* precedent to justify taking their land—their submission to Governor Pownall. The only reason they were still here, he reminded the Penobscots, was by the sufferance of the Provincial Congress at Watertown, which had guaranteed them six miles on either side of the river from the head of tide.

Lincoln later reported to the authorities in Massachusetts how the Penobscots were upset upon learning the rights granted them at Watertown were only six miles on each side of the river. "They appeared to be much hurt and disappointed," he wrote. Then he had honed in with an ingenious argument. A mere six miles, he maintained, would give them no hunting grounds at all, for settlers would soon crowd in from all sides. If they gave up their Watertown claim, the state would give them a larger tract upriver and two islands in the ocean at Penobscot Bay near their ancient summer campground at Naskeag Point.

"We don't think it right to remove further upriver" was the Indian reply.

Lincoln retorted: "You have our proposals from which we shall not depart."

"We expect to be paid," said the Indians.

"We do give you more land and better for hunting. What further consideration do you desire?"

"Blankets, powder, shot, and flints."

To General Lincoln, here was a perfect opener. The ensuing palaver settled on 350 blankets, 200 pounds of powder, and a proportional amount of shot and flints, which, with some offshore islands and a promise of land way up in the boondocks, would be the final price the Penobscots received to hand over their six-mile strips on both sides of the Penobscot River which were absolutely prime settlement land.

For forty-three miles up to the Piscataquis River on the west and eighty-three miles up to the Mattawamkeag on the east, new territory was becoming available that Massachusetts could sell. True, the Indians were doing it reluctantly and surrending only half as much on the west as on the east and keeping their "Old Town" at Indian Island and their "New Town" at Passadumkeag, but this had to be a tremendous bargain. The commissioners didn't say so publicly in their report back to Boston. They merely urged the consummation of the pact as soon as possible by having the agreed-upon supplies sent forthwith, having a commissioner complete and obtain the deed in which the Indians "would sign a relinquishment of all their right and intent to the lands agreeably to the above contract," and, while the commissioner was at it, listen to their complaints "in regard to the fraudulent conduct of a French priest among them."

This latter affair was the influential John Neptune's personal problem. He had given the priest thirty-seven beaver skins to market for him in Boston and the priest, he believed, had pocketed the money. Neptune wanted the money and felt the state owed it to him because the priest had been appointed by the state. The advice of General Lincoln and his colleagues was that taking care of this problem would "have a tendency to secure, not only their [the Penobscots'] obedience but their confidence and esteem."

Present when this original agreement was signed were four witnesses, there to certify the Indians' consent: Colonel Jonathan Eddy, settler William Colburn, and two ministers, the Reverend Daniel Little and the Reverend Seth Noble.

It was the Reverend Little, in the long run, to whom the Commonwealth entrusted the responsibility of delivering the agreed-upon supplies to the Penobscots and securing their final ratification of the treaty. He did so in 1788 after an initial attempt in 1786 by General Lincoln had been unsuccessful because the Indians were away on a fall hunt. At that time, the store of blankets, powder, etc., had been left with a John Lee of Castine, who said he would bring them to Old

Town upon receiving instructions. Another reason for the two-year delay can be seen in a message from Governor John Hancock to the General Court in May 1788, informing them, "I have appointed the Reverend Mr. Little to execute the business, who had been long conversant with those Indians," but now that Little was ready to proceed, the chief executive had to add: "After every effort of mine, I fail in the procurement of money...." and, therefore, he had to ask the lawmakers for public funds. Undoubtedly Hancock received them, since the Reverend Mr. Little and his party were on Indian Island by the third week in June 1788.

The minister had the supplies, plus a parchment on which the Massachusetts solons had recorded what they called their "gift of land" to the Penobscots. However, the Indians were not being so easily cajoled into accepting what they saw as a land grab. Their spokesman was Orsong Neptune. He told Little: "If anybody takes any land from us, it must be King George, for the General Court and General Washington (at Watertown) promised we should enjoy this country." Furthermore, he added, that while at Kenduskeag, the tribe had had "not a right understanding of matters" and had been "pressed to make that treaty contrary to our inclinations."

So the Reverend Little was sent away empty-handed. In addition, Orsong had fired a parting verbal shot at him personally. Asking the interpreter, "Is not Mr. Little a minister?" and receiving an affirmative answer, the Indian then declared, "Brother, ministers ought not to have anything to do with public business."

The upshot: This first cession of Penobscot territory, some 200,000 acres, was put off until 1796, and the 1790 federal statute, enacted meanwhile, was ignored by Massachusetts. Their "sweetheart deal," as we know, was never submitted to the U.S. Congress for approval.

The Penobscots had tried their best to resist. Park Holland, the noted surveyor, upon being sent up the east branch of the Penobscot River in 1793 to mark off the very tract that had been designated a "reserve" for the tribe, encountered hostility and obdurance. To act as a guide, he had hired Sabattis, "an old and very respected Indian of the Norridgewock tribe," who spoke some English, which most of the Penobscots still did not. At Old Town, though, their party was accosted by one English-speaking native threatening them with a gun if they went any further. It turned out he was a Maliseet, showing off his courage to impress a Penobscot woman he had come for, and he desisted when Sabattis said: "Shoot old Sabattis, you want shoot anybody."

Nevertheless, the Penobscots made it plain they did not want Holland and his group going upriver. He convinced them they were only planning to survey Penobscot land so whites couldn't trespass, and they finally let him continue. But at Mattawamkeag, the party was stopped again and told by the Penobscots the river was their river and they didn't want whites traveling up it.

Their argument was: "For bye and bye the white man would come and buy a little of their land, then a little more, and the farther the white men go up, the farther the beaver and moose would go.... Poor Indian would have no land and no moose meat."

Once more, Holland talked his way past them. What he didn't say was that his job also involved surveying for the land speculators Henry Knox and William Bingham, a task he proceeded to accomplish with help from John Marsh and old Sabbatis.

The ineluctability of what was happening could be gleaned from a statement by Governor John Hancock, issued in March 1788, of why the treaty with the Penobscots was of great consequence, "For though perhaps a very small force may subdue or extirpate that tribe of natives if they should commence hostilities, yet the effecting it would be more expensive and troublesome than the completing a treaty respecting their lands would be..." and "much more consistent with humanity to conciliate their affections, than to subdue them by force."[4]

The idea that natives should never be allowed to keep possession of any considerable amount of their original holdings was widespread, even if they had fought on the American side as in the District of Maine.

Land speculation was in full throttle Down East. At first in Maine, the biggest player was Henry Knox, who ended up with close to 2.5 million acres, and then, because he couldn't handle the finances, sold out to his Philadelphia friend William Bingham, a U.S. senator and the largest landowner in America, while still retaining a share of the action if the project proved successful. Thus we find the "Squire of Thomaston" writing to Bingham in 1796, when it appeared the nettlesome problem Massachusetts was having with the stubborn Penobscots had finally been solved.

"As to the Indian lands," Knox wrote, "no opinion can be had of the Committee or other persons in the legislature as to price. It is however probable they will be sold in single townships at pretty high prices. Some play may be formed at the time of sale to purchase as many as we think proper, and we ought to purchase many of them, at any rate at which they will be sold."

Deep in his own affairs in Maine, having retired as secretary of war (he had followed Benjamin Lincoln) where he had been responsible for Indian matters, how much attention did Henry Knox give to the indigenous natives of Maine? This question was raised repeatedly 200 years later during the Land Claims Settlement debate and answered by opponents that he most certainly knew about the Penobscot Treaty of 1796 (as the above clearly indicates) and most likely the Passamaquoddy Treaty of 1794 (Knox had visited their lands as a member, with Benjamin Lincoln, of the commission to determine the St. Croix boundary), and, they adamantly argued, took it for granted those agreements did not have to be ratified by Congress since the law he had promulgated in 1790 did not apply to any of the eastern states.

This was mere guesswork (or wishful thinking), seeing that Knox left no record of his opinion on the exact subject of the Non-Intercourse Act and its application to the Maine

This 1788 painting by Thomas Davies, a British officer, shows an encampment of nomadic hunters with their conical bark shelters at Point Levy, opposite Quebec. Maine Indians were living in a similar fashion, and indeed, the Indians pictured here may have been descendents of Maine Indians who had earlier fled to Canada.
NATIONAL GALLERY OF CANADA, OTTAWA.

Indians. He did, however, express a thought identical to Benjamin Lincoln's, that the Penobscots had given up their land to Governor Pownall. This Knox had stated publicly in 1784 when he and Lincoln had made an abortive attempt to talk to the Penobscots and had later recommended to the General Court "an assignment of such lands to the Indians as may be necessary to their happiness...." Generally regarded as considerate of the Indians, at least those in the west whom his subordinates had to fight, Knox does not seem ever to have expressed his private views about the tribes in Maine.

Curiously enough, Benjamin Lincoln, who'd had the same responsibilities in the War Department as Knox, did pen a set of *Observations on the Indians of North America* in the year 1795. Lincoln's document was printed by the Massachusetts Historical Society as a response to remarks by a Doctor Ramsay to that same society, where he had insisted on "the impractability of Indians being civilized" and that "ere long they will cease to be a people."

The first premise Lincoln accepted, stating: "On the whole I am fully in opinion with my friend Dr. Ramsay that the Indian nations will never be civilized...." But he didn't

agree they would be annihilated. Here was a military man who had had considerable contact with Indians throughout the country, not only as secretary of war, but as a negotiator with the Penobscots and later, on behalf of the federal government, a negotiator with the southern Indians.

Although he always struck a hard bargain in his negotiating, he saw their point of view. "They believed they were placed on these lands by the Great Spirit," he wrote. "No one has a right to dispossess them.... The attempts which have been made to that end have left the worst impressions on their minds.... They say to us, Where are the good effects of your religion? We of the same tribe have no contentions among ourselves respecting property; and no man envies the enjoyment and happiness of his neighbor."[5]

But since Lincoln believed civilized and non-civilized people could never possess the same territory, he felt, unlike Dr. Ramsay, that the Indians would "continue retiring before the enlightened husbandman, until they shall meet those regions of the north into which he cannot pursue them."

His final prediction was that in their northern enclave, "being now in the possession of a country fitted by nature, to the life of a sportsman, they will probably continue as a people until time shall be no more."

The irony was that the general's forecast of a wilderness exile ended for the Passamaquoddy not far from the developable property he had bought in Dennysville, Maine. Once that tribe, out of financial desperation, had sold the bulk of their lands in Washington County, they stayed in close proximity to their white neighbors, both at Sipayik (Pleasant Point) near Eastport and Motahkmikuk (Indian Township) next to Princeton. They never quite moved beyond the reach of "civilization."

Yet they had always been a peripatetic people, practicing cyclical migration from the coast, inland, and back, seagoing in their homemade canoes, and changing villages from time to time. For many years, they had used Milltown, opposite present-day Calais, as a spring village but left when it was destroyed by Colonel Benjamin Church and his rangers in 1704. St. Andrews, which had been a Passamaquoddy summer fishing village for 10,000 years, was still occupied until the Revolution, which brought many if not most of them from Canada to Machias. Finally, the postwar exodus of Tories to what became New Brunswick led to the choice of Pleasant Point as a stopping place from which parts of the tribe eventually spread west to Indian Township.

Historically, the range of Passamaquoddy lands was huge, both in New Brunswick and Maine, stretching from the lower St. John River Valley on the east to the Union River (at Ellsworth) on the west and north to Danforth and the Schoodic Lakes. Archaeologists have estimated their presence in the Passamaquoddy Bay area to date from at least 3,000 years ago.

The end of the Revolution saw a beginning split in their ranks and territory due to the fact that half the land was in New Brunswick; some members did stay on plots the British provided at St. Andrews, Milltown, and near Vanceboro on the Canadian side. The British, nonetheless, allowed "American" Passamaquoddy to come over and hunt porpoises off St. Andrews. Porpoise, in the Passamaquoddy diet, has been described contemporaneously as "a rare sort of soul food."

All in all, the Passamaquoddy were to lose 80 percent of their original territory. In 1786 Massachusetts held a public lottery auctioning off townships Down East, notwithstanding that the state didn't have title to twenty of them. The most northeasterly of these were still in the possession of the Passamaquoddy.

To those of the tribe who remained on the American side, this should have been "a time of reward," as Susan MacCulloch Stevens put it in her work, *Passamaquoddy Economic Development in Cultural and Historic Perspective*.[6] They were expecting the promises made to them by Colonel John Allan as the representative of the U.S. government would be kept.

Unhappily, they weren't. Mrs. Stevens, the late wife of latter-day Passamaquoddy Governor John Stevens, wrote that ten years after the Peace Treaty of 1783, "the Indians were destitute, in large part because of the war, and were beginning to make threats of retreating to Canada and joining the British who had not completely given up the thought of regaining some territory. Allan went so far as to have the Indians take his two young sons as hostages one winter, as proof of his sincere intentions to make the government honor the obligations he had made on its behalf. In an eloquent appeal to the Massachusetts legislature, he pointed out that the Indians still had letters from Massachusetts and General Washington promising that "the widows and children of Indian veterans would be cared for, that the Indians should be guaranteed free exercise of religion and supplied with a priest...that they were to have exclusive rights of the beaver hunt and that the wanton destruction of game by white hunters was to be curtailed. In addition, ammunition was to be provided for fowling in times of emergency, fair trade was to be established and regulated, and an agent was to reside near them to assist in business dealings and to redress wrongs."[7]

This last was of great importance to the Indians. One of the main reasons the Passamaquoddy (and Penobscots) joined the American cause was their anger over the dismantling of Fort Pownall and its trading post by British naval captain Henry Mowatt in violation of the English government's treaty with the Maine tribes.

Now, in the early 1790s, the Passamaquoddy were desperately seeking to be accepted as "brothers and children under the protection and fatherly care of the United States government."

The best deal they could obtain was the one Allan finally secured through Massachusetts in 1794, when they sold off most of their land.

Several decades later, for a brief period during the War of 1812, it might not have mattered anymore whether they were under Massachusetts or even the U.S. federal government. In a repeat of what happened during the Revolution, the British captured Castine, but in this instance, almost the entire Down East region of Maine came under their control and they raided as far inland as Bangor, which they easily captured and ransacked after routing the American militia at the Battle of Hampden. The Treaty of Ghent in 1814 required them to evacuate all of their Maine conquests, but while the occupation lasted, the British commander declared the local inhabitants to be henceforth subjects of the king.

In 1816 Captain Lewy, a Passamaquoddy sub-chief, was the first of his tribe to move west to Indian Township, establishing himself on an island in the east branch of the St. Croix River.

The overall chief throughout this time—and top chiefs were selected for life—was the celebrated Francis Joseph Neptune, who was also considered a shaman. It has been said that when he made his remarkable musket shot at Machias, the Americans watching the event declared it "unbelievable!" The Indians cried out: "He has powers!"

Shaman or not, Chief Francis Joseph Neptune was not able to do much in the way of magic for his people in the postwar period. In 1804 it was reported by Massachusetts Governor James Sullivan in his history of the District of Maine that those natives at Pleasant Point led "a wretched life, feeding on clams and other shellfish" and were hungry and cold—due in large part to the lack of wildlife, decimated by non-Indian hunters in the area. By 1816 all of the 250 to 300 Passamaquoddy were living on public charity.

Soon the dispenser of that largesse, such as it was, would change. Maine broke away from Massachusetts finally and officially in 1820. No doubt with an inward sigh of relief, the lawmakers in Boston turned over their responsibilities for the "Eastern Indians" to their newly empowered counterparts up north.

NOTES

[1] George Otto Trevelyan, *The American Revolution.* Edited by Richard B. Morris. New York: David McKay and Company, 1964, page 424. First published in 1899.

[2] Ibid.

[3] As cited in *The Ancient Penobscot* by the Honorable John E. Godfrey of Bangor, Collections of the Maine Historical Society, 1st Series, Vol. 7, Bath, Maine, 1876, page 7.

[4] *Baxter Manuscripts: Documentary History of the State of Maine,* 2nd Series, Vol. XXII. Portland, Maine: Fred L. Tower Company, 1916, page 463. Collections of the Maine Historical Society.

[5] Collections of the Massachusetts Historical Society of MDCCXCVIII, Vol. V, pages 6–12. Boston. Reprinted by John H. Eastburn, 1835.

[6] Susan MacCulloch Stevens, *Passamaquoddy Economic Development in Cultural and Historical Perspective.* Mount Vernon, Maine, 1973.

[7] Ibid, page 48.

14

MAINE IN CHARGE

*T*he first act recorded by Maine government at its
highest level—governor and council—toward the
Indian population inherited from Massachusetts occurred on
May 5, 1820, less than two months after Maine officially
became the twenty-third state.

An order was signed by William King, Maine's first governor and the politician who had effectively engineered the
breakaway from Massachusetts. It read as follows:

> The bearer Mary an Indian woman not being able to walk and
> being desirous of returning to her friends at Penobscot the person
> having the direction of the Stage from Brunswick to Gardiner or
> Hallowell will have the goodness to convey her to either of the
> above places and present their amount to.... William King.

Thus it was that Dr. Jacob Perkins was reimbursed $3.50—the
"Stage Fare, etc." for "Mary, an Indian woman" and also
for her sister who accompanied her—$1.75 each from
Bowdoinham to Hallowell. How Mary and her sibling then got
from Hallowell to "Penobscot" was never explained in writing.

During those early years of Maine's statehood, and for
many years afterward, the governor and council had responsibility for Indian affairs. The *council* no longer exists, having
been abolished in 1975. Originally, under English rule, the
council in Massachusetts was the upper body of the general
court, but not publicly elected, its members chosen by the
lower house of representatives and subject to gubernatorial
veto. After 1783 and statehood, Massachusetts inserted a senate in its place, yet kept the idea of an "advise and consent"
body to check the powers of the governor, particularly on
appointments. In Maine it was called the executive council
and it consisted of seven members elected from districts by the
majority party legislators. In Governor William King's day,

that party would have been the Jeffersonians, who called themselves *Democrat-Republicans,* as opposed to the *Federalists* of Washington and Hamilton.

Getting organized to deal with the Indians, and particularly their land, was a first order of business for Maine's new administration. "Agents" were needed and Mark Trafton of Bangor was appointed, not only to supervise the Indian Territory but all public lands on the Penobscot and its branches. William Vance was given a similar responsibility on the Schoodic (St. Croix) River.

On January 16, 1821, a delegation of Penobscots composed of the tribal lieutenant governor, John Neptune, and five other chiefs came to Portland. They met with the governor and council, and the Maine officials heard Neptune's complaints about fish weirs set up by whites that were ruining the Indians' fishing and trespassing lumbermen cutting on Indian land.

Most of the very earliest examples of issues to come before the governor and council, however, seemed innocuous and routine. They were asked, again in January 1821, to settle the account of Joseph Treat, who had been sent up to the St. John River by the legislature the previous fall with John Neptune as his guide in order to explore the Aroostook country. Presumably, this was Lieutenant Governor John Neptune whose wages were one dollar a day plus $10 for a new birch-bark canoe and paddle—$65 in all for the trip. In November the governor and council heard from Jonathan D. Weston, Esq., the appointed agent for the Passamaquoddy, asking for money to buy a woodlot that would provide the local Indians with firewood.

Two bills received in 1822 and 1823 shed light on the history of a unique Maine institution. The first bill was for the payment of $20 to Samuel F. Hussey for boarding Penobscot Indians during the 1822 session of the legislature (then held in Portland), and the second for expenses for boarding two Penobscots, Neptune and Francis, during the 1823 session for eighteen days.

Here, indeed, was proof that the practice of allowing representatives of the two principal tribes to attend legislative sessions had its start at the very dawn of the state's existence. Some historians think it may have been a carry-over from Massachusetts. Note that where the Penobscots are concerned, *several* persons seem to have been in paid attendance. These may have been representatives of two main factions beginning to develop known as the Old Party and the New Party. Nowadays, each tribe has only one representative.

In 1824 trouble brewed on the Penobscot lands and an extensive document from Samuel Call, Jr., agent, showed how complicated the problem of protecting Indian property could be. Call had found two teams of six oxen each and twelve to fifteen men logging on Indian property—having already cut 1,200 logs—and he asked if they had a permit. "After some hesitation, they said they did not," according to Call, but told him he should go to Old Town and check with Daniel Davis, the brother of his fellow agent, Jackson Davis, and a Mr. Dudley, who did have a permit. Call checked and found Daniel Davis and Dudley had no permission to cut, although they informed him Jackson Davis had said it was okay. Before Call could charge them as trespassers, they came up with a permit, hastily signed by Jackson Davis and predated 1823. When questioned, "Mr. Davis declined giving me copies or any information on the subject," Call reported. The perplexed agent sought instructions from the capital—and soon, before the logs were removed.

An agent's life was never easy. Jonathan Weston was soon under fire from the white inhabitants of the town of Perry who asked for his removal, particularly because he not only allowed cutting in Indian Township to exceed $500, the limit set by the legislature, but let "five teams with large crews from New Brunswick" haul out $3,000 worth of timber, which he, as agent, had the right to sell. "It appears mysterious," the petition of William Frost and others complained, "that the Indian agent utterly refuses to sell to American citizens at any price and should sell to British subjects over whom we have no control to prove *the sum* he receives."

A corresponding beef was submitted by William Norwood and concerned the wood lot Weston had purchased for his charges. When Norwood found twenty-eight to thirty wigwams on his land, he ordered the Passamaquoddy off, but they insisted they were on the land the state had bought for them and refused to leave. Weston backed the Indians, so Norwood went to the legislature, which ordered a survey that showed the land was his. He had also been awarded an assessment of $12.50 for the wood the Indians had cut, Norwood said, but Weston still hadn't paid it.

A petition from all of these local folks recommended Peter Goulding, Esq., of Perry to replace Weston.

But almost as soon as Goulding was appointed, Governor Albion Parris (Maine's second governor) received a letter stating: "I understand the Eastport traders have set the Indians out to make opposition to [Goulding].... The Indians have been told by the Eastport traders that Mr. G. will not let them have the money in advance as heretofore and that they will not be able to have their powwow in June."

Sure enough, a petition from the Passamaquoddy, themselves, against Peter Goulding soon arrived, except their complaint, it turned out in this case, was that he wouldn't let them have any say on agreements with others for cutting grass and timber on their lands.

They said they viewed this "to be one of our unalienable rights, so long as the title to the Township remains in the said tribe, to have a voice to be heard." Then they added they "were entirely satisfied with J. D. Weston" and would be happy to have him back.

Agents came and went. Goulding, by the way, stayed, and when he was attacked by whites in 1827—on the same grounds as Weston, that he allowed "foreigners" to cut—the Passamaquoddy defended him, adding a postscript to the letter from their leaders: "Indians be very glad no let'm white people in this town cut wood on their lot."

Among the names of the many agents who served during

this first decade of Maine's existence was one that stands out—Colonel Joshua Chamberlain. But this was not the hero of the Civil War. This was his father, who had fought in the War of 1812 and had been court-martialed and acquitted after the Battle of Hampden, before moving to Brewer in 1817. There, his someday-to-be immortalized son listened to Indians who encamped in his father's backyard in birch-bark wigwams, heard stories of Mohawk attacks and of the frightful spirits who haunted Katahdin, learned some of their language, and later climbed Katahdin in spite of those bloodcurdling tales.

No sooner was the appointment of the elder Colonel Chamberlain made than a petition came from the Penobscots to remove him, signed by the tribal governor, John Attean (but not by the tribal lieutenant governor, John Neptune). The letter said the tribe wanted Thomas Bartlett of Old Town for the job.

A letter from a Bangor lumberman, Amos Roberts, to Edward Kent, a prominent local lawyer and Whig politician who later became governor of Maine, contained hints of the hidden ulterior motive. Roberts declared, "The Indians are completely united in Bartlett." But another letter sent to Governor Enoch Lincoln, equally biased in the other direction, stated, "Amos M. Roberts is a young man in trade with Richard Bartlett, a brother of Thomas. They are both engaged in lumber and other speculation." More importantly, they had had an altercation with Chamberlain.

On February 17, 1829, yet another petition came from the Penobscots. This time, it declared: "...there has been art and deception used to make our minds disaffected against Colonel Chamberlain and by these means they have wrongfully obtained our names to a petition requesting his removal...." Signed again by Governor John Attean, this new missive insisted the Penobscots were now "well satisfied" with Chamberlain and "preferred him to any other man."

A lawyerly comment from Edward Kent aptly summed up the thoughts of an outside observer vis-à-vis the job of attending to the tribes. Wrote Kent: "I can only add that during the last summer I was the distributor of a small sum among certain families in the tribe [Penobscot, from a private contribution from Brunswick], and if the trouble and vexation of the agent is in proportion to that I experienced in this small matter, his office cannot be a sinecure."

Another noted Mainer commenting about the Penobscots at this period was Seba Smith, the editor of the *Eastern Argus* newspaper, and later a writer and political humorist of national note. In September 1825 he visited Indian Old Town and has left us a vivid word picture of the scene.

He begins by writing of the "small island, which has been the headquarters of the Penobscot tribe of the aborigines from time immemorial and which is still cherished by this fading remnant of a fading race, as the sacred spot where their forefathers loved to dwell, where their council fires were lit, and their pipe of peace was smoked, where their light canoes played over the water as buoyant as the wild duck which they pursued, where they sunk to rest, generation after generation, and mingled their bones with the dust."

Transported from the mainland by batteau, Smith and his party landed in time to witness a funeral procession. They had just set foot on the island when they were startled by a gunshot announcing the appearance on the river of fifteen to twenty canoes, full of Indian men. One Penobscot woman, possibly for a joke, told Smith: "Maybe Mohawk coming." But then another said, "Maybe one dead and they coming to bury him." It turned out to be a *her*, a young girl who had died of consumption upriver, and Smith watched as the canoeists took out a "plain rough box, somewhat in the shape of a coffin," which a number of women then carried by the cords fastened around it to the meetinghouse. Everywhere in the village there was silent weeping. Smith commented on the great attention paid by the Indians to the "ties of consanguinity," as if the deceased were a relative of everyone. Later, learning of another death in the tribe a day or two previously, Smith editorialized that "the tribe is gradually dwindling in numbers, which seems to be the inevitable fate of all the

This replica of a bark wigwam shows a rectangular shelter made of poles and sheets of bark. Some were large enough for several families. Other Wabanaki wigwams were conical or domed. MAINE STATE MUSEUM

aborigines, where civilization approaches them"—hardly an original thought, and he echoed Benjamin Lincoln by going on to add the Penobscots would certainly die out, "unless compelled to migrate to the more friendly shelter of some distant wilderness."

He watched a group of Penobscot men dig a grave for the poor victim of tuberculosis and how, in digging, they several times came upon decaying bones in their overcrowded burial ground. He also described the decaying wooden crosses that marked the graves. Mentioning the tribe's still active proclivity for wandering, he wrote of their spending the cold winter months in the forest, "where they can procure wood for their fires without much labor," and their scattering in different directions in the summertime. The past summer, surprisingly, he reported, some of them "traversed the grand canal of New York with their canoes and visited Albany." They were still living in bark- or board-covered wigwams in 1825, had a meetinghouse (church), a house for their governor, a Roman Catholic priest who visited a few times a year, and a school, which was now closed, but there was talk of establishing another one.

When it was time for Smith and his party to leave, the bat-teau that had brought them was not available. An Indian offered to convey them in his birch-bark canoe. While the whites sat huddled on the bottom of the potentially tippy craft, the Indian stood erect, paddling them across, "with a steady nerve and strong arm."

The closed Penobscot school, with its promised but uncer-tain reopening, had its counterpart on the Passamaquoddy reservation.

Only the situation was much more complicated and intense, essentially an educational drama that lasted almost a decade and had ramifications spreading well beyond the small Down East community of Perry in which Pleasant Point was located—in fact, the conflict reached Maine's then capital of Portland, Boston, and even Washington, D.C. Pressure from outside was mounted by the Maine governor and the Indian agent against tribal traditions, including hereditary chieftain-ship and the use of the Passamaquoddy language, and involved a clash of religions, too—between Protestants and Catholics. The result was a culture war within the Passamaquoddy tribe, itself, over how its children should be raised.

The beginning of this strife can be dated to a communi-cation to the Maine state governor and council on May 21, 1821, from the Reverend Elijah Kellogg, Sr., of Portland, ask-ing for an introduction to the Passamaquoddy chiefs. The good reverend, a veteran of the Revolutionary War and the Battle of Bunker Hill, for twenty-four years had been the pas-tor of the Second Parish Congregational Church in the state's largest city. He was not a stranger to controversy, the creation of his parish having been occasioned by a split in the original First Parish Church's congregation, but assuredly nothing he had ever been involved in—and that included failed business investments with his wife's merchant family, the McLellans— had ever prepared him for what he would encounter among the Passamaquoddy. Sixty years old when he emarked upon this adventure as a Protestant missionary to the Down East region on behalf of the Society for the Propagation of the

Gospel, his top priority was to create a school in which Passamaquoddy children were taught to read and write in English, to become self-sufficient farmers, and to enjoy the "benefits of civilization."

Kellogg's name has a certain resonance in Maine history, but that is mostly due to the fame of his son, the Reverend Elijah Kellogg, Jr., who became nationally known as an author of popular books for boys. In a true tale of Maine's early years that often sounds like fiction, the elder Kellogg is forever linked with a Passamaquoddy native named Sock Bason (Jacques Vincent), usually referred to as Deacon Sockabason since no priest was available for the universally Roman Catholic Passamaquoddy flock, and he would read them prayers. Although not a tribal chief—that honor belonged for life to Francis Joseph Neptune—Deacon Sockabason was clearly influential, married the chief's daughter, lived in the only framed house on the reservation, and was the most fluent in English of his people.

His encounter with Kellogg occurred as soon as the minister arrived on June 10, 1821, and Sockabason was not friendly. He said he wanted Passamaquoddy youngsters to learn French, not English. "God gave Indians his language and his religion," he told Kellogg, "and I no alter what he say."

It took Kellogg a while to learn Sockabason was harboring a grudge against the state governor and council, who had rejected his request to be given a particular wood lot. When Governor King told him the Passamaquoddy should learn English, the Indian defiantly shot back, "We won't learn English."

Kellogg also learned of Sockabason's reputation for being "proud and fond of power and of money and of gain," but, too, that he was bright and talented. Among the Passamaquoddy, he was the most adept at agriculture and was already raising three acres of potatoes. His need for a plow was the means Kellogg used the following year to win his allegiance by getting the state governor and council to grant him the funds to buy one—and six hoes, as well.

Denny Sockabason, daughter of Francis Joseph Neptune and wife of Deacon Sockabason, painted by a British officer at Eastport, 1817.
ABBY ALDRICH ROCKEFELLER FOLK ART MUSEUM,
COLONIAL WILLIAMSBURG FOUNDATION, WILLIAMSBURG, VA.

Upon his return from a trip to Boston, where he was admonished by the bishop of the Catholic diocese not to cooperate with Kellogg, Sockabason announced he would send his son and daughter to the Protestant school when it was built, and he set about recruiting other pupils. Thanks to a grant from the Maine legislature, received in 1823, the Reverend Kellogg constructed his school and was ready to open classes by 1824.

The minister's report that year was as positive as could be. The desire of the children to learn was equal to his expectation, he wrote, "considering the hostility of their Indian habits to my errand among them (to say nothing of the horror of losing their religion), their submission to order and progress in the alphabet...and in getting their untutored tongues around

181

words, the most ragged with consonants...."

There were at most sixty children in the village and Kellogg had an average of "perhaps twenty-five" attendees. "The prejudice of the tribe against learning English is subsiding," he wrote hopefully. Through private funds he had been able to "clothe about sixty of the Indian children with a cotton shirt and gingham frock...," and had given $75 of the $100 from the state governor and council to the poor and indigent, with the remainder deposited in the Eastport Bank. Of another $75 he received for promoting English and agriculture, $43 had gone to Indians who raised potatoes and other vegetables, and $32 had gone for his board and washing during the sixteen weeks he stayed, until the Indians and their families departed into the wilderness at hunting time, and he closed up shop. Afterward, Sockabason would be his caretaker and receive $5.

Commuting seasonally from Portland, Kellogg would appear at Pleasant Point in the spring once it was certain the Passamaquoddy had returned from the winter hunt. In May 1825, with his school again open, the Protestant-cleric-turned-"superintendent-of-schools" ran into yet another unexpected obstacle. The tribal people were angry at Sockabason and threatening to boycott the school. The crisis was hardly improved when a Catholic priest, Father Byrne, showed up to make trouble, wanting to teach the children Latin, and insisting that at the very least no girls should go to school. Then the priest lured the children to his own school by reading to them from an old Indian manuscript.

It was reported to Kellogg the old Indians were saying: "Now no children who walk to church walk to school to learn English. Priest, he say so."

Although Kellogg suspended his teaching for about five weeks, he later resumed it. One of the trump cards he now played was his receipt of federal money to spend on clothing and a potato cellar, plus grants from the state. Also, he had Deacon Sockabason squarely on his side and acknowledged how important that was in his report.

The singular attitude in which Sockabason presents himself, standing like an oak of the mountains, braving the storm of prejudice, superstition, and persecution, must touch the heart of the legislature and give them an increasing interest in emancipating these wretched beings from their present degradation.

That October he received a letter from the deacon, who addressed him as Father. "You been here five months in school, now you walk Portland," the Passamaquoddy stated in his own handwriting. "Some old Indians give me much trouble because I will have school...say to Governor Parris and his councils I friend to your school and send you soon next spring and help the Indians all he can. Nobody make me give up his school."

The federal money Kellogg dispensed came from the Bureau of Indian Affairs in the U.S. War Department, which had been established by Secretary of War John Calhoun and put in the hands of Thomas L. McKenney, a career military man. Although born of a Quaker family, McKenney had been head of volunteers in the War of 1812, and in 1816 was appointed by President Madison and then re-appointed by President Monroe as head of the Superintendency of Indian Trade.

Because of his crackdown on fur traders who cheated the Indians, McKenney ran afoul of a powerful senator from Missouri, Thomas Hart Benton, and his office was closed by Congress in 1822. Two years later, the Bureau of Indian Affairs was created—and has been controversial ever since—but McKenney managed to survive in the job for six more years, until Andrew Jackson fired him for resisting his Indian removal policy.

The money McKenney sent to Kellogg came from a $10,000 annual appropriation first voted by Congress in 1819 "for the civilization of Indians." From his office in Washington he would write Kellogg, to whom he dispatched $150 every year, asking for a report on the Indian school, "the general health of the children, their advances in the work of civilization," and, incidentally, any material about the local

*Poling and paddling a birch canoe up a rapid stream.
Note the baby on a carrying board amidships.*
MAINE STATE MUSEUM

Indian chiefs. McKenney was a scholar, as well as an administrator and negotiator, who published a magnificently illustrated two-volume study, *The Indian Tribes of North America.* In June 1825 he wrote Kellogg, asking him to collect Indian oratory for a book that Samuel S. Conant of New York wanted to publish. And he also requested: "With the view of preserving in the archives of the government whatever of the aboriginal man be reserved from the ultimate destruction which awaits his race...an alphabet and grammar...and chapter in language, neatly penned on sheets of octave size and put up between thin board or thick paper."

Kellogg never indicated whether he shared the generally held feeling, as expressed again by McKenney, that all Indians, including *his*, were doomed to extinction. The good reverend soldiered on at Pleasant Point. In March 1826 Governor Albion Parris informed him he was sending "$50 for relief of the sick and indigent and $100 for the improvement and instruction of said Indians in English and encouragement and assistance in agriculture." There was also $75 to erect a "cooper's shop" and for purchasing cooper's tools to teach the Indians how to make barrels.

Native Americans porpoise fishing.
COLLECTIONS OF THE MAINE HISTORICAL SOCIETY, 1997.42

The state governor added, "the above appropriations [were] made by the Legislature principally through your influence and recommendation.... You will assure the Indians of the interest felt for them by the government of the state."

But included, too, was a warning that, "all further assistance will be withheld if they refuse to send their children to school or if they oppose the wishes of the government of the United States and of this state in instructing them in agriculture and the mechanic arts."

The state governor's strong wording may have been prompted by a letter recently received from the three selectmen of Perry (one of whom was Peter Goulding). They had gone to the school and heard the children "read and repeat English" and sing psalms, and "we were pleased with their performance especially when we know what an unnatural race they are and the great attempt made this season by all the artifice of the Catholic priest to overthrow the school which interrupted it about five weeks."

Despite this "support" from the top, Kellogg's worst moments were yet to come.

The following year, the new bishop in Boston, Benedict

Fenwick, instructed the Passamaquoddy that if Kellogg was spreading religion, "you must have nothing to do with him, nor suffer him to come among you.... But if his views be simply to teach [you] to read and write and should not go beyond that, I shall not object to his being received by you."

Seemingly, a compromise had been reached, but the Church showed its power (possibly after learning that Protestant prayers and singing were still going on at Kellogg's school) by withholding the visit of any priest or the bishop himself from a major ceremony the Passamaquoddy held upon the election of a new tribal lieutenant governor. Indian visitors—Penobscots and Maliseets—came from "Away" to join in the weeks-long festivities, yet without Catholic clergy present, "no matches are made, no marriages are made, and the great carnival breaks up under this *awful dispensation*," Kellogg complained. The word was out that Bishop Fenwick, who had taken an active interest in proselytizing in Maine (he was to create the town of Benedicta in southern Aroostook County), would now not visit unless the school were closed. "So my poor school was made the scapegoat to carry away all the sin of the flock's being left like sheep without a shepherd," Kellogg bemoaned.

The year 1828 started with an attempt by the leaders of the tribe to have the War Department disown Elijah Kellogg, Sr. The reverend believed they were trying to secure the federal money for themselves, and was able, after receiving word from McKenney, to disabuse them of that notion with the news that the funds, if relinquished by Maine, would go to Indian schools in the Southwest.

While the politicking went on at a higher level— Governor Parris vouching for Kellogg to Secretary of War James Barbour—the Catholic faction on the scene took actual physical action. There were now two priests at Pleasant Point—a Father Vergil Barber and Father Smith. Together they marched to the Protestant school to take it over. Kellogg said they couldn't, that it belonged to the secretary of war. They replied that it belonged to the Passamaquoddy tribe.

Not only was there a war of words, but the two priests took a "stock of wood" and broke open the lock. Kellogg had it repaired. Then Father Smith smashed down the door with an axe, and the two priests removed the books and school supplies inside and prepared to run a Catholic flag up the flagpole. Kellogg promptly announced he would teach out of Deacon Sockabason's house and would provide clothing only for the children who came to him to be taught. All summer long two schools operated. Two widows to whom Kellogg had given blankets returned them, saying they would lose their souls otherwise. The tension got to Father Smith, who had a nervous breakdown and was replaced by Father James Fitton. One of the priests, unidentified, was heard to say Kellogg "should be shot." When the Protestant minister walked about in the village, children would aim their fingers at him and pretend they were firing guns. Kellogg, now sixty-seven years old, began to think about retirement, but he stayed on for two more years, the continued turmoil notwithstanding.

The two governments in Maine and Washington, D.C., withheld their funds almost to the end of the next year and when Kellogg received the aid, he also received appreciation for helping to bring the funds back. But also involved was an extraordinary trip that Deacon Sockabason and others took to Washington in the fall of 1829.

The story was told by Thomas L. McKenney in his memoirs, actually in a footnote discussing the influence of storms on the travels of Indians and their arrival in North America.

When McKenney was director of the Bureau of Indian Affairs, he was informed one day that a party of Indians had arrived in D.C. and had come in their canoes by way of the Potomac. There were five of them who were conducted to his office.

> To the questions—to what tribe did they belong and what business had brought them to Washington, I was answered that they belonged to the Quoddy tribe, away down toward sunset where the land stops in the East, meaning the neighborhood of Eastport, Maine.

McKenney claimed their visit to D.C. was "very unexpected to them." They had gone out in two birch-bark canoes to shoot porpoises when a storm came up and forced them out to sea. After being blown about for two or three days and nights, they spotted a vessel, rigged up white shirts to their paddles, and caught the attention of the crew, who picked them up. They were by then off the Virginia Capes.

"The principal was DEACON SOCKBASIN [*sic*] who spoke English tolerably well," McKenney went on. "His name had been made familiar to me by various communications bearing his signature on matters relating to their schools."

McKenney next related that he gave them the means to sustain themselves and get home. The canoes stayed in Washington, one of them conveyed by McKenney to the War Department, and the other hung up in the passageway over the door of his office, until it was sent to the Columbian Institute and displayed "to attest in how frail a vessel human beings may be driven by a storm, upon the ocean, for at least 1,000 miles."

McKenney's conclusion—and apparently his main interest in relating the story—was that if the Passamaquoddy could survive the storm Sockabason described to him, it was "not unreasonable to conclude that other adventurers on the deep blue sea"—meaning Indians in the distant past—might have had similar experiences.

This footnote has to be puzzling.[1] For it is also known that on this 1829 visit of Sockabason's to D.C., which hardly could have been as accidental as McKenney believed, the Passamaquoddy "deacon" managed to meet with President Andrew Jackson—no admirer of Indians—and received a grant of $300 through the good offices of Old Hickory. The Reverend Kellogg was to administer the funds, but half could be paid to a priest if the Indians agreed. However, at that point in time, there was no priest at Pleasant Point.

The following year, 1830, a priest did arrive, Father Michael Healy, during the second week in July—after Kellogg had started his school. Again, there was agitation against the

Protestant school, and Kellogg, who was approaching seventy years of age, at the end of the summer decided he had had enough.

His resignation essentially signaled the final round in the fight for the type of school he'd wanted, but the coup-de-grâce wasn't delivered until 1833. Most unusually, Maine, in this era, had a Roman Catholic congressman, Edward Kavanagh, the first of his religion to hold office in New England, and Kavanagh arranged for a $200 yearly grant from the War Department for civilizing Indians. The money went to Bishop Fenwick this time and was used to pay a French-born priest, Father Louis-Edmond Demillier, who stayed ten years at Pleasant Point as a schoolmaster and priest, running things as the Catholics wished.

What long-term effect this "culture war" had on the adaptation of the Passamaquoddy to their new situation under the United States remains a matter of conjecture, or argument. So does another issue this entire nine-year-long incident poses— the literal infusion of some, albeit limited, federal funding for one of Maine's tribes. While not raised during the Land Claims Settlement debates, this precedent does seemingly militate against the position that the federal government had left the East Coast Indians' status as the exclusive province of the states.

Bishop Fenwick's ultimate success in gaining control of the school and religion situation at Pleasant Point may seem to have been based on a compromise. Yet as far as the Passamaquoddy were concerned, Bishop Fenwick's preoccupation had to do with ending Protestant competition. When the bishop visited Maine's third state governor, Enoch Lincoln, in the summer of 1828, he presented him with a full-scale plan for better *Catholic* schools and churches for the Maine Indians, and the proposal was submitted to the legislature.

Still, lurking behind the harsh feelings aroused on the Passamaquoddy reservation by the controversy was a definite division of opinion among the native people. How far should they move toward the goal the preponderance of state leaders

appeared to have set for them—to "civilize," or at least mod-
ernize them, and make them *self-reliant*, like other Americans?
Was their clinging to Catholicism just a symptom of their
wish to cling to their own culture? Should they choose tradition or adaptation? Within a few years, a pronounced break
would occur: an Old Party and a New Party would emerge.
Paradoxically, the New Party contained the traditionalists and
the Old Party the modernists. The divide would become a
geographical one, as well, with the New Party heading north
to settle on the tribe's territories at Indian Township.

Earlier, while the Reverend Kellogg was having his troubles at Pleasant Point, the Penobscots were initiating their own
Old Party–New Party squabbles. These were more a matter of
personality than of religion or philosophy. The problem essentially arose as a power struggle between the tribal governor,
John Attean, and the tribal lieutenant governor, John
Neptune. It was exacerbated by the fact that Neptune had
seduced Attean's wife, allegedly to publicly humiliate his superior, and then, with his supporters, left to set up camp on a
small number of acres of land belonging to the tribe in Brewer,
where he remained with his common-law wife Molly Molasses
for several decades.

The land in Brewer had come into the Penobscots' possession in 1818 while Maine was still under Massachusetts. It was
part of another "treaty," brought on by the Penobscots' need
for money. They sold the Commonwealth most of their land
along the Penobscot River, but kept four townships near
today's Millinocket, in addition to a "gift" of the parcel in
Brewer.

They were even to lose these four townships in 1833, in
the final major transaction by which the state acquired Indian
lands. A publication by the Pleasant Point Bilingual Program
covering Penobscot history, as well as Passamaquoddy,
Maliseet, and Micmac histories, describes the event this way:

> ...the State sent two men to buy whatever land they could from
> the Penobscots. These men got the tribal governor and three oth-

ers to sign a deed selling all four Penobscot townships for $50,000—less than $1 an acre. Other members of the tribe found out about the sale and found out that the four who signed had been secretly promised new homes. They protested to Maine's Governor Smith, but he didn't listen. The State later sold the townships and Millinocket now sits on one of them. Also around the same time, the tribe was talked into selling five of their islands. It never was paid for some of these islands.[2]

The two men involved were Amos Roberts and his sidekick Thomas Bartlett, for we find the state governor and council on June 21, 1832, receiving a bond from both men, attendant upon their appointment as commissioners "to purchase such of the lands belonging to the Penobscot Tribe as they might be disposed to sell." Amos Roberts is well known in Bangor history as one of the prime "lumber barons" during the period when that city was the lumber capital of the world.

By the end of the first two decades of Maine's new independent status, the local Indians, rather than quietly fading into non-existence, had made their presence known. Maine's Governor Enoch Lincoln, himself, had even written an extensive poem that included them. Well, to be exact, it included the long-since-departed "Pequawketts," who had inhabited Fryeburg, where he had resided for a number of years. But he could have been voicing the unspoken resentments of his contemporary Penobscot and Passamaquoddy constituents when, in his epic verse, *The Village,* he had a "painted chief pour forth his rankling rage and sullen grief," as follows:

> Ye spoilers of all which the red man possessed,
> Why disturb ye my shade in the peace of the graves?
> When ye came oer the big rolling waters a far.
> We received you as brothers and gave you our food;
> But you burst on our heads with your thunders of war.
> Ye plundered our wigwams and drank of our blood,
> Ye robbed from our hunters and the wilds of their game,
> With our wives and our children, ye drove us away.
> To our chiefs with the furies of discord ye came
> And incited our tribes with each other to prey...

May famine, disease and contention abound,
Till our lands you restore and our wrongs you repair.

Enoch Lincoln was the son of a governor of Massachusetts and the brother of another Bay State governor. He had to have had a good deal of poltical acumen, and it shows in other parts of the poem when he describes Indian torture of prisoners in gory detail, as if to show he isn't just a one-sided "Indian lover." Not that his poem, which also included a very early blast against slavery, had much to do with his political problems. Rather, these involved a rift in his own party and an executive council that wouldn't approve his appointees. So, after three successful one-year terms (he was extremely popular, particularly for his tough stand on the northern boundary question), he declined to run for a fourth time, only to die suddenly at the age of forty while still in office.

Politics were fairly raw in those days. Newspapers, for example, were designed to be partisan and were run on behalf of the two main parties, which by then called themselves Democrats and Whigs.

The *Eastern Argus,* where Seba Smith had been editor, was Democrat to the core. The State of Maine, as a whole, was likewise controlled by the Jeffersonians and Jacksonians, but Edward Kent had managed to get himself elected as a Whig in the late 1830s for a two-year term. The *Eastern Argus* would not concede Kent might do anything right. On October 12, 1838, they printed on their front page a letter which apparently had originated with a Penobscot named Sebattis Neptune, along with the editorial comment that, "Gov. Kent is just about as successful in talking Indian as in governing the state—and in both, seems inclined to favor a dangerous increase of *Executive Power.*"

The letter bore the heading "GOV. KENT AND THE PENOVSCOTS" and began:

The Penobscot Indians, imbibing a little of the republican spirit of the age, or snuffing the air of the Canadian rebellion, lately determined to oust their hereditary Governor, and put in his place a chief of their own selection. It appears that the old dignitary, on account of alleged peculation, intemperance, and sundry other peccadiloes, *had got himself in very bad odor* among his subjects. They accordingly judged that the time had arrived *"when in the course of human events it became necessary"* to dissolve all allegiances and fidelity to him.

A Council of forty was summoned from the neighboring tribes, the Passamaquoddy and St. Johns, to be present at the ceremony of deposition. The old *humbug* of hereditary succession was set aside, as better fitted for their...half-clothed forefathers, than for enlightened, civilized Indians of the nineteenth century: yet not without opposition, for there still remained many sturdy advocates of the established system who protested against so dangerous an innovation.

In this state of insubordination and outright revolt, the old Governor looked round for an ally. Emperor Nicholas would gladly help a brother despot in distress, but was too far off. *A Bull from his holiness the Pope* could not be got over in season.... He found an ally nearer home. Governor Kent appeared as the champion of his fallen fortunes, and thundered down upon the loco foco Indians several peremptory letters, threatening them with *Sheriffs, Balls,* and a THOUSAND BAYONETS, if they did not desist from their leveling designs, and go home....

There followed an alleged copy of a communication to Sebattis Neptune and the other troublemaking Indians assembled at Old Town. Essentially, Kent warned them that the "new liberty pole must not now be raised.... If the pole is raised, Indians will fight and *I have one thousand guns and bayonets,* and I will send Sheriff and soldiers to take you all.... I take no sides with either party, but if you will not mind me, then certain I send guns and men on the Island."

To the writer's (and no doubt the *Eastern Argus's* editors') delight, the Indians disobeyed the chief executive, elected their "citizen governor," danced around the "liberty pole which they had erected as a symbol of their new principles," and pow-wowed for two weeks before everyone went home.

Governor Kent, it was then predicted, would follow the deposed chief into retirement.

Partisan and exaggerated as this "letter" might have been, the future for both Maine tribes and their members seemed as unsettled as could be, split as they were, once the prelude to the U.S.'s own great civil war commenced in the next two tempestuous decades.

NOTES

[1] Thomas L. McKenney, *Memoirs,* vol. II. New York: Paine and Burgess Company, 1846, page 29.

[2] *Maine Indians: Brief Summary: People of the Early Dawn.* Pamphlet prepared by Pleasant Point Bilingual Program, Title VII, Perry, Maine. Joseph A. Nicholas, director, text by Alberta Francis. Page 23.

15

THE 1840s AND 1850s

*W*hen the late J. Russell Wiggins, retired editor of the *Washington Post*, Maine transplant, a dedicated opponent of the Land Claims Settlement, made his statement that the Maine Indians might have joined the Cherokees, et. al., in exile across the Mississippi if they hadn't been under the Pine Tree State's protection, this bit of hyperbole merely may have been Wiggins's way of saying to the Passamaquoddy and Penobscots (and later the Maliseets): *See how fortunate you were. Now, shut up, go home, and drop your case.* As history, the comparison was more than a trifle skewed. Oddly enough, the politician held most responsible for the forced exodus of Native Americans between 1832 and 1850, whch included the tragic "Trail of Tears," was President Andrew Jackson. We have seen he was aware, at least, of the Passamaquoddy, met with Deacon Sockabason and others, and endorsed their request for aid by sending it on to Congress. What he communicated on that occasion seemed hardly the words of a totalitarian fire-breathing Indian hater who would gladly have routed them out from their ancestral lands in New England and shipped them west.

"Recollecting that this tribe, when strong and numerous, fought with us for the liberty we now enjoy," the seventh president's message stated, "I could not refuse to present to the consideration of Congress their application for a small portion of the bark and timber of the country which once belonged to them."

One wonders if the story of Jackson's consideration, when spread through "Indian Country" in Maine, accounted for the fact that in an 1837 census shortly afterward, and yet at the height of the "removal" episode, the data gleaned from the Penobscots revealed that the political makeup of the tribe was two-thirds *"Democrats, Jackson men, as they say,"* and the remainder Whigs. The total number of Penobscots, incidentally, as reported by John Neptune before the 1840s began, was 95 families and 362 persons. The article detailing such news in the *Lincoln Patriot* of Waldoboro added that "party spirit runs high" on Indian Island and that this small, reduced tribe, reflecting Jackson's comments about the Passamaquoddy, could once have fielded 2,000 warriors.[1]

Despite an occasional piece in the newspapers, the Indians of Maine no longer loomed large in the minds of its citizenry. Their fighting potential had dwindled to a ridiculous handful of braves; they had lost their role as a buffer or balance of power vis-à-vis the English in Canada; whatever of their land was useful and desirable had been taken from them; they were, all in all, really sort of piteous, existing on handouts from the gentlemen in charge of state government who, since 1832, were now operating out of a nice, new, grey granite, Bulfinch-designed capitol building in Augusta.

Those exalted honorables had much more serious problems than any posed by a few poor Indians, and chief among them at the start of this era was the question of where the northern boundary of the State of Maine would be: where they wanted it—somewhere near the St. Lawrence River—or where the British wanted it—about halfway down Aroostook County at a line drawn through Mars Hill. The state, on its own, had almost gone to war against Canada, marching its militiamen north to build a stronghold at Houlton and, finally, forts at two strategic spots, one on the Aroostook River, one on the St. John River, naming them respectively in bi-partisan fashion for two Maine state governors, John Fairfield, Democrat, and Edward Kent, Whig.

The cooler heads who eventually prevailed and prevented a military conflict were dominated by Daniel Webster, after he became U.S. secretary of state, and Great Britain's Lord Ashburton, born Alexander Baring and, it so happened, a large-scale landowner in northern Maine. On August 9, 1842, in the sweltering heat of Washington, D.C., both negotiators constructed a compromise known to history as the Webster-

Ashburton Treaty, which formally went into effect on November 10 of that same year.

Maine's Governor John Fairfield declared his "deep disappointment" with the pact, but the state as a whole, helped by a hush-up payment of $1.5 million for its *lost* acres in Canada (3.2 million of them) and some adroit lobbying by one of their congressmen disbursing a secret State Department slush fund, did accept the *fait accompli*.[2]

Unnoticed amid the turmoil was that the addition once and for all of the entirety of Aroostook County to the state had given Maine new populations of Indians—small bands of the Maliseet and Micmac tribes—who, since time immemorial, had occupied these lands.

They were to remain pretty much invisible, except to local folks, until the latter part of the twentieth century.

In 1920 a French priest, L'Abbé Thomas Albert, published *Histoire du Madawaska*, which touches upon the native population of the upper reaches of the St. John River Valley. The entire area, prior to its being divided by the Webster-Ashburton Treaty, covered some 12,000 square miles, and its vast wilderness was the domain of the Maliseet, who, with their close cousins the Passamaquoddy, were known to the French collectively as *Etchemins*. Father Albert describes a small village called Madoeskak, *la demeure du chevalieresque Malecite* (home of the chivalrous Maliseets), which was still in existence when the French Acadians, originally forced from their homes in Nova Scotia by the English and then again displaced by Tories in New Brunswick, arrived in large numbers. That particular Indian village of Madoueskak, according to Father Albert, was the most important of the entire Maliseet tribe, which was spread all along the St. John River. By 1920 the Canadian city of Edmundston had taken over the site, and its post office occupied the exact location where the Indians had held their great councils. Also in the vicinity were Micmacs, and the name Madawaska, itself, we learn, is of Micmac origin—from *madawes*, meaning porcupine and *kak*, or place, denoting *the land of the porcupines*.

The author also tells of Mohawk raids, those fiercest of Iroquois fighters advancing this far north on at least two occasions to exterminate the Maliseets. Out of one such episode comes a story—or legend—repeated over the centuries, of the young woman Malobiannah, whose fiancée was killed in a battle in which she, herself, was captured by the invaders. Forced to help navigate them down the St. John, she quietly planned her revenge, then tricked her captors into letting her lead them over Grand Falls where they all perished. As Father Albert comments: "The Maliseet heroine has since been sung in verse in the Abenaki, French, and English languages..." and he further suggests that Greek history, so rich in noble gestures, offers none as "grand and sublime as the simple and little known sacrifice of this obscure daughter of the woods."

Most of these Maliseets apparently were among those who went to Machias and fought with John Allan. How many came back north or stayed and mingled with the Passamaquoddy is not known, and their numbers, which totalled only thirty in 1850, fluctuated greatly because of their "*genre de vie nomade*," wrote Father Albert, their "type of nomad life."

Father Albert, too, spoke of them retiring into "the shadow of the last oaks of the ancient forest, and with a haughty frown, waiting for the death of their race."

Once the boundary question was settled, Maine public life experienced a number of other burning issues, mostly reflective of what was going on in the rest of the country.

One of these issues was anti-Catholicism. However, if the Maine Indians were noticed enough to be hated during the spate of virulent anti-Catholicism that roiled Maine in the 1840s and '50s, they were most certainly despised as Indians, not Catholics. The principal animus of the Protestants who joined the "Know-Nothing" movement, as it has been dubbed, was against recent immigrants, almost all of them Irish. Called what they were because when asked about their movement, they answered: "I know nothing," these fired-up bigots entered politics, in Maine and elsewhere, as a third party and were not averse to violence. Churches were burned in Bath and Bangor, and a priest, Father John Bapst, tarred and feathered in Ellsworth. Two other issues, sometimes linked to this one (or having the same supporters), were slavery and temperance. In 1851 Maine passed the first "prohibition" law in the United States. Anti-slavery, including total "abolition" of the practice, was probably the strongest of these trends. The political uproar in Maine, as in the rest of the country, over these three issues was extensive. Parties broke up and formed again in new configurations until the Republican Party fused together a number of elements. The ferment was extreme as the nation lurched toward the election of Abraham Lincoln, and Maine government, reflecting the shifts in tradition, exchanged its Jeffersonian roots in the Democratic Party for that new Republican group, the Grand Old Party, or G.O.P., as it is still called today.

Here and there a few voices were raised on behalf of Maine Indians amidst the swirl of stirring political events engrossing the only media of the day, the newspapers. One such voice in Maine was that of a dissident Quaker named Jeremiah Hacker who published a periodical strangely called the *Portland Pleasure Boat*. Under a subheading he printed whenever he mused about the tribes: "Lo! The Poor Indian," he published the following thoughts on December 12, 1847, about a Penobscot named "Captain John," described as the "grandson of Sabattas," who is not otherwise identified. This Captain John, it seems, was currently in jail, having gotten drunk on Thanksgiving Day and been caught stealing a $2 cane. He was slated to linger behind bars until March, when the court's term would begin and he could be brought to trial. Hacker editorialized:

> The pale-faces can steal the Indians' beavers, moose, deer and other game, rob them of their hunting grounds and their fathers' graves, and teach them to get drunk and steal; but if the poor Indian steals so much as a walking stick, after they have taught him the art, he must be locked up in prison and wait months for a trial, and then, perhaps, be sent to State Prison!

In a sardonic epilogue to these remarks, the editor, who today might be called a "bleeding heart" by his detractors, added the fact that a $100 bail would gain Captain John his temporary freedom, "but probably, there is not Christianity enough in the city among those who are able to bail him out...."

By contrast, in that same year of 1847 a different sort of story involving Maine Indians appeared in several newspapers. It seems that members of the Penobscot tribe, at least, were in the habit, particularly during the summer, of leaving Old Town and camping out, even in urban settings like Portland. A group of them had set up their wigwams near Portland Bridge and, as they no doubt did everywhere, drew a crowd of onlookers.

Among them, in this instance, were two young factory girls who thought that one of the Indians, of particularly non-Indian appearance, looked enough like them to be their lost brother, who'd disappeared as an infant. And so it turned out to be. He was James Wilbur, a baby stolen from outside a house in Sandy River near Farmington, by an itinerant hunter and sold to Indians, who had raised him, first under the name of White Jim, and then James White. The year before, he had married a young Indian woman, Mary Francis. The reunion of this young man and his Indian bride with his long-grieving parents made for great human-interest copy, with the implication that "Lo! The Poor Indian" would most likely now become white in more than name.

Three years later, in May 1850, Jeremiah Hacker was back at it under the "Lo! The Poor Indian" rubric, with another broadside—that was not so much a Captain John sob-story type as it was a reflection of *"liberal"* thinking on the Indian issue at the time.

Hacker started off in his usual condemnatory way, stating: "...no nation was ever more criminal in the neglect of its duty toward a crushed and almost ruined people...", which leads up to "and if there is any virtue in legislation, the legislature of this state should not permit the session to close without taking this matter into consideration and *action.*"

The matter was brought to his attention in a conversation he had "with one of the Penobscots...one of the most intelligent of that tribe I have ever met with. He has the soul of a true [Indian], the spirit of his noble ancestors still lingers in their son."

More to the point was this Indian's analysis of the root cause of his people's poverty. Here, once more, are echoes of the conflict among the Passamaquoddy when Reverend Kellogg was jousting with Bishop Fenwick and his priests for control of the Pleasant Point school. Now, almost three decades later, Hacker was hearing from his Penobscot informant a decidedly similar discourse, based on the theme that ignorance was at the bottom of the tribe's poverty.

"This ignorance," Hacker wrote, "is in a great degree chargeable to their priests who teach them the Latin or Indian language instead of the English. He thinks the priests do this purposely to keep them in ignorance and maintain their power over them."

Editor Hacker then offered his support for a solution—told to him by his Penobscot interlocuter—that the tribal representative to the legislature in this coming session intended to ask for a bill "that an English school be established among them."

That intelligence drew the editorial comment: "The time has now arrived and opportunity is now offered by the Indians, themselves, for the whites to overcome this evil..." give the Indians "an equal chance in the world to improve..." and then, while and because the Penobscots were asking for action, "let the lawmakers at Augusta see if they cannot do one good thing, and do it quickly."

Did they do it—did they create an English-speaking school on Indian Island? It is hard to tell from the skimpy records of those days (legislative debates were not transcribed, nor were roll call votes). Nothing appears in the laws passed of 1850, although that year the legislature did institute an omnibus education bill, setting up a statewide school system and requiring all towns to participate, However, in 1853, a resolve *was* passed, granting $200 to the superintending School Committee of Old Town "in maintaining a school at the Indian village on Oldtown Island for the education of the Penobscot Indians." This is the first mention of a payment by the state for a Penobscot school—and note the money is going to a nearby white school committee, not to the tribe itself nor to a Catholic diocese. This may well have been the start of teaching done in English. By 1855 the legislature was giving $350 to the Old Town School Committee for the Penobscot school, and the same year they offered $100 to support "schools among the Passamaquoddy Indians, if in their judgment the amount can be advantageously used for that purpose."

Later entries showed the legislature sending more money, $250, for Passamaquoddy schooling, but directing it to school committees in Perry and Princeton and requiring them to report back results to the state governor and council.

Education for the Penobscots had also expanded, reaching beyond Old Town. Starting in 1858, money was sent, as well, to the school committee in Lincoln to supervise a school for Indian children, and the next year, in a still further move, the lawmakers designated $2 for "each and every Indian child that shall attend the school" in the little Penobscot River village of Greenbush, halfway between Old Town and Howland.

Two reports to the legislature at the end of the decade in 1860 seemed to make it clear the instruction was in English. James A. Purington, the Penobscot agent, declared he had "no hesitation in saying that the money ($250 to Old Town and $100 to Lincoln) had been judiciously expended" and "the results [in the case of Lincoln] fully answer all reasonable expectations." The whole system handled fifty-four students from five to twenty-four years of age who studied reading, writing, arithmetic, and geography for about twenty weeks. It should "be continued," he urged, because "it will be a power-ful means of improving the language, elevating the character, and improving the condition of this people."[3]

The only downside reported from Old Town when a *female instructor* ran the school from May 14 to October 12, was a two-week interruption by a "*varioloid*" (smallpox or measles) outbreak among the tribe on Indian Island.

The Passamaquoddy agent, George W. Nutt, was not quite so upbeat about the two schools under his jurisdiction. The one at "Peter Dennis Point [*sic*]" near Princeton had twenty-five students and, according to the local school committee, they were making "rapid progress," but the entire school was conducted in a room at the priest's house and "was entirely too small and unfit for a school room."

The problem at Pleasant Point seemed to be the teacher, a Mr. Stickney, who did not appear all that interested. "I think it would be much better to employ teachers who are more acquainted with the manners and customs of the Indians," advised Nutt, who also advocated for funds to build a suitable schoolhouse at "Peter Dennis Point."

Both documents contain more than a report card on Indian schools. They cover progress in agriculture, census data, health status, employment, welfare, and other government-type measurements of the tribes. Scarlet fever, we learn, had been a problem the past year at Pleasant Point; worse had been an outbreak of smallpox affecting seventeen Passamaquoddy, two of whom died. The Penobscots had only one confirmed case of smallpox, although "considerable" unnamed sicknesses. Passamaquoddy numbers fluctuated: 451 in the fall of 1859, dropping to 442 in May 1860, then rising to 553 in November 1860. The problem in counting, the agent felt, was that, "this tribe seems to have no fixed home, but wander about from place to place as suits their convenience for the time being." In winter they left Pleasant Point, he explained, because they had "no wood lot from which to keep their fires." The Penobscots, on the other hand, according to their agent, appeared more sedentary. Two-thirds of them resided on "Old Town Island," which had forty-three framed houses on it, three barns, a chapel, a council hall, and "a schoolhouse in poor repair." The upstream islands were

Opposite are three woodcuts by Father Eugene Vetromile, said to have been made around 1865 to illustrate his book The Abnakis and their history. Or, Historical notices on the aborigines of Acadia. *New York, J. B. Kirker, 1866.*

Courtesy of the Abbe Museum

home to twenty-nine scattered houses and fifteen barns. Livestock included eighteen pigs, twenty-five head of cattle, and three horses. "As is well known, the tribe has a nominal government of their [*sic*] own and retain[s] certain ancient customs and usages," the agent saw fit to add.

James Purington ended his report with a suggestion for tougher legislation to crack down on the sale of liquor to Indians (in a state already dry by law). Then, he both lauded his charges—"they are chaste in their habits and generally kind in their intercourse with each other"—and released some of his frustration in dealing with them: "The Indians are naturally jealous, and this jealousy is sometimes inflamed by the selfish motives and insinuations of the whites to such a degree that the refusal of the agent to comply with all their demands, however unreasonable, is attributed to some personal motive on his part and from this cause he is often much embarassed in the discharge of his duties."

These two reports were submitted in compliance with a resolve passed by the legislature on March 17, 1860, asking for an annual "state of the tribes" presentation in writing. Now that it seemed they might not vanish, after all, the Maine legislators may have felt the time had finally come to learn more about how their homegrown Native Americans were faring

Certainly, throughout these decades, a steady drumfire of items had come before them relating to the Passamaquoddy and Penobscots, enough apparently to keep a standing committee busy.

For example, one item the committee addressed was the question of what to do about a road through Indian Township, the Baring and Houlton Road, "the great thoroughfare from the waters of the St. Croix to the Aroostook country by way of Houlton." They were reminded the heavy loads on it

Panaubsket Alnambay Udenek, Old Town Indian Village

Lewis Island, Indian Village on the Schoodic Lakes

Sibayk Alnambay Udenek, Pleasant Point Indian Village

necessitated annual repairs, but "that portion of it passing through the Indian Township...is not subject to taxation." In other words, it was a direct cost to the state and if anyone sought to change that arrangement, Land Agent Samuel Cony argued, "it would hardly comport with humanity to divert any portion of the meagre funding of the Passamaquoddy tribe to that purpose...."

Or when the state began to create game protection laws, the men in Augusta had to remember to exempt the Indians from their restrictions, due to treaty obligations. For example, in an 1853 bill to preserve moose and deer, no penalty was to be levied upon the Indians unless they were hunting *"with or for persons forbidden to hunt by this act."*

A fairly complex issue was brought to the 1854 Legislature by Seth W. Smith, who was then the Passamaquoddy agent. The issue involved a complication arising from the 1794 treaty Massachusetts had signed with the tribe. Here was a loose end popping up sixty years later. It dealt with two small pieces of land among the parcels "granted" to the Passamaquoddy. Areas where a question of title remained were 100 acres at Nemcass Point, and all of Pine Island (in Big Lake), both of which were claimed by the white owners of Hinckley Plantation (today Grand Lake Stream), and a number of islands in the Schoodic River near Townships 6 and 7, claimed by the owners of these townships.

Agent Smith reported that since the Indians had been on Pine Island for thirty years and Nemcass Point had been an Indian village for many years in the past, the Passamaquoddy case was solid there. The question of the Schoodic River islands was shakier. Townships 6 and 7 had actually been granted to the mega-landowner William Bingham prior to the Treaty of 1794. There were fifteen islands worth $2,000. The Indians and the owners had each occupied them at different times and an exact ownership had never been resolved.

Nor did it appear to be after the matter was brought to the legislators' attention. Nemcass Point was another story. On

An engraving of "The Penobscot Belle" from the January 1848 issue of
The Ladies Repository. MAINE HISTORIC PRESERVATION COMMISSION

March 14, 1859, they provided $50 for "fencing purposes on
the lines of the Indian lands at Nemcass Point."

Three weeks later, $300 was voted to repair that "great
thoroughfare" through Indian Township.

In all of this period, we catch only a few eyewitness
glimpses of the Indians that go beyond official communications or bits and pieces in the press.

One was from Benjamin Browne Foster of Bangor who, in
August 1847, wrote in his diary:

> This PM, we rode to Oldtown. Crossed in the ferry. Set up two or
> three coppers for the Injin juveniles to shoot at with their bows
> and arrows...Went into the grave yard. Some of the crosses at the
> head of the graves had carved on them the figures of birds. Found
> one new-made grave and, while we were looking round, the bell
> in the Catholic Chapel began tolling. Concluding there was to be
> a funeral we left the yard and went over to the Chapel. We were
> refused admittance. We were told it was a Frenchman—"some
> Fraunchman," as they expressed it—who resided on the island.
> Presently there issued from the opened door an Indian bearing a
> long cross with the image of Christ sculptured on it, about one
> foot in length, following him a man with a black cross, probably

for the grave. Next, a man with the coffin, covered with a white cloth, under his arm. Then, indiscriminately, the mourners and others. We left without following.[4]

Almost two years later, Foster went back to Indian Island. Here is his word picture of the Penobscots in February 1849:

Have just returned from the pleasantest visit to Oldtown Island that I ever made.... It was somewhat frosty and overcast; noses, ears, and extremities were cold, yet we kept good hearts.... Hitched teams and called into a wigwam to warm. Roamed from house to house calling or looking in on the natives engaged at basketmaking when employed at all. At length called at their priest's in rear of the chapel. A comfortable, well-furnished parlor, and a gentlemanly, obliging occupant, clad in a long black gown and four-cornered cap. After enjoying the caloric questioning and conversing with the priest, he put on a black cloak and accompanied us to the house of [?], a blind, intelligent, old Indian, ninety-five years old. The priest addressed him in French (he, the priest, is a Frenchman). The old man spoke to us in good English and offered a paper setting forth his virtues and necessities, to which we responded by our charities.... The priest shew us the interior of the chapel, a coarse building decorated with some equally large, coarse pictures of the annunciation, nativity, crucifixion, etc. Our ignorance and curiosity asked a sight of his missal which lay near by, which he exhibited us. Latin scripture, printed in red and black.[5]

The years passed. The 1850s had almost ended when the *Portland Transcript* printed an "Editorial Excursion to Aroostook," a trip by its staff up the Penobscot River that included a stop at Indian Island. Since this newspaper called itself a *"journal of literature,"* as well as news, the work they printed was a long piece, full of descriptive and at times quasi-poetic writing, not the usual more staccato "journalese" of a regular daily. After inspecting General Samuel Veazie's sawmills north of Bangor, and seeing "the steel teeth rushing remorselessly through the sturdy logs, sub-dividing them with horrible din, into boards, clapboards, shingles, and laths...an immense vegetable slaughterhouse," the author embarked, along with thirty-one others of their "Editorial party" upriver to Old Town, where during a short stopover, he and two companions boarded a canoe and were paddled across to Indian Island by a young Penobscot.

Of the one-story houses he encountered there, he wrote, "Some of them are quite dilapidated while others are neatly painted and have a very comfortable appearance." Walking by the small Catholic church, they entered a house and received a friendly welcome from some women, one of whom said they knew Portland and that it was a "very big city." The writer noted that the people were decently clad, some even foppishly so, and he considered that the tribal people he saw were living in "tolerable comfort" off hunting and fishing and state government annuities, and had made considerable strides toward becoming civilized. He reported:

> One old Indian who approached our party was greatly puzzled as to our character.
>
> "You Englishmen?"
>
> "No."
>
> "You commissioners?"
>
> "No—editors."
>
> "Ugh! You make newspapers. Learned men; have great minds!"
>
> Here was a compliment to the profession! But the old fellow was evidently a wag, and we fear he was only poking fun at us. He took a bow and arrow which one of our party had purchased, and pretended not to know their use, asking, with sly humor, if the bow was a fiddle!

Once the writer and his fellows resumed their trip up to Maine's recently acquired *new frontier* in Aroostook, they also found amusing the names some of the Indians listed as owning land on the islands they were traveling past. "There were 'Saul Ninepence and Tellus Molly, his wife,' 'Molly Olesole,' 'Peol Thunder,' and many other equally funny euphonics."

The writer's poetic nature was finally allowed to blossom and cap this brief episode. It happened on their return trip from Aroostook, coming down the Penobscot this time, seeing a real-life moment of Indian life, as if frozen in time, and as glorified in books of adventure and romance.

> It was near the hour of sunset, when the softened light gave a roseate hue to wood and water. The surface of the river was as calm as the face of a sleeping infant, and the wooded shores of an island just opposite the point we were passing, were mirrored in its depths, like a painted forest.—Moving along this island shore were ten or twelve canoes, filled with Indians, on their way to their winter haunts in the woods.—It was a hunting party, going up for the winter, with all of their goods and utensils. As they silently glided up the smooth river beneath the gorgeously tinted trees, they seemed to be stealing away from the world of care and labor to which we were reluctantly returning. We almost envied them their exemptions from the troubles of civilized life until the thought of their exposure to cold and hunger, the dreary life of the woods in mid-winter, as portrayed in Hiawatha, came to our relief, and we went contentedly on our way.[6]

Incidentally, *The Song of Hiawatha* had been published three years earlier by Portland's own Henry Wadsworth Longfellow, and this epic poem—essentially about Ojibways, also Algonquins like the Maine Indians (although the poet used an alien Iroquois hero's name for his protagonist)—was an immediate national and international bestseller. In Susan Jeffers's introduction to her beautifully illustrated children's version of the story of *Hiawatha,* she stated that, "Longfellow had known the Chief of the Ojibwa tribe and had seen the last few Algonquins in Maine."[7] The first part was true enough. In 1850 the poet wrote a letter of introduction for this chief, who was visiting England, to his friend Arthur Mills, a lawyer and member of parliament, saying he was "presenting to you a Chief of the Ojibway Nation by [the name of] Kah-ge-ga-gah, or if you prefer the English, George Copway," and he added, tongue-in-cheek: "Do not be alarmed and think that he will burst into your drawing room with a war whoop. On the contrary, he is a man of peace."

The other half of Ms. Jeffers's statement, however, is harder to prove—i.e., any Longfellow connection with the

Indians of Maine. He'd read about them, no doubt, may have heard firsthand accounts from his grandfather, General Peleg Wadsworth, a veteran of the Revolutionary War Down East, and had even written about them in several poems. Yet nothing in his letters has revealed a meeting with any of them and long before *The Song of Hiawatha* came out, he had moved to Cambridge, Massachusetts, where he wrote the work, basing it on the Indian researches of Henry Schoolcraft and the rhythms of the Finnish poetic saga, *The Kalevala*.

Besides, that expression of hers, "the last few Algonquins in Maine" is highly puzzling. By 1860 it had become plain that "Lo! The Poor Indian" was in Maine to stay.

NOTES

[1] *Lincoln Patriot,* Waldoboro, Maine, 7 April 1837.

[2] Francis Ormond Jonathan Smith, U.S. congressman from Maine, was known as F. O. J. Smith and by his nickname of *Fog* ("suited [to] his ability to cloud or transform issues to suit his own ends," it has been commented). The State Department, at his urging, employed him as an agent with a secret slush fund to win over influential Mainers to accept the Webster-Ashburton Treaty. Later, he and Daniel Webster had charges brought against them by Congress but were both exonerated.

[3] "Report of the Agent of the Penobscot Indians to the Governor and Council," printed in *The Laws of Maine, 1860.* Stevens and Sawyard, Printers to the State.

[4] Benjamin Browne Foster, *Downeast Diary.* Orono, Maine: University of Maine Press, pages 48–49.

[5] Ibid. Pages 170–71.

[6] *The Portland Transcript,* 28 October 1858, Vol. XXII, No. 29, pages 226-27.

[7] Susan Jeffer, *Hiawatha.* New York: Puffin Pied Piper Books, 1983.

16

OLD JOHN NEPTUNE AND OTHER NOTABLES

In his diary for August 23, 1847, Benjamin Browne Foster wrote: "Went on board the *Governor Neptune*, the Oldtown and Passadumkeag steamer."[1] The young Bangor resident, then sixteen years old, cited a number of interesting details about the flat-bottomed, low-built vessel—that its boiler had the dimensions of a cooking stove, that her paddle wheel in the stern was strange looking, that the fare to Greenbush was 25 cents—but not a word of wonder that a craft transporting passengers on the state's major navigable river would bear the same name as a still-living local Indian, and a highly controversial man, at that.

Now, it can be argued the owners of the steamboat had in mind that known figure of the American Revolution, the Passamaquoddy Governor Francis Joseph Neptune, but the fact is that *Governor Neptune* immediately calls to mind the Penobscot John Neptune, arguably the most famous of all Maine Indians, thanks in large part to Fannie Hardy Eckstorm's enduring eulogy of him in her book *Old John Neptune and Other Maine Indian Shamans.*[2]

The Neptunes crossed tribal lines, for we find them not only among the Passamaquoddy and Penobscots, but the Maliseets, too. Tribalism, for Native Americans, was never racial; new recruits were always welcome, even whites, and in the South, even blacks.

The Neptunes, as their name implies, were connected with water. Their totem animal was the eel, which inhabits both salt and fresh water. In the Penobscot pecking order, the *eel* folks were not necessarily at the top—those clans from which hereditary chiefs were chosen. The real elite were the *frog* and the *squirrel*. Apparently, a custom had been to make the holder of the highest position—called "governor" by the nineteenth century—a member from a land animal clan; the second-in-command then would be a man from an aquatic animal family.

The Neptunes were generally reputed to be magicians—*m'teoulinos*—shamans, as in the old days, and were thus powerful personages if not exactly the upper crust of the tribe.

But like many Indian institutions, this one always had a certain flexibility, no "foolish consistency." Joseph Orono, for example, was neither a *frog* nor a *squirrel;* he was a beaver and also about three-quarters white. Dying in 1801, allegedly at an age greater than a hundred, he left a gap that it took the Penobscots five years to fill. Had Orono's only son lived, he might have been elected. Instead, the tribe went to the Attean family of the *squirrel* clan and chose Attean Elmut in 1806 (there are numerous spellings of Attean—Aitteon, Atien, Etien—all varieties of *Étienne,* the French equivalent of Stephen). This "Old Aitteon" died around 1809; actually, he committed suicide, stabbing himself in a fit of depression during a sea voyage to Boston. After an interim, he was eventually succeeded by his son, John Attean, elected tribal "governor for life" in 1816. The tribal lieutenant governor chosen to serve with him was John Neptune.

Through various publications over the years, probably more is known to posterity of these two Penobscot politicians than many, if not most, of the Maine state governors of the nineteenth century. Indeed, one of those early chief executives, our second state governor, William D. Williamson of Bangor, had a considerable acquaintance with the nearby Penobscot tribe, and included a large section about the two men in his pioneering *History of the State of Maine.*

It is a piquant experience to read a passage of Williamson's in which, with the decorous and tactful language of the starchy Yankee lawyer that he was, he details possibly the most sensational event of post-statehood Penobscot Indian history. Here is how Williamson detailed the clash between Attean and Neptune:

> If female continency and chastity be seldom solicited or violated, there have been instances of lascivious intercourse, attended with

fearful evils. An affair of this character, a few years since, happened at a chief's camp, or hunting wigwam in the forest, between his wife and an under chief, when the husband was absent. The shrewd native, suspecting the crime, made her confess it, and then forgave her; determining to wreak his vengeance only on the adulterer. Once they met and strove to take each other's life, in a combat with knives; nor were they without great difficulty separated. These transactions occurring, while the two men were at the head of the Tarratine (Penobscot) tribe, have divided it into dire parties, who are not yet reconciled.[3]

The splashy knife fight may or may not have taken place, but it certainly made for dramatic reading when Williamson wrote about it in 1832. The theory that John Neptune did what he did—seduced his superior's wife—as a political statement, trying to put down his boss publicly, has been doubted. For one thing, the traditional leadership pattern in Algonquian tribes was not necessarily that of number-one leader and a second-in-command; tribes often had nearly co-equals—an overall chief and a war chief—so Neptune may not have felt he was inferior to Attean, rather, that in personal authority he far outranked him. Fannie Hardy Eckstorm quoted Williamson as writing that John Neptune was "the most lascivious man in the whole Penobscot tribe," and that Williamson had known him for years. She, herself, described him as "a man ruled by his own desires, a man of the flesh."[4]

The incident with Attean's wife happened in either 1826 or 1827, and John Neptune was no playful young buck. According to Fannie Hardy Eckstorm, "He was nearing sixty years, he had a wife and children and grandchildren, already well grown."[5] Neptune's act was considered an "unpardonable sin."

Although he might once have overawed his fellow tribal members with his reputation as a *m'teoulino*, John Neptune was disgraced as an adulterer. Governor Attean's wife was with child, and it would not have been Neptune's first illegitimate offspring. He'd already had more than a few with Molly Balassee (known as Molly Molasses). But the way Fannie described it: "The situation was as hideously tragic as a Greek play. The tribe rose outraged and indignant, the governor would have taken Neptune's life and Neptune fled from him; his own conscience must have driven him into the wilderness, relentless as a Fury...."[6]

That wilderness eventually turned into the Penobscot land in Brewer, and he ultimately took half of the tribe with him and settled there in 1832. Fannie Hardy grew up in Brewer, where her grandparents had arrived in 1835. She never knew John Neptune personally, but stories about him abounded in her household, which he and Molly had often visited.

His reputation was such that it made the white newspapers. An announcement in the *Bangor Courier* on November 27, 1851 was startling enough in itself: "John Neptune, age eighty-seven, married to Miss Mary Paulsoosup, seventy-three," but the writer then played snidely on Neptune's well-known prowess as a hunter—saying he'd not too long ago bagged $500 worth of game and "he became so elated with his success that he could not refrain from hunting among the women."

Another writer, David Bugbee, in an 1848 piece called "Voices from the Kenduskeag," told a tale from Neptune's younger days. The Indian was in Boston with General John Blake, the Penobscot agent under Massachusetts from 1811 to 1819, before Maine's statehood. Neptune was, in Bugbee's words, dressed in "a splendid scarlet frock, confined about the waist by a girdle of wampum, Indian leggings or stockings and beautifully beaded mocassins." A young lady present at an event they were attending asked to examine Neptune's garb. General Blake said she could do so, but warned her: "Remove yourself as soon as possible because he's an exceedingly wild fellow." A surreptitious wink was then exchanged between Blake and Neptune and, as the damsel studied the Penobscot's garments at close quarters, the agent held onto the big, brawny Native American. When, abruptly, he let go, Neptune seized the maiden and announced: "Now, you my [woman]!" She shrieked, and with both men no doubt trying to restrain their mirth, Neptune released her.

Portrait of John Neptune, now hanging at the
Tarratine Club in Bangor. Maine State Museum

John Neptune was always pictured as a big man, around 225 pounds. A newspaper writer named G. T. Ridlon described him as "most picturesque and attractive...a person of commanding presence, being of good stature and of enormous circumference at the equatorial region." His complexion was a "genuine copper."

In those early days, Brewer, also the home of Joshua Chamberlain's family, was said to have had more Indians living in it than whites. Manly Hardy, Fannie's father, was a noted woodsman and a hunter almost as equally renowned as John Neptune, himself.

Grandfather Hardy was in the business of buying furs and other articles from the Indians, so they were always in and out of his house. An oft-repeated family tale of John Neptune in their home took place on a very cold night when the "Old Governor" came in "tired and chilled," sat by the fire, became drowsy, then slumped face down on a bed of burning coals. Fannie's grandmother, alone with him, leapt forward, grabbed

Molly Molasses (Balassee), photographed in 1865 at the age of ninety. MAINE HISTORIC PRESERVATION COMMISSION

him by the belt and, despite his significant girth and the fact that she was half his weight, swung him up from the embers before he could be badly burned.

The Brewer in which the Hardys and Neptunes lived had been, in Fannie's words, "an ancient Indian resort." The earliest French maps named it *Niove* or *Nioue*, and Champlain may well have seen it from Kenduskeag Stream on his trip up the Penobscot. After Massachusetts, in the 1818 treaty, gave the Penobscots two acres there in perpetuity, Maine neglected to honor the arrangement, with the result that "the Indians at their pleasure occupied any unfenced site in the town that was suited to their manner of life and provided fresh water and firewood," using seven Indian campgrounds in all.[7]

Young Manly would go off to these wigwam clusters to play with Indian children, including John Neptune's grandchildren, and in later years, he would hunt with them, often the only white man they allowed in their company. Fannie told how her grandfather and the Old Governor would sit by that same fire where he had nearly been burned and "chat familiarly; for they were excellent friends." Molly Molasses would come, too, a sort of sourpuss, "but always a faithful friend of Hardy." With them on occasion would be her beautiful daughter Sarah. Fannie asked: "How much of their history did my grandparents know? They knew that Molly, though several times a mother, had never had a husband; but did they know her children were fathered by 'Old Governor?' Did they know the handsome Sarah was his own daughter? Did they know why the tribe was divided and half of it living in Brewer while the other half lived in Old Town...?"[8]

The one certainty, she felt, was of their total ignorance concerning John Neptune's and Molly Molasses's *m'teoulino* status among their people. Calling them the "two greatest shamans of their time," she marvelled that her no-nonsense Yankee forebears, who pooh-poohed ghosts and demons and witchcraft and magic, could entertain these friends by their hearthside without the slightest suspicion of their other natures, "Which shows how little any of us knows about Indians," Fannie concluded.

In continuing this discussion, Fannie later added, "With Indians you know only what they will let you know." She did so at the start of a chapter she called "Behind the Looking Glass." Her own father, when discovering on the pages of Charles G. Leland's *Algonquin Legends of New England,* the feats of "'J. N.,' the great magician," could not credit such tales. The Indians had been having fun with Leland, making up a lot of nonsense, he insisted.

Fannie, herself, might have stayed equally skeptical if she hadn't learned about the concept of *m'teoulino* from an old Indian woman she never identified, and become acquainted with a world where her grandparents' "fireside friends" loomed as fantastic, extravagant spectres in a dream universe, despite their being flesh and blood personages met with on an every-day basis.

Stories about John Nepture are told *in front of,* as well as *behind,* the looking glass.

Seba Smith presented an example of the former, in a small magazine called *The Rover* which he published in New York in the mid-nineteenth century, as a reprint of an article from a Somerset County, Maine, newspaper, the *Skowhegan Clarion*.

The setting was in Kennebec River country, west of Moosehead Lake, in the immediate vicinity of Moxie Stream and Moxie Pond. John Neptune, always an individualist, was far from his family's traditional hunting grounds in the Kenduskeag Valley near Bangor, and he had set up camp at the foot of Moxie Pond. That fall he did very well, both in hunting moose and beaver, but particularly in his trapping, so that by the time he prepared to leave, he had forty beaver skins, sixty otter, eighty sable, and two hundred muskrat ready for sale. Or so Neptune reported. Knowledgeable critics later contested those figures as too high for a single trapper to handle. Yet the main thrust of the narrative was the robbery of Neptune's goods by a party of white hunters and the burning of his camp as an attempt to hide the crime. Since the canny Indian had marked his furs with a special insignia ("a snake cut up and down the skin") not discernible to others, he set out to find them, believing they had been put on the market by the thieves. For two years he had no success until, one day in the town of Embden, he discovered a skin that bore his private marking, learned who had sold it to the dealer, notified the authorities, and received back the bulk of his property the robbers had not yet tried to sell.

Fannie Hardy Eckstorm, speculating as to the date of this incident, wondered whether Neptune's hunting in the distant Kennebec region was connected to his being turned out of office in 1838, or had happened earlier, or ever happened at all, although Lewis Ketchum, another well-known Penobscot, did tell her a similar story about the Old Governor.

Another John Neptune story *in front of* the looking glass concerned a court case in Bangor, in which the Old Governor appeared as a witness for the firm of Wadleigh and Purinton, who were being sued by General Samuel Veazie over a real-estate purchase involving former Indian land. After none other

Clara Neptune told the story of her grandfather-in-law, John Neptune,
outwitting Pamola when he ventured up the sacred mountain, Katahdin.
COLLECTIONS OF THE MAINE HISTORICAL SOCIETY

than Daniel Webster, the lawyer for Wadleigh and Purinton, had examined Neptune, he was cross-examined by Veazie's lawyer, Jere Mason, and the following exchange occurred:

Mason: "Who brought you to this courtroom?"

Neptune: "Wadleigh and Purinton."

Mason: "Did they tell you what to say?"

Neptune: "Yes."

With this straightforward answer from their own witness, the Wadleigh and Purinton people were said to have started squirming.

The opposing lawyer bore in relentlessly.

Mason: "What did they tell you to say?"

Neptune: "They told me to say what I knew about it."

And that throwaway line was reputedly delivered by Neptune "with the true dignity which sat so naturally and gracefully upon him."[9]

Other John Neptune exploits, still told, definitely stemmed from the *other side* of the looking glass. Katahdin, the Penobscots' sacred mountain, was never climbed by them, nor approached too closely, because of the Indians' tremendous awe of this highest peak in Maine and the ferocious monster, Pamola, who inhabited it. All, that is, except for John Neptune, according to a story told by Clara Neptune, his granddaughter-in-law.

In Clara's narrative, John Neptune was a mighty traveler who ventured even to the western tip of Lake Superior, deep into the territory of the Chippewas. He feared no man and no beast and that included supernatural ones like the "evil God of Mount Katahdin," whose head was as large as four horses, with the body and feet of an eagle, capable of clutching a moose in one claw and lifting such weighty prey up to its den on the Four Fools Trail, where it devoured its victims—animals or humans, as the case might be.

During one night of the Moon of the First Snow, John Neptune, having left Chimney Pond, was traversing the trails of the great mountain unafraid, when he came to a fork in the path; he was aware that Pamola might be watching, but unaware Pamola had spotted him.

To the left, Four Fools Trail, Neptune knew, *would* take him past Pamola's den. Yet to the right, the Tracy Trail was covered by a thick fog (called Pamola's Plumes) and Neptune reasoned that Wuchowsen, the Wind Bird, had been ordered by Pamola to lay down this dense pea soup so he would go left. For that reason, the Old Governor plunged into the fog, which was then whipped up into a blizzard. Blinded, the Penobscot *m'teoulino* summoned his *baohigan*, or animal spiritual messenger, who guided him to an abandoned shack equipped with a strong, heavy door. Safely inside, Neptune stayed overnight while Pamola vainly expended all of his might and that of nature in trying to force open the entrance. At dawn the hideous eagle-beast departed and the secret of Neptune's successful defense was revealed. He had poured water around the bottom of the door and it had frozen fast. Or, rather, it may have been his helper's idea, for Clara always ended her story by saying: "Dat ol' Gov'ner, wasn't he lucky he got such a smart Boohigan?"[10]

An even wilder yarn about John Neptune, immortalized by Fannie Hardy Eckstorm, was the famous incident of the *"wiwiliamecq."*

A *wiwiliamecq* was an underwater creature of humungous size, twenty to thirty feet long, most akin to an overgrown snail, but also described as a sea serpent, a lizard, even a crocodile, or a hippopotamus, and poisonous to the touch. There were said to be some in the bigger lakes in Washington County; one lake specifically cited was Spednic Lake, up along the New Brunswick border, not far from Indian Township. But the location of John Neptune's epic fight with a *wiwiliamecq* has always been pinpointed as Boyden's Lake, in the town of Perry, where Pleasant Point is located.

As the oft-told story goes, John Neptune took on the shape of his *baohigan,* snake or eel in this case, and did battle with an antagonistic Micmac chief whose baohigan was that crocodilian-slimy *wiwiliamecq,* and the underwater wrestling match so thrashed the lake that it turned brown from the dislodged bottom mud. The Indian name for Boyden's Lake is Neseyik—meaning *roily* and *muddy.*

After Neptune vanquished the Micmac chief at Boyden's Lake, he allegedly dragged the man's body ashore at Muddy Lake Point and tied it to a tree with yellow birch twigs.

Fannie Hardy Eckstorm believes this folk legend goes way back into Down East Indian time. That it could be attached to John Neptune by the Penobscots and Passamaquoddy of the mid-nineteenth century illustrates probably more than any other fact the force of his personality. Nor was he, himself, the shy modest type who might have tried to sidestep the notoriety. No doubt he encouraged these tales of his shamanistic prowess. Any good politician would—and, despite the problems he had brought on himself by womanizing, notwithstanding the disgrace he had suffered among his peers, he stayed in the public limelight.

A miracle—call it a political miracle—happened next in the Old Governor's real life, although no one knows exactly how. That is to say, after seducing John Attean's wife, then being exiled off Indian Island, Neptune somehow contrived to reforge an alliance with the man he had wronged and who might have killed him. Together, they reasserted their claims to be tribal governor and lieutenant governor of the Penobscots for life, offices to which they had been elected in 1816. Then, in 1838, a revolt against their rule erupted. While an ancillary issue in this dispute was the maintenance of the office-tenure-for-life tradition, the real heart of the matter was the school question. The Old Party, led by Attean and Neptune, was for an English school; the New Party, under Tomar Socalexis and Aitteon Orson, wished to stick with the priests and, presumably, French and Latin, with a minimum of accommodation to the prevailing American culture. With the help of votes from the Passamaquoddy and Maliseets who attended a conclave at which the quarrel was decided, the more reactionary traditionalists prevailed. Attean and Neptune were ousted and the Maine legislature, the following year, decreed biennial elections for tribal leaders.

The split continued for decades. Attean and Neptune refused to relinquish their titles and, for that matter, their power. The laws of Maine record a legislative act as late as March 11, 1858, appropriating $50 for the Penobscot agent to pay for the "equal benefit of John Attean, former tribal governor, and John Neptune, tribal lieutenant governor." A year later, on March 5, 1859, the Augusta lawmakers were dispatching $25 to John Neptune "as a salary for services as governor of the said tribe." Both disbursements, by the way, were from the Penobscots' own tribal funds.

John Neptune died in 1860. The Old Party–New Party dispute did not die with him. On February 21, 1866, the Maine legislature again had to intervene in Penobscot affairs, setting out in white man's law a pattern these people were now to follow in electoral procedure. On "the second Tuesday of September annually," they would vote as if in a primary election, with the "old and new party, so-called," each selecting their own candidates for office and governing "alternatively, commencing with the old party for the year eighteen hundred and sixty-seven, and the new party shall have no voice in the selection of candidates for said offices" and no vote in the years when the Old Party held sway. This process would be reversed when it was the New Party's turn to rule. The agent was also directed to preside over these arrangements.

A portrait of John Neptune in his final years was drawn by Henry David Thoreau during a visit to Maine in 1853.

The famed naturalist met the Old Governor at the latter's home, a humble "ten-footer," and the Indian was sitting on his bed in one of the two rooms of the house. "He had on a black frockcoat and black pants, much worn, white cotton shirt, socks, a red silk handkerchief about his neck, and a straw hat. His black hair was only slightly grayed. He had very broad cheeks, and his features were decidedly and refreshingly different from those of any of the upstart Native American party whom I have seen. He was no darker than many old white men. He told me that he was eighty-nine; but he was going moose-hunting that fall, as he had been the previous one."[11]

Alas, that is all we see of this notable figure through the talented pen of the Concord iconoclast. Thoreau spent most of his time talking to Neptune's son-in-law, Tomer Nicola, "a very sensible Indian," in large part because "the Governor, being so old and deaf, permitted himself to be ignored, while we asked questions about him." Tomer Nicola, a descendant of "Half-Arm Nicola," a wounded refugee from the 1724 raid on Norridgewock, had married Mary Malt, one of John Neptune's legitimate daughters. Among their nine children was Joseph Nicolar (note the slightly changed spelling), the groundbreaking Penobscot author of *The Life and Traditions of the Red Man*.

On a different trip to Maine, this time in 1857, Thoreau met another well-known Penobscot, Joe Polis, and he wrote a good deal about him, because they went together into the Maine woods. Polis had been one of John Neptune's backers in the Old Party–New Party strife over the school, personally leading a group that physically prevented the priest and the anti-school faction from cutting down a liberty pole on Indian Island, erected as a symbol in favor of secular education.

Arriving by riverboat in Bangor in 1857, Thoreau commented:

> We had hardly left the steamer, when we passed Molly Molasses in the street. As long as she lives, the Penobscots may be considered an extant tribe.

Then, he was taken by his relative, Deacon George Thatcher, to Indian Island and he continued:

> The first man we saw on the island was an Indian named Joseph Polis, whom my relative had known from a boy, and now addressed familiarly as "Joe." He was dressing a deer-skin in his yard. The skin was spread over a slanting log, and he was scraping it with a stick, held by both hands. He was stoutly built, perhaps a little above the middle height, with a broad face, and, as others said, perfect Indian features and complexion. His house was a two-story white one, with blinds, the best looking that I noticed there, and as good as an average one on a New England village street. It was surrounded by a garden and fruit-trees, single cornstalks standing thinly amid the beans.[12]

Asked if he knew of a good Indian guide to take Thoreau to the Allagash Lakes by way of Moosehead and return via the East Branch of the Penobscot, Polis replied: "Me like to go myself, me want to get some moose," while he kept on scraping at his hide. Thoreau described the answer as coming "out of that strange remoteness in which the Indian ever dwells to the white man."[13]

They left the next day by stagecoach. Polis had arrived from Indian Island, bearing his canoe on his head, and his only other baggage was an axe, a gun, a blanket, a store of tobacco, and a pipe. With the canoe lashed across the top of the coach, they set off for Moosehead Lake, through Garland, Sangerville, Abbott, and Monson. "The Indian sat on the front seat," Thoreau wrote, "saying nothing to anybody, with a stolid expression of face, as if barely awake to what was going on.... He never really said anything on such occasions.... His answer...was never the consequence of positive mental energy, but vague as a puff of smoke, suggesting no responsibility, and if you considered it, you would find you had got nothing out of him. This was instead of the conventional palaver of the white man and equally profitable."

What Fannie Hardy Eckstorm, who never had a lot of respect for Thoreau, found irritating many years later, was that when Joe Polis did speak, Thoreau didn't listen very sensitively to him. It all had to do with a story Polis told in order to bolster his argument concerning why they should rest on Sunday, a story which Thoreau recorded in his book, *The Maine Woods*, with a certain amount of disdain. He called ceasing activity in the woods on the Sabbath equivalent to traveling in *"slow coaches."* Such phrasing was most annoying to Fannie. She claimed Thoreau "had come into the Maine woods to study the Indian" and, in his response to Joe Polis, had "blundered," turning the Indian off, causing him to clam up or, as she put it, "shutting the mouth of the man who could have told him all he wanted to know."

With deliberate irony she described Thoreau, while camping at Kineo, being so inspired by seeing a piece of phosphorescent wood that he wrote four pages on the phenomenon. Moreover, she considered him a "poor woodsman," and a *woodsman*, like her father and her special hero, John Ross, the master river driver, was the type of person she most admired.

Joe Polis was said to have been a shaman; in one case, by Clara Neptune, his niece, and in another by Manly Hardy, Fannie's father, who knew him well and said of him, "Joe Polis would have been a powwow man, if they had such things in these days."

His authoress daughter, in reporting this remark, revealed her own true feelings about the Indian shamanism she had discovered—that it was real, indeed. Her father, she wrote, would "never have believed that in the lives of his old friends were these secret chambers to which he was denied admittance."[14]

Another of Henry David Thoreau's guides has also survived through his and Fannie's writings. Joseph Attien does not appear to have been a *m'teoulino*. But he was a politician, apparently a good one, selected to be the Penobscots' (Old Party) governor, first in 1862 before the Maine legislature intervened, holding office for seven years and missing an eighth term when it became the New Party's turn by law. His death by drowning in 1870 was the occasion for one of Fannie's stories in her book *The Penobscot Man.*

Once more, Fannie made use of an opportunity to scold Thoreau, stating, "If ever Henry David Thoreau showed himself failing in penetration, it was when he failed to get the measure of Joseph Attien." She claimed "Thoreau hired an Indian to be aboriginal. One who said, 'By George!' and made remarks with a Yankee flavor was contrary to his hypothesis of what a barbarian ought to be," and the fact Attien was so long remembered after dying tragically at age forty-one meant he "must have shown promise at twenty-four," when he guided Thoreau.

Attien, in addition to his other attributes, was one of river driver John Ross's men. That he was an Indian did not keep him from being a crew chief and captain of one of the six- or seven-man boats they used in running the river. On the Penobscot Log Driving Company "drives" that John Ross superintended, men made their reputations through their own abilities, and Joe Attien, a 225-pound giant of a man, was one of the most respected by Indians and non-Indians alike.

According to Fannie's account of his tragic end, entitled "The Death of Thoreau's Guide," the men blamed one of the Yankees, whom they called "Dingbat" Prouty, for the fatal accident. They did not believe Prouty had any place being in Joe Attien's crew instead of Joe's cousin Steve Stanislaus, and when Attien's boat ran the rapids at Blue Rock Pitch, it was said Prouty had somehow put the Penobscot governor (which Attien was at the time) up to this act of daring. Others claimed John Ross, himself, had ordered the boat to go over. Whatever the origin of the reasons for Attien's exploit—and as crew chief and "a waterman of his reputation," he could have refused even John Ross—Joe Attien took a boatload of seven men, instead of the usual six or even four when working in dangerous waters.

Fannie wrote: "It was a very simple accident.... There was a long, lean boat, blue without and painted white within...like a huge fish, half out of water; within her the line of red-shirted men, their finny oars fringing her battered sides...hard red knuckles, tense on the oar butts, sun-burned faces under torn brims, or hatless; sun-scorched eyes winking through sun-bleached lashes...." They were suddenly in the churning white water, paddling like mad, pushing off boulders with their iron-tipped settling poles—

"And then was their black fate close upon them," Fannie continued. The boat did not "swing to the current; she was too heavy...." Flung across the raging torrent, Attien and his crew were swept up by the full force of the river, the boat crashed against a sunken rock, was stove in, and swamped, with Joe Attien standing on the gunwhales, trying desperately to keep his boat and the knot of men who clung to it from swirling down a series of falls below.

Six days later, they found Joe Attien's body—precisely where Manly Hardy had precicted they would—in Shad Pond. His boots were hung on a pine tree and a cross cut on the bark—"a strange but sincere memorial of a good man," to quote Fannie. She included a photograph of Attien in *The Penobscot Man*, a dark-eyed burly figure in a suitcoat jacket, dress-shirt, tie, and brimmed hat, solemn-looking, moustachioed in the style of the time (1862), and obviously a person of strength and character, as the writer had made clear in her paean to him.

Another photograph in the same edition of her book features four Penobscot males, two seated, two standing, dressed as elegantly as Joseph Attien, although hatless, wearing frock coats and waistcoats, three of the four sporting gold watch chains, and all wearing bow ties and white dress shirts. They are perhaps recognizable as Indians, but certainly demonstrate the extent to which these Penobscots had adapted outwardly to the white man's ways. Two of those pictured figure in

Fannie's stories—Lewey Ketchum, another crew chief for John Ross and the Penobscot Log Driving Company, and Sebattis Solomon, "Black Sebat," whose derring-do, when John Ross and his gang were contracted to run logs down the Connecticut River when no one else would, became legend. Fannie tells Black Sebat's story to illustrate the temper of the Penobscot man. On a dare, Black Sebat and three other Penobscots ran Canaan Falls, north of Hartford, and despite the suicidal nature of their mad feat, all but one survived, including Black Sebat. Fannie, in relating this true tale, makes her final paean not to any single individual Indian, but to the entire essence of the world she knew—the lumbering era of the Maine Woods at its Penobscot River epicenter and of the original inhabitants and how, by the end of the nineteenth century, they had found a new place in what the region had become—at least for a moment in time.

Of that famous boat plunge north of Hartford, she declaimed grandly: "Four Penobscot Indians, men who have no country, in the face of dangers which they fully comprehend, cheerfully elect to die for the honor of the tribe.... The honor of the tribe, the fame of the West Branch Drive, the reputation of the Penobscot man, were the ideals that beckoned them."[15]

That the Penobscots seem to predominate in the panoply of Maine Indians whose memories have survived them into the flow of the state's history and folklore is perhaps most due to their having a Boswell in the form of Fannie Hardy Eckstorm. Another woman writer, but of our time, has recently contributed a few Boswellian touches of her own. Bunny McBride, formerly of Hallowell, now of Kansas, published two books in the 1990s, *Molly Spotted Elk* and *Women of the Dawn,* that brought out of the shadows another group of Maine Indians, this time all females. We have met at least one of them already—Molly Molasses—and another, Molly Ockett, has been mentioned. Her name graces a host of tourist landmarks in western Maine: Molly Ockett's Cave, Molly Ockett Mountain, Molly Ockett Trail, Moll's Rock, Mollywocket Brook.

Molly Ockett was not a Penobscot but a Pigqacket, and Molly Mathilde, another of the four Mollys cited in *Women of the Dawn,* was apparently part Kennebec, part Maliseet, daughter of the historic Chief Madackowando and the wife of the French nobleman, the Baron St. Castin. Yet Donna Loring, an outstanding contemporary Penobscot woman who has served her nation as their legislative representative and police chief, is happy to praise them all. "Penobscot women, like all Wabanaki women, have been the guardians of their people," she wrote in a reaction to Bunny McBride's book, and pointed out how the four profiled women all possessed "energy and power" that made them transformative in how they affected the lives of others, including non-Indians.

In her introduction, Bunny McBride explained that the four women were each given Christian names of Mary, which Wabanakis, whose languages interject *l* for *r,* would pronounce *Maly*—or more acceptable to English ears, Molly. The four Mollys cover four centuries of Indian history in Maine, from the seventeenth- to eighteenth-century period of settlement and warfare to the mid-twentieth century, where "show business Indians" were still in vogue. These women led difficult if not heroic lives, and so it is only fitting their personages should emerge more fully from the forgetful past and we should be able to range Molly Mathilde, Molly Ockett, Molly Molasses, and Molly Dellis (stage name: Spotted Elk) alongside those males of whom we have heard a good deal—Madockawando and Robin Hood and Metacomet and Francis Joseph Neptune and Deacon Sockabason and Orono and John Neptune and Joseph Attien, etc.

Longfellow praised Molly Mathilde's incomparable beauty and charm in a poem entitled "The Baron St. Castin." Molly Ockett, renowned as a healer using native medicine and a clairvoyant, has long been remembered for having cured a future vice president of the United States, Hannibal Hamlin, as an infant, and predicting a great future for him. Molly Molasses was a symbol to Thoreau of the everlastingness of the Penobscot people. And Molly Dellis Spotted Elk led an unimaginably adventurous life that took her from the obscurity of Indian Island, Maine, to New York City and Paris at some of the most exciting moments of the twentieth century.

An amazing phenomenon is the keenness of interest that causes authors to explore these colorful figures, to resurrect the biographies of individuals within a segment of the Maine population that is now so overwhelmingly in the minority. It is as if collectively, the tribe, nation, and bands we still have with us are as sharply etched as the memorable personalities they have produced.

NOTES

[1] Benjamin Browne Foster, *Downeast Diary.* Orono, Maine: University of Maine Press, page 49.

[2] Fannie Hardy Eckstorm, *Old John Neptune and Other Maine Indian Shamans.* Orono, Maine: University of Maine Press, 1980 (reprint).

[3] William Durkee Williamson, *The History of the State of Maine.* Two volumes. Hallowell, Maine: Glazier, Masters, and Company, 1832, Vol. 1, page 500.

[4] Eckstorm, *Old John Neptune,* page 121.

[5] Ibid.

[6] Ibid, page 124.

[7] Ibid, page 3.

[8] Ibid, page 5.

[9] David Norton, *Sketches of the Town of Old Town.* Bangor, Maine: S. G. Robinson, Printers, 1881.

[10] "John Neptune's Encounter with Pamola," by Marion Whitney Smith, *Down East Magazine,* February-March, 1956, pages 15–16.

[11] Eckstorm, *Old John Neptune,* page 166.

[12] Henry David Thoreau, *The Maine Woods.* Reprint edition arranged by Dudley C. Lunt. New York: Bramhall House, 1950, page 18.

[13] Ibid.

[14] Eckstorm, *Old John Neptune,* page 186n.

[15] Fannie Hardy Eckstorm, *The Penobscot Man.* Originally published in 1924. Somersworth, New Hampshire: New Hampshire Publishing Company, 1972 (reprint).

17

Elsewhere in Indian Country

*T*he Wabanaki tribes inhabiting presentday Maine were not simply a bunch of provincials, lost in their copious woods. They were noted travellers, on rivers and even on the Atlantic. Their contacts extended far to the west. Francis Parkman writes of them in *La Salle and the Discovery of the Great West* as having been among the companions of the noted French explorer of the Mississippi in the 1670s and '80s. Indeed, there is a rowdy story told (but not by Parkman who was a prudish Boston Brahman) of La Salle and some Wabanaki canoeists on one of the Great Lakes sighting a far-off stretch of land. In answer to the Frenchman's query as to its name, the Indians answered "Michigan." As we know, Michigan it has remained to this day—an enduring Wabanaki joke for in the Passamaquoddy language, *Mitch I Gun* means "human waste"—*feces*, to be exact.[1]

The Wabanakis prime contact with the West, historically, was through constant warfare with the Mohawks. But there were also interactions with this segment of the Five Nations of the Iroquois that were not hostile. Such was the Wabanaki Confederation, also known as the Great Council Fire, established at Caughnawaga in Quebec Province, near Montreal. The date for its formation remains fuzzy—generally given as 1749, but as a regular gathering on the banks of the St. Lawrence, it may have been started many years earlier. In any event, it was a going concern almost two decades before the English conquered Canada, drawing tribes from Maine and the Maritimes to meet with Mohawks, Ottawas, Hurons, Montagnais, and other western tribes.

The settlement, itself, at Caughnawaga had been founded in 1676 as a refuge for Iroquois converts to Catholicism. So the Mohawks there were not exactly the same as those who had been preying upon the Maine and Maritime tribes. In point of fact, by 1700 the wars among the Iroquois and the Wabenakis had been ended by a treaty. Both sides held that the other had submitted, and a sort of pecking order was established geographically, each tribe to the west of any other being deemed an "elder brother" and the farthest east of them all—the Micmacs—treated as an infant sibling. Allegedly, the Micmac representative at the Great Council Fire was required to dress up as a baby! Nevertheless, unity was stressed, as well; the Penobscots had two words for the gathering: *Bezegowaki*: "those united in one"; or *Gizargowak*: "completely united."

The Wabanaki Collection at the Huntington Free Library in New York City contains records of the frequent interaction between the tribes in Maine and this federal-like body in Canada. In August 1825 a request was made to the State of Maine by the son-in-law of Passamaquoddy Governor Francis Joseph Neptune for funds to travel to a "general meeting in Montreal." Not just for himself, either, but for Passama-quoddy, Penobscots, and St. Johns (Maliseets), "thirty in all." Whether the state came up with money for such a delegation was not recorded. But in 1847 the tribal governor, John Francis, son of Old Francis Joseph, was seeking help to go to "Konowango in Canada" himself.

It may have been in 1849 that the Passamaquoddy, in the throes of their intra-tribal Old Party–New Party struggle, asked for assistance from the Grand Council. Through their local agent, J. Sylvanus Leland, they sent a letter to "the King of the Seven Tribes at Caughnawaga and to the Grand Council of Chiefs and Representatives about to be assembled at the Grand Fire at Caughnawaga." Their hope was that "the long-pending difficulties among the Passamaquoddy tribe of Indians may at this session of the Council be settled on a firm basis."

Complaints followed against a certain Sabbattis Neptune, who, upon returning from attendance at a Caughnawaga session, had stirred up trouble, leaving the tribe "in a state of ferment, notwithstanding his promise to be '*all the same as one brother.*'" Several times he had cut down and burned liberty poles erected by the governor. So would the Grand Council

Chiefs please end "the mischievous machinations of said Sabbattis."

An answer recorded from the Caughnawaga chiefs started by stating that an earlier response through "the ancient custom of sending our words to our brethren by wampum belts" had been misunderstood, so they were now doing it in writing. The advice they gave was "to follow your same and unaltered mode of living as heretofore—to strictly follow the Roman Catholic religion...follow and adhere to the same government, listen to and obey your chiefs, listen attentively to the good advice of your Missionaries...be very careful of your lands, do not sell or dispose of them but keep them for use and the use of your children...."

The latter point was strongly emphasized in a letter dated July 31, 1865, addressed to John Francis, who was still tribal governor. Don't allow white people to take "possession of your land" and also be careful of selling them wood. These admonitions were repeated again and again, stressing Iroquois experience "as a burnt child dreading the fire." They had heard the *governor and authorities of the State of Maine* "where you hold your lands are trying to get you to sell your lands on the pretensions of making you rich.... You will impoverish yourselves.... Therefore be firm...never sell an inch of ground.... You will always be independent."

No voluntary sales of Passamaquoddy land were made—then or since—and where they lost land involuntarily, the whole Land Claims Settlement can be seen to have resulted.

Nevertheless, they probably didn't need the Caughnawaga chiefs to buttress their own deep feelings. Indeed, they had already begun to feel disenchanted with the confederation after groups of Penobscots and Passamaquoddy who had moved to the Canadian location, returned home and began agitating against the great peace council. Three years earlier, as a matter of fact, the Penobscots began the Wabanaki pullout from the confederation. In 1862 Aittion Orson was said to have come back from Caughnawaga, gone into the Council House at Indian Island, laid the wampum he'd brought back

A view of Caughnawaga near Montreal, site of the Great Council Fire,
where Maine tribes met with Iroquois and western tribes for many years.
Illustrated here are the ruins of the ancient fort of Sault Saint Louis.
From Souviens canadiens: album de Jacques Viger.

on a table, and had Nicholas Sockabesin throw it out the door, where the tribal members let the beaded belt lie on the ground, signifying an end to their participation. The Passamaquoddy ended theirs in 1870 when Joe Lola and their keeper of the wampum, Captain Sapiel Selmore, attended for the last time.

By then the original purpose of the Great Council Fire—to keep the peace between Iroquois and Algonquins—had lost all meaning. So much had happened in the intervening century and a quarter that the landscape of "Indian Country" had become almost unrecognizable. The Indians of Maine had been reduced to a mere remnant of the powerful people they had been as late as the American Revolution.

Elsewhere in the United States, the same pressures were being exerted against all Indian tribes, with similar results, as their way of life was sometimes violently, sometimes non-violently, impacted.

It is an epic, often tragic story, told many times from many points of view. For our purposes, since the Maine tribes cannot be understood in total isolation, there are highlights of this sustained national drama that set a context for the still *unsettled* Indian–non-Indian relationships throughout the U.S. How much the Maine Indians knew at the time of what was going on is, no doubt, unanswerable. But that sweep of history—out of which legal and governmental concepts like *sovereignty, nation-within-a-nation, allotment,* and *termination* arose—far less flashy than the battles and the killings, but far more important, can now be seen in several centuries of retrospection.

An interesting figure to start with, on the government level, is Thomas L. McKenney, the first American federal bureaucrat appointed to deal directly with Indian tribes on a sustained basis. That is, in heading the office in Washington, D.C., called then, as now, the Bureau of Indian Affairs.

We have met McKenney before, through his involvement with the Reverend Elijah Kellogg and "Deacon" Sockabason of the Passamaquoddy. But years prior to that long-running incident, McKenney had begun his career in charge of "federal regulation of U.S. Indian Trade with the Indian Tribes."

The U.S. government, by asserting itself in trying to control all trade with the Indian tribes, really had the best of intentions. They sought to keep the Indians from being cheated and, if there were an ulterior motive here, it was to keep the Indians happy in order to maintain peace. McKenney wrote of his agency in his memoirs: "Its tendencies were kind and merciful.... The system was one of pure humanity...without reference to profit; and receiving in exchange from them, their furs and peltries, at fair prices...." Individual traders and companies, he charged, "operated to place [the Indians] amongst the unobstructed, full and unmitigated blaze of a consuming avarice."[2] Unlike those private parties, the feds banned the use of whiskey or other alcohol as a trade item.

McKenney wrote that his reports (which protested the use of whiskey and recommended stringent enforcement of regulations) "were not regarded in the light of very friendly interpositions.... I was not in favor either with the private trade, or with the more formidable power concentrated in the companies." That antagonism soon materialized in the blustering, bullying form of U.S. Senator Thomas Hart Benton, fronting for the Missouri Fur Company.

Unable to browbeat or intimidate McKenney, Benton resorted to a legislator's ultimate weapon. He introduced a bill to abolish the offending office and, in 1822, was successful.

In the interval, McKenney had not only struggled to keep Indian trade aboveboard, but also had managed to wrangle a $10,000 yearly appropriation from Congress to help Indian tribes cope with problems. It was out of this money that he had made federal grants to Kellogg and Sockabason. Two years after McKenney was out of a job, he was approached by Secretary of War John C. Calhoun about organizing a new bureau in his department, which would have *overall* responsibility for Indian affairs. Given McKenney's experience, his good reputation among the tribes, his military experience (he'd been an army colonel), and his political loyalty as a faithful Democrat, he seemed an ideal choice. It took some persuasion on Calhoun's part, since McKenney, stung by his experiences with Thomas Hart Benton, was on the verge of emigrating to Mexico. However, on March 11, 1824, he finally accepted, and the Bureau of Indian Affairs had its first leader and began its tempestuous career.

McKenney would have been called a "liberal" in today's media. But the "liberalism" of his time was of a two-edged sort. Some Americans at that time—Andrew Jackson, Thomas Hart Benton and others—made no bones of the fact they just wanted the Indians' lands and resources, and thus the Indian was simply to be pushed out of the way. And in the 1820s this meant across the Mississippi to an ostensible wasteland called "Indian Country." McKenney's different view was not necessarily opposed to their removal from their homelands, but it had two less inhumane facets: 1) That any Indian removal was to be voluntary on the Indians' part; and 2) That it was to be accompanied by the type of efforts he had made among the Passamaquoddy to help them become more "civilized."

McKenney spoke of "the perishing consequences to the Indians of a near connection with a white population..." and that "their degradation and extermination will be inevitable if left where they are."

He pointed out that in the eastern coastal states from Maine to South Carolina, only 6,000 Indians remained. In Virginia, of the once-powerful Powhattans, only a pitiful forty-seven still lived within the Old Dominion's boundaries.

"*Brothers,* some of you believe you have a sovereign right over all within the limits designated for your occupancy," McKenney would state in opening a set speech when sent south to talk major tribes like the Creeks, Choctaws, and Cherokees into pulling up stakes for their own good. Then he would add: "Do you not see the degrading nature of the relation in which you stand to the whites...? Are you not aliens—and even worse, though living in the heart of your country?"

With the Creeks, he had some success. Then hardball politics, Thomas Hart Benton-style, raised their ugly spectre. McKenney received a visit from the famous Sam Houston, who wanted the BIA chief to help him land a federal contract to supply the "emigrant Indians." At $55 per head, the total package was to cost $4.4 million for removing these people and sustaining them for a year. When McKenney told the Texan it would be a conflict of interest for him to get involved, Houston angrily threatened retaliation.

But McKenney's real nemesis was Andrew Jackson who, once he succeeded John Quincy Adams as president, set about to end his predecessor's policy of pursuing Indian removal on a voluntary basis only.

McKenney felt the pressure and expressed it: "Alas! The hour was even then rapidly approaching, when, on the question of their removal, they were to have no will of their own. The mandate went forth and submission, or death, was all that was left...their lands were wanted and they must surrender them...." He added a personal note, too. "I would rather be one of these persecuted sons of the forest...than to have had any agency in thus forcing them, under such forms, from their country...."[3]

Eventually McKenney was fired by Jackson for resisting his

policy, which enabled the southern states, particularly Georgia, to evict the Indians from their own lands by armed force and march them west on the infamous "Trail of Tears." It was an episode in American history that has raised several knotty, enduring issues. The idea that the Indians could save themselves by becoming *civilized* doesn't stand up to close scrutiny given the fact that the Cherokees, in particular, were actually more civilized than many of the white Georgia rednecks who dispossessed them. They were literate, they lived in houses, went to church, produced newspapers, had farms, grew cotton (kept slaves), ran businesses, etc. The Cherokees had a capital called New Echota and a constitution patterned after that of the United States. In the *City Directory* of Portland, Maine, for the mid-1840s, we even find an unexpected item announcing that John Ross, chief of the Cherokee Nation, was vacationing at Cape Cottage, Cape Elizabeth, one of the tonier spots in Maine for summer visitors.

This whole imbroglio brought troubling questions to the fore, most obviously those of the Indians' status in this country and of federal–state relations where they intersected in the matter. Jackson harped on the notion of states' rights, at least at this stage of his career. McKenney, in his early discussions with Old Hickory on the subject, reported him as sympathetic to the plight of "civilized tribes" like the Cherokees, "but to encourage them to the idea, that within the confines of a state, they may exercise all the forms and requisites of a government...he does not consider can be advantageous to them, or that the exercise of such a right can properly be conceded."[4]

McKenney, himself, seemed in agreement with his boss's position on the "nation-within-a-nation" issue. He asked in his memoirs: "What would New York say if the Six Nations (Iroquois) wanted to establish within her limits a separate and independent government...? Would they assent to have their citizens rendered liable to be arraigned at the bar of an Indian court of justice and to have meted out to them the penalties of their criminal code?"

His answer to himself was that, by going beyond the

Mississippi, the tribes would no longer have any problems with state authority.

Yet Indian problems with *state* authority, a hallmark of the Maine Indian Land Claims Settlement, remain a constant contention in our present courts.

The legal ramifications of the 1838 move by the State of Georgia have been described by U.S. Supreme Court Justice Stephen Breyer as "a collision between law and morality on the one hand and desire and force on the other."[5]

Justice Breyer's concise history of the Cherokees' battles with Georgia also crosses the border, as the issue did, into the South's pre-Civil War position on how far it would tolerate federal intervention into its affairs. Nor was this conflict about slavery (after all, the Cherokees had black slaves, too). Georgia was upset over the feds' failure to live up to a promise made in 1802 to extinguish Indian title to all tribal lands in the state.

When Georgia first went ahead on its own, attempting to usurp land owned by the Creeks, President John Quincy Adams denounced its actions and threatened military force. Georgia's governor, George Troup, called out the state militia. But no shots were fired because the Creeks voluntarily ceded their territory.

Nevertheless, a pattern of defiance, armed if necessary, had been established from the state level. After Jackson's election and particularly after 1829, when gold was found on Cherokee lands, Georgia became especially emboldened. The Georgia legislature passed laws to confiscate Cherokee land, to nullify Cherokee laws (like one that required licenses for white Georgians to enter their territory), and to prohibit meetings of the Cherokee legislative council. It ordered the arrest of any Cherokee who argued against emigrating west and forbade Cherokees to dig for gold on their own land. The power question was thus raised in the most forceful of manners. Whose laws were to prevail on land both Georgia and the Cherokees claimed? Who was to be the sovereign? And could it be the United States of America had no say?

The Cherokees refused to accept the actions of the

Georgia lawmakers. They did what Americans have always done in such situations. They went to court.

Their lawyer was the best money could hire, the Virginian William Wirt, a former U.S. attorney general, prosecutor of Aaron Burr, and constitutional law expert par excellence. His case seemed an open and shut one. Treaties signed by the U.S. were the law of the land and here was a state openly challenging one the feds had with the Cherokees. Also, there was recognition *then*, 150 years before the Maine Indian Land Claims case, that the 1790 Non-Intercourse Act had been violated.

However, Wirt's problem was to decide in which court to sue. Doing it in a Georgia court would be hopeless; a lower federal court, located in the same venue, would be little better. So he had to go straight to the U.S. Supreme Court to present the Cherokees' plight and seek redress.

Technically, the only way he could do it, under the Eleventh Amendment to the Constitution, was to represent the Cherokees as citizens of a *foreign country* bringing a lawsuit against a state.

The Supreme Court's decision in *Cherokee Nation v. Georgia* has had ramifications for Native Americans ever since it was rendered in 1831. What has echoed down through the ages has been the dictum expressed in Chief Justice John Marshall's majority opinion that the Cherokees *could not be a foreign power*, since all Indian tribes, to use his words, were "*domestic dependent nations.*"

Much of the U.S. government's subsequent policy toward its Indians, as well as a great deal of jurisprudence, has been based on that cryptic definition, which shut the door on the high court's willingness to hear the Cherokees.

Another viewpoint expressed in *Behind the Trail of Broken Treaties,* a 1974 book by Vine Deloria, Jr., Indian author, activist, and lawyer, has resurrected the opinion of a different Supreme Court judge, Justice William Johnson, who sat in on that case. Deloria calls it "Perhaps the clearest description of the nature of Indian political existence...."[6]

241

Justice Johnson had agreed with Marshall the Cherokees were not a foreign country. But his view of their status was more nuanced than the *domestic dependent nation* definition. He wrote strikingly: "Their condition is something like that of the Israelites, when inhabiting the deserts. Though without land that they can call theirs in the sense of property, their right of personal self-government has never been taken from them, and such a form of government may exist though the land occupied be in fact that of another...."[7]

Deloria also quotes from the dissenting opinion of Justice Smith Thompson who declared, apropos the Cherokees, "it is not perceived how it is possible to escape the conclusion that they form a sovereign state. They have always been dealt with as such by the government of the United States; both before and since the adoption of the present Constitutution...."

Thompson contended, too, that Marshall's own definition still allowed these "domestic dependent nations" the "rights of self-government and a clear legal right to occupy their traditional lands."

John Marshall did not escape the Cherokee–Georgia conflict simply by turning away the case William Wirt tried to bring directly to him. Circumstances dictated otherwise. Three months after the *Cherokee Nation v. Georgia* decision, the Reverend Samuel Worcester was one of eleven New England missionaries among the Cherokees whom Georgia arrested for refusing to take an oath to uphold state laws. Sentenced to several years of hard labor by a Georgia court, most accepted a pardon from the state governor by taking the oath. Worcester refused and Wirt now brought his case before the U.S. Supreme Court, where it was accepted. Arguments were heard from February 20–23, 1832, although Georgia failed to appear and announced it would not recognize any decision of the court.

The verdict was straightforward. "It is the opinion of the Court that the judgment of the [Georgia] Superior Court must be reversed and annulled." Worcester was to go free, because Georgia's laws had "no force" in Cherokee territory.

History records Andrew Jackson's sardonic remark: "John Marshall has made his decision. Now, let him enforce it."

Marshall's lament, "our Constitution cannot last," may have had some validity to it, given the president's unwillingness to back up the U.S. Supreme Court, had it not been for an unrelated federal–state crisis shortly afterward when South Carolina said a law its legislature passed had "nullified" a federal tariff the Palmetto State didn't like. Reversing his states' rights stance, Jackson received a congressional mandate to enforce the federal law and South Carolina backed down. The Supreme Court soon received word the president would support any decision it made, including *Worcester*, but before it returned to session, the plaintiff, himself, accepted a pardon from Georgia in return for dropping his suit.

Jackson played a dastardly role in the shameful denouement to this story. After a small group of Cherokees were induced to sign a "treaty" giving up their land to Georgia, Old Hickory refused to intervene. No federal troops would uphold the Cherokee Nation's treaty rights and almost all were forcibly deported to Oklahoma, as were other southeastern tribes.

Traveling through the United States during this period was the French aristocrat Alexis de Tocqueville. In his monumental study of our ways, *Democracy in America,* he mentioned Indians from time to time. The Frenchman noted the resemblance between the "political institutions of our German ancestors [the Gauls] and the wandering tribes of North America," but didn't hold out much hope for the Native American's future. "All the Indian tribes who once inhabited the territory of New England—the Naragansetts, the Mohicans, the Pequots—now live only in men's memories," he wrote, then added, "I have met the last of the Iroquois; they were begging...."[8] He witnessed the exodus of the Choctaws, saw them crossing the Mississippi, "and the sight will never fade from my memory." The sight was of the Choctaws in the dead of winter, having "neither tents nor wagons," carrying their wounded, sick, newborns, and elderly "on the point of death," getting into boats to cross, without a "sob or complaint," and the most poignant touch of all: the dogs they left on the opposite bank beginning to howl at being abandoned and plunging into the icy waters "to swim after their masters."

However, de Tocqueville's sharpest comment was reserved for American policy in general: "Half convinced, half constrained, the Indians go off to dwell in new wildernesses, where the white men will not let them remain in peace for ten years. In this way, the Americans cheaply acquire whole provinces which the richest sovereigns in Europe could not afford to buy."[9]

Lewis Cass, secretary of war under Jackson and Democratic presidential candidate in 1848, stated the matter quite baldly. In order for the Indians not to become extinct, "it would be necessary that our frontiers cease to expand and the savages settle beyond them"—a situation he deemed unlikely.

That the east–west frontier expanded right up to the Pacific, every school child in America knows. That the Indians never did become extinct, we also know to be a truism. So what *was* done with them?

The road to the present in the philosophies and programs the federal government has used in dealing with the "Indian problem" is littered with milestones—more like gravestones— of policies that didn't work and took a heavy toll on those they were alleged to help—the Indians. Words like "allotment" and "termination" are now but dim memories, dredged up by historians of the zigzags of federal policy toward the tribes. Who remembers the Dawes Act, named for Massachusetts U.S. Senator Henry L. Dawes, who thought he was doing the Indians a favor by teaching them the virtues of "selfishness?" Carlisle College, if remembered at all, is done so for Jim Thorpe's football prowess, not as part of a concerted effort to separate Indian children from their parents and drill into them, as if they were juvenile West Pointers, the white man's *superior* culture.

John Collier's name is all but forgotten today, except by such sensitive Indians as Vine Deloria, Jr., for he was the

BIA director under the New Deal, who strove valiantly to let Indians be themselves and run their own affairs. Was the Indian Claims Commission, finally established by law in 1946, after many years of trying, really a big step forward in settling Indian land claims, or just an impediment, as it seemed to Tom Tureen in prosecuting the Maine Indians' claim? Who could believe today that the hated "termination" attempts, started in the Eisenhower administration, of stripping the tribes of their independent status and their link to the federal government would finally be halted by Richard Nixon?

Among the more polemic of current American Indian writers, it is fashionable to accuse white Americans of concerted, deliberate *genocide* vis-à-vis the native tribes. Certainly, there were those who acted upon the statement that "the only good Indian is a dead Indian." In Maine we had our James Cargill who, when acquitted of murdering peaceable Indian men, women, and children, cynically demanded scalp bounties for his victims. But in defense the argument is offered that no announced, official intent existed, as in Nazi Germany, to wipe out an entire people, and that many "righteous Americans" were friends of the Indians, like Thomas L. McKenney or Helen Hunt Jackson, author of *A Century of Dishonor,* who blew the whistle on the 1864 Sand Creek Massacre, or Warren K. Moorehead, the archaeologist who condemned the allotment frauds in Oklahoma and issued *A Plea for Justice,* his 1914 book detailing his experiences as a conscientious member of the Board of Indian Commissioners.

Even Henry L. Dawes expressed no intent to harm the Indians; he simply believed *selfishness* was the root of advanced civilization and couldn't understand why Indians were not motivated to possess and achieve more than their neighbors. His belief in the civilizing power of private property was absolute and, to him, to be civilized was to "wear civilized clothes, cultivate the ground, live in houses, ride in Studebaker wagons, send children to school, drink whiskey, and own property." On the latter score, his "allotment" scheme was guaranteed to do exactly that. The Indian

Country west of the Mississippi, given to the displaced "civilized tribes" like the Cherokees, Creeks, Choctaws, etc., was to be broken up into individual allotments, so that each Indian would have his or her own homestead. The "surplus" tribal land not needed for this purpose was to be sold to the U.S. government and redistributed to non-Indians.

Senator Henry Teller of Colorado saw Dawes's bill in a different light. Its real aim, he argued in debate, was "to get at the Indians' land and open it up for resettlement." In February 1887 the Dawes Act became law, was not repealed until after the Meriam Report of 1928, and caused Oklahoma Indians, alone, by 1934 to lose almost three-quarters of their land—a reduction from 138 million acres to 47 million acres. Land theft, yes, but genocide?

The use of such emotional language was concurrent with the rise of Indian activism that emerged in the 1960s as long-simmering Indian grievances began to come to a boil. In the interim a period of passivity had seemingly set in among the tribes, compounded by a steady loss of population and dependency on others once their traditional modes of living were no longer possible.

Maine, itself, was something of a backwater, and the condition of its tribes and bands in the latter half of the nineteenth century and first half of the twentieth century was close to invisible—a mere curiosity, if noted at all.

Lives of quiet desperation—to use Thoreau's expression—were being lived among the Penobscots, Passamaquoddy, Maliseets, and Micmacs, and the rest of the state and the world barely noticed.

NOTES

[1] This is according to ssipsis (Eugenia Thompson) and Georgia Mitchell in the glossary of their book, *Molly Molasses and Me*. Brooks, Maine: Little Letterpress, Robin Hood Books, 1998.

[2] Thomas L. McKenney, *Memoirs*. New York: Paine and Burgess Company, 1846, page 19.

[3] Ibid, page 161.

[4] Ibid, page 249.

[5] Justice Stephen Breyer, *The Cherokee Indians and the Supreme Court*, *Journal of Supreme Court History*, Vol. 25, No. 1. Boston and Oxford, U.K.: Blackwell Publishers, 2001.

[6] Vine Deloria, Jr., *Behind the Trail of Broken Treaties*. Austin, Texas: University of Texas Press, reprinted 1985.

[7] Ibid, page 114.

[8] Alexis de Tocqueville, *Democracy in America*. Perennial Classic Edition. New York: HarperCollins, 1969, page 321.

[9] Ibid, page 325.

18

THE TRANSITION

*I*n 1920 Carl Milliken of Island Falls was governor of Maine, and on February 29 of that year he received a startling communication from the Passamaquoddy Tribe. It was a petition signed by sixty-four members and it began: "We, the undersigned members of the Passamaquoddy Tribe of Indians, humbly beg the State of Maine to use her influence against making Indians citizens of the United States."

The rumor was rife in Indian circles that Congress intended to enfranchise the Indian population in the country and, indeed, in 1924 it did proceed to pass such a law. But ahead of time, the Passamaquoddy were serving notice they were happy with their present status. "We are wards of the State of Maine and we want the Passamaquoddy Tribe to remain as a relic of the state," the petition continued, going on to cite as authority for their action the name of one of Maine's most revered political figures, Governor Milliken's fellow Republican, James G. Blaine. "Once we received kind advice from [the] Honorable James G. Blaine, president of the Indian Defense Association of Washington, D.C. He advised us to stay in the wigwam. By doing so the government will always help us. We are satisfied with our lot as Indians...." The Passamaquoddy were careful to point out they meant no disrespect to the U.S.A. Their patriotism and loyalty was cited back to the days of Colonel John Allan in the Revolution. They noted they had raised fourteen men to fight for the Union during the Civil War and in World War I, twenty-four out of a hundred Passamaquoddy males had gone into the service. Left unsaid was the fact their own tribal governor, William Neptune, and another prominent tribal leader, Sabattus Lola, both had had sons killed in France. Their plea ended: "Please use your influence. If the law be already passed, let us be exempt from it."

Chief William Neptune. COLLECTIONS OF MAINE HISTORICAL SOCIETY

There is no record of what Governor Milliken offered for a response when, three days later, Neptune and Lola paid him a visit at the statehouse to deliver their protest in person.

As it turned out, they received their U.S. citizenship in 1924, along with the rest of the country's Indians, but their full rights as Maine citizens did not come until much later. In fact, the State of Maine did not even allow the tribes to vote in federal elections until 1954, and their ability to vote for state representatives and state senators was not sanctioned until 1967. Yet what the episode in 1920 seems most to indicate was that this small group of people Down East feared any change in their situation, bad as the status quo might be, suspecting it might bring even worse conditions. Washington County, Maine, where they were located, was one of the poorest sections of one of the poorer states in the U.S., and poverty there, as among their white neighbors, engendered a sort of deep-dyed conservatism, which they had come to share.

It may well shock Americans to learn some Indian groups did not clamor for full inclusion as citizens of the U.S.A. Even today, in certain western tribes and among various segments of

Indian clothing such as that of the Micmac mother and son on the left, photographed in 1865, reflects several centuries of contact with the French. The Indian boy on the right is wearing a traditional headdress of upright feathers. MAINE STATE MUSEUM

the Iroquois, it is said the older people will not vote, reserving a sense of nationality for their own people. The Navajos, and others, solved this potential problem of dual loyalties during World War II by having their nation declare war separately on the "Axis" of Germany, Japan, and Italy.

Until 1924 the tribes in Maine were still juridically in a condition of limbo, vis-à-vis the federal government, which generally ignored them, while they continued in a relationship of subservience under a state government that paid them a minimum of attention through a system of state-appointed agents. These were essentially welfare directors, doling out a limited largesse, derived mainly from sales of the Indians' own timber, to a population kept, for the most part, perennially in need. On occasion, complaints against agents were tendered to the state governor and council, with requests for the miscreants to be replaced. Whether particular individuals were kept or not, the system essentially remained in place until the Land Claims Settlement. The state legislature from time to time, also had the habit of ordering the agents, especially Passamaquoddy ones, to sell Indian land and use the proceeds for the funds they paid out to their charges.

The two tribal representatives to the Maine legislature rarely rocked the boat. Although not allowed to vote nor to participate in committees, they *could* address the lawmakers. One such occasion, in 1887, was so notable it is still remembered. Lewis Mitchell, elected by the Passamaquoddy who were then a tribe of 530 persons, stated plainly: "We remain as a nation yet," in defending the Passamaquoddy position that their treaty rights had been violated.

Elucidating these gripes, Mitchell cited various instances in which land guaranteed to the tribe in their 1794 treaty with Massachusetts had been taken from them, including "a mile [-wide] strip, eight miles long, given to a rich man worth probably half a million dollars for a road." Other examples included a wood lot at Pleasant Point, which the legislature had ordered sold at auction, and a claim they lost to a man named Granger, who had disputed their ownership of islands in the St. Croix, an action that cost them, or their trust fund, $2,500.

Going back into history, Mitchell detailed for the legislators the extent of the original Passamaquoddy hunting grounds, lands that comprised most of Washington County. "Just consider today how many rich men there are in Calais, in St. Stephen, Milltown, Machias, East Machias, Columbia, Cherryfield, and other lumbering towns," Mitchell said. "We ask ourselves how they make most of their money. Answer is, they make it on lumber or timber once owned by the Passamaquoddy Indians.... How many of our privileges have been broken; how many of our lands have been taken from us by authority of the state?"

His plea for the state "to be just to a few friendless and helpless Indians" was no doubt listened to politely by the elected officials gathered in Augusta, who then went on to other public business.

But the Indians have remembered.[1]

Maine, itself, never a prosperous state, followed a generally conservative pattern of living after the Civil War. Lumbering and farming were the primary economic factors, but generally in decline, and a change to tourism and the pulp and paper industry occurred only slowly. The predominant political mode was the nearly total control of state offices by the Republican party.

The late-nineteenth century saw the creation in a few small cities of textile and shoe manufacturing, and an influx of immigrants, primarily French-Canadians, to work in these mills. For the most part, such developments did not affect Maine's two major Indian tribes, except that some shoe and textile mill jobs were available to the Penobscots in the Old Town area and some paper company jobs to the Passamaquoddy. In Aroostook County, where the Micmac and Maliseet Bands remained, economic life was nearly entirely agricultural, which meant potato farming, with jobs for harvesting the spuds and a market for Indian-made potato baskets.

The state was still essentially rural, heavily forested, and becoming all the more so as abandoned farms grew back into woods. Fishing and hunting, formerly open to all with no regulations, became more of a business as sportsmen from "Away" came in search of recreation and were willing to pay for guides and accommodations and a chance to catch and shoot their fill of wild creatures. In short order, "game laws" were issuing from Augusta, and one of the first Indian–non-Indian clashes of the era arose as a result, ending in a law case that one day would affect the Indian Land Claims litigation.

On January 14, 1891, a Passamaquoddy tribal member named Peter Newell was arrested for hunting in Township 6

Indian guides competed with white guides for business and faced the same restrictions when new "game laws" were issued.
MAINE STATE MUSEUM

during a closed season and for having two deer in his posses-sion. More than a year later, on April 19, 1892, his case was finally settled by the Maine Supreme Court, which heard his appeal.

There was no question of Newell's guilt. He acknowledged he had killed the two animals in clear violation of Maine statutes. But, he argued, he had a lawful right to do so "by reason" of the superior legal status of various treaties made between his tribe and Massachusetts, commencing in 1713 and ending in 1794.

Or rather, Newell's attorney, George Hanson of Calais, made these arguments for him. An early defender of Indian rights, Hanson tried to put pressure on Maine by appealing to Massachusetts. The thrust of a petition to the governor and council of the Bay State Commonwealth, signed by all male Passamaquoddy over the age of twenty-one, stated that Massachusetts, in the act of separation granted to Maine in 1820, had guaranteed the latter would carry out all the for-mer's obligations toward the tribes within its territory. The privileges of free, unencumbered fishing and hunting by the native populations was to continue unabated. And so it had until 1869, when Maine laws were passed setting seasons and forcing Indians to obey them, too. "This clearly was a violation of our agreement [with Massachusetts] and a great in justice to us, for it took away and still takes away our chief means of support for several months of the year." The Passamaquoddy said they had never "released their rights"— unlike the Penobscots—by agreeing to ratify the Maine–Massachusetts Treaty. They also declared vehemently, "We are as much a tribe as are the Cherokee or Sioux."

This last point was all-important to them for *State v. Newell* rested on the Maine Law Court's decision that the present Passamaquoddy tribal people could not be counted as descendants of the "contracting Indians" who had had hunting and fishing rights reserved for them in the treaties of 1713, 1725, and 1749. The court stated, "There has been no continuity or succession of political life and power. There is no mention in the treaties of a tribe called 'Passamaquoddy Tribe,' and we cannot say that these present Indians are the successors in territory, or power, of any tribe named in the treaties, or are their natural descendants...."

Hanson's appeal to Massachusetts to intervene was no more successful than Peter Newell's arguments had been in Maine.

The year of 1892 does not seem to have been a propitious one for the Passamaquoddy. The Indian agent did change when Charles A. Rolfe replaced H. C. Munson (accused of mishandling money the year before, but exonerated), and Rolfe's report to the state governor and council made for gloomy reading. Scarlet fever had broken out at Pleasant Point. "During the summer," he continued a litany of woe, "measles were quite prevalent and many of the families were prevented thereby from making their usual trip to Bar Harbor and other summer resorts, where they have hitherto earned quite a sum of money by the sale of fancy baskets, furs, etc. The sale of coarse, heavy baskets has been largely cut off this season, and in September. I found many asking for aid that had not been obliged to do so before.... It is an undoubted fact that the Indians are growing more helpless every year. Fur-bearing animals are now almost extinct. Sportsmen are growing to like white guides better than Indians. The courts have debarred them from the old privilege of fishing and hunting except in open season...."

It was not for want of trying to find ways to sustain themselves that the tribe was suffering. The *Portland Board of Trade Journal* carried the following item around this time: "The Passamaquoddy Indians, one of the most progressive native tribes in this country, have started a new enterprise, giving exhibitions of aboriginal life," and it described the first event, which took place at Eastport. Sopiel Mitchell opened it, speaking in the Passamaquoddy tongue, war-whooping, and flourishing a knife and spear so eloquently, the article reported, that he didn't need an interpreter.

An opportunity presented itself when the State of Maine's game laws withdrew their protection of the seals proliferating in Casco Bay that had become a nuisance to fishermen. A bounty of fifty cents, later extended to a dollar was placed on these marine mammals. Proof of each animal's demise was to be its nose, cut off and presented to the authorities. Since the Passamaquoddy were the state's premier seal hunters, and despite the distance to Casco Bay, they entered the competition with such gusto that by 1900, the seal population in and around Portland Harbor had been decimated. Four years later Passamaquoddy were still bringing noses to the Portland city treasurer and collecting money, until it was finally detected that many of the noses were bogus, made up of sealskin pieces with the hair burned off of them, "nostrils" burned in, and catgut added to simulate whiskers. The Portland landlubber had already paid out several thousand dollars before the deceit was discovered. The enterprising natives were arrested and the bounties discontinued soon afterward.

A few years earlier, in 1887, the Passamaquoddy from Pleasant Point had started holding encampments on Campobello Island and providing "novel and interesting amusement for the boys during the summer evening." One can picture

*A rare photograph showing Franklin Delano Roosevelt, as a young man, on a
canoeing outing from Campobello with local Indians. The future president
had numerous interactions with the nearby Passamaquoddy.*
COURTESY OF DONALD SOCTOMAH

among these vacationing youngsters who strolled about and
traded with the Indians for spruce gum and baskets five-year-
old Franklin Delano Roosevelt. Certainly FDR was acquainted
with the local Indians. Tomah Joseph, a Passamaquoddy arti-
san, made a canoe for him and a number of handsome carvings on birch bark, now exhibited at the old Roosevelt sum-
merhome. On view, too, is a 1920 (the year Franklin ran
unsuccessfully for vice president on the Democratic ticket)
photograph where he posed alongside Passamaquoddy Tribal
Governor William Neptune. What FDR's early exposure to
Maine's Indians may have contributed to the more enlightened
federal policies introduced at the Bureau of Indian Affairs by
John Collier in the 1930s is a matter for interesting conjecture.

The American Friends Service Committee's resource book,
The Wabanakis of Maine and the Maritimes, referring to the
period under discussion as that of "An Invisible People," has
stated: "The places that Wabanakis were permitted to occupy
were usually remote and isolated. There were few jobs nearby;
unemployment was high and poverty was the rule. Housing

A group of Pleasant Point leaders in the 1920s–1930s, posed for the camera. Note the swastika on the collar of the figure to the right. The hooked cross is an ancient Indian symbol and bears no connection here to its use in Germany during this period.
MAINE STATE MUSEUM

and roads were poor. Access to education and decent food and medical care was difficult...."[2]

But hard as life might be, the Wabanakis were able to keep their sense of existing in "separate, cohesive communities." One way, adopting a non-Indian sport, and excelling at it, was through their championship baseball teams. The tribes played each other, and the Penobscots produced one player of such outstanding ability that he not only starred for a national professional team, but had the team name changed in his honor.

In 1897, when Louis Sockalexis went to Cleveland, the team was called the Spiders. After he left, the "Cleveland Nine" became the Indians. Sockalexis, who began playing as a kid on Indian Island, continued in a college career, first at

Louis Sockalexis, photographed after his retirement
for a postcard sold to tourists who
visited Indian Island.
COURTESY OF THE *BANGOR DAILY NEWS.*

Andrew Sockalexis, Lewis's brother, was himself an Olympic marathon
runner. He is pictured here with his trophies in front of his home on
Indian Island. MAINE HISTORIC PRESERVATION COMMISSION.

Holy Cross and then at Notre Dame, and was an overnight sensation for Cleveland.

The *Sporting News* on April 24, 1897, called him: "THE BEST ADVERTISED PLAYER IN THE BUSINESS."

Two weeks later, the *New York Journal* printed a poem about him, "Merry Sockalexis, who can bat and knock the home run, who can scalp the blooming umpire, etc," with Indian imagery on display everywhere, in the media and in the stands. He was greeted with war whoops and Indian yells, likened to an eagle when circling the bases, to a plunging bison on the prairies starting out on a home-run ball, and arousing the bleachers to a scalp dance in the eighth by stretching a single into a double. By June, *Sporting News* declared him "the most popular player in the league...." Alas, his stardom was to be as fleeting as his speed on the field. The season was not even half over when he was dropped from the team, a lame ankle being given as the reason, but it was no secret that alcohol had become an insuperable problem for him. The *Sporting News* that had so admired "Sock" revealed, "Sockalexis had succumbed to the curse which had been the bane of his nationality ever since civilization put whiskey in the reach of the aborigines."

Sock went back to play in Cleveland in 1898, but only in twenty-one games, and in 1899 a mere seven games. A visit to the minors was no less disastrous, since he simply couldn't control his alcohol addiction.

In 1898, while Sockalexis was still a celebrity, *Sporting Life* printed a dispatch from Old Town, Maine. It told of a wedding attended by four hundred people, mostly Indian Island inhabitants, at St. Joseph's Catholic Church. The bride was Josephine Newell and the groom John Ranco, both of a "proud lineage in the Penobscot Tribe," but the real stars of the show were one of the groomsmen and one of the bridesmaids: Louis Sockalexis and Cornelia T. Crosby, better known in Maine as "Fly Rod," the most famous female fishing guide in the country.

It was stated, "Although the bride was the handsomest

maiden on the island and the groom a...Phoebus Appolo [*sic*], the gaunt Sockalexis and his white partner attracted the lion's share of attention from the assembled braves and woodsmen.... In the dancing that was one of the best features of the reception, the tawny rightfielder and Miss Fly Rod were frequent partners, and a more graceful pair never flitted over a waxed floor than the man of [native] blood, with a civilized exterior and education, and the daughter of civilization who elects to spend her days in the wilds with rifle and rod."

In time Sock went back to Indian Island, mastered his drinking problem (which allegedly had abruptly begun after some deliriously celebrating Cleveland fans took him to a bar and he tasted his first whiskey), married, did some baseball coaching, worked in the woods, and died of a sudden heart attack in 1913. In 1915 a Cleveland newspaper ran a contest to rename the Spiders. The winning entry: the "Cleveland Indians," was specifically suggested by a fan to honor the first American Indian to play in the majors.

Those years on Indian Island have also been documented in the biography of Molly Spotted Elk, born Mary Alice Nelson on the Penobscot reservation in 1903.[3] In 1913, the year of Louis Sockalexis's death, she was a ten-year-old girl growing up in the endemic poverty where the tribal people shared their meager supplies of food, including rations from the state of half a barrel of molasses and half a barrel of salt pork. Like most poor Mainers, they got by, but there were differences. The Penobscots traveled more, entertaining tourists at summer resorts, dancing, and, above all, selling the baskets they'd made during the winter months. Sweetgrass braiding parties at which the women produced these sales items were held almost every night, complete with refreshments and music for songs and a dance. Their isolation and sense of community was all the stronger because Indian Island in those years had no bridge connecting it to the mainland. A ferry—a fourteen-passenger bateau—costing two cents per person each way—was the only means of getting back and forth, except if you canoed or—quite dangerous—swam and dealt

Molly Spotted Elk (also known as Molly Dellis and née Mary Alice Nelson), vaudeville dancer and movie actress.
COURTESY OF MOLLY'S DAUGHTER, JEAN ARCHAMBAUD MOORE.

When Indian Island could only be reached by boat. Here, a passenger is being transported to Old Town in a canoe.
MAINE HISTORIC PRESERVATION COMMISSION

Penobscot women making their beautiful baskets at Indian Island.
MAINE HISTORIC PRESERVATION COMMISSION

A street scene on Indian Island, early twentieth century.
MAINE HISTORIC PRESERVATION COMMISSION

Indian Island School and pupils, 1910.
MAINE HISTORIC PRESERVATION COMMISSION

Saint Ann's Church and convent, Indian Island, early twentieth century.
Most Penobscots are Roman Catholics and still workship at Saint Ann's.
MAINE HISTORIC PRESERVATION COMMISSION

A Penobscot band of the era. Maine Indians have always been musical.
MAINE STATE MUSEUM

*The Penobscots putting on a minstrel show, a popular form of
entertainment at the time (if now highly politcally incorrect).*
MAINE STATE MUSEUM

Above and Below: In 1920, when Maine celebrated its 100th anniversary as a state, a prominent feature of the Portland festivity, held June 26 to July 5, 1920, was the Indian encampment at Deering Oak Park.
COLLECTIONS OF MAINE HISTORICAL SOCIETY

A Penobscot fishing with a spear, circa 1911. The wooden spear is traditional, with a metal prong replacing the earlier ones of bone. MAINE STATE MUSEUM

with the strong Penobscot River currents. When the ice was thick enough, the crossing could be done on foot, yet in early fall and spring, the passage on thinner ice could be much more dangerous than swimming.

While in her teens, Molly first left the island and began her career in vaudeville. It is significant she took the stage name she did—based on an animal—the elk—never seen in Maine. For at that time all Indians, in white American eyes at least, were western Indians and the Maine tribes, for a long period, donned the trailing feathered headdresses of Plains groups like the Sioux whenever they put on shows for tourists or engaged in public ceremonies.

Another recent publication, a fascinating compilation of news articles and comments, has been put together about the

Expert Passamaquoddy seal hunter Joe Lola, seen with some of the hides he has stretched for drying. Lola also won fame by brazenly making a cold call on the major of New York City and trying to sell him Indian baskets.
COURTESY OF DONALD SOCTOMAH

Passamaquoddy by their former representative in the Maine legislature, Donald Soctomah, and it presents a vivid picture of his people during these "invisible years."[4] The specific epoch covered is 1890–1920 and the work is full of lively human interest stories, like the exploits of Joe Lola, who had the effrontery to call on the mayor of New York City unannounced and try to sell him baskets, or the travails of Lewis Mitchell, the renowned orator and legislative representative, when he ran the St. John River Falls rapids in his canvas canoe and his companion, Xavier Francis, was drowned, and when Mitchell was arrested for possessing seagull wings, but claimed exemption from the Maine game laws protecting the birds.

Information on political events and tribal culture, too, in this era provides a keen sense of the Passamaquoddy struggle to survive as themselves, despite the predictions of pundits nationwide about the sorry future of Native Americans.

In 1928 the federal government decided to take a look at overall Indian conditions in the U.S., and Dr. Lewis Merriam of the Brookings Institution, a think tank in D.C., was hired to supervise the survey. In the *Meriam Report* the allotment program was finally seen for the catastrophe it had turned out to be. Indian health was bad, the *Report* said, the general death rate and infant mortality excessive, diets inadequate, housing unsanitary, water bad, income low—a national scandal, in other words. Characteristically, the Maine tribes—as non-federal responsibilities—had not come under this searching light, but their conditions were no better, if not worse.

John Collier, as director of the American Indian Defense Association, helped prompt the *Meriam Report* by fighting an attempt, ultimately thwarted, to take away Pueblo lands in New Mexico. In 1933, FDR made him commissioner of the BIA.

Collier did not ignore the Maine tribes.

During the summer of 1934, a young woman working in his office was sent to Maine to report on the Penobscots and Passamaquoddy. Her name was Gladys Tantaquidgeon, and she was a Mohegan from Connecticut. She also had ties to Maine. It had been through Professor Frank Speck, the anthropologist extraordinaire who had studied the Penobscots and written a classic book about them, that Gladys was able to attend the University of Pennsylvania.[5] Thanks to Speck, as well, Molly Spotted Elk was at Penn the same time, the 1924–25 school year, and they worked together in Speck's cluttered office. Symptomatic of the times, both these Native American females were domiciled at International House, as if "foreigners."

Two separate visits—to the Penobscots and the Passama-quoddy—were included in Gladys Tantaquidgeon's report, parts of which were published in a BIA magazine called *Indians at Work.*

Some history and geography began the Penobscot piece—that they were the most numerous of the Wabanaki tribes, did not settle at Old Town until 1669, that the centennial anniversary of the St. Ann's mission chapel on Indian Island was celebrated in 1933, that for over fifty years, nuns of the Order of the Sisters of Mercy had been teaching in the Indian Mission School there, that the Penobscot language was closely related to the extinct Norridgewock dialect, that Penobscot unmarried young men were specially trained for running power and long distance endurance, that wampum had played a big role in their culture, and that shamanism was important to them.

Present conditions (as of 1934) were elucidated. Writing in a section called "Social Status," Gladys noted, "Years of close association with the neighboring whites have not robbed the modern Penobscots of their distinctive innate qualities and we find the Indian characteristics predominating." Their language, at that date, was still in use and despite some intermarriage with whites, there was "a strong tribal consciousness." However, it was pointed out that, "In past years the attitude of the whites toward the Indians, with but few exceptions, has been antagonistic." Nor could this ill feeling in Old Town be chocked up to anti-Catholicism, then rife in Maine, since this mill town was inhabited by many co-religionist Franco-Americans and Irish.

Other sections of the Tantaquidgeon report on the Penobscots covered "Education," "Economic Life," "Health," "Arts and Crafts," and "Ceremonial Life."

That year, seventy-eight pupils were at St. Ann's and five Penobscot boys were at the elementary school in Old Town, the latter via a concession granted by the legislature through the efforts of a local Indian Women's Club organized on the island. The St. Ann's school seemed to be in good shape, well lit and ventilated, with running water, flush toilets, swings, see-saws, and up-to-date textbooks and other classroom equipment. At least twenty Penobscots attended Old Town High School, two girls were at the University of Maine, and one boy was attending Dartmouth College. Jobs were still scarce (this was during the Great Depression). A few men worked at the Old Town Canoe factory, and some worked in a paper mill or woolen mill. Federal projects employed others doing road work. But basket making was the major trade, and it was under intense competition from cheaper Indian baskets out of Canada and baskets sold by Gypsies passing themselves off as Indians. Miss Tantaquidgeon suggested a trading post on Indian Island with Penobscots in charge.

She found the tribe on the whole to be "dependent and insecure as a group," and went on to state: "Under their present form of government, as wards of the State of Maine, they cannot be otherwise." A particular problem where state authorities had let them down was in the matter of sanitation and potable water. In 1933 state authorities had condemned their wells, yet a year later, as Gladys wrote, "no attempts had been made to furnish them with pure water." In frigid weather they had to go down to the river, break the ice, and fill buckets to carry to their homes. They were pleading for a sewerage system and also for the services of a resident nurse. That some of the old ceremonial dances were being revived was a more positive note the Mohegan writer was pleased to observe.

Visiting the Passamaquoddy, Gladys Tantaquidgeon actually spoke in her native tongue and then in English on the occasion of a celebration for a new tribal governor-elect. Since neither her Mohegan nor her English remarks could be understood by everyone, the master of ceremonies, Joseph Neptune, translated. A short concert by the nine-piece Passamaquoddy band followed, plus a war dance under the leadership of governor-elect Joseph Nicholas. At the end of the evening, as the band played the "Star-Spangled Banner" and all arose, Gladys wrote she saw "something pathetic in the closing scene." Her words still have a harsh and poignant ring, as she described "this mere handful of Indians bravely carrying on the battle against the culture-destroying forces of a civilization that for centuries has sought to crush the very soul of the Indian, and in this 'land of the free' deprive him of his natural privileges."

Conditions were certainly deplorable at both Passamaquoddy reservations. On the cultural level she singled out the disappearance of the old native-made costumes and the adoption of "the Plains Indian influence, especially the war bonnet, which has swept New England and, I fear, is here to stay." Down East, too, the reservation wells had been tested and condemned by state authorities, with nothing done a year later and the people still using the contaminated water. An outbreak of typhoid fever had resulted and as many as twenty tribal people had died. Children were undernourished; tuberculosis and venereal disease were constant threats; the housing stock was "so old and in need of repair that the Indians suffer from the cold in winter. There are holes in the roofs and sides, and window panes are broken in some." A number of families had no beds, no mattresses even, and slept on the floor, using old coats to cover themselves. The milk or cocoa and crackers served at the school by the nuns was sometimes the only food the children had. Gladys spoke warmly of a priest, Father Murphy, who was trying to secure federal aid, particularly for a better school than the one-room affair they had.

The starkness of the Tantaquidgeon report went on and on: 95 percent of the Passamaquoddy were on relief roles; "The group at Peter Dana's [sic] Point are very poor and only a few families at Pleasant Point are self-supporting." A single person, man or woman, was given $1 a week to live on; a family of four, $2, and a family of six, $4. Moreover, as Gladys related, "They are obliged to patronize the stores of the sub-agents [who work for the state] who charge top prices for their staple groceries."

One of the biggest problems for the Indians was the need to pay $1.15 for a license to hunt or fish. A trapper's license might cost them $10. So subsistence hunting and fishing no longer provided an automatic lifeline.

At both locations the Passamaquoddy language was still in use. "Practically no English is heard on either reservation and even the children revert to speaking their native tongue as soon as they leave the classroom." Some children actually spoke Passamaquoddy to their teachers, one of the nuns reported.

Above, the Horace Nicholas family home at Pleasant Point.
Below, the Wallace Nicholas family at Pleasant Point,
the father showing off one of his fine snowshoes.
MAINE STATE MUSEUM

*The Passamaquoddy mission school in the Peter Dana Point
section of Indian Township, 1930s.*
MAINE STATE MUSEUM

*Every summer Maine Indians went to the
wealthy resort of Bar Harbor to sell baskets and
other items. This is their encampment at
Bar Harbor, shown in a stereoscopic image.*
MAINE HISTORIC PRESERVATION COMMISSION

Prior to John Collier's administration, such a situation would have outraged the bureaucrats at the BIA. But his was not a philosophy of assimilation at all costs. The Indian Reorganization Act of 1934, for which Collier became known nationwide, sought to give Indian tribes the maximum of self-government and allowed them the revival and enjoyment of their own cultures, if they so desired. Unfortunately, Collier's hands were pretty much tied where non-federal Indians like those in Maine were concerned.

On May 26, 1935, a letter from Miss Mina H. Caswell of South Portland presented the BIA with a series of questions whose answers she needed because she had been contracted to write a history of the Maine State Health and Welfare Department and planned a chapter on "the Indians of Maine as wards of the state."

She had seven queries, ranging from, "How much has Congress to do with the Maine Indians?" through, "Were the Maine Indians affected in any way by the senatorial investigation in 1929–32—or the report of the Meriam Commission in 1928?" to "How will the Quoddy project affect the Passamaquoddy living in that section?"

In typical government fashion, her inquiry was "bucked" to a lower-level expert to prepare a memorandum as the basis for a reply bearing the commissioner's signature. On June 18 the director of Planning and Development, who signed himself only as "Ryan," sent a memo to his superior, Fred Daiker, an assistant to Collier, assigned to write the return letter for their boss. Apparently, Ryan had accompanied Gladys Tantaquidgeon on her trip to Maine the previous summer. He also mentioned contact that had occurred between the Maine State Health and Welfare Department and the BIA in the fall, "because of complaints made to us of conditions among the Passamaquoddy."

The finished product from John Collier went to South Portland about a month later. He answered Miss Caswell's questions point by point, but the general thrust was that his bureau had very little to do with Indians on "long-established state reservations." For the BIA to consider the Maine Indians, Congress would specifically have to authorize federal jurisdiction and provide an increased appropriation. Neither the Senate investigation nor the *Meriam Report* had touched upon Maine Indians. However, because of new federal legislation passed in 1934, the Wheeler–Howard Act (by which the Indian Reorganization Act was commonly known) and the Johnson–O'Malley Act, there conceivably could be some help. Under the former, Collier felt, the Maine Indians, if they so desired, "could vote probably for Indian tribal organization." If they did so, the Johnson–O'Malley Act, which allowed the BIA to contract with state and territorial agencies to provide "education, medical attention, agricultural assistance, and social welfare" to their Indians, might be open to them. In the matter of the proposed Quoddy tidal dam, Collier said he knew practically nothing about it but presumed "it would no doubt open an opportunity for labor on the part of the Indians."

That the potential opportunities mentioned for the Maine Indians by John Collier were not seized upon became evident two years later when more BIA officials went Down East and reported back.

One of these reports, because of its literary author, rises well above the usual no-nonsense precision of governmental language. D'Arcy McNickle, then administrative assistant in the BIA, had just published his first novel, *The Surrounded*, now considered a pioneering classic of Native American writers. Whether in expository prose or fiction, McNickle, son of an Anglo-Irish father and Cree mother and brought up on a Salish (Flathead) reservation in Montana, was always eloquent. The D'Arcy McNickle Center for American Indian History at the Newberry Library in Chicago is named for him. Most of his writings—and his three novels—deal with Indians in the West, but his piece on Maine so well captures a spirit of place that it is worth reproducing the opening in its entirety.

Here at Eastport, Maine, on the Bay of Fundy, old ocean shows his strength.

Standing on a height of land, one watches the tidal course rush with the speed of a mountain river. Blue water leaps high where cross-currents meet. Foam flecks the eddies. One gets dizzy with watching.

At low tide a ruin of shattered rock shows how sledge-like is the pounding of water on a resistant shore. A brown scum of seaweed marks the tidal crest. A thousand white gulls flash upward, then drift downward again.

That is Passamaquoddy, where Army Engineers have undertaken to deal directly with ocean's elemental forces. They would literally put a harness on old ocean—a harness for half a million horses! Something to match Paul Bunyan and Babe, the blue ox.

Counterpoised against this epic geographical background, McNickle then juxtaposes: "And here on Passamaquoddy, within earshot of the tidal roar, lives a rather forlorn band of Algonquin-speaking Indians...."

To illustrate that among the four hundred denizens of Pleasant Point, many spoke nothing but their native language, McNickle described: "Four-year-olds playing in the dust open their eyes wide to a question put to them in English. They say something in Indian and continue the play—friendly, but not impressed by a visitor who doesn't know how to talk in accustomed ways."

The poor housing Gladys Tantaquidgeon mentioned gave Pleasant Point, in McNickle's opinion, its "forlorn effect." The best of the homes were not fully sealed inside, the foundations were not banked up, wood was scarce, and the polluted well water was still polluted...and being used!

"Except for emergency projects, one cannot understand how these people survive." Some men had been working on the Quoddy project, reducing those on relief to 90 percent, yet recently the work at Quoddy had been shut down. Of the $49,000 spent by Maine on the Passamaquoddy in the last biennium, only a small part had gone to health, education, and similar social services and none into capital investment.

The one good thing the legislature had done for the tribe since 1935 was remove the hunting and fishing license fee. "They may hunt, *in season*, as free as they like," McNickle reported. "And in the country surrounding the Princeton reserve, there is abundant game—moose, deer, bear—and fish. Strange fact, but they will be enjoying conditions as much like their ancient life as perhaps any Indian group in the U.S."

McNickle also visited the Penobscots. He saw them as "more kindly dealt with by time and fortune" because of their proximity to Bangor, "one of Maine's best cities." But their advantage over the Passamaquoddy was only "relatively favorable." They still lived in "crumbling houses" and health conditions were far from satisfactory. The state had built a water and sewage system for them, but McNickle felt "a thorough-going program of social planning" was needed. "The philosophy of the State is the familiar one of passively doling out funds for essentially unproductive services."

A set of half-a-dozen recommendations accompanied McNickle's narrative. First off, it had to be determined legally "whether or not Indian Reorganization Act funds can be used for state reservation Indians who did not vote on the Act."

If not, some educational assistance could be given, some qualified Penobscots and Passamaquoddy should be hired by the Indian Service, markets should be developed for their baskets, better housing provided for both groups, economic and social organization developed for both groups, and clean water arranged for the Passamaquoddy.

McNickle's caveat was that assistance "beyond the simple measures indicated here" could not be offered "within the present scheme of jurisdiction."

A final—and discouraging—coda to this well-meant effort under John Collier's revamped New Deal BIA was contained in a memo to Collier from Assistant Commissioner William Zimmerman. It was dated October 22, 1937. Zimmerman had gone to Maine, perhaps because of McNickle's report, spent a day each on the reservations, and then had a discussion with Norman McDonald, Maine's director of public welfare. His conclusion: "...this office should take no formal steps, not at this time at least, to assume jurisdiction over the Maine Indians. I am confident that we could do a better job than is now being done, but I see no hope of obtaining approximately $100,000 a year, which is the amount now being spent by the state."

That such a move was even contemplated in 1937 borders on the amazing. That it would have been revolutionary, too, for the Maine Indians, was summed up for Collier by Zimmerman at the end of his memo. "In my conversations with the leaders of the two groups, I gathered that they were interested in the work being done by the federal government for other Indians, but they definitely regarded themselves as state wards and are not anxious to be placed under federal supervision."

The State of Maine, on its part, did not stir at all from its lethargy toward its native tribes until some five years later. In 1942 the subject was finally tackled in the Ninety-First Maine Legislature by the Legislative Research Committee, a special standing "study committee" which, every session when the lawmakers weren't in Augusta, examined various topics of public interest. The 1942 Indian study was dubbed the *Proctor Report* for Ralph W. Proctor of Auburn who, as a special assistant to the group, wrote it. Reading its findings in retrospect, one is struck by its thoroughness—and its bias, which was to try to find a way to make the Maine Indians conform more to white society. "Is it time to break up the reservations?" Proctor rhetorically asked, through the devices of vocational training and off-reservation work for tribal members. Also, should Maine introduce a sort of mini-Dawes Act, allowing the allotment of individual homesteads to Indian families, entailing "definite ownership of land to those who will work it.

Another finding was that although Congress had granted all Indians in the U.S. the right to vote, "neither the Maine attorney general nor the state supreme court were willing to give a definitive ruling allowing Maine Indians the vote," since the state constitution said Indians "not taxed" couldn't vote. Further findings revealed that the Passamaquoddy had never been compensated for islands granted them by Massachusetts but lost through the Granger court case; and that their trust fund had been denuded when their bank accounts were impounded in 1933, and receipts that should have gone to them went into the general fund. The next legislative session in 1943 did take some minimal action: $2,000 was voted to reimburse the Passamaquoddy for the fifteen islands in the St. Croix, and money used to pay legal fees in the Granger case put back in their trust fund. Yet in 1945 the state began depositing all receipts to the Passamaquoddy trust fund into the state's general fund on the grounds that Maine was spending more on the tribe than the annual receipts of the trust fund.

The years of World War II showed the Maine Indians in more or less their "invisible" holding pattern, except for the large percentage of their young men who went off to serve in the armed forces. One other *contribution* they made to the war effort was quite unconscious on their part. In 1944 and 1945 German prisoners were brought to Maine and camps were established near Houlton for potato harvesting and in the North Woods, including a site at Indian Township for cutting wood for the paper companies. Security wasn't very strict at the logging sites, but escapes were non-existent. "We had been told the forest was populated by wild Indians who would not hesitate to kill escaping prisoners," one of the Germans explained, "and we had no reason not to believe these stories." The prisoners at Indian Township no doubt knew otherwise. Cases of fraternization were not unknown and resulted in one Indian child with the name of Ritter.

If the Passamaquoddy and Penobscots were deemed "invisible" in this period, despite their official representation in Augusta, the Indians in Aroostook were not on anyone's radar screen.

Regardless of the fact that the Maliseets had had a presence in the Houlton area long before Joseph Houlton arrived in 1807, the municipality, itself, seventy-odd years later was recognizing them as merely anonymous "Indians," chiefly in paying for their burial costs. Before the end of the nineteenth century, an "Indian Reserve" had been located in Houlton, meaning at least five families living together. An "Indian Reservation" next came into being along County Road, not far from the city dump. When evicted from this site in 1916 by the owners of the land, the "Indians" removed to "The Flats," which was closer yet to the dump. There, they lived in obscurity, one of their chief economic activities the making of baskets for the potato harvest. Since "the County" farmers depended on a steady supply of these receptacles, it became a widely accepted practice in Aroostook to allow Indians onto private land to obtain the brown and yellow ash they needed for their basketry. One name of an early Maliseet leader to survive these misty times was Doctor Peter Polichies—not a medical doctor, but a man with special healing powers because he was the seventh son of a seventh son, a powerful combination in various Indian cultures.

The other native people in Aroostook County, the Micmacs, scattered at several locations—Presque Isle, Fort Kent, and Houlton—were more obscure in the general Maine scene than even the Maliseets.

But there were still some stirrings beneath the placid surface of the 1930s. In 1933 Florence Nicola Shay, a Penobscot and descendant of Old Chief John Neptune, wrote and somehow self-published a very short book. Entitled *History of the Penobscot Tribe of Indians,* she later had it re-issued in 1942.

This feisty lady had had the temerity to write to President Franklin Delano Roosevelt and complain that the State of Maine had taken away her right to vote. Living in Connecticut, she had had no trouble voting in the presidential election of 1928, she wrote. But returning to Maine in 1930, she was turned down by the clerk in Old Town when she tried to register and he had cited to her "an obsolete law of Maine...and in that law, we [Indians] are classed with criminals, paupers, and morons."

Her letter to FDR was answered by Fred Daiker at the

BIA. He told her the Indians of Maine had the right to vote, but had to register, pay a poll tax (Maine had one until 1973), and meet whatever educational requirements the state demanded (since declared unconstitutional).

In her 1942 edition of her book, since the voting situation hadn't changed, Florence protested, "I have four sons and I feel the government has not the right to draft my boys without giving us the right to vote.... We are a segregated, alienated people and many of us are beginning to feel the weight of the heel that is crushing us to nothingness...."

The letter to FDR had also requested federal help in building a bridge from Indian Island to Old Town. Fred Daiker replied that this matter was entirely a state responsibility. Commenting, Florence wrote: "I hardly think that the state would consider giving us a bridge but we have not asked for any yet."

There was no lack of problems to be aired: the Penobscot language was almost gone; the skill of basket-making was dying; kids who went to white schools were dropping out because of "inferiority complexes"; their agent lived in Eastport, out of reach, and the local subagent lived in Augusta and was no help on weekends; homes still needed repairs; children needed dental care; houses needed sanitation; and, moreover, "Our last Rep. in 1941 was merely recognized as a 'visitor,'" she wrote, referring to the action of the Maine legislature in expelling the two Indian non-voting delegates from their seats in the house.

Yet Florence Nicola Shay wasn't just waiting passively. In addition to her book and letter to the president, she was helping to organize a women's club on Indian Island dedicated to bettering Penobscot welfare, education, and social progress, and they had not only become affiliated with the Maine Federation of Women's Clubs but also the General Federation of Women's Clubs on the national level.

Her philosophy had a distinctly modern touch: "Progress is the word now for the younger generation and they are beginning to realize it. The time of the war paint and scalping

Indian is gone forever and if they hope to exist they must compete with the white man, so they are acquiring all the education they can...."

NOTES

[1] Lewis Mitchell's entire speech has been reproduced in *The Wabanakis of Maine and the Maritimes,* published by the Maine Indian Program of the New England Regional Office of the American Friends Service Committee, 1989, pages C–46–49.
[2] Ibid, page A–19.
[3] Bunny McBride, *Molly Spotted Elk.* Norman, Oklahoma, and London: University of Oklahoma Press, 1995.
[4] Donald Soctomah, *Passamaquoddy at the Turn of the Century, 1890––1920: Tribal Life and Times in Maine and New Brunswick.* Printed with funding from the Maine Humanities Council and the Passamaquoddy Tribe of Indian Township in 2002 (all proceeds to the Passamaquoddy Cultural Heritage and Resource Center).
[5] Frank Speck, *The Penobscot Man.* Orono, Maine: University of Maine Press, 1997, reprint.

19

JUST BEFORE THE STORM

A closer look at Florence Nicola Shay's words in 1942 concerning the future of her Penobscot tribe, where she says *the time of the war paint and scalping Indian is gone forever*, does not really suggest she wanted her people to assimilate; she wanted them to *compete* with the white man.

And a further examination of the *Proctor Report* of the same year, revealing language such as, "The Indians are shiftless, take no care of their houses or their land and little of themselves.... The whole impression one gets is of slackness, lack of pride or initiative," gives promise of a continuing attitude of disdain or worse, unless they do become whites in mind, spirit, and action.

Proctor has a few words, too, for Florence Nicola Shay, pejorative ones, wherein he considers her the ringleader of "a small group (15 percent)" of Penobscot malcontents who "aren't satisfied with their treatment." He chides her for complaints in her book about unfulfilled treaty obligations, saying she forgets "that the terms of the treaty are antiquated and that the present appropriation exceeds many times what it would cost to meet the terms of the treaty literally."

Official handwringing over the stubbornness of the local tribes was nothing new in Maine. As early as 1852 a Governor's Report on Indian Affairs referred to their "native slothfulness" and stated confidently that they would stay "in a condition bordering on pauperism...until their habits have been changed."

Another Governor's Report in 1890 recommended "enforced education, enforced labor, enforced allotment on proper land."

State responsibility for these surviving tribal people had been shifted around from the state governor and council to a joint executive–legislative committee and, after a brief, rather inexplicable sojourn from 1929 to 1931 in the Forestry Commission, finally to the Department of Health and Welfare. The Legislative Research Committee's decision to study the situation in 1942 showed at least a subliminal dissatisfaction with that arrangement, which nevertheless continued.

In 1949, because of complaints received from the Penobscots, Governor Frederick G. Payne sent his administrative assistant, John H. Welch, to Indian Island with orders to give him a written report. Welch met with the tribal council and his work drew the ire of Commissioner David Stevens of the Department of Health and Welfare, who snippily and bureaucratically objected that since Maine law did not provide for a tribal council, Welch had, in effect, been listening to a mere ad hoc committee. What had ostensibly gotten Stevens's goat was that the Penobscot leaders had said they'd never had any serious problems with the department "until Mr. Stevens took over."

Another black eye for Health and Welfare occurred at the start of the 1950s. A poorly planned, slapdash attempt to provide better Indian housing emptied almost the entire Passamaquoddy trust fund. Homes on which $8,000 per dwelling had been spent deteriorated so that soon they were worth only $2,500. Finger-pointing in the statehouse hallways, while it might have included comments about slovenly Indians who did no maintenance, must have contained gibes, too, about shoddy workmanship and incompetent supervision by a department that had allowed such a fiasco.

Serious discussion of the need for a separate Department of Indian Affairs first surfaced in 1952.

David Stevens, still commissioner of Health and Welfare, attempted to scotch all talk of that sort. On August 4, 1952, he sent a long report to the Legislative Research Committee and did allude to a possible *Division* of Indian Affairs under his aegis. Dave Stevens, in his time, was considered the most powerful and effective bureaucrat Maine ever had. A beanpole-tall, gaunt, Ichabod Crane-ish figure, he never minced words and insisted the Indians as a whole weren't supportive of a separate department, except for "only a very local and aggressive minority group at Indian Island."

Several years later Stevens went on to become the commissioner of the Department of Transportation and his position was filled by a medical doctor, Dean Fisher, who had a fairly crusty bedside manner, himself. In 1954 Fisher predicted the state's Indian reservations would not last—that "education, economic pressure...and intermarriage will eventually bring an end to the reservation system in Maine," and that the Indians, themselves, were looking forward to its dissolution.

The concept of "termination" had gained credence nationwide, and during the Eisenhower years became professed federal practice. In hindsight, the fact that Maine's first Democratic governor since the 1930s, Ed Muskie, could consider such an outcome a solution should not come as a surprise, given the temper of the times. The headline, "MUSKIE WOULD CLOSE INDIAN RESERVATIONS" appeared in the *Portland Press Herald* on January 12, 1956. Muskie's statement at a news conference that the prospect was "worth exploring" followed his two-day visit to the Passamaquoddy, where he inspected housing that "should have been torn down, rather than repaired." It was the governor's opinion that the younger Passamaquoddy were interested in owning land. Although the Indians, if they all left the reservations, would be integrated with the rest of Maine's citizens, Muskie said, they would still receive services "available to white people in similar economic circumstances."

Quashed repeatedly (Ed Hinckley, the first Indian commissioner, thinks eight to ten times), the idea of a separate Department of Indian Affairs still wouldn't die, particularly given that the reservations didn't fade away.

More deliberate action began with the 101st Maine Legislature, 1962–64, when an Interim Committee on Indian Affairs was created. Even this early in the soon-to-be raucous '60s, a feeling had reached Augusta that a need for change was in the air. The chairman was a Republican state senator from rural Penobscot County, Clyde Hichborn, who years later switched to become a Democrat. In either party, Clyde was quite liberal in his views about Indians.

When the next legislature, the 102nd, opened in 1965, it had a Democratic majority thanks to Lyndon Johnson's landslide. From the previous Interim Committee came An Act Transferring Indian Affairs to the Governor and Council. An Orono Democrat, Keith Anderson, put in An Act Providing Funds to Create a Division of Indian Affairs in the Department of Health and Welfare; and from Representative Warren Cookson, a Republican from Glenburn, came two bills: one proposed the transfer of Indian education from Health and Welfare to the Department of Education and, most importantly, one proposed An Act Creating a Department of Indian Affairs.

This latter bill won out for eventual consideration.

Warren Henry Cookson had all the credentials of a quintessential Maine, small-town conservative. A graduate of Bangor High School, he served in the army in World War II, then came home to a life of public service—town manager of Lincoln, town manager of Milo, and in his own town of Glenburn, selectman, road commissioner, school board member, state representative for six years, VFW, American Legion, Masons, etc., parishioner of the Glenburn Covenant Church, and active Republican. Not exactly the biography of a revolutionary.

But there is a saying of Victor Hugo's often quoted in the Maine legislature about "an idea whose time has come." So it seemed with the notion of a separate department-level agency to deal with Indian matters. When Cookson's bill emerged from the State Government Committee, it bore a 12–1 Ought to Pass recommendation. The lone dissenter was Representative Richard Berry of Cape Elizabeth, a maverick Republican businessman and transplant from Malden, Massachusetts.

Dick Berry notwithstanding, the measure had clear sailing in the house where it was enacted 123–0 and found equal acceptance in the senate.

The department's future, once it was up and running, was not to be so smooth.

Its commissioner, by law, had to be a person qualified by "experience, training, and demonstrated interest in Indian affairs." Consultation with the tribes was not required. Governor John Reed and the council chose Edward C. Hinckley, who had majored in Cultural Anthropology at Harvard and, after a stint in the army, picked up a Master's in Education, also at Harvard. He had taught in BIA Indian schools in Utah, Arizona, and Nevada, and had worked for the Indian Health Service. The Maine Indians may not have known it, but they were getting a friend to run the first (and only) state agency ever to handle Indian matters in this country.

Ed Hinckley's individualistic ways would often prove startling to Maine's staid government as it was constituted in the mid-1960s. When he told Niran Bates, head of the bureau responsible for arranging office space, that he wanted his office in Augusta, the veteran bureaucrat, surprised, blurted, "We thought you'd want to be out there with your Indians." Novice politician he might have been, but Hinckley knew he had to be where the center of action was.

He, himself, was a doer—a creator of action. In a letter to me, Ed wrote: "The fact that I was able to assist in developing unique working relationships between the Penobscot and Passamaquoddy tribes and a number of significant federal government agencies (EDA, DHUD, OEO, etc.) *before* the claims case had even found an entry into the country's judicial system is of immense satisfaction to me," and added, with the humility of hindsight, "but of little relevance to almost anyone else."

It was certainly not of *little relevance* that some federal assistance was being added to the fairly meager state effort. These were the days of Lyndon Johnson's nationwide War on Poverty and its programs, particularly the Community Action Program grants, were the first crack the tribes had at money from Washington since the Reverend Kellogg had brought funds to the Passamaquoddy. Hinckley credits Stan Tupper, who was the state's First District Republican congressman, with having engineered an arrangement by which Penobscots and Passamaquoddy each had their own CAP agencies, rather than being lumped in with non-Indian poor in Penobscot and Washington Counties and having to compete for Title II funds.

U.S. Senator Edmund Muskie helped, too. In the Economic Development Act, this savvy, veteran lawmaker was able to insert three words to make Maine Indians eligible for its provisions. The original draft of the law included services to "tribes recognized by the federal government"; Muskie simply added, "or state governments," and so the Penobscots and Passamaquoddy came under EDA and the water and sewage projects its federal grants could provide.

Yet many of the old ways hung on. One of Ed Hinckley's first tasks was to fill the job of Indian agent for the Passamaquoddy. The previous holder of the post, the notorious Hiram Hall, had been violently hated by the Indians for the tyrannical way he exercised his power, best illustrated by the story that when a pregnant Passamaquoddy woman had leaned on his truck while arguing with him, he'd driven off, dragging her fifty yards down the road. Hall had died suddenly of a heart attack, which, it was said in "Indian Country," had been brought on by accusations of fraud against him. As a replacement, Ed Hinckley found a teacher and wildlife aide named Arnold Davis, and suffered the agonies of the Augusta bureaucracy when it took six months to get the appointment through the personnel system, only to discover he and Davis had very different philosophies about how Indians should be treated.

Davis didn't seem too far behind Hiram Hall when he was quoted in the press as saying: "They're [the Indians] like rats in a barrel as long as they're out there on the reservations, living on welfare."

So the first big brouhaha for the new commissioner came when Hinckley fired Davis for "insubordination." Davis appealed, but the action was upheld, a situation Ed now describes as "one of the more grueling experiences of the time."

In the long run, the department's *budgetary* problems were to prove far more severe. A dirty little secret none of the legislators knew was that Health and Welfare had many times run out of funds in its Indian account, but in a huge operation had found money to cover the shortfall. Ed Hinckley would have no such option.

And then the state governor changed. The election of 1966 saw Republican John Reed replaced by Democrat Kenneth Curtis. But this should have been a change for the better. Curtis, at age thirty-five the youngest governor in the country, had once been the EDA administrator in northern Maine, was sympathetic to the Indians, and was supported by them. John Stevens has been quoted as saying: "Ken Curtis got into office as governor. He was helpful, once he was educated a little, so we started dreaming of what we might get him to do."[1]

Therefore, it had to be disappointing to Ed Hinckley that his budget requests for additional needed funds were not met by the governor, who was starting his first term with a hostile Republican legislature determined to make him go back on his campaign promise that he wouldn't raise taxes.

Uncharacteristically, the "liberal" governor's first budget did not even give the new department as much money as his predecessors had allotted Health and Welfare for the Indians in the past. Determined to go beyond merely running a handout operation, Ed Hinckley had asked for some hefty increases—$280,000 for developmental programs and $550,000 to upgrade the woeful infrastructures on the reservations. Nor was he particularly quiet about his frustration when his requests weren't met, making statements that he felt like "a man chipping away at an iceberg with an icepick," and that if his job were just to continue doling out welfare, the department shouldn't have been created. "I'm beginning to feel like the kid that didn't ask to be born," he said publicly.

Such asperity, sincere as it was, didn't sit well in the collegial atmosphere of the Augusta statehouse. Worse, by January 1968 it was revealed that Indian Affairs had overspent its budget.

Grudgingly, the state made up the $18,000 from its general fund. Then, the department exceeded its allotment again, this time by $50,000. An emergency appropriation act took care of that shortfall.

When Hinckley presented his 1969 budget, the Appropriations Committee jumped on him. Its most veteran member, the crusty Democratic "professional politician" from Lewiston, Louis Jalbert, called the commissioner's inability to stick to his budget "close to defiance." Trying to defend himself, the embattled department head said he had the support of the governor, who had asked him, "If you stop spending, will people suffer?" Told "Yes," the chief executive, according to Hinckley, ordered him to continue giving relief to the tribes and the money would somehow be found.

When yet again, the department was discovered—in mid-March, 1969—to be heading for a $40,000 to $50,000 gap, the senate chair of the Appropriations Committee, Richard N. Berry, hit the roof. "What an example, what a pattern, what a route to follow for other department heads," he thundered. "If you think your cause is just, spend all the money you wish." More drastically, he introduced an order to take legal action against Hinckley as a violation of Title 5, Section 1583, of the Revised Maine Statutes, which forbids a state official from ignoring an appropriation limit, under penalty of a fine equal to the overspending and a jail term of up to eleven months.

But things never went that far. One of Berry's fellow Republican senators, Peter Mills, Sr., protested it would look to the rest of the country as if Maine were "picking on a very, very small minority tucked down in the corner of the state."

Several months prior to this latest outburst, Ed Hinckley had offered his resignation to Governor Curtis, stating, "If the price of getting the extra money means my job, then that's the way it's got to be." Ken Curtis demurred—at *that* juncture—

but the repeated problems in the department set in motion the idea that ousting Hinckley might have to be the price of emergency funds for the Indians.

The tribes, themselves, did not want to see Hinckley go. In full regalia, including western war bonnets, they demonstrated in the statehouse. John Stevens said Hinckley was "the only one in recent memory who has not been an agent or commissioner against the Indians." The legislature was accused of "bigotry and callousness." Despite the uproar, Senator Berry let it be known he would drop his charges against Hinckley if the governor accepted Hinckley's resignation.

When, on March 20, 1969, Ed Hinckley did submit a resignation, it *was* accepted. But Curtis also made it clear he would brook "no curtailment or interruption" of programs on the reservations, plus he would oppose any measure to hurt the Department of Indian Affairs. Moreover, he hired Ed Hinckley back as an advisor until a new commissioner could be hired.

The search, it was announced, would follow a policy instituted by Hinckley of seeking consultation, if not approval, of the tribal governors and councils. Such a step away from paternalism was only one of various innovations Hinckley had introduced. Another was the creation of Indian-run housing authorities on each of the three reservations. Previous housing had been built without the slightest Indian input and had proved to be infamously substandard. Several federal programs allowing for self-determination had been put in place, as well, with state Indian department help, like the Community Action Program agencies and a stand-alone U.S. Department of Commerce redevelopment area on Indian Island.

A more intangible development was the start of the *Maine Indian Newsletter* whose editor, Eugenia Thompson, the Penobscot woman who called herself *ssipsis*, was a direct descendant of John Neptune and Joseph Nicolar. In the '60s she was married to Ken Thompson, who worked for Ed Hinckley in the Department of Indian Affairs, and it was from their home in Freeport that the *Newsletter* was published.

Hinckley remembers working on it when he was still in Nevada, prior to leaving for Maine to take up his new job.

The white writer Alvin Josephy, Jr., noted for his books about Indians, in an essay entitled "New England Indians, Then and Now," stated that during the 1950s, he worked for Time–Life, where there was an actual (if unspoken) ban on stories about Indians.[2] "Back in those innocent days, it was a rare non-Indian who knew that there were still Indians living on Indian land in New England," he declared. "Such ignorance kept the Indian communities there even more submerged, powerless, and neglected than those on reservations in the West."[3] Conversely, the New England Indians lived in their own isolation from other Indians, whether in neighboring states or far-off regions of the U.S. "In the course of the momentous events that began in the 1960s," Josephy continued, "the Indians of New England returned to full public view, some of them joining in solidarity with Indians from other parts of the country to assert the dignity, pride, and spiritual strength of their traditional Indian values and tribal heritages."[4] The *Maine Indian Newsletter*, the bound volumes of which exist on the shelves of the Maine State Library in Augusta, offer a treasure trove to the historian of the attitudinal changes then in ferment. Even now, some of the material makes for sizzling reading.

Listen to the words of a Frank Growling Bear (Nicola)— a Penobscot folksinger—in a lyric of his that starts with the couplet: "The French and Indian Wars do still go on today; Amid the woods of Maine, the land of Penobscot Bay."

The meaning of *French and Indian* Wars becomes clearer in the next stanza when he singles out Joseph E. Binnette, the state representative from Old Town who "Downs Indians to the ground, in his polished Frenchman style."

Ironically, the late Joe Binnette, although ostensibly Franco-American, was, as some of us who served with him in the legislature knew, an Irish orphan boy adopted by a Franco family.

Growling Bear goes on:

He's an ethnic Representative in the Congress Halls of Maine
The group he speaks for is the white, normal or insane.
He downs all helpful bills, which help Indian ways
This unrefined Indian hater will have his justice day.

Other verses strike other pejorative notes, based on issues in Maine affecting the tribes, such as:

The white supreme non-Indian has showed his lesson well
Of how he saved the Penobscot [River], by polluting it to hell
With the hoardful Great Northern, snatching Indian property
And the lily white scummed tanneries, pumping colors in the sea.
The white supreme Maine government, telling Passamaquoddy tribes
That their vast landhold's unsettled, till their population dies.

There is an editorial note following this entry, advertising that "Frank Growling Bear has a strong voice that will be heard and his music strikes many a guilty chord in those who are doing wrong to the native people."

Printed, too, was an outburst by Tim Love, self-described as a Proud Penobscot (later a tribal governor on Indian Island), sounding what once would have been an unthinkable sacreligious and heretical note that "Even on our Penobscot Nation stand the very symbols of our destruction: the Christian churches...raping and pillaging Mother Earth."

Editor Thompson followed this same trajectory back into Indian identity and included pieces written by herself but published under her Indian name. In one of them entitled "The Earth Is My Mother," she did not sign her work just *ssipsis*, but *ssipsis ganesahoway*—using the latter Penobscot word meaning "carries a big rock," so she could say in her prose poem, "I am not a giant. I am only a little bird. I carry a big rock peacefully. Sometimes I feel like throwing rocks, but I would be afraid that I would lose my name and lose my territory and damage my Mother."

Harking on the past seemed to instill strength and eloquence to Indian voices as they made themselves heard in the late '60s and early '70s.

From ssipsis, again:

We were also called Red Paint People before that [being called Penobscots]. The red meats of the salmon and the lobster were our chosen sustenance along with the red strawberries. We covered ourselves with red paint, dancing in happiness and peace. In death, the red fire consumed our bodies and our ashes were mixed with red clay.

sipsis could seek to embarrass the Maine establishment even when Passamaquoddy John Stevens was Indian commissioner. In a well-publicized demand, she insisted the state follow its treaty obligations to her tribe to the letter. The Penobscots had to receive, among a long list of items, 500 bushels of corn, seven barrels of clear pork, 100 yards of blue broadcloth, 100 pounds of gunpowder, 150 pounds of tobacco, and six boxes of chocolates. Stevens's sheepish answer was printed in the *Newletter*. The department had no money for such items. "If I did buy this material," he argued, "this would mean someone else has to do without...."

Maine Indian attitudes of resentment, long pent-up, appeared openly in print. Councilman John Sapiel was quoted as saying in a letter: "I speak as an Indian and not an apple"—apple—*red on the outside, white on the inside*—an Indian term of derision for a tribal member who tried too hard to assimilate. One anonymous column sarcastically proposed creating a Department of White Affairs, run by Indians, that would look upon white people as savages unless they adopted the Indian way of life and religion.

Young Donnie Francis, who helped start a *Nee-Dah-Bah* ("My Friend") Club for Indian youth, was quoted in the same vein. "The people on my reserve are just starting to wake up and realize they are Indians, not white people...mostly it's the young people who are starting to realize this...there are still a lot of the old people, mostly your parents, who believed the only way is the white man's way and these people are the ones we have got to prove to that we are Indians, not white people."

The Indians' oft-hidden sardonic sense of humor came into full display in the *Newsletter*. The following was a set of *funny definitions*:

"Priest: Mafia boss in funny clothes."

"VISTA worker: a White liberal without money."

"Indian Department teacher: The only good Indian is an all-White one."

"Equality: An Indian living in a Black ghetto operated by Mexicans and owned by Whites."

Nothing and no one was sacred. When Maine's revered U.S. Senator Edmund S. Muskie let his home state tribes know of his vote to return Blue Lake and its surrounding lands in Kit Carson Forest to the Taos Pueblo in New Mexico, *ssipsis* quipped editorially, "I hope Senator Muskie will help whenever we get around to asking for the return of Mount Katahdin."

The shocking idea that Katahdin had not been saved for all Maine people by the unselfish act of former Governor Percival Baxter, who'd bought it with his own money and given it to the state, was bruited again under the heading "WAR CHIEF RANCO STATES PENOBSCOT SOVEREIGNTY: QUESTION BY KATHY PAUL":

"Kathy: How did we lose Mount Katahdin?"

"Chief Ranco: Mount Katahdin was taken through the Governor of Maine, who was at that time Governor Baxter."

Land lost was frequently mentioned in the *Newsletter*. A bumper sticker, proclaiming "MARSH ISLAND IS PENOBSCOT INDIAN LAND," was cited. Marsh Island was nothing less than the land on which the municipality of Old Town is located. The genesis of the Penobscots' beef was the eighteenth-century settling of John Marsh, their interpreter, on a lot of land granted to him by the tribe because they liked him. They saw their action as giving a small part of Arumsunkhungan Island to a friend as a present. Yet when Marsh brought his deed to the Massachusetts General Court to be ratified, it included the entire island and, in Indians' eyes, the general court exploited their initial generosity to Marsh into a claim for all of the Penobscot Valley. Such seeming perfidy and ingratitude still rankled after two centuries.

To underscore the point, ssipsis made a newsworthy if fruitless gesture. She marched into the offices of the municipal officials in Old Town and presented them with a parchment document—an eviction notice. Needless to say, it was ignored.

Another attempted show of Penobscot sovereignty, given significant coverage in the *Newsletter*, involved a young tribal member named Martin Neptune. He had been the founder of the *Nee-Dah-Bah* Club and was listed on the editorial board of the *Newsletter*. An activist, he had been involved with Operation Mainstream and TRIBE INC., the latter an effort by the four Wabanaki groups to set up a joint school using a former federal facility on Mount Desert Island. U.S. marshalls had arrested him in Maine by order of a federal court in Connecticut for failing to report for induction when drafted. His legal defense was to pre-figure arguments made in the Maine Land Claims case. Neptune simply maintained he was not a U.S. citizen since he was born to full-blooded Penobscot parents resident on Indian Island. The position of his American Civil Liberties Union lawyers was that the Penobscots had never been conquered by the United States and had never voluntarily ceded their lands. Next came back-up claims: that states could not enter into treaties; only the U.S. president and Senate could; and that the Penobscots still owned their territory "under a separate and distinct sovereignty."

Support for Neptune's contention was reported from far afield. The six-nation Iroquois Confederation publicly announced its support for Neptune's position that the U.S. had no right to force U.S. citizenship upon Indians, subject them to the draft, or make them fight in foreign wars. One of their more outspoken members, Wallace "Mad Bear" Anderson, a Tuscarora, dogmatically maintained that *forced citizenship* violated international law, various treaties, and the concept of Indian sovereignty. The draft was applicable solely to Indians who voluntarily became American citizens. Mad Bear's idea of appealing to a higher authority than the U.S. was popular. The Penobscot tribal council seriously considered petitioning the United Nations for membership. The Tuscarora firebrand ominously warned the white population, "Someday you may be on trial before an international tribune to answer for your crimes against my people."

This catch-all threat of his had been reprinted in the *Newsletter* from an Indian publication, *Akwesasne Notes*, put out by the Iroquois, and now considered by historians to have been the leading pioneer organ in the U.S. (circulation 50,000 in 1968) for advancing a radicalized indigenous view that began sweeping through Native Americans in the 1960s.

But where Martin Neptune's plea was concerned, the Indian Rights Association, itself seen as a radical organization by conservatives, did not agree. Its Law Committee issued a statement, re-issued by the *Newsletter*, in which the group's litigation experts saw "no merit in the legal position taken by Mr. Neptune. He is a citizen and must be subjected to all U.S. law, whether he approves of it or not. Old treaties and customs, however venerable, are rendered ineffective by subsequent acts of Congress."

Since the U.S. District Court took a similar position in the Neptune case, on the grounds he was indisputably a U.S. citizen, they added the opinion it was "unnecessary to determine at this time the Constitutional validity of those treaties..."—that is, the agreements made between the Penobscots and the States of Maine and Massachusetts.

The pages of the *Newsletter* were often filled with discussions of the eighteenth- and nineteenth-century treaties. These pieces were constant reminders of the means by which Maine Indian land, in Maine Indians' eyes, had been "lost." The surrounding white communities, so accustomed to the placidity of their Indian neighbors, laid the blame for the change in them on "outside agitators." Those stirring up the Passamaquoddy were listed in the local press and dutifully re-reported in the *Newsletter* as:

*Peter Dana Point's tribal governor, John Stevens, and Regina Nicholas
participate in a sit-in on U.S. Route 1 to protest the cutoff of state benefits,
particularly milk for children and medical help for the elderly.*
©1969 BANGOR DAILY NEWS, USED WITH PERMISSION

"A certain young lawyer who had come to town"
"Those draft-dodging VISTA boys"
"The new director of the Community Action Program"
"Newspaper reporters and magazine writers"

On the political front, the Indians were likewise becoming
engaged. A letter was posted in the *Newsletter* about an election in State Senate District 27—or, rather, in the Democratic
primary, between Richard Broderick of Lincoln and Michael
Pearson of Old Town. The writer posited: "I don't believe anyone will vote for Broderick, do you?"—then added, "Pearson
is the first person to fight discrimination openly in Old Town,
that's for sure."

Mike Pearson, a school teacher, won that Democratic
nomination handily and went on to a distinguished career in
the Maine senate. Dick Broderick, along with his wife Faye, at
one time the Democratic national committeewoman from
Maine, had been among a group of citizens from Lincoln and
Enfield suing the University of Maine at Orono to prevent the
giving of scholarships to Indian students.

Governors John Stevens and Kenneth Curtis at Peter Dana Point in
September 1970, a year before Curtis appointed Stevens to the post of
Commissioner of Indian Affairs. PHOTO BY STEVE TAKACH

So ssipsis's publication could and did discern a difference
between whites—that some could be helpful. Governor Ken
Curtis was an example. Some of the history made in that era
came back to me when Curtis was quoted in the *Newsletter*
saying he would seek a resolution from the 1969 National
Governors' Conference calling on Congress to abolish the dis-
tinction between federal and state Indians. As one of his
staffers, I helped write that resolution and was with the governor at the Colorado Springs meeting where he got it approved.
In 1968 he had asked U.S. Senator Robert Kennedy, a special
friend, to have his Subcommittee on Education hold hearings
in Maine, and Kennedy, before his assassination that same
year, had responded by sending two of his staff to help him
seek ways of bringing federal Indian benefits Down East.

Extralegal action, too, took place in 1968 when Passamaquoddy patience ran out. The Georgia–Pacific paper company had long been logging on land in Indian Township that
the tribe contended was its territory. To add insult to injury,
G–P refused to hire Indian crews to produce this pulpwood

for its mill at Woodland. The age-old dispute between the two parties saw no signs of being settled and so the Passamaquoddy, donning war paint and feathers, attacked the G–P crews in the woods, causing them to bolt and leave behind expensive equipment in Indian hands. After further negotiations, Georgia–Pacific announced on October 8, 1968, that they had hired three all-Indian crews.

A year later another neo-warpath sprang into being when the State of Maine, experiencing Department of Indian Affairs budget problems again, cut off certain aid to the Passamaquoddy, including milk for children and medical supplies for the elderly. Thereupon, Route 1 through Indian Township was suddenly barricaded and a toll established, $1 for cars and $2 for trucks, the fees to be used to make up the missing state funds, which, within a remarkably short period of time, were reinstated.

These, indeed, were turbulent years and the turmoil on the national scene—the rise of "Red Power" in tandem with the Black revolt over civil rights—formed a backdrop to the astonishing Land Claims upheaval soon to erupt in Maine. The outbursts by Indian activists nationwide made headlines, whether it was Wallace "Mad Bear" Anderson leading his Tuscaroras into the Department of the Interior Building to make a citizen's arrest of the Secretary of the Interior, or the invasion and holding of Alcatraz, or the occupation of the Bureau of Indian Affairs offices, or the tragic shoot-outs at Wounded Knee, giving the late '60s and early '70s an aura of revolutionary fervor that affected all of "Indian Country," even those forgotten remnants in the East. When the "Trail of Broken Treaties" march on Washington occurred in 1972 and led to the BIA takeover, "Eastern Indians participated in substantial numbers," according to Vine Deloria, Jr.[5] The initial idea for the cavalcade to D.C. had been to present "Twenty Points" for reforming the tribes' relationships with the federal government. One of these points (number seven) was asking "mandatory relief from treaty violations by state governments."[6]

Quite apart from such dramatic events, Maine was to witness a much more radical and revolutionary redress of grievances on behalf of its own Indians and in an entirely legal and ultimately non-violent manner. No one knew it then—Indian or non-Indian—but the stage was being set for the granddaddy of all historic white man versus Native American land claims arguments.

NOTES

[1] Robert H. White, *Tribal Assets.* New York: Henry Holt and Company, 1990, page 29.

[2] Included in *The Pequots in Southern New England: The Fall and Rise of an American Indian Nation,* Laurence M. Hauptman and James D. Wherry, Editors. Norman, Oklahoma: University of Oklahoma Press, 1990.

[3] Ibid, page 10.

[4] Ibid, page 13.

[5] Vine Deloria, Jr., *Behind the Trail of Broken Treaties.* Austin, Texas: University of Texas Press, reprinted 1985.

[6] Ibid, page 51.

20

Aftermath I

*F*rom the standpoint of an outside observer, who better than Alvin M. Josephy, Jr., the Time–Life editor, to pen an apotheosis of sorts, once Jimmy Carter signed the Settlement Act, of what had happened in Maine.

"I remind you of the shock waves that radiated out from the Maine land claims case of the Penobscots and Passamaquoddy," Josephy began his wrap-up.[1] "In a real sense, that was history coming back to haunt the nation, but equally significant, it was a landmark moment in the course of Indian–white relations."

It was an impact felt everywhere in the U.S, recognized by an expert in the field like Josephy, that led naturally to his opinion expressed in the paragraph below of how much change Maine, itself, started feeling in the aftermath.

> Until a short time before, it had been the tradition of most non-Indians in Maine to ignore the soul-searing prejudice, discrimination, deprivation, and injustices endured by the Maine Indians, who could expect little, if any, interest or protection from the state government. Many remember a brutal episode in which non-Indian hunters bullied and committed murder in an Indian community, apparently certain they had nothing to fear from Maine justice. Well, no more. Thanks to the Penobscot and Passamaquoddy claims fight, non-Indian perceptions and attitudes toward Indians experienced what one might term a rapid evolution for the better in Maine.

I remember, myself, as a legislator, one immediate palpable difference in Augusta. While, in my day and in my Democratic caucus, strong sympathy existed for the Indians and there was a great deal of collegial respect for their representatives in the house, it had still been a struggle to get those representatives seated after several failed attempts previous to 1975. Following the Land Claims Settlement, the Passamaquoddy and Penobscots, no longer dirt poor, did something a number of big-time commercial and industrial lobbying groups did in the state capital—they threw a reception for lawmakers.

It was held at one of the plusher hosteleries and was a very swanky affair: free booze, great hors d'oeuvres, etc., and the place was packed. No one wanted to miss what had become the social event of the season. I vividly recall noticing with a touch of irony the presence of the Honorable James Dudley of Enfield, our Democratic Custer-type Indian fighter, who had joined with Faye and Dick Broderick to try to take away Indian scholarships at UMO, and who had fought me, his party leader, when I was seeking to seat the Indian representatives. But there was old Jim (who uncannily resembled W. C. Fields), chomping away on the expensive shrimp and other goodies the Indians had provided. These receptions continued for several years, always crowded and looked forward to, then, alas, they ceased.

As Alvin Josephy, Jr., concluded, following his praise of events in Maine: "But all, we know, is still not well."

A pronouncement on the settlement by John Stevens had sounded a note of optimism, albeit a cautious one, that did not necessarily preclude some rough patches ahead. "The most important thing that has come out of all this," the Passamaquoddy leader was quoted as saying, "is hope. Now we have a future, not just a past."[2]

On paper the money part of the $81.5 million settlement was divided as follows: Trust funds were set up for the two tribes to be held by the federal government and invested by the secretary of the interior with the concurrence of the Indians. The sums allotted this way were $12.5 million to each tribe in general and an extra $1 million each for their elderly. The tax-free income from these trusts was to go back quarterly to both parties. Also, money was restricted for land acquisition: $26.8 million apiece to the Passamaquoddy and Penobscots and another $900,000 for the Houlton Band of Maliseets.

These must have seemed like breathtaking sums to people who had until recently been living for the most part off welfare handouts. How would they spend it?

Robert H. White, in his book *Tribal Assets,* covers four tribes that entered into the full maelstrom of American free enterprise. The Passamaquoddy were one of the four tribes chosen for a case study à la Harvard Business School (the others were the Mississippi Choctaws, the Ak-Chin of Arizona, and the Warm Springs of Oregon). "To spend any time among [them]," the author declared "...is to believe that the private sector...offers Native Americans a better way out of poverty and powerlessness than does the public sector."[3]

Regardless of the fact that the resources the Maine tribes had to invest came from the public sector, they did make conscious decisions to spend part of their disposable income on economic development. Some money had to go for land, anyhow, and while its wood products—lumber and pulp—were marketable, it was a slow way to make a substantial profit. Describing how the Passamaquoddy divided up their nest egg, White reported it was roughly split in thirds—for land, for low-risk securities that returned a yearly dividend of $400 to $800 a year to each tribal member, and for entry into businesses. As their consultants, they hired Tom Tureen and his partner Barry Margolin, who had led them through the Land Claims process, and this arrangement morphed into Tribal Assets Management (TAM) with the addition of Tom's Princeton classmate, Egyptian-born Swiss investor Daniel Zilkha, and Yale-educated lawyer-businessman Rob Gips.

The first enterprise for the Passamaquoddy was their acquisition in Washington County of the Northeastern Blueberry Company (NEBCO). They came across this 2,000-acre blueberry farm while out searching for land to buy, paid $2.2 million of settlement dollars for it, and still own the operation today.

The most famous of their ventures with TAM, however, was the Dragon Cement purchase. Its complicated, audacious financing and successful denouement did, indeed, become a case study at the Harvard Business School. Through former Governor Ken Curtis, contact was made with the Cianbro Company, headed by Curtis's political friend, Alton "Chuck" Cianchette, owners of the only cement plant in New England. The tribe, helped by a BIA guarantee of a bank loan (which TAM discovered could be tax-exempt under the 1982 Indian Tribal Government Status Act), bought the plant, which was located in the seaside town of Thomaston, 125 miles south of Passamaquoddy country. When they sold it in 1988 to a Spanish outfit, *Cementos del Norte*, for almost the same amount as the whole Land Claims Settlement, a cool $81.3 million, they made something like a $60-million profit.

With such a success story, TAM was soon besieged by other tribes seeking investment assistance. A Wisconsin band of Chippewas used their services for a $23.7-million purchase of a manufacturer of electronic test equipment. An eastern band of Cherokees in the Carolinas took over the largest mirror company in the United States via a junk bond-leveraged buy-out arranged by TAM. Closer to home the Portland-based partners worked with the Penobscots, putting them together with SHAPE, INC., a Kennebunk-headquartered manufacturer of cassettes. Thus was born Olamon Industries, established on Indian Island.

A statement to the Maine press on November 1, 1983 by Penobscot Lieutenant Governor Joseph Francis expressed his *nation's* intention to devote itself to "economic development" big-time. He spoke of the possibility of selling Penobscot timberland to French investors. However, a closer look at the reason for Francis's making such remarks reveals a complexity of issues that, in a sense, get to the very heart of the contradictions embedded in the momentous settlement agreement.

For Joseph Francis was reacting to reporters' questions after a ruling from the U.S. Supreme Court had adversely affected the Penobscots and, to be blunt, was about to cost them one-quarter of their operating revenue.

What happened was the U.S. Supreme Court had refused to hear an appeal by the Penobscot Nation of a decision handed down from the Maine Supreme Court.

It all had to do with gambling on the Indian Island reservation.

Since 1973 the Penobscots had been openly conducting games of chance known sometimes as *beano*, sometimes as *bingo*. Lots of organizations did so in Maine—churches, fraternal organizations, veterans groups, etc.—but the Indians were attracting overflow crowds with far bigger pay-outs than the others, raking in as much as $50,000 a month. They were doing this—having single "high-stakes" jackpots up to $10,000—despite a Maine law passed in 1943 limiting single jackpots to no more than $200 and a total evening's take to $1,000.

In October 1982 the state, in the persons of Arthur Stilphen, commissioner of Public Safety, and James Tierney, attorney-general, finally initiated an action to end what they deemed a flagrant flouting of Maine law. They went to Kennebec County Superior Court and received a judgment against the Penobscots. The tribe, with Tom Tureen as its lawyer, appealed the ruling to the Maine Supreme Court.

A young lawyer of Penobscot ancestry, Mark A. Chavaree, Esq., in a paper on "Tribal Sovereignty" written later, described this case, *Penobscot Nation v. Stilphen,* as "the first opportunity for a court to interpret the meaning..." of the all-important phrase *"internal tribal matters"* in the settlement legislation. The Penobscots were arguing that "high-stakes beano (or bingo)" was exempt from state law because the proceeds were used for the *internal tribal matter* of funding tribal operations. Also, that language in the settlement notwithstanding, they derived power from federal common law to exercise this example of tribal sovereignty.

Maine's top court emphatically disagreed.

Its opinion, issued in June 1983, delivered by Chief Justice Vincent McKusick, affirmed the state's position that the controlling language in the settlement legislation made the Indians citizens of Maine, not a "nation within a nation"—their local government essentially was no different from any

Maine municipality—and the Penobscots had to obey the gambling regulatory laws like everyone else. The court declared unequivocally that the operation of gambling games "was not an 'internal tribal matter' within the meaning of the state legislation enforcing the Settlement Act."

Chief Justice McKusick, a highly respected and thoughtful jurist, seemed unusually pointed in some of his language. One section reads:

> Maine has a legitimate government interest—having nothing to do with its own financial needs—in preventing the Penobscot Nation's beano games. The tribe's interest in beano, by contrast, is purely financial. And, in point of fact, the Penobscots would have nothing to sell if high-stakes beano were not prohibited throughout the rest of Maine.

The Indians' argument that the state's only regulatory function was to insure honest games, and their games were scrupulously honest, was met with the rejoinder, "A motorist may not run a red light simply because no one else is entering the controlled intersection."

The most quoted part of the Maine Supreme Court's reasoning related to the contention that since the beano revenue paid for tribal matters only, it *was* an internal tribal matter.

McKusick rather tartly rejected the notion by stating that if the Penobscots could do anything criminal as long as it "turns a profit for the Nation," this would violate the overall spirit of the Settlement Acts, as well as common sense.

From a legalistic point of view, another landmark feature of the decision was its ruling on the ambiguous language in the Settlement Act that defined *internal tribal matter*. Unlike many pieces of legislation, this one gave only examples: an Indian tribe in Maine could decide its membership without state interference; it could control hunting and fishing by its own members on its own property; etc. But McKusick's wording, citing one of those learned law principles that make laymen's eyes glaze over—in this instance the *ejusdem generis* rule—was that a general term (i.e., *internal tribal matters*) followed by a list of illustrations "is ordinarily assumed to embrace concepts similar to those illustrations." Unequivocably, *beano* was not included in the *general term*. It had "played no part in the Penobscot Nation's historical culture or development," was not a traditional practice, and was only to make money. Ergo: the phrase *internal tribal matters*, "embraces only those matters illustratively illustrated in the statute and other matters like them."

With fifteen years' hindsight, Mark Chavaree still maintains the Maine Supreme Court in *Penobscot Nation v. Stilphen* "overstated the changes to tribal sovereignty intended by the Settlement Acts." The argument still rages on, as it did then, until temporarily squelched by that 1983 refusal of the U.S. Supreme Court to take up the Penobscots' appeal from the McKusick court's decision.

Three days after first speaking to the press, Tribal Lieutenant Governor Joseph Francis, on November 4, 1983, again made news with a defiant notice that the Penobscots would take their high-stakes beano games to Connecticut and open a far bigger operation on the tiny Pequot reservation in the rural town of Ledyard.

No one knew it then, but a lot of history was to result from such a hookup—nothing less than Indian gambling on the ultimate scale of a Foxwoods, setting off a spontaneous movement to build Indian casinos throughout the country.

As a lead-up to this development, it is helpful to know that at least half a decade before the final settlement in Maine, Tom Tureen and his group of poverty lawyers were busy elsewhere, too. Once Judge Gignoux had ruled that the Maine tribes fell under the Non-Intercourse Act, "Tureen sent his partners on a trip around the East Coast to find out what Indian tribes might have had similar histories," to quote Kim Isaac Eisler in his book, *Revenge of the Pequots*.[4]

One that fit the bill nicely was a group of fifty-five Pequots on the Mashantucket Reservation where their ancestors had been since 1667, and where, also, the State of Connecticut in 1855 had sold 1,000 of their acres without receiving the approval of Congress. Barry Margolin of Tureen's staff sat down with Richard "Skip" Hayward, chief of the Pequots, and interested him in letting the Maine lawyers also seek redress for his tribe. Until 1980, however, and the Maine settlement, not much was done; then, following the success in Maine, the Pequot case was moved forward and, once more, ended with a negotiated agreement, rather than litigation: federal recognition of this "small" tribe and an act of Congress giving the Pequots $900,000 and land—not particularly valuable land, originally theirs, which they could buy back from the present-day white owners at inflated prices. That legislation was initially vetoed by President Ronald Reagan. Yet a second, amended version finally received his approval.

Now, back to the shutting-down of the Penobscots' high-stakes beano in November 1983. Kim Eisler maintains that "At the time of the ruling, he [Tom Tureen] already had an alternative plan" since by then the Pequots had won their case.[5] The unexpected element was Tribal Lieutenant Governor Francis's spilling the beans about a move to Connecticut without sufficient consultation with others. His own tribal governor, young Tim Love, caught by surprise, admitted no contract had been signed with the Pequots for the $2.5-million gambling hall Francis had described as ready to begin construction "as soon as we can pour the concrete," and which would seat 3,500 people (as opposed to the maximum of 1,000 players the Penobscots drew on their "Super Bingo" nights). Nevertheless, Love was quick to add: "But if I were a betting man, I'd put my money on it."

The Pequot leader, Skip Hayward, was much more circumspect. A *Portland Press Herald* article quoted him as saying: "We are trying to study things very carefully before we get involved." Kim Eisler relates that Hayward was actually furious. His people, mostly Baptists and Jehovah's Witnesses, had strong religious objections to gambling, far more so than the mostly Catholic Penobscots. Although Judge McKusick's language in the *Stilphen* decision had rightly stated beano or bingo had never been part of Maine Indian tradition, gambling as such certainly had been since time immemorial and did not carry a stigma. That the Pequot chief soon changed his mind was due to a trip Hayward took to Florida, where he witnessed firsthand how high-stakes beano had totally transformed the fortunes of a poverty-stricken Seminole tribe.

The Pequots' giant bingo parlor opened on July 5, 1986. Money was borrowed from banks, backed by a Bureau of Indian Affairs guarantee, and the Penobscots helped with an $800,000 loan. The Maine tribes also received a four-year management contract to run the games, and so instant and stunning was the success of the venture that the Pequots bought them out after only two years.

By 1988, however, all quite legally, the Penobscots, themselves, were back into *high-stakes bingo.*

Once again the U.S. Supreme Court played an important role, through a Riverside County, California, case, deciding that, as a general rule, state and local governments could not regulate gambling on Indian reservations—an action allowing Indians in at least eighteen states to run high-stakes bingo games.

Initially Maine Attorney General James Tierney said the ruling had no legal impact in Maine due to the Settlement Act, but then added an unusual caveat. There was "a policy question," the attorney general said, "which is...Maine now has the only tribes in America that are unable to gamble." And he openly urged the legislature to at least give the state's Indians permission to conduct high-stakes bingo.

As a former house majority leader, Tierney was, of course, aware of a bill legalizing beano or bingo on Indian reservations that Governor Joseph Brennan had successfully vetoed in 1985. Helped by the attorney general's encouragement, it was resurrected in 1987 and passed anew. The only effort to stop it was made by Representative Mona Hale from Sanford, claiming her constituents feared unfair competition to their bingo games. Mona's motion against enactment was defeated by an overwhelming vote of 134–5. The Penobscot representative was the late Priscilla Attean and, in the debate, she spoke in her usual sincere and elegantly simple manner. Among other things, Priscilla said: "I know many of you are thinking, 'Yes, the Penobscots are rich or they should be, with their investment programs.' That is far from the truth. Yes, we do have investments, but at this point in time, the rate of return is so low and most of the profits are channeled into economic development...." Until their long-range goals could be met, they needed the high-stakes revenue they had lost.

Added the "Dean of the House," the veteran Appropriations Committee member from Lewiston, Louis Jalbert: "Their real estate doesn't have fair-market value—it's held in common—they can only sell to each other," the point being the Penobscots couldn't levy property taxes.

In the senate, there was not even a recorded vote; the bill was accepted, as legislators say, "under the hammer," with a single whack of the presiding officer's gavel to show the vote was unanimous.

On this occasion the new state governor, John R. "Jock" McKernan, had no problem signing the measure.

On October 11, 1987, the Penobscots, now lawfully able to offer thirty-six games a year, reopened their high-stakes parlor. The Passamaquoddy later followed suit and installed their own high-stakes gambling at Indian Township.

Meanwhile, the euphoria generated by the tribal economic development trend in Maine was reaching its peak. Robert White's *Tribal Assets* has its opening chapter at a ribbon-cutting ceremony in Pleasant Point, where the Passamaquoddy had just completed a factory to manufacture high-tech housing with Makroscan, a Finnish company. The $5-million joint venture had been financed 50–50 so flush was the tribe during 1987, and the prospects for the state-of-the-art enterprise seemed unlimited. Wayne Newell, a Harvard-educated tribal leader, had come from Indian Township and declared: "This is a great victory for the Passamaquoddy," adding, given his deep interest in the tribe's culture, "But no matter where we go, we must remember we are Passamaquoddy and never forget the richness of our heritage."[6]

A year later, another chapter of *Tribal Assets* reported, this particular project had gone belly up—due to unforeseen government regulations and changes in the market. The Dragon Cement plant was still doing well, its highly profitable sale still a year away, while another manufacturing opportunity, making automobile trunk-lining mats for Gates Formed Fibre Products of Auburn, Maine, was in the offing. But the Passamaquoddy now understood that ventures into American and worldwide capitalism were definitely not risk free. The Penobscots were to learn the same hard lesson, particularly in a "flyer" they took with Schiavi Homes, a Maine maker of manufactured housing. The Penobscots did well by loaning money to the Pequots but, according to Chief Barry Dana, a loan to a California tribe of a similar six-figure amount was never repaid.

The intricacies of Maine's Implementing Act did carry seeds of discord. One step the bill took was to wipe out the Department of Indian Affairs. Although many of the services hitherto provided by the State of Maine were now to be assumed by the federal government, the need had been recognized for a mechanism to allow communication and interaction between the tribes and the state.

The quasi-governmental device worked out in the act was the Maine Indian Tribal–State Commission (MITSC). This section of the statute set up a nine-member organization, described as "inter-governmental," comprised of four members designated by the state, two by the Passamaquoddy, and two by the Penobscots. The ninth member, to serve as chairperson, would be chosen by the other eight. Funding was provided by the parties, 50 percent state, 50 percent tribal. Not until 1983 were the first meetings held and the first chairperson came on board in June 1984. He was that same Maine businessman, Alton "Chuck" Cianchette, who had played a key role in selling the Dragon Cement Company to the Passamaquoddy.

The MITSC's responsibilities were to cover five areas: 1) To measure the effectiveness of the Settlement Act and the state's relationship with the tribes; 2) To recommend lands to be added to tribal territory; 3) To promulgate fishing rules on certain bodies of fresh water within Indian territory; 4) To recommend fish- and wildlife-management policies on non-Indian lands as they may affect those resources on Indian territory; and 5) To recommend extensions to existing reservations.

Quietly at work since 1983, the Maine Indian Tribal–State Commission has been a focus for the unsettled matters implicit in the painstakingly hammered-out compromise incorporated in the settlement. Yet while its work has been generally unnoticed, its sessions have often been stormy. In 1996 the 117th Maine Legislature created a Task Force on Tribal–State Relations to "explore ways of improving the tribal-state relationship and the effectiveness of the MITSC." The group was also asked to explore adding the other two Indian entities in the state—the Houlton Band of Maliseets and the Aroostook Band of Micmacs—into the equation.

The title of their report pretty much told what they had discovered:

AT LOGGERHEADS
The State of Maine and the Wabanaki

An equally frank, if not stronger, indication of the difficulty, can be found in the report's "Prologue." Printed there is a lone statement from one of the task force participants, the Honorable Margaret "Dolly" Dana, tribal council member from Pleasant Point. "I am a Passamaquoddy and I am distinctly different. I need to be treated as such," she starts out, and goes on to say: "It has been sixteen years since the Land Claims Settlement Act has been passed.... I view the Settlement Act as a way to push us out of existence as Passamaquoddy people. I felt it then, I see it now. It was not an honorable act...."

Her recommendations? "Simple. Recognize us as a different people, with different views, different ways of doing things, and understand we do it the way it seems, feels right for us.... We just want to be able to conduct our affairs with-

Copy of a notice posted on fishing waters in Maine Indian-owned territory, displaying rules falling under the authority of the Maine Indian Tribal–State Commission.

out outside interference. In every aspect of our lives, we need to control our destiny if we are to continue to survive as Passamaquoddy people. Until the State of Maine can see and understand this there will be no peace, no harmony, no balance, no future...."

Stressing that Passamaquoddy within the confines of their land are in one jurisdiction and the State of Maine is in another, Margaret Dana finally asks: "Can we really live side by side like this? We can. We just have to make the effort."

The Maine Indian Tribal–State Commission has soldiered on and yet exists, in spite of frequent internal dissensions, lack of strong state backing, weak authority, and only a single part-time staff person. A perusal of its history shows that in 1988 Chairman Chuck Cianchette, also a former state senator,

314

questioned the need for the commission's existence. Among his arguments: the state did not take an active interest; MITSC had not had to use its one real power, that of making fishing rules for fresh water in Indian Territory; and there was perceived duplication with other governmental areas. Cianchette called for a high-ranking meeting of both sides to discuss possibly disbanding.

Chuck's challenge most likely had been for effect, to get people talking and thinking. Five months later MITSC met and unanimously voted to retain the Pittsfield businessman as its chair for the next four years. Fifteen years since, the organization remains active.

With limited resources, it has striven to carry out its assigned functions. Recommending additions of land to the tribal holdings is one of the more important ones. Neither the Passamaquoddy nor the Penobscots went right out and bought the 150,000 acres each tribe was allotted under the Settlement Act. In the act, itself, areas were designated from which land could be bought for Indian territory, to be held in trust by the U.S. government. MITSC helped in 2001 when the Passamaquoddy wanted to add to their official "Indian Territory" any land in Township 19 MD in Washington County they could purchase before the year 2020. They were specifically interested in 465 acres adjacent to their blueberry fields. After MITSC gave its unanimous approval, Passamaquoddy Representative Donald Soctomah submitted a bill to so amend the Implementing Act and it became law.

Township 19 MD, incidentally, is just north of Columbia Falls and officially has *BPP* added to its nomenclature, which makes it *Middle Division, Bingham Penobscot Purchase*, right out of Maine history and William Bingham's 2.5-million-acre splurge of land buying after the Revolution. Also in this same township is a small body of water, Grassy Pond, where the regulation of fishing is under the jurisdiction of MITSC. Two bass are allowed per day and ice fishing for every species is allowed from January 1 to March 31, but salmon, trout, togue (lake trout), and bass cannot be taken under the ice prior to

Indian leaders meet with Governor Angus King and (center, front row) Cushman Anthony, former state representative and chairman of the Maine Indian Tribal-State Commission. In the back row are Penobscot Representative Donna Loring, Governor King, Maliseet Chief Brenda Commander, Passamaquoddy Governor Richard Doyle, and Penobscot Chief Richard Hamilton. In the front row are Micmac Chief Billy Phillips on the left, and Passamaquoddy Representative Donald Soctomah on the right.
COURTESY OF MITSC

December 31. The range of waters, both in Passamaquoddy and Penobscot territory, in which such detailed rules are promulgated, stretch from Maine's Atlantic Coast to the Canadian border.

Among its other activities, the MITSC has raised money for a video on the Wabanaki people, promoted a Wabanaki Day at the legislature, supported removing a "sunset" provision that might have ended the Passamaquoddy Tribal Court's jurisdiction over Class D and E crimes, looked into amending federal law to let Passamaquoddy hunt porpoises, and given its blessing to a proposal to grant special Maine license plates to tribal members—a bill that didn't pass.

In 1993 the most sensitive of issues—casino gambling—first came before the commission. They were asked to approve a Passamaquoddy plan to buy land in the city of Calais and add it to Indian territory. The stated purpose was "economic

316

development," but everyone knew the ultimate goal was a casino. Unanimously, the commission recommended approval, as long as the Calais City Council agreed.

And that the Calais City Council had already done, by a unanimous vote in December 1992, informing the legislature it was for a $10 million hotel and casino.

The legislation needed under Maine law to permit such an enterprise came up for a house vote in April 1994. In undoubtedly one of the lengthiest debates of the session, it was soundly defeated—fifty votes for, ninety-six votes against—despite the impassioned pleas of the legislators from Washington County who saw it as an economic boon for one of the poorest counties in the state, if not the entire country.

Some years later, when a legislative attempt was made to rectify a state supreme court decision concerning a parcel of Indian-owned land in Albany Township near Bethel, the argument—that if it legally became "Indian Territory" the Passamaquoddy might build a casino there—was enough to defeat the bill.

Diana Scully, who serves as part-time executive director of the MITSC, initially feltmutual relations within the commission had improved to a degree since the publication of *At Loggerheads*. Diana has been its secretariat practically since its inception and has watched it struggle over the key point of contention—restricting tribal sovereignty—deliberately built into the settlement, itself. Since it is the Settlement Act and its very language that puts the two participating entities *at loggerheads,* she saw an improvement in the fact they both beganreviewing the settlement, talking about its effectiveness, discussing ways in which it could work better, and considering whether it should be changed in one fell wholesale swoop or by stages.

It is a job that requires *consensus,* which has been the traditional Indian method for taking action. The language relating to municipalities, in Diana's words, was *a sore point from the beginning,* with the Indians believing their having the powers of a municipality to be an *addition* to their existing sovereignty under federal law, and the state regarding the municipal powers to be a *replacement* for any Indian sovereignty, except for "internal tribal matters," a term never solidly defined. Another post-loggerheads task considered by the commission was whether to redraft this section of the Implementing Act and add more examples of "internal tribal matters." For instance, the settlement law was rather definite on fish and wildlife matters. The Indians wanted to see a similar specificity with regulatory questions regarding air, water, and land. It was also noted that the federal act spoke more of preserving tribal cultures, and the Indians wanted to see this same emphasis in the state act.

Albeit a tiny quasi-governmental agency known, at best, to a mere handful of people in Maine, the Maine Indian State-Tribal Commission has served as a fulcrum for trying to balance the inconsistencies of a political solution to possibly the most far-reaching crisis in the history of the State of Maine. That event, which technically ended with the flourish of Jimmy Carter's quill pen, happened more than two decades ago and, so it now seems, was no more than another truce in a complicated Indian-non Indian warfare that has persisted for nigh onto four centuries. The battlefields are different now—they are not the deep woods and the edge of settlement, but the courthouses and the media—where one side—the State of Maine—sees an end of conflict, and the other side—the tribes—sees ongoing restlessness and disenchantment.

But at least within the frail body of the MITSC, kept alive all this while despite the pessimism of its chairman in 1988, talks *can* take place, even when war clouds loom. Nor have Maine's Indian-non Indian relations been all doom and gloom. Progress happens, and it will be well to explore that aspect, too, as we move into further examination of the post-settlement years.

NOTES

[1] Alvin Josephy, Jr., "New England Indians, Then and Now," in *The Pequots in Southern New England: The Fall and Rise of an American Indian Nation*, Laurence M. Hauptman and James D. Wherry, Editors. Norman, Oklahoma: University of Oklahoma Press, 1990.

[2] Robert H. White, *Tribal Assets*. New York: Henry Holt and Company, 1990.

[3] Ibid, page 273.

[4] Kim Isaac Eisler, *Revenge of the Pequots*. New York: Simon and Schuster, 2001, page 81.

[5] Ibid, page 103.

[6] White, *Tribal Assets,* page 14.

21

AFTERMATH II

*T*o date in the Maine Indian Land Claims Settlement story, almost all focus has been on the Penobscot Nation and the Passamaquoddy Tribe. Brief mention was made that Congress included another Maine Indian group in the final legislation, namely the Houlton Band of Maliseets, who received funding of $900,000 and, at the same time, were recognized by the federal government, and in Chapter 15, a brief bit of their history was given. Since then, still another Maine Indian group has been added, the Aroostook Band of Micmacs, who gained federal recognition in November 1991 and who also received $900,000 in funding with which to buy land.

These two tribal "bands" are kin-based segments of far more populous tribes living farther north and east, mostly on reservations, in Canada. The Maine branches were the southernmost of their people, and the territory on which they roamed and hunted was primarily Aroostook County.

The Maliseets have six First Nation communities in Canada and only one, the Houlton Band, in the U.S. The term *band*, pretty much interchangeable with *clan*, is a label originally supplied by the Canadian bureaucracy in a legal document known as the Indian Act. Other names exist for the Maliseets as a whole. Throughout the history of the Down East Maine–Maritime region, we hear them referred to as the St. John Tribe, reflecting their close ties geographically to the St. John River. One of their own names for themselves is *Wolastoqiyik*, or "People of the Beautiful River." *Woloostook*, their term for that river, spawned *Aroostook*. Yet *Maliseet* is actually a Micmac word meaning one who talks slowly or incompletely, reflecting the way the Maliseet language sounds to a Micmac. Theirs is an Algonquin tongue nearly identical to Passamaquoddy (the *Pestomuhkatiyik*, or "People of the

Pollock-Spearing Place"), to whom they are first cousins, at the very least.

Among themselves, the Maliseets use the term *Skijin* ("The People"). One of the thoroughfares on their reservation outside of Houlton is Skijin Road, and I have seen a New Brunswick license plate with the lettering SKIJIN.

Like all northern Indians, the Maliseets relied almost exclusively on hunting and fishing for food and roamed over huge areas of land. Houlton, first settled by Americans in 1807, was a site on the Meduxnekeag River the Maliseets had frequented since time immemorial. When the availability of game diminished and a spur of the Canadian–Pacific Railroad reached Houlton in the 1870s and helped set off the boom in potato growing, Indian families began to stay in the town.

The long-time existence of their "Indian Reserve," west of the Military Road built to Houlton during the bloodless "Aroostook War" of 1839, became a major argument for including the Maliseets in the original Maine Indian Land Claims Settlement. Anthropologist James Wherry, in a 1979 paper he wrote for the Maliseets to buttress their claim, stated: "...governments in the United States have never established reservations for the Maliseet bands living in Aroostook County, yet this curious lacuna of government involvement in Indian affairs did not affect the conceptions of common folk who applied the term "Indian reservation" to the settlement of the Maliseet bands in Aroostook County."[1]

In the 1960s the Association of Aroostook Indians was formed as a joint effort of the Maliseets and Micmacs to improve their poverty-stricken conditions. The Houlton Band took the leadership role. One precipitating factor was the infamous "Pink Lady" incident in Houlton in which nine tribal members died from drinking canned heat mixed with Kool Aid. The local indifference toward the Houlton Indians was expressed by the editor of the *Houlton Pioneer*, explaining why he didn't give much coverage to a story that made headlines in other parts of Maine. "No big deal," he said, "it wasn't a concern.... If it had been white people, the whole town would have gone into mourning."

When, as Maliseet Chief Brenda Commander told me, the "Indian grapevine" picked up news of the Penobscot and Passamaquoddy claims against the State of Maine, the Maliseets decided to see if they could also be involved. A member of the Houlton Band, Fred Tomah, took part in the negotiations. In an interview with him, I asked how, against all odds, did it happen they were successful? Rather mysteriously, he answered: "We had connections getting federal recognition." Further questioning drew forth the names of U.S. Senators John Melcher of Montana and Daniel Inouye of Hawaii, important members of the Select Senate Committee on Indian Affairs, which was handling the Maine case. Inouye, the World War II Japanese-American war hero, was quoted by Fred as saying the State of Maine "had dirty hands" in this instance.

Once it was decided to include the Maliseets, a sticking point became whether or not the 5,000 acres they could buy with the $900,000 could be federal trust land and thus not subject to state and local taxes. On record is a letter to the Senate Committee protesting such a tax-free arrangement, allegedly sent at the suggestion of the attorney general's office in Augusta. A supporter of the Maliseets, on the other hand, anthropologist Willard Walker of Wesleyan College, charged that a plan to put the 5,000 Maliseet acres in severalty (i.e., individual ownership) was "an arrangement that, like the Dawes Act, would inevitably result in the return of the 5,000 acres to non-Indian ownership" if the Indians couldn't pay their taxes.

This particular bullet was dodged and so was the requirement—forced on the Penobscots and Passamaquoddy—of being juridically treated as simply another municipality in Maine.

Land was bought in Houlton—not without some opposition from the community, and in 1987 the Maliseets broke ground on a major facility to house their own government services. The band has over fifty employees, a number of them non-Indians. They presently own more than 800 acres and include in their real estate an income-producing housing project in Bangor, Maliseet Gardens, mostly for senior citizens. In one instance, when Houlton voted down a bridge in their part of town, the Maliseets built it and then had a battle over whose name it would bear, a local farmer's or one of their own.

Despite having been accepted in the Land Claims Settlement, the Maliseets were not made members of the Maine Indian Tribal–State Commission, nor do they have a representative in Augusta. A bill in the Maine legislature to give them this same status did not pass in the year 2000. However, Brenda Commander insists, "We do not give up easily, but just keep plugging away," and still feels a sense of progress compared to her people's plight before the settlement and federal recognition.

The Micmacs in Maine (they often use the phonetic spelling of Mik'maq, which they prefer) are not concentrated in a single community, as the Maliseets are in Houlton. Some members of their band do live in Houlton, but others are in Caribou, Fort Kent, and especially Presque Isle. They were denied inclusion in the Land Claims Settlement precisely because, at the time, they had no documentation to prove their claim to Maine land. The signing of that agreement in 1980 was, for them, "a day of agony and frustration," and, moreover, it also signalled an unwanted break with the Maliseets and the demise of the Association of Aroostook Indians. Worse still, since the settlement mandated the end of the Maine Department of Indian Affairs, they lost what few benefits they got from the state.

Treated like *off-reservation* Indians, living in shacks and trailers in scattered locations around "The County," the Maine Micmacs, in their lives of "fierce independence," had terrible statistics: 75 percent unemployment rate, 95 percent school drop-out rate, 70 percent alcoholism rate, 68 percent of families in poverty, and an average life expectancy of forty-five years.

Beginning in 1985 the Aroostook Micmac Council petitioned the U.S. government for federal recognition. Three years later the BIA replied "they were not in a position to respond to the [Micmac] petitions at this time." Helping the band in their efforts were Dutch-born anthropologist, Harald Prins and his writer-teacher wife Bunny McBride, the Pine Tree Legal Assistance office in Augusta, and a Washington, D.C., law firm. Prins and McBride had been asked to research the gap in knowledge that had left the Aroostook Band out of the Maine Land Claims Settlement—a process that took them almost ten years. McBride has described how she and her husband would get up at 4:00 A.M., leave their Hallowell home, and four hours later arrive in Aroostook County. "We'd stay for two or three days, working deep into the night, sleeping on a foam mattress on the office floor. We each took home $80 a week. We spent a lot of time with the Micmacs in their homes, sometimes overnighting with them."[2]

Their persistence eventually paid off, even after the initial defeat of their first bill in Congress. On November 26, 1991, at long last, the Aroostook Band of Micmacs were granted official federal recognition. There were rumors beforehand that President George H. W. Bush might veto the measure, but eventually he signed it. The Micmacs, too, received $900,000 to enable them to buy land.

Despite the sparseness of their population in Maine, the Micmacs form one of the largest aggregations of Indians in North America—some 25,000 strong. In Canada, where the term for tribal groupings is "First Nations," the Micmacs have twenty-eight separate entities spread over four provinces (Quebec, New Brunswick, Nova Scotia, and Prince Edward Island). Their language is Algonquin, but fairly different from the Abenaki speech of the rest of Maine's Indians, containing influences of Cree and Montagnais. In Aroostook it is estimated that 44 percent of the Micmacs speak the native tongue as a first language.

That was certainly the case when I went to visit Micmac elder Bernard Jerome and his wife Ramona at their home in

Presque Isle. Although both were fluent in English, they felt much more comfortable using Micmac when they spoke to each other. Bernard explained there were two dialects in the Micmac language. Since he originally came from the Gaspé Region in Quebec Province, the French had influenced his use of his own language, while Micmac bands in Nova Scotia and New Brunswick were influenced by the English over the past several hundred years.

Many of the Micmacs in Aroostook County originally had come from the Canadian provinces, as he and his wife had. Although largely congregated in Houlton, Caribou, and Presque Isle, there were "clusters" in the small towns of Easton, Limestone, Stockholm, New Sweden, and Bridge-water. Following the Micmac Settlement Act of 1991, a new criterion for membership in the Aroostook Band was that a person had to have been born in the United States, thereby obviating the danger of a rush of immigration from Canada to take advantage of the band's federal recognition under U.S. law.

Of the $900,000 the band received to buy land, not all had been spent, Bernard told me, in discussing how things had changed since the settlement. Their first purchase had been a place he called Spruce Haven on the Doyle Road between Presque Isle and Caribou, where they built a community building; other parcels acquired were 80 acres and 100 acres in Caribou and 110 acres in Littleton. This was a long way from the 5,000 acres they were entitled to buy.

"We never rush into things," Bernard remarked.

One had the impression of a highly conservative people, made somewhat nervous by sudden good fortune. Bernard emphasized that a Micmac child born in Aroostook in 1991 would still have a lot of traditional values in his or her life. "The *Micmacness* will come out," he said, "and not a reservation mentality, but a broader understanding." These days, the opportunities for that child would not be limited to making baskets, picking potatoes, or doing perpetual manual labor. Young Micmacs are going to the university, the high school drop-out rate has diminished, living conditions have improved. "The world is opening up. We now have options."

A clever if oblique approach to the perennial problem of alcoholism is also being tried out on Micmac youth. Although, as Bernard expressed it, many are "caught at an age, not sure what to believe," they have an interest in traditional drumming, but in order to participate in ceremonies, they have to be off alcohol and/or drugs for four days. Otherwise, they will spoil the purity of the ceremonies.

One of the new Micmac ceremonies, held close to home at Spruce Haven, is the celebration each November 26 of the day the Aroostook Band received its U.S. government recognition.

Clearly, the post-settlement transitions of the four Indian groups in Maine seem, at a cursory glance, to have been positive. At least as compared to the past, they are generally acknowledged to be so. The Indians are out from under their utter dependency on the State of Maine, as in the case of the Passamaquoddy and Penobscots, or from the petty tyrannies of municipal general assistance directors, which was the last recourse of the Maliseets and Micmacs. The Hiram Halls are gone. Even those Aroostook peoples, less than 1,000 in number, run their own small governments and the two bigger tribes run operations as complex as many a good-sized municipality.

It is a bit ironic, therefore, that the most contentious uproar to date in the post-settlement period has derived from the very fact the Penobscots have their own Department of Natural Resources and it measures water quality, especially in the Penobscot River. Their fight with the state over jurisdiction has resulted in litigation going all the way to the U.S. Supreme Court (which declined to take the case). Demonstrations, marches, Indian defiance, threats of jailing, etc., kept the issue in the headlines in a fashion not seen since the days of the Land Claims Settlement controversy.

On occasion, this dispute has been referred to under the acronym of NPDES, which stands for the letters of a federal environmental program, the National Pollutant Discharge

Elimination System, administered by the U.S. Environmental Protection Agency. The trouble began when the EPA in Washington began an effort to turn its duties of regulating discharges over to the states, thus avoiding duplication of permitting for dischargers. The Penobscots' agency, their Water Resources Program, which had worked nicely with the feds, was opposed to having Maine's Department of Environmental Protection assume sole responsibility. They said they feared the state group might be too close to the powerful paper companies, who discharge into the Penobscot, and thus not as tough as the EPA.

Their opposition had an effect. The EPA, on the verge of transferring its powers to the state, reversed course and decided to keep operating NPDES in Maine. Governor Angus King was reportedly livid at the news.

A counterattack was waged with the paper companies in the vanguard. On the grounds the Penobscots and the EPA had been conspiring in secret, attorneys for Great Northern, Georgia–Pacific, and International Paper went to court under a *Maine* statute—the Freedom of Access (to information) Law—and demanded to see records of all communications between the Indians and the EPA.

"No way," the Penobscots responded. "That's an *internal tribal matter* under the Settlement Act. We do not have to comply."

But Judge Robert Crowley of the Maine Superior Court did not accept their reasoning. *Turn over the documents or go to jail,* he told the tribal leaders, who now included the Passamaquoddy chiefs. Furthermore, until his ruling was followed, each tribe would be fined $1,000 a day. The one caveat was that the jail terms and fines would be suspended if his decision were appealed to the state supreme court.

In response Barry Dana, the Penobscot's young governor, holding up a bottle of yellowish water taken, he said, from the Penobscot River that morning, dramatically declared: "The paper companies don't want our documents.... They're after the continued right to pollute the river."

May 2002, Maine Indian protestors marching to Augusta at the
climax of their fight with the state and the paper companies
over water cleanup and sovereignty issues.
COURTESY OF DONALD SOCTOMAH

The paper companies had pleaded just as vociferously. "The Penobscot Nation argues we will not be allowed onto Indian Island to review records. This position is unacceptable and not in compliance with the requirements of the Maine Freedom of Access Act...." They'd also condemned "an effort by the Maine tribes to assert environmental authority, both inside and outside of their territories."

The latter point had led the state, through its attorney general's office, to enter the case on the side of the paper companies. Assistant Attorney General Bill Stokes said Maine was "concerned with distinctions about 'internal tribal matters' that could figure in future relationships between the tribes and the state"; i.e., the old bugaboo about the key, ambiguous clause in the Settlement Act.

"They do have sovereign power," Stokes agreed. But the courts would decide how extensive or how limited that power would be.

In challenging the paper companies' complaint that they were being kept off Indian Island, the Penobscots' lawyer, Kaighn Smith, mounted a strong defense. Smith contended that any action by the paper companies to obtain tribal records might involve the ransacking of tribal computers, the rifling of tribal files, etc., and that such action would constitute *an outright invasion* of tribal sovereignty. The argument was so effective that the opposing lawyers pulled back, denying an intent of "entry into the tribes' reservations" and requesting only to have the available documents brought to them "at a location of the tribes' choosing."

The state supreme court sanctioned this supposed compromise; however, in upholding Crowley's ruling, all action against the tribes was again stayed until they could appeal to the U.S. Supreme Court.

After that route failed, and Crowley's ruling still prevailed, a further attempt, orchestrated by Governor King, sought accommodation. The spectacle of Indian leaders being jailed in Maine for promoting cleaner water was hardly one the governor relished.

An agreement literally was in the works when, on May 11, 2002, the Penobscots and Passamaquoddy stunned their counterparts in Maine government by announcing they were pulling out of the negotiations. They would turn over the documents.

Almost two weeks later, they did—with a colorful and attention-getting flourish. A two-day march to the statehouse in Augusta symbolically started thirty-three miles away at Norridgewock, the site of the famous massacre of their fellow Abenakis in 1724. Drumming, chanting, flying tribal flags, some fifty tribal members marched along the Kennebec River and reached the capitol moments before the court order's deadline expired. A gathered crowd of their compatriots and supporters cheered Barry Dana when he still insisted, "We are not municipalities!"

Since those documents were handed over, nothing more has been heard of them. Their use as a ploy to interpret the tribes' sovereignty under the Implementing Act has passed into the law books and merely joins a body of decisions, such as the earlier *Penobscot Nation v. Fellencer* case, in which the tribe's sovereign power to fire a non-Indian employee, despite

Maine law, was upheld. The grey area of opposing views on the powers delineated in the settlement remains as confusing as ever, and the NPDES stalemate has not been totally solved.

"At loggerheads," to be sure, is one condition prevailing in tribal–state relations in Maine—the one that gets most head-lines—yet positive elements *are* in the public mix. The legisla-ture, itself, in this regard seems light years ahead of where it was when I was there in the 1970s and '80s.

For example, Passamaquoddy Representative Donald Soctomah put in a bill to expunge the word "squaw" from place names in Maine because it is offensive to Indian sensi-bilities. Protests immediately mounted, above all in the Greenville area where *Squaw Valley* is a well-known local ski area and resort. It seemed an amazing shock to some non-Indians that among Indians the word has assumed a highly pejorative connotation, referring to a female sex organ, and has often been hurled at their women as an insult. Arguments by opponents that *squaw* was a perfectly harmless word fell on deaf ears, since they failed to produce in person the Indians they had quoted saying it was innocuous. The bill passed over-whelmingly.

An event *far more of a first* in Indian relations for Maine government took place on March 11, 2002. On special occa-sions joint sessions of the house and senate are held in the statehouse, the most hallowed being the state governor's annual appearance to deliver the "State of the State Address." Nowadays, too, the chief justice speaks on the "State of the Courts," and the chancellor of the University of Maine System on the "State of Public Higher Education."

To this prestigious list, that March 11, 2002, reputedly as the inspiration of House Speaker Michael Saxl, was added the "State of the Tribes Address to the Joint Session of the 120th Legislature." The newspapers rightly called the event "historic."

So did the legislature in a resolution it passed "recogniz-ing" both this gathering and the Wabanaki people, specifying the *Passamaquoddy Tribe*, the *Penobscot Nation*, the *Houlton*

Band of Maliseet Indians, and the *Aroostook Band of Micmacs* as playing "a vital role in the life of the state" and existing as "an integral part of the social, economic, and legal fabric of the state...."

Such events always contain a certain pomp and pomposity. Elaborate language is used, the gathering of both legislative bodies formally orchestrated, delegations sent to invite the guest speakers—in other words, as much fanfare as is ever seen in Maine. The appearance of the Indian leaders on March 11 not only brought such tokens of respect, but fairly electrified the staid chamber when they arrived in their native dress (the real thing, not western war bonnets). Symbols of tribal culture were much in evidence throughout the proceedings—a wampum belt made of quahog shell, an ornate peace pipe, plus eagle feathers waved during the opening prayer and the Penobscot chief's speech.

A past Penobscot representative, Butch Phillips, gave the prayer to open the event. Phillips intoned a traditional Indian blessing: "Creator, we thank you for many gifts. Mother Earth, lands, birds, fish...." He waved his eagle feathers. "For ancestors, precious families, bringing together leaders of these two governments...."

The three tribal governors who followed him with speeches picked up on the theme of environmental quality implicit in Phillips's prayer—not unintentionally, either, since the fight with the state and the paper companies was then in full bloom. Nor were these Indian orations merely congratulatory that a historic occasion was taking place. Contemporary political content was packed into their words, which were laced with trappings of cultural difference as sharply contrasting as the Indian costuming and symbolic insignia were to the plain Yankee décor of the statehouse surroundings.

"*Aguwan psite yu wen ehyit,*" Chief Richard Stevens of Indian Township started off in Passamaquoddy, saying, "Good day to everyone who is here," as he held up his wampum belt. "In my culture holding the wampum belt is the most significant sign of truth. When a person speaks while holding the

Former Penobscot Representative Butch Phillips gives a traditional Indian blessing before the first State of the Tribes Address, held in the House of Representatives Chamber, March 11, 2002. PHOTO COURTESY MITSC

wampum belt he speaks from the heart and speaks the truth."

Delving into history, Stevens admitted the state had not always treated the tribes well, "but we are still here and we are a part of Maine." And they had been around for 12,000 years, he emphasized, his ancestors having seen the retreat of the ice age and the last of the woolly mammoths.

Then, to press his point, there was the *current* "State" of his "Tribe" at Indian Township—not good, with unemployment close to 50 percent and an average life expectancy of only forty-eight years—and this despite having made, as he said, "great strides in the past four years because of the willingness and desire of this legislature and the people of this great state to work with the tribes."

Tribal Governor Richard Doyle, the Passamaquoddy leader at Pleasant Point, pulled no punches at all. Showing his elaborately decorated peace pipe, he said, "I'm here to make peace," and then flat out declared the 1980 Settlement Act "a failed experiment" since it had not settled questions of tribal jurisdiction. Wading into the fight over river-discharge regulation, he harped on fish that were unsafe to eat, declared the duty of the tribes was to protect water quality, and defiantly

Drummers join in at the Hall of Flags, after the first State of the Tribes Address, March 11, 2002. PHOTO COURTESY MITSC

proclaimed, "If I must be in prison, so be it. My people will be forever."

The final speaker was Barry Dana, *sagamore* or chief of the Penobscots. "I am a Penobscot," he began. "I am a human being of the Penobscot River." Much of his talk was given over to the importance of that river to his people. The Wabanaki legend of its creation was repeated for this distinguished audience—how Glooskap smacked Oglabamu, the greedy giant frog who had sucked up all the region's water, and thus released the streams that now course through Maine. He spoke of the Penobscots' canoeing their river to go to Katahdin, their sacred mountain, travelling its bounds between Millinocket and Searsport, gathering medicinal plants on its banks, praying for the return of salmon to its waters, protecting the eagles, turtles, dragonflies, "our relations," that inhabited it, and working for the day when their children could once again eat all the fish out of it they wanted and not be scared off by warnings of pollution. "It is time to unlock the chains of fear since the settlement," he concluded.

The frank rhetoric notwithstanding, the event, itself,

concluded in a spirit of friendliness and sheer excitement that such an occurrence had transpired in Maine. Everyone went together to a special lunch provided in the statehouse Hall of Flags, where booths set up by Indian groups distributed information.

Even a usually cynical reporter for the Portland newspaper had to conclude: "In the end, however, it was the unprecedented nature of Monday's speeches and the way in which tribal leaders presented themselves to the legislature that left a lasting impression on those who witnessed the event."[3]

It was impossible not to glean a sense of some progress from the materials offered that afternoon. Copies of the *Wabanaki Legislative Update* were available (this publication, itself, is an innovation since I served in the house) and the earliest of the issues carried a two-page spread of photos from "Wabanaki Day" at the statehouse in 1999, which put the tribes now on a par with other Maine groups that organize efforts to tell their stories firsthand to the lawmakers. Both tribal representatives, Donald Soctomah (Passamaquoddy) and Donna Loring (Penobscot), were upbeat in their assessment of their accomplishments in the previous session. The big news of the 119th Legislature was the passage of the Offensive Names Bill, and Donna Loring was also pleased with a resolution honoring Wabanaki women. She had high hopes, too, for a bill she was sponsoring to mandate Maine Indian education in grades K–12 throughout the state. Donald Soctomah saw another bright spot in an archaeological project at Meddybemps in Washington County where cooperation between state, federal, and private agencies and the Passamaquoddy proved effective. In the same vein, a bill was passed to study threats to Maine Indian archaeological sites and to create legislation for their increased protection.

In their 120th Legislature report, the two Indian representatives had even more important news to announce. The Native Education Bill had passed—no mean feat when there is a longstanding tradition in Augusta of opposition to mandating new programs for the state's local schools. Donna

A legislative resolution has stipulated that the Maine State Museum shall include portraits of outstanding Indians for public display in the Statehouse. Maine State Museum *Chosen for the first four are (clockwise from upper left):*
SOPIEL SELMORE *(c.1800–c.1900), of Pleasant Point and Perry, was the Passamaquoddy "Keeper of the Wampum Records." He was the last traditional wampum belt reader and a tribal spokesman.Around his neck he's wearing a Wampum belt used in tribal diplomacy.*
JEREMIAH BARTLETT ALEXIS *(1854–1930) was also known as Jerry Lonecloud in his "Wild West Show" performances. A member of the Aroostook Band of Micmacs, he was born in Belfast, Maine, and died in Halifax, NS.*
VIVIAN F. MASSEY *(1927–1998) was the first woman Penobscot Nation Representative to the Maine State Legislature. She also served on the Penobscot Tribal Council, as Tribal Clerk, and on the Indian Education Advisory Board.*
TERRANCE (TERRY) CLAYTON POLCHIES *(1941–) was the first Tribal Chief of the Houlton Band of Maliseet Indians, 1979–82), helped gain U.S. federal recognition for the tribe, and served as its chief during the Land Claims Settlement period.*

Loring called it "the most comprehensive bill enacted on Indian history in the country" and said she had received requests from other states interested in copying it. A Maine Native American History and Culture Commission was established by the law to help prepare for the introduction of these courses, and among the handouts in the Hall of Flags was a list of those on this Wabanaki Study Commission, with appointees from the four tribes, the Maine Department of Education, and the University of Maine.

The university, with an active Native American Studies program on its Orono campus, had brochures promoting its course offerings. The program is open to all students, while a Native American Scholarship program is offered primarily to members of the four Maine Indian groups. They are buttressed by a Wabanaki Center that works closely to support these Indian students. Special mention was made in the material of success stories, like that of Betsy Tannian, a fifty-six-year-old Penobscot mother, who went to college at UMO after her children were grown, and who had just won a highly competitive Morris K. Udall Native American Congressional Internship; and like that of Passamaquoddy Gail Sockabasin, who was on a fellowship from the Kellogg Foundation Leadership Program, studying language immersion, for which she had travelled to Hawaii, a state known for its success in restoring a native tongue.

On the University of Maine table was also a flyer advertising that "American Indians at UMaine" were sponsoring a charitable race, the "Fiddlehead 5K Run/Walk," exhorting students to "Run for Indian Education."

What a change from the old days, I couldn't help thinking, no matter what strains and difficulties lay ahead.

NOTES

[1] James Wherry, *The History of the Maliseets and Micmacs in Aroostook County, Maine.* Preliminary Report, No. 2, June 1979. Prepared for the Association of Aroostook Indians.

[2] Edgar Allen Beem, *Boston Globe Sunday Magazine,* 3 June 2001.

[3] *Portland Press Herald,* 12 March 2003, pages 1B and 3B.

22

―

LOOKING AROUND I

Six months prior to the epochal *State of the Tribes* event in Augusta, the emphasis placed on the Penobscot River by Chief Barry Dana naturally took center stage when the Fourth Annual Maine Rivers Conference was held at Indian Island. The Penobscot Nation hosted the meetings, which were held in the gigantic Sockalexis Bingo Palace. This huge, aluminum-sided building doubled as a community center, but its major purpose was loudly broadcast in its signage: "HIGH-STAKES BINGO" and in a proud boast: "THE ORIGINAL INDIAN BINGO."

Inside its cavernous space, one noticed how all of the light fixtures were shaped like dream catchers, those net-filled circles that are now an undifferentiated universal symbol of North American "Indian-ness." Large, real dream catchers, decorated with feathers and furs, were hung on the walls, along with bingo posters announcing events like "FALL FESTIVAL BINGO" and specialties like the "PATRIOT GAME," using stars-and-stripes flag symbols to cover cards (the conference, by the way, was taking place the weekend after September 11, 2001).

Across from the Bingo Palace, large-scale construction was in evidence. This turned out to be a $1.4 million Tribal Office Facility, financed by the Rural Housing Service of the U.S. Department of Agriculture. Next to the Bingo Palace, itself, was a modern sewage treatment plant and a little beyond that, a handsome school complex. On the surrounding black iron fence was a poster in red and yellow, declaring the area an "ALCOHOL AND DRUG-FREE SCHOOL ZONE."

Some of the environmentalists who had flocked to the conference from all over Maine commented on that austere fence, which gave a prison-like quality to an otherwise attractive setting. Barry Dana wryly explained their first superintendent, a lady "who was very strict," had insisted upon it.

The Penobscot chief, a trim, black-haired, intense man in his forties with a pony-tail, was the welcoming speaker and also an important participant in the proceedings. It was, perhaps, no accident that the conferees were coming to Indian Island. The NPDES fight was raging and here were potential allies in Maine's white environmental community.

While, in one way, Barry was simply "preaching to the choir," in another way, he did present a fresh approach, one I hadn't heard as such in similar gatherings. His topic on the first panel was "Spiritual Connections: People and the River."

After having introduced us to the "small but very unique and talented Penobscot Nation," he launched into *his* people's connection to the river, the problems of connecting biology and spirituality, "struggling with western science" and translating concepts of Indian ideology such as "The people are the salmon, and the salmon are the people."

This sense of "spirituality" was illustrated in an ineffable manner by an almost "shaggy dog" story (i.e., one without obvious meaning) that Barry told. It had to do with a group of non-Indians who had come to seek "spirituality" among the Native Americans and were put to work scraping a hide with the idea of making a drum. After a while they became impatient and asked, "When are we going to talk about spirituality?" At the end of the day, when the drum was done and the disappointed whites still wanted to talk spirituality, it was revealed to them that the process they had just gone through—the manufacturing of the drum—was an *example of spirituality*—that "native spirituality connects with everything we do," Barry said.

He talked about his youth, growing up on Indian Island, fishing, swimming, and—heavily underscored by his tone of voice—eating fish—all activities in the once far more pristine Penobscot. This was an entrée to the problems with today's river—the warnings on consumption of the river's fish, the dioxin count in the sediment at Lincoln Island, the unsightly stain at the outfall of the Lincoln Pulp and Paper Company— and right into the controversy raging with the big paper companies—plus a bit about the Penobscots' trek every Labor Day, paddling sixty-five miles upriver and then running to Katahdin, as a "symbol of conviction" for maintaining tradition in today's lifestyle. "Our whole life was drawn from the river," Barry summed up.

After adding it was "very encouraging to be in a room with people who are of the same mind," the young-looking chief said, with a deprecating smile, he had just talked twenty minutes longer than he ever had in his life.

The Penobscot wasn't the only river discussed that September day. April Francis, a Passamaquoddy, talked to us about the St. Croix, which stood in the same relationship to her people as the Penobscot did to Barry Dana's. It, too, had become a dumping ground for toxins, and her people wanted it back to its pristine state of 120 years ago, when it was called the Schoodic. And other river systems, like the Saco and Presumpscot, with no direct present-day tribal connections, were discussed, although in the case of the latter stream, it was noted that Chief Polin, a Pequaket, had in the eighteenth century walked to Massachusetts to plead with the general court to protect its fish. A prime goal of the Friends of the Presumpscot was to remove some of the dams that now clogged the waterway. Barry Dana had also made it plain he wanted to see the Penobscot dam-free.

Another river system environmental group—the Meduxnekeag River Watershed Coalition—represented a merger of Indian and non-Indian support for water cleanup in the Houlton area. Its director had begun her work doing baseline studies of the river for the Houlton Band of Maliseets, and the tribal role in watershed protection is a strong component of the overall effort.

Later that day, we went out with Dan Kusnierz, the manager of the Penobscots' Water Resources Program, to look at a pollution site. At Costigan, an above-ground gasoline leak had spilled into the river. According to Dan, it had been discovered by Mike Bear, a Penobscot sub-chief and avid fisherman, who had smelled gas and noticed a sheen on the water. The

Maine Department of Environmental Protection was alerted, but they said it was marsh gas and when John Banks, Dan's boss, said nonsense, the state officials allowed it might be spillage from a motorboat. The Penobscots kept investigating, however, until a leaking pipe from a nearby gas station was unearthed.

Starting in mid-May and lasting until mid-October, Dan said, his office did a lot of monitoring of the river—100 sites—testing for e-coli, measuring temperatures, dissolved oxygen, color, pH, turbidity, plankton blooms, mercury, dioxin—pretty sophisticated stuff, and they shared their findings with the state DEP, which didn't do much monitoring, he added. Warnings, like those about not eating fish, were posted publicly by the Indians, and we saw them right at the roadside rest-stop in Costigan next to the site where the gasoline leak had occurred.

Back at the Bingo Palace in the evening, we conferees were introduced to other aspects of modern-day Penobscot life. Several videos were shown and the most fascinating was one filmed in 1992, "The Year of Indigenous People," when a group of young Penobscot canoeists travelled to Alaska with a 27-person war canoe and paddled against 8- to 10-mile-an-hour currents upstream from Athabaskan village to village, averaging 35 miles a day, connecting with the local Indians whose native language was totally different from theirs. This *Journey into Tradition* was for the Penobscot youth a new version of their annual sacred run and a symbolic re-connection with ancestors in a "land bigger and more enormous" than many of them had anticipated. It was a way, too, of showing western Indians the great canoe skills developed by their eastern brethren. The mixing of native cultures was reciprocal, with the locals introducing the visitors to their famous "potlatch" gift-giving ceremonies. The greatest challenge for the Penobscots was said to have been adjusting to Athabaskan food, like whale fat.

Several subsequent trips of mine to Indian Island helped round out a snapshot in time of the Penobscots at the beginning of the twenty-first century. The new Tribal Office Facility hadn't yet opened so my first meeting with Barry Dana took place in an older building adjacent to the Sockalexis Bingo Palace. The name Sockalexis was enshrined here, too, in a wall plaque dedicated to the famed athletic Sockalexis brothers—Louis, the fabled Cleveland Indians baseball player, and Andrew, a champion runner—both of whom were inducted into the American Indian Athletic Hall of Fame.

Other items catching my eye were paintings on the walls by Barry Dana, himself, and by the seemingly ubiquitous ssipsis (Eugenia Thompson). Hers were cutout figures in an arresting, distinctly Indian style, one of them of Grandmother Moon. Examples were displayed, too, of a Penobscot handicraft I had seen—and greatly admired—when visiting the small Indian Island museum: canes whose carved handles were beautifully sculpted warrior heads and faces, in full color.

Construction was going on inside here, as well—the conversion of a large interior space into a gymnasium, complete with basketball court, for the Penobscots' Boys and Girls Club, an organization Barry was promoting (he has children of his own). One tribal member we ran into was a tough-looking motorcyclist, whose daughter, Barry told me, had gotten her biker father to take an interest in the Boys and Girls Club.

With an eye to the language in the Settlement Act regarding *municipalities*, what might have been a discussion with the city council chair or head selectman in any Maine community was quite different here, despite some parallels. The job of overseeing the Penobscots' complex of governmental institutions did follow familiar civic paths to a degree, but only to a degree.

Right from the start there was a candid statement from Barry that the Penobscots paid no property taxes. The perennial problem of most local officeholders in Maine of preventing taxes from rising was thus transcribed into a broader but no less nail-biting worry of where does the money come from to keep the services going. More than in any Maine town or city, the federal government helps meet Indian Island's needs.

The $1.4-million grant from the U.S. Department of Agriculture to build the equivalent of a town hall was but one example. Since the BIA recognition of the tribe, funds now came from HUD for individual and congregate housing, from the U.S. Department of Education for schooling, from the Indian Health Service for medical care, from Health and Human Services for social and cultural programs, etc. Money from the bingo games also contributed greatly—obviously not a source available to any municipalities in Maine but, then again, the Penobscots receive precious little from the state—a mere $30,000—for the biggest of local expenses—school funding. The rest of their education dollars come from D.C.

Barry, who grew up on Indian Island, went to a two-room schoolhouse. Its replacement is as up-to-date and well-equipped as the finest elementary school in the state. But here, too, the difference is palpable, if subtle. The entire student body shares a single heritage that in the past it was taught to scorn. Today's goal, Barry said, is to encourage children to embrace the idea that it's all right to be Indian—to urge them, "Be proud of who you are."

Bringing back the Penobscot language has been a goal fostered by the Federal Administration for Native Americans. A language grant has been received from that agency, but the problem of restoring Penobscot is exacerbated in that most of the native speakers have died. Barry admitted he is "envious hearing the Passamaquoddy," who have done so much better in retaining their language.

The Penobscot School does have cultural programs for its students: drumming, singing, trapping, storytelling, and a three-day campout for the children. The preponderance of the teachers is still non-native (80 percent to 20 percent), but the school board, run by the Penobscots, makes every effort to hire its own where it can.

The difference in schooling from his day, Barry said, has been "huge." There is a large increase in the number of Penobscot youngsters going on to college. After grade school, the students can attend any high school they want; most of

Barry Dana, the dynamic young governor of the Penobscots, has achieved high recognition in Maine as a spokesperson for the Indian tribes on various contentious issues, from water quality to casino gambling.
PHOTO BY DAVID A. RODGERS

them choose Old Town, Orono, or the private Catholic school, John Bapst, in Bangor.

All the trappings of a modern education are now open to these Indian children, from Head Start to computer literacy, and they are taking advantage of it. To demonstrate his commitment, Barry organized at his own expense a celebratory dinner for Penobscot graduates, adults included, at the end of the school season, at which I was the guest speaker.

Economic development is an activity some Maine municipalities work hard at, while others scarcely bother to seek businesses. Although the Penobscots have been extremely proactive in trying to promote jobs for themselves and revenue for their communal coffers, the record has been spotty.

Barry told me with a rueful smile the Penobscots had first been offered the Dragon Cement deal that had made so much money for the Passamaquoddy and the blueberry operation still making money for their Down East cousins. "We haven't been smart," he said, but quickly added, "We haven't been too stupid, either." Their loan to the Pequots in Connecticut was successful, and revenues keep coming in from land they've bought in Maine—60,000 acres now in federal trust and some 70,000 in fee simple (on which they have to pay taxes). Disappointments have included the Schiavi Homes fiasco and, ultimately, after they nursed it along for sixteen years, the cassette-making plant at Olamon Industries on Indian Island.

The Penobscots continue to be entrepreneurial. Barry mentioned several potential projects in the works. One is to bottle water from a source on their Carrabassett property and another is the wind-power proposal of an Italian company, also to be located in western Maine.

A highly successful endeavor of theirs, I learned, was the Maine Indian Basketmakers Alliance, a cooperative for selling all-authentic Indian baskets made in Maine, spearheaded by Theresa Hoffman. It has a sales outlet on the main street of Old Town, on the way to the Indian Island Bridge.

Another project dear to Barry Dana's heart is to raise funds for a much-enlarged museum on the Island, one that will serve as a federally approved repository for Penobscot and other Indian artifacts found in the region. Fire protection is a must in this regard, he said.

We also talked about the Penobscots' Department of Natural Resources. The Penobscot Nation employs five game wardens to cover hunting and fishing on its properties, which are spread all over northern Maine—whole townships in the Carrabassett, Matagamon, and Mattamiscontis regions, and east of Lincoln, and up the Penobscot where all the islands above Indian Island belong to them.

This discussion naturally tailed off into the NPDES dispute, which at that time had not come to any resolution. Barry said he had gone to Millinocket to speak to the owner of Inexcon, the parent company of Great Northern, and found the man didn't even know his lawyers were suing the Penobscots. He also said the tribes wouldn't mind working with the state if the state would apply stricter water quality standards, such as how to measure the mixing zone discharge outlets; the state allowed up to 4.5 miles; the tribes wanted the toxins measured at the pipe egress. That was a deal-breaker, the state DEP allegedly had said.

The paper companies were likewise fearful the tribes might be delegated power to license their discharges, if the EPA kept its authority. Playing hardball, the paper companies had threatened they would only drop their case against the tribal leaders under the Maine Freedom of Access Law when the feds actually gave up their enforcement duties to the state. On top of this impasse, a possibly even bigger fight was about the tribes' jurisdiction over Penobscot River waters. The Indians contended their ability to enforce environmental quality also included the east and west branches of the river. The state said no, that the Settlement Act only stipulated the main stem.

While Barry claimed housing had improved significantly on Indian Island, they were now facing a common municipal problem in Maine—a housing crunch. They were simply running out of space as more tribal members sought to find housing on the reservation (Barry, himself, lives in the town of Solon). Even with some federal grants for new homes, there is no place on Indian Island to put them. The tribe has voted to buy land in nearby Argyle, but money is needed to develop the infrastructure, and the case would be the same if they tried to use Orson Island just upriver, which they already own. The problem of housing—particularly affordable, subsidized housing—was compounded by the fact Penobscot houses can't be mortgaged, since they must pass to the tribe, if sold. A tribal lending agency—the Four Directions Development Corporation—had been created to deal with this problem.

Barry Dana grew up in the '60s, participated in "Unity" gatherings of Indians in New York, Canada, Maine, and Oklahoma, and in other of that era's awareness-raising events in which Native Americans marched and agitated. He went to the University of Maine at Orono, received a B.A. in Education, studied forestry, too, then worked as a probation officer, using wilderness experiences as a means of dealing with troubled kids. His deep connection to nature stems in part from these earlier experiences.

Finally, I asked him about the Settlement Act and he spoke of tribal members, including his own mother, who had opposed it. One man, in particular, Dana Mitchell, claimed it was illegal and when, early on, the tribal authorities gave a per capita payment of $700 to each member, he refused to take it. Mitchell's argument was the settlement remained illegal as long as he didn't accept a per capita payment from it. Barry said some Penobscots cynically referred to the settlement as the "1980 Lawyers Employment Act." The goal now of the tribal chiefs, Barry said, was to amend it.

Re-elected in September 2002, Barry Dana had a former chief, Francis Mitchell, for an opponent, and one of the issues was Mitchell's promise of more per capita payments to tribal members. They were to come from money the tribe didn't have yet—from the profits of a proposed Indian gambling casino in Maine, an idea resurrected in sensational fashion after the Calais and Albany Township failures—and an issue to be discussed at length in a subsequent chapter.

Barry, who had told me of his opposition to earlier per capita payments, had made no mention of them in his announced platform, which was: "We have moved into a new era where relationship building is key to our success. If the state of Maine is going to recognize our sovereignty as a federally recognized tribe, if the voters of Maine are going to accept a tribally run casino, if the lawmakers will pass necessary legislation that honors our sovereignty and cleans up our rivers, then I must have your support and your vote to continue."

Maine Indian politics can be very volatile, but Barry Dana got his vote of confidence.

Running unopposed on that same ballot was Donna Loring, the Penobscot Nation's representative to the legislature.

Like Barry Dana, she, too, did not live on Indian Island. At one time, Donna had held the leadership of the Central Maine Indian Association, an organization formed to speak for Indians in Maine who had left their reservations. One of the first things I learned when I met her at her house in Richmond was that the Penobscots and Passamaquoddy handled this issue of residence differently. An off-reservation Passamaquoddy cannot vote in tribal elections. Penobscots can.

But Donna had grown up on Indian Island and, in answering my standard question about the settlement's effect, she dwelt first on her memories of life there beforehand. "Prior to the Land Claims, we didn't have a heck of a lot," she said candidly. No running water existed until the late 1960s or early '70s. She remembered carrying water in galvanized buckets on a pole and dumping "honey buckets," since there was no sewerage, either. Nor was there a bridge to the mainland until 1959.

When the river froze, the Penobscots would lay a sawdust path across the ice to the Old Town shore and go back and forth across it. In the spring, you took your life in your hands, she said. Walking over, you might suddenly hear a booming sound behind you. You'd turn and look and the ice was gone, then you'd "have to jump from ice keg to ice keg." The memory brought not a smile to the face of this petite, serious-looking woman whose erect bearing bespoke her service in the military and the years she spent as the police chief on Indian Island, but only a terse comment: "Having to live—having to live like that? C'mon, state of Maine. What's happening?"

Whereupon, she touched on the history of her people, that they were the first to come in contact with Europeans (going back to Verrazano, if not John Cabot) and, as she put it, "They [the Europeans] had the most time to assimilate us." With a trace of an ironic smile, she added, "It's a real miracle. We're still here."

Her view of tribal history was grounded on the critical fact that the Penobscots, generally ignored by the federal government, had been "taken over" by a state. Maine, as the successor to Massachusetts, had to assume its prior treaty obligations. "Without the mandate from Massachusetts," Donna said, "Maine could have done away with us." In defense of this rather harsh statement, she offered the infamous case of Malaga Island, a settlement mostly of African Americans and mulattos off Brunswick, Maine, literally demolished by the state in the first decade of the twentieth century, and its inhabitants forcibly removed to an insane asylum.

Donna's sensitivity to the position of other minorities in Maine and the country had been heightened by her position as coordinator of tribal, state and international relations and her work with Rachel Talbot Ross, a leading Maine African-American activist with whom she traveled to Vietnam and also met with South African officials. Outside of Maine, Donna has likewise been an Eleanor Roosevelt International Fellow, traveling to Chile under their auspices, and a Fleming Fellow of the Center for Policy Alternatives in Washington, D.C.

Such a wordly background and sophisticated connections, plus experience overseas in the army, adds a dimension to her role in the legislature. The derivation of this governmental arrangement for Indians, unique in the U.S., still remains a bit of a mystery, she conceded. Donald Socotomah had done some research on it, finding the Penobscots and their council had been in the habit of visiting governors, both in Massachusetts and Maine. Also, she mentioned the emissaries sent to the Caughnawaga Great Council Fire. The first documented Indian representative in Maine seemed to have been in 1823, and Donna thought they had existed even earlier; certainly they were meeting with the British prior to the Revolution.

As an aside, a piece of information I later discovered may be of pertinence in clearing part of the historic mist. In the Huntington Free Library's Wabanaki Collection, one of the documents, dated February 5, 1843, bears on the issue. In a letter sent from Augusta, presumably to the two tribes, signed by an Isaac Sanborn, he starts by writing about many complaints in the capital "from both whites and Indians because so many Indians come here as representatives." This was during a period when the Old Party–New Party division had

Donna Loring, the highly respected Penobscot representative to the legislature, who has also been the police chief on Indian Island, a military aide-de-camp to the governor with the rank of colonel in the Maine National Guard, and chair of the Maine Commission of Women Veterans.
JOSE LEVIA/LEWISTON SUN JOURNAL

erupted. Consequently, Sanborn continued, there was a petition at the legislature "...to restrict you to *one representative from the Quoddy tribe* and *one from the Penobscot tribe* and that they may be chosen by ballot as white men choose their representatives, and now brethren, we hope this will meet your approbation and that you will come together, all parties in good friendship next fall and choose one representative which will do all the business of your tribe here in good faith." (Emphasis mine.)

Donna, in providing me with historical background, referenced that Old Party–New Party split. She spoke of Joseph Nicolar, who had married Old John Neptune's daughter, and their two daughters, Florence and Lucy, the latter of whom had gone into show business, like Molly Spotted Elk, as Princess Watawasu, a celebrated singer. Then Donna brought into the story her own grandmother, a non-Indian, Hazel Curtis of Brownville Junction, disowned by her family for marrying an Indian, who, as a strong Baptist amid a basically Catholic population, had teamed up with "Lady Lucy" and other mavericks, including Lucy's sister, the pioneer agitator

Florence Nicola Shay, to push for Penobscot voting rights and, most of all, a bridge to the mainland. Their women's group drew *internal* opposition, however, once they promoted access to public schools off-island. They "got grief" from Catholics, Donna said, because of the Catholic Church's long monopolistic tradition of providing education to the Penobscots. Eventually, the legislature agreed to allow young Penobscots to attend non-Indian local schools, and just as eventually, Indian Island did receive its bridge.

But gains were few and far between in those pre-Land Claims days. Their struggle to receive federal help, in particular, ran up against opposition from already established "federal tribes," mainly in the West. The BIA's attitude was: "There's just so much federal money. You guys fight over it." And they did. Donna's solemnly pronounced opinion followed: "Prior to the Land Claims, it was not a pretty picture." Less than one-quarter of the people on Indian Island had houses. Now, they all enjoy federally financed housing and, although some Penobscots claim the Land Claims had nothing to do with it, she was sure those two elements—the Land Claims and federal programs—were "absolutely linked."

Yet the money from D.C. wasn't a pure panacea. All of the Land Claims dollars hadn't come to the Penobscots directly; only $12.5 million of their share hadn't had to be spent on land and, aside from a single per capita distribution, they had tried to use it to generate economic development. But they were not entrepreneurs, had no direct experience handling money and markets, had made some bad investments, but were learning, and now they had created their Four Directions lending institution, making loans to help start new businesses.

Although not part of our discussion, the proposal for expanding Indian gambling in Maine from high-stakes bingo to a Foxwoods-sized casino in the southern part of the state had already surfaced by then. Donna, I knew, supported the idea. Her thoughts on gambling per se had previously been made public in one of those reports she and Donald Soctomah issued periodically in Augusta at their own expense and concerned the Albany Township debate; her piece appeared under the heading: "Excerpt from My Legislative Diary" and was the story of the bitter clash over LD 2607, An Act Concerning Previous Passamaquoddy Indian Legislation.

The bill was actually a technical piece of legislation related to the Land Claims that added a small portion of land—eight acres—to territory owned by the Passamaquoddy in Albany Township, but it blew up into a fight over gambling because the Passamaquoddy revealed they intended to build a Super Bingo hall there. Opponents in the region contended this would be turned into a casino. Despite a 10–3 Ought Not To Pass committee report, the bill passed the house. Passage in the senate turned out to be a different matter.

"Saturday, April 8, 2000, was the day from hell," Donna wrote. "Not because we lost the Passamaquoddy bill in the senate but because we were treated so shabbily and degradingly. No citizen of this state should ever have to sit through such a verbally abusive attack as Representative Soctomah and I did. It was the hardest thing I have ever done to sit there helpless and listen to these self-righteous, pompous senators talk so degradingly about my people and gambling in the same breath...."

Many of the arguments made then, and in the same pejorative tone, were to be echoed in Maine two years later after the release of a far more explicit and extensive Indian casino gambling plan. The Albany Township debate presaged many of the same emotional elements. From her point of view, Donna came away with the feeling, "When the smoke had cleared, it was yet another Indian massacre."

Such strong feelings were exacerbated by the fact the debate had entirely skirted the "government-to-government" aspects of the issue. "The purpose of the bill was to complete the legislative process that the legislature, governor, and the Passamaquoddy Tribe had intended," she wrote. "The senators chose to focus on the gambling issue, not the government-to-government relationship that is a high legal priority. The obligation they have to a government-to-government relationship is far greater than Albany Township. Since when did a disorganized town or any town have the power to turn a treaty agreement between governments around?"

As for her *personal feelings* about gambling, she added: "Please understand when I say I am not pro gambling. It is mostly that I am for making native people economically self-sufficient. I certainly am not for making my people look like criminals just because we are desperate to find something that economically works for us." She then cited an attempt made in that very same session to get legislative help—a sales tax break—and how some of the very same senators who condemned them on gambling had shot them down on tax relief. She also listed the many bills dealing with already legalized gambling in Maine that had been handled that session.

Her *last words on the subject* included: "I heard a lot of mean-spirited, negative words during that senate debate and they were calculated to hurt and to criminalize. I left the senate chamber feeling personally attacked...."

"Don't criticize us. Don't criminalize us. We are just trying to survive."

Among other official positions held by Donna Loring is that of a military aide-de-camp to the governor, which carries with it the rank of colonel in the Maine National Guard. In addition, she is chair of the Maine Commission of Women Veterans. The patriotism of Maine's Indians is legendary, and that they can rise above the hurts they often feel inflicted upon them to rally around their fellow Americans is nowhere better exemplified than in a poem Donna composed and published in the *Tribal Representatives Legislative Update* right after September 11, 2001.

Entitled "Ten Thousand Eagles," it begins:

> Ten thousand eagles flew that day across the bright blue sky
> To meet the spirits on their way from fiery smoke filled tombs.
> They soared above the dark, black clouds
> Billowing from the earth and hovered for a moment there
> And saw the face of doom.
> Ten thousand eagles gathered and swooped down beneath the

clouds.

They found the spirits one by one and plucked them from their plight.

They carried each new spirit through the black and hate filled clouds...."

And ends:

May our spirits soar on eagle's wings above the dark black clouds
of hatred, murder, and revenge that keep us hatred bound.
Ten thousand eagles flew that day as all the world stood still.
The eagles flew above those clouds
Perhaps some day
We will.

Another Maine Indian woman leader is the appropriately named Brenda Commander, chief of the Houlton Band of Maliseets. Her directions, given to me over the phone, to the tribal band's government offices on the outskirts of Houlton were precise and easy to follow, and it wasn't her fault I first went to the wrong place. What misled me was the sign for SKIJIN RD. This was in typical wide, rolling Aroostook farmland—the heart of potato country—and at the end of Skijin Road was an extra-large white farmhouse, so I said to myself: *This must be it.* There were a few cars and some farm machinery around, some outbuildings, but, to my amazement after I'd parked and approached, the imposing structure was clearly empty.

Thank God for car phones. I was soon apprised of my error, drove down into a hollow, took a sharp left, and ended in a more modern-looking complex containing a two-story, two-sectioned building of log-cabin-style wooden construction, with a railed balcony, and a paved parking lot full of vehicles. The van next to me bore a tribal logo and the title Maliseet Health Department.

Inside the place was bustling with busy people. Brenda was located, and this dark-haired, friendly woman ushered me into her spacious office. Not surprisingly, it was full of Indian articles—a dream catcher, a tomahawk, stunning handmade baskets, a western headdress, a double-headed American eagle sculpture, framed pictures of children, and a shovel, emblematic of the first dirt dug on projects built by this obviously rejuvenated group of more than 700 Native Americans who had once lived in total obscurity amid the potato lands of central Aroostook County.

Brenda, who grew up in Houlton, was quick to admit that the inclusion of her band in the Land Claims Settlement and the resulting federal recognition had "helped tremendously."

We discussed that momentous breakthrough for the Maliseets at some length. One of Brenda's assistants, Sue Desiderio, joined us and I was made aware of (and later given a copy of) the extensive documentation put together by James Wherry, which the Houlton Band had presented the U.S. Senate as justification for being included—at the last minute—in the settlement. Brenda gave particular credit for this success to one of her predecessors as head of the band, Terry Polchies, and credit also to Fred Tomah and Aubrey Tomah, other tribal members, and—she made sure to mention—the support of the Penobscots and Passamaquoddy.

In talking to Brenda and Sue, one had the feeling that their people, prior to the Land Claims, had been a tight-knit minority, turned inward because of poor living conditions and the hostility, both implied and expressed, of the white community around them. They had large families, Brenda said. In her own household, she had six brothers and three sisters. Her mother stayed home to take care of them. And her mother's attitude was: "You don't have to go to school." Indeed, the local schools didn't expect much from Indian children nor pay much attention to them.

Sue, who was blonde, having had a mother who was half-Indian and a father who was full-blooded, added that a day didn't go by in her childhood without her father talking about the family's Maliseet heritage.

The official count of Houlton Band members was 743. They do an enrollment once a year. Newborns are registered. The criterion for membership is a direct lineal descent from

Brenda Commander, the popular chief of the Houlton Band of Maliseets, whose members have seen a considerable improvement in their status since the days when they were consigned to a "ghetto" near the town dump.
COURTESY OF BRENDA COMMANDER

original members of the band who were on the rolls at the time of the Land Claims Settlement in 1980.

James Wherry's report contained extensive genealogical material on the Houlton Maliseets, documenting the early twentieth-century ancestors of today's families, with surnames such as Tomah, Polchies, Bear, Sappier, Paul, Devoe, Joseph, Francis—some of which also occur among the Penobscots and Passamaquoddy.

Discussing those old days, Brenda thought families might have been organized in clans, but not with animal totems, as among the Penobscots. James Wherry refers to the anthropological concept of a *Deme* community—or, in his definition, "a group of individuals living in close proximity who would be related by a series of bilateral kinship relationships." This arrangement was symptomatic of the northeastern Algonquin tribes, he alleged.

Such scholarly language aside, the memories of Brenda and Sue were simply of family groups living together in a single vicinity and of activities then—and important still—like trapping, basket making, and collecting fiddleheads in the spring. Basket making, using pounded ash, still had a major impact, and Sue commented that until she went away from Houlton, she never realized how much she would miss the sound of wood being beaten into strips.

The 1980 settlement gave the Maliseet Band $900,000 with which to buy land. They have not rushed out to do so and, consequently, the $900,000 has grown to $2 million. But some parcels have been bought and developed, like the tribal office compound where we were meeting. Also, the land on Skijin Road and the abandoned farm, a place now reserved for storage while plans for its future are developed. On the other side of the bridge built across the Meduxnekeag River is their housing project, Maliseet Riverside Village, which now gave the tribe a permanent living space. Wherry's report had given a detailed history of the way in which the Maliseets in Houlton had been forced to move from place to place in the community.

At the tribal headquarters were offices for an entire array of services: health department, finance, education, natural resources, sanitation, social services, child care, food pantry, forestry, EPA liaison, and water quality—a mini-government of impressive breadth for so few people. They have some 800 acres to manage, day care, Head Start, a three-year language grant from the Administration of Native Americans to teach their children Maliseet and, obviously, they are light years ahead of where they once were when it comes to managing their own affairs.

As always, there were difficulties. One advantage, Brenda said, was not having municipal status and the complications it brought. But on the other side of the coin, they had no representative in the legislature, were not members of the Tribal–State Commission, and had not been invited to speak at the State of the Tribes event at the statehouse. This last statement was delivered tersely by Brenda with an open hint that a like omission would not be duplicated in the future.

The dispute between the Penobscots and Passamaquoddy and the State of Maine over controlling water quality was brought into our discussion. The Maliseets, too, have a quarrel with the state, although it has not yet made the headlines. The Meduxnekeag River runs right through their property and they feel they should have "concurrent jurisdiction" over its regulation. The state maintains it has "full jurisdiction."

This and other sore points have led to talks with the feds about the validity of the Settlement Act and the Maine Implementing Act. Apropos the State of Maine, Brenda said: "They feel they control us. We're saying, 'No, you don't.'" The Maliseets are seeking more sovereignty, more police power, a tribal court, etc. "Our leaders are told: 'You don't have any authority,'" Brenda complained.

Early on in our meeting, Brenda had told me I should talk to Fred Tomah, in part because he had been on the negotiating team that had worked out the Maine Implementing Act. It was arranged by phone I would go to see him as soon as I had finished speaking with Brenda and Sue. His background knowledge would help clarify for me the exact legal situation of the Houlton Band in an area of law and politics that is not only complex but frustratingly murky. "Be prepared to stay awhile," Brenda warned me when I was about to leave. "Fred loves to talk."

His was one of the houses at Maliseet Riverside Village. Built on a hill was a tract of single-family houses, resembling any modest suburban settlement in the U.S. Fred at once ushered me downstairs into his "work room," where he built the baskets on which "I earn my living," as he told me. There, we had a rambling conversation for several hours.

One key message he was trying to impart concerned a piece of state legislation finally passed in Augusta on April 13, 1982. Since I had been a member of the house then, yet had no recollection of it, I made myself a note to look the bill up later. When I did, the position of the Maliseets juridically came more into focus.

What seemed plain from that debate on LD 2076, An Act to Amend the Maine Implementing Act with Respect to the Houlton Band of Maliseets was that the tribe was entirely under state law. The bill's chief defender in the senate, Judiciary Committee Chair Senator Dana Devoe of Penobscot County, stated in emphatic terms the Maliseets had been given no sovereign powers in either the federal Settlement Act or the Maine Implementing Act. They could not even have a tribal judge or special fishing and hunting rights.

Behind LD 2076, which was really a clarification of the law, Devoe said, were "weeks and weeks and months and months of very hard negotiations between the Maliseets and the Maine attorney general's office." The thrust of the measure, co-sponsored by the two lawmakers from Houlton, a Democratic senator and a Republican representative, simply provided that if the Maliseets bought land in Maine, it could not become "trust land" under federal law, and not taxable, unless the local governing body approved; it also required a PILOT (Payment in Lieu of Taxes) fee be paid to the local body out of a $100,000 fund set aside within the $900,000 the Indians had received from the feds.

Ironically, this information only came to light in debates when first a house member and then a senator tried to kill what many people saw as an innocuous "housekeeping" measure. Had they done so, Fred Tomah probably would have been happy, although those two, Representative Edward Kelleher and Senator Andrew Redmond, had been two of the strongest opponents of the Settlement Act. Both were again unsuccessful here. I blush to say I was recorded absent on the roll call vote in the house, but assuredly I would have voted for the bill since it did have the approbation of the Maliseets, the governor's office, and bi-partisan majorities of the Judiciary and Taxation Committees.

It was hard, not being privy then to this knowledge, to follow Fred's tales of various land transactions—fights with Houlton and Littleton over taxes, trying to deal with a major problem Indian landholding has had all over the country—that if taxes on it can't be paid, it is "repossessed," so to speak, or "alienated" from the Indians by non-Indians. In any event, they lose their land, which is what all of this legal wriggling

Not only a savvy constituant, Fred Tomah is a skilled basketmaker and argues against a sales tax on Indian baskets: "You can't tax culture."
PHOTO COURTESY OF THE HOULTON BAND OF MALISEETS

around was meant to prevent, while at the same time assuring Maine town fathers they're not going to have land taken off their tax rolls completely should Indians buy it.

Legal wriggling around was very much the sense I had of what Fred felt about his experiences on the negotiating team that had devised the Maine Implementing Act. Obviously, he didn't much care for the final product. He complained of not having had any involvement "until it was in its final form." His voice filled with emotion as he vented his anger on Section 6204—"the knife that went through your heart." Subtitled Laws of the State to Apply to Indians' Lands, this section is a single, if run-on, sentence that declares: "Except as otherwise provided in this act, all Indians, Indian nations, and tribes and bands of Indians in the State and any lands or other natural resources owned by them, held in trust by them by the United States or by any other person or entity shall be subject to the laws of the State and to the civil and criminal jurisdiction of the courts of the State to the same extent as any other person or lands or other natural resources therein." Fred derisively called it "the cement that would forever protect Maine"—protecting it from a *"third-party interest,"* namely the aboriginal rights of the Indians, which the Maliseets had never given up, he said. Only the U.S. Congress could take those rights away. Since they hadn't done so in the federal act, the federal act and the state act were not in compliance as the law required them to be and therefore—although he put it as a question, "Can we kill the Maine Implementing Act?"—it was plain he would like to take that question to court.

It was an interesting session, there in Fred Tomah's basement workshop, with evidence of his traditional skill of basket making all around us, talking portentously of laws and legislation and legal maneuvers. What was perhaps implicitly more noticeable here than in previous discussions elsewhere, due to Fred's directness, was the restlessness beneath a status quo the Maine Indian tribes acknowledged to be treating them much better than in the past. Better, but not good enough.

This striving for improvement, I asked myself—was that something new in Maine Indian life, brought on by their success in the Land Claims, a subtle interjection of one of the values of their white neighbors? I thought of all the bills now introduced into the legislature by the Indian representatives each year. Fred Tomah had one he was promoting, himself. Take the sales tax off Indian baskets—"You can't tax culture," was his argument. Proudly, too, he told me how much in taxes the Houlton Maliseets paid the City of Bangor on their rental property—$80,000 a year. They were players. Another $5 million went into Houlton's economy.

If I hadn't known where I was, hadn't had access to the history of the Maliseets in Aroostook County, hadn't had Fred's baskets before my eyes, I might have thought I was back campaigning in southern York County with a savvy constituent who wished to talk issues about which he knew a lot more than I did.

My next interview took me forty-three miles north to Presque Isle. This part of Aroostook County has a different feel from the rest of New England. Geographically, I'm reminded of Nebraska by the rolling hills and wide open spaces. Culturally, we political cognoscenti in Maine call the stretch I was on "the Bible Belt," a section of Protestant fundamentalism evident in the many churches in the small towns—Littleton, Monticello, Bridgewater, Mars Hill—that succeed each other along Route 1. Except for the architecture, you might think you're in Tennessee. Presque Isle, once the home of a major air force base, is more of a melting pot, and a gateway to the upper reaches of the St. John Valley, an area nearly all Acadian French and Roman Catholic.

Religion was thus on my mind, at least subliminally, when I went to visit Bernard Jerome, the Micmac elder who had agreed to meet with me in the unavoidable absence of the Aroostook band's chief, Billy Phillips.

Bernard's wife Ramona answered the door, invited me in, and asked me to wait. Her husband was on his way home from Spruce Haven, she informed me, and though I had no idea then what Spruce Haven might be, my ears picked up when she mentioned that he'd been there cutting wood for the *sweat lodges*.

The very term, *sweat lodge*, was like a jolt to my imagination. I was sitting in a typical American home (the Jeromes's house was in a project of military housing, built for the air force, and later turned over to the tribal band) and, suddenly, my mind contained images of Indians somehow in the West, indulging in mysterious rites in special picturesque structures out on the plains. When Bernard arrived a few minutes afterward and we had a chance to talk, my mental picture changed considerably. Sweat lodges were pretty much universal among North American Indians and nothing was unusual about the

Micmacs having them in Aroostook County.

They are a mechanism for "healing and purification," Bernard told me, and operate much like a sauna, with water being poured on twenty-eight heated stones (representing the twenty-eight Micmac tribal bands) to create the steam inhaled by the participants. There is a healing lodge for every season and four separate ceremonies to commemorate those different parts of the year. Lodges may also occur once a week or at least twice a month. They afford an opportunity for Micmacs to pray to their ancestors or to the Creator. The construction is of a twelve-sided, dome-shaped building, eleven feet across, produced in a stylized manner from east to west and then north to south. In the old days, the frames were birch saplings; today, any wood available is used, Bernard told me, and he emphasized that before the wood was cut, an offering of tobacco was presented to Mother Earth. Their sense within a lodge was they were inside the womb of Mother Earth, being warmed by the sacred fire, and that the heat was a "new form of life," entering the body, bringing a "good feeling" to one's entire system.[1] This activity brings them a sense of relaxation, reduces anxiety, and allows people to "believe in themselves."

A courtly gentleman sporting a small, thin moustache, Bernard Jerome spoke with quiet enthusiasm about what was an important cultural and *religious* practice for his people, who were also nominally Roman Catholics, for the most part.

The two sets of beliefs, seeming to complement each other rather than clash, had been in existence since 1610, when the great Micmac chief, Membertou, had converted to Catholicism. One year later, in 1611, according to Bernard, the Micmacs actually concluded a treaty with the Pope, recognizing the growing influence of the Catholic missionaries in their midst. Not the least of the priests' power lay in their immunity from the diseases Europeans unwittingly imported—smallpox, plague, measles, etc., that killed off Micmacs on as large a scale as they did the other tribes in eastern North America. Since the shamans were helpless against these deadly outbreaks, they lost their influence.

Nevertheless, a sense of the supernatural imparted by native medicine men remains strong among present-day native people and these traditional ways are especially strong among Maine's Micmacs.

Bernard told a story about his own grandfather, off in the woods, hearing a crow calling and calling, then saying to his trapper companions, "Look, I've got to go. Something has happened in my household." Sure enough, after traveling sixty miles, he arrived home to find his son had died.

Bernard's mother was a devout Catholic, he said, but still she would tell that story.

Young Micmacs, he went on, are caught in an age where they don't know what to believe. Yet they seem most interested in their culture. While not as interested as the elders in the sweat lodges, they are strongly attracted to drumming, another mainstay of *spirituality* among native people, and some of these youngsters have traveled to ceremonial events in other states and in Canada.

Among the Micmacs, cultural programs for youth—like how to make a drum—are now conducted, exposing these young people to their own and other native traditions. A Micmac Interpretation Center contains stone tools, 6,000 to 7,000 years old, and, unique to the Micmacs, examples of that hieroglyphic writing first developed by a French priest, Father La Clerq, around 1690.

The Aroostook Band of Micmacs received its federal recognition from Congress in a document registered as Public Law 102–171, and dated November 26, 1991. It declared that the Aroostook Band, represented by the Aroostook Micmac Council, "is the sole successor in interest, as to lands within the United States, to the aboriginal entity generally known as the Micmac Nation which years ago claimed aboriginal title to certain lands in the State of Maine."

The law then stated the band had not been included in the Maine Indian Land Claims Settlement Act of 1980 "because historical documentation of the Micmac presence in Maine was not available at that time."

Once the appropriate documentation had been presented, thanks to the work of Harald Prins, his wife Bunny McBride, and others, this legislation was necessary to override the provision of the 1980 Settlement Act that extinguished all Indian claims in Maine, except for those of the Penobscots, Passamaquoddy, and Maliseets. Stating the Aroostook Band of Micmacs was similar "in both its history and its presence in Maine," to the Houlton Band of Maliseets, the law declared it "is now fair and just" to give the former the identical settlement as the latter. Then followed the same sort of complicated, legal dance spelled out between the federal Settlement Act, the Maine Implementing Act, and the Micmac Settlement Act that has rendered this whole business dizzyingly confusing to laymen. The upshot, in simple terms, was the Aroostook group received $900,000 to buy up to 5,000 acres of land, and became eligible for federal funds. Included in the bill, too, was the federal stricture that tribal members had to be U.S. citizens.

Had the change helped the tribe? Bernard Jerome, like his counterparts in other tribes, readily admitted there had been benefits. Certainly, more access to education and medical help was offered, and native people were gaining skills by administering the programs. Young Micmacs were going to the University of Maine, the high-school dropout rate was not as bad, and living conditions had improved.

What I didn't hear from Bernard was the usual, "But...." Quite possibly, he was too much of a gentleman to bring up negative points in a discussion with a stranger. The farthest he seemed to go in that direction was to say they "hadn't seen the full results yet," and "education was only starting to sink in." Bernard, in describing his people, emphasized their culture had evolved with changing environments, and during their long history they had always co-existed with others, intermarrying with other Indians and even non-natives and, as he put it, "molding ourselves on a daily basis." So he seemed quite laid-back, and not as anxious as some who had talked to me, about making overt changes to the present Maine Indian–state arrangements.

NOTES

[1] Micmacs do not go naked into the sweat lodges, Bernard Jerome told me; they wear shorts.

23

Looking Around II

or various reasons, eight months elapsed before I visited the Passamaquoddy. In a sense, it was like going to see two tribes, because they have two reservations, fifty miles apart, with two tribal councils and separate governmental operations, although a mechanism exists, a *Joint Tribal Council*, for collective action. My first stop was at Indian Township, the most rural of all Indian sites in Maine.

This is interior Washington County, a land of endless trees, undeveloped lakes, and distant mountain silhouettes, close to a wilderness in many places. Upon leaving the little town of Waite, spying the road sign for Indian Township, one notes practically nothing but forest until "The Strip" is reached. I remembered "The Strip" from that 1953 fishing trip with my dad. We had headed out on Route 1 from the airstrip at nearby Princeton, past abject poverty—wretched shacks—bordering a handsome body of water, whose name I had since learned was Lewy Lake. Moreover, in no way could I have known I would pass the exact spot where some twenty years later a white man named Plaisted, the owner of tourist cabins on this lake, was to so rile up a pair of Indian brothers, the Stevens boys, George and John, that the ruckus caused eventually led to an epochal turn of American law vis-à-vis Native Americans.

My first stop in the township was at Mikhu Lodge, where I was staying. Actually a set of cabins on the shores of Lewy Lake, it is owned by a Passamaquoddy woman, Molly Neptune Parker, and her non-Indian husband, T. C. Parker. Molly, whose brother Bobby Newell is the present tribal governor at Indian Township, also owns a takeout restaurant on the premises and, in addition, holds down the job of child welfare coordinator for the tribe and is a champion basket maker. T. C., a former police chief in Waldoboro and Ashland, had been chief of public safety on the reservation and a county deputy sheriff before ill health forced his retirement. It was T. C., the ex-cop, who first filled me in on a serious local problem—the problem of drug abuse among young people in Washington County—especially the misuse of the painkiller Oxy-Contin, which, ground down into powder, was being snorted like cocaine or mixed with liquid and injected into veins like heroin. Several Indian youths had died as a result. Nor was the practice confined to Indians. "Washington County is the world capital of Oxy-Contin!" I was told.

Our conversation was fairly wide-ranging. T. C. had been a devoted outdoorsman until emphysema curtailed his activities in the woods—he did say he was the only deputy sheriff he knew of to serve a summons while lugging a portable oxygen tank—and he talked about the traditional trapping that some Passamaquoddy (he specifically mentioned a Dave Sockabason) were still doing—muskrat, beaver, and otter—and the depradations on deer by coyotes, which were worse than in southern Maine because the varmints there had pets and small game more available to them. People in Washington County were too poor, for the most part, to own pets, he said, and local rabbits and partridge were now scarce. When he was trapping coyotes, T. C. added, his best bait was partridge feathers, arranged to look like a live bird.

In discussing traditional Indian activities, T. C. opined it was too bad I couldn't speak with his father-in-law, now in a Calais nursing home. The old man had forgotten his English and spoke only Passamaquoddy. But I could talk with his mother-in-law, who lived nearby, if she were willing. A phone call made the arrangement and I was soon speaking to Mrs. Irene Dana, "ninety years young," who was in a wheelchair due to diabetes that had forced the amputation of both feet.

Her home was one of those on "The Strip," brick houses that in the late 1960s had replaced the shacks I'd seen a decade and a half earlier. It seemed like a sturdy and comfortable dwelling.

She was three weeks out of the hospital, following her

operation. One of her granddaughters, Belinda Gabriel, was with her, helping out. Mrs. Dana told me she had so many grandchildren, she couldn't count them all. In mentioning diabetes, she remarked that a lot of people on the reservation seemed to have it, possibly because of the change from their old-time diet of game and wild foods and the fairly sedentary life they currently lived. Unlike many diabetics, she showed no signs of obesity—she was tall and slim—and when she started talking about her past, she emphasized how she had loved hunting, fishing, and trapping, insisting that, contrary to stereotype, Passamaquoddy women were rabid sportswomen.

Our conversation naturally dwelt a good deal on the past. She commenced by saying Indian Township "wasn't much of anything them days," but quickly followed by adding, "things were better like years ago.... We was happy.... Nowadays, I don't know." In a sentiment commonly heard in many American households, she complained the local "kids are lazy, don't want to do anything except watch TV and play video games." Her generation had skating, sliding, snowshoeing, and home cooking; "Oh, that was lovely." Now, since the Land Claims, "people expect so much. A lot of people who never wanted to be Indian, wants to be Indian."

Belinda then volunteered the information that DNA testing had become a requirement for tribal membership.

Harking back to the past again, Mrs. Dana remembered when Route 1 was a dirt road and when she'd had a horse— "It was so nice riding horses"—they'd go on the ice with them, but there were no horses now. They'd had working horses, too, to transport wood, and would have to go six miles to get hay. They made ash and sweet grass baskets, too, selling some at the Fourth of July celebrations in Princeton, where they always "had a good time, but they don't do it anymore." Until recently she had taught basket making at the Abbe Museum in Bar Harbor, along with her daughter Molly. Her own mother had taught her the skill. As a child, she had gone to school in Princeton, a very small school, then had quit to help her mother. Her father used to sing in Indian and accompany himself with a sort of horn, sounding like a rattle, that he hit against the side of a chair. "That was so nice," she said smiling, remembering how she would dance, too.

Another thing about the old days she loved was riding the train between Princeton and Eastport. It also went to Calais. Belinda swore she'd never heard about that train before.

Switching to the present after a phone call from the Indian Township Health Clinic checking up on her condition—was she taking her medicine?; "Yes, the bottle's empty,"she said. "They take care of the elderly good."

One change she'd seen was that not so many young people left here now to go into military service. She and Belinda could only count three, while in the past many more had done so. The kids stayed here, Mrs. Dana said, even though there were no jobs. "The ones that get out do good for themselves," she stated, particularly referring to the growing number who went on to college and even graduate school. It was no surprise to hear her add: "Family life is pretty strong here."

This charming nonagenarian lady who seemed up on everything told me that quite a bit of intermarriage with whites occurred these days, almost half and half. To be on the tribal census, which entitled you to services, you had to be at least one-quarter Passamaquoddy. Last week, she said, a couple from California had stopped at the tribal office and declared they were related to a certain member. "They thought they'd get lots of money," Mrs. Dana commented disapprovingly. Then, she smiled that great smile of hers. "They're wrong."

One point in this discussion was about the interchange between Indian Township and Pleasant Point. Mrs. Dana was of the opinion that "people here feel Pleasant Point is different." Yet people from Pleasant Point lived in the township now and "our people move there, too," she said, a phenomenon also described by T. C. Parker. The ex-police chief put a political spin on it, saying the recent tribal election that brought Bobby Newell back to power had caused some of his opponents to head for Pleasant Point. Newell had succeeded incumbent Richard Stevens, illustrating what T. C. pictured as the ancient rivalry between the Newell and Stevens families. Bobby Newell, who had once been tribal governor for a term at Pleasant Point, illustrated most dramatically in his own person this back-and-forth transfer of populations.

I talked with Bobby at the tribal office, which is housed in a rustic but strikingly decorative building close to the bridge that connects Indian Township with Princeton. I had met him a dozen years before when he had served a previous term as governor here. Now he was obviously older, stouter, a dark-haired, intense, middle-aged man of visible energy and charisma and, not so visible, controversy. He invited me to order breakfast, which was brought to the office, and then bluntly began our chat with the statement that he would like to change the Land Claims Settlement. The good part, Bobby said, was that "it took us away from our dependent state." The bad part—no surprise to me—was that much-disliked clause limiting the tribe's sovereignty. Going back to the treaties the Passamaquoddy had signed with the whites, he insisted they "reflected we're not a municipality." Those old treaties with Indians were to be good as long as the grass grew and the rivers flowed. "Well, the grass is still growing and the rivers still flowing," Bobby declared emphatically. "We don't need a referendum to build a casino," he argued. "We have a treaty with the State of Maine. They have violated the agreement by not honoring our tribal government and allowing the Passamaquoddy to do what they wanted—even if it included a casino—on trust land."

Then, this emotional chief of his people voiced a kind of war-whoop substitute for battle I'd only read about in Native American publications until then. "If the State of Maine government continues to ignore our rights, we may have to go to the World Court."

He assured me—and I assured him I knew it was true— that a number of North American tribes had already taken their grievances to the World Court and the United Nations.

Our discussion, however, was far from being all harangue.

370

Bobby revealed some interesting tidbits of history, including tales of the Land Claims battles. He described Governor James Longley "pounding on a table and screaming: 'I don't understand why you want a nation within a nation,'" and Bobby slyly saying: "When are you going to leave office, Governor?" Once, after Bobby had been quoted in the press speaking derogatively of Longley, there was a knock on his door—he was then living at Pleasant Point—and one of his children went to answer it and came back and said, "There's some old white guy to see you." The volatile governor of Maine, instead of sending one of his angry rebuttal letters as he famously did to any and all detractors, had come in person to dispute Bobby!

Bobby also spoke about the infamous Don Gellers, calling him, "Right, wrong, or indifferent, the first attorney who stood up for Indian people." That he was set up by Danny Bassett on the marijuana bust was also well known, Bobby claimed, but it set the stage for Tom Tureen to take over. We then went further back into Maine history with the reference to an article in *Ramparts* magazine that Bobby said was titled "The Royal Screwing of the Passamaquoddy."

He talked of a governor of Maine—unnamed—alleged to have said at a time when the tribal people were totally wards of the state: "Make them speak English or don't feed them." Earlier, in Andrew Jackson's time, there had been a request, he said, to have the Maine tribes lumped in with the Cherokees and others being forcibly removed to Oklahoma. Going back still further, he spoke of the fears of the people of Calais during the War of 1812 that the Passamaquoddy would join the British, and later, after the Civil War broke out, that the Indians would join the Confederates who had their agents just across the border in Canada and who actually did attempt a raid on Calais. To the contrary, the Passamaquoddy enlisted in the Union army in numbers that were the highest percentage of population of any community in Maine. The well-known patriotism of his tribe was stressed. The last American killed in World War I was a Passamaquoddy.

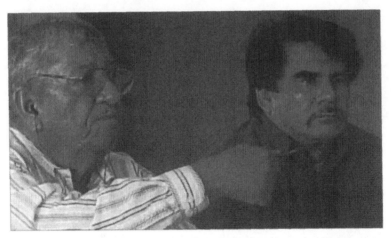

The Newell and Stevens families of Indian Township are said to be long-term rivals. But here, side by side, are two of the best-known Passamaquoddy leaders: John Stevens on the left, and Bobby Newll on the right.
COURTESY OF DONALD SOCTOMAH

And did I know there had been Passamaquoddy code-talkers in World War II? John Stevens's father had been one. Working in tandem with a fellow tribe member, they scouted German lines and relayed information to each other in their indecipherable native tongue. On a certain occasion, John's father was with a white lieutenant on a mission and when the officer was wounded, carried him back to safety, although wounded, himself.

The same tribal headquarters building where I ate my eggs and bacon while listening to Bobby Newell was also the site of my interview with John Stevens. More of an elder statesman now, he is still an important member of the tribal council. The reputed Newell–Stevens family rivalry was certainly absent in both of the discussions I had with these Passamaquoddy leaders.

My acquaintance with John went back twenty-five years to the time I had worked as an assistant to Governor Ken Curtis. John had become the first Indian to head up the state's Department of Indian Affairs. His feelings for Ken and that era, 1966–74, were warm and nostalgic. Bobby Newell, too, had made an exception to his charge that the State of Maine always held the tribe back by praising Ken as the governor who had "showed respect and kept his word." John Stevens had also served under Governor James Longley and had very different stories to tell about him.

But first he gave me a mini-biography of himself, how he was born at Indian Township, grew up here, went to high school in Princeton, and what it was like then. "Hardly anybody was working," he said. "Jobs were seasonal, blueberry raking, driving logs on the rivers, no running water, no sewers, health bad, a lot of hunger...." John joined the marines, went to Parris Island, somehow survived the training. "Rough as the military was, it was better than here—you could get to the movies—there were streetlights...." A veteran of combat in Korea, John came home and became convinced of the need to make a change. First off he attempted to get the Catholic Church, which played a strong role in Passamaquoddy life, to be, as he said, "more helpful." He convinced the parish priest to become board chairman of the first tribal housing authority. The biggest stumbling block to progress was the notorious tribal agent Hiram Hall. Then Ken Curtis got elected. A visit was arranged for Governor Curtis, the speaker of the house, the president of the senate, and other key legislators to inspect the reservation's housing, which was in lamentable shape—only fifteen houses for eighty to ninety families, with no more than two bedrooms in each for the large Indian families, and those shacks along "The Strip" had weeds growing through the floorboards and, in half the cases, floors of mud.

A law was passed in a referendum approved by the people of Maine—the first of its kind in the state's history—to create a housing authority to supply funds to build new homes for the tribe. John remembered a problem that arose when Attorney General James Erwin, a conservative Republican and later Ken Curtis's re-election opponent, tried to stop the project, claiming the state owned the property since it bordered Route 1, which had been built on land that had been taken from the Indians by eminent domain. The project, held up for six months, finally did go through and resulted in those brick edifices, still extant, like the one in which I interviewed Mrs. Dana.

Other reminiscences from the Curtis years included the fact Ken had helped open his alma mater, the Maine Maritime Academy, to Indian students, plus an interesting sidelight on the Land Claims. Toward the end of Curtis's second term, the case had not really developed far, but one day John, as Indian commissioner, got a call from the governor and a request to learn more about it. With him he brought Tom Tureen, who explained everything and they spent an entire evening discussing the matter. "Ken took it very seriously," John said. "He thought we had a case."

Not so Governor Longley, who told John it was a "phoney thing." John continually warned him he should seek an accommodation, for if the Indians filed a lawsuit on all 12 million acres, "the state would be bankrupt in four days." Then, as John put it, "We gave up our club for us to be good guys."

After the Land Claims fight was all over and Governor Longley was dying of stomach cancer, he summoned John to his summerhouse in Litchfield and apologized—an apology, John noted, that never appeared in print.

A question I had for John about his tenure as commissioner of Indian Affairs concerned an incident that *did* appear in print—ssipsis's request to him to substitute the actual original items in the Indian treaties—blankets, gunpowder, corn, etc.—for money payments. John laughed and said his comments then and now were not printable.

The whole idea of giving up modernity just didn't sit well with him. For instance, Indian mothers were using disposable diapers for their babies. Should they go back to making diapers out of buckskin? "*You* can go back. I just came from there," he told ssipsis privately. "I'm not carrying 'honey buckets' or getting water out of the lake."

ssipsis does live that old-fashioned life, in accordance with her ideals, at Albany Township, he added.

John Stevens, on the other hand, had just returned from

Wayne Newell of Indian Township is a key educational and cultural leader among the Passamaquoddy. One of the first of his people to go to college, Wayne is a Harvard graduate and also a scholar of native traditions.
COURTESY OF WAYNE NEWELL

having the most up-to-date treatment for prostate cancer any American could have. He had no apologies for pushing the Passamaquoddy into the modern world, although grousing a bit like Mrs. Dana about children hooked on TV. Nevertheless, they now had a hundred Passamaquoddy students at the University of Maine.

This veteran leader of his people, first elected tribal governor when he was seventeen years old, could state in summary, "I'm so proud because we're making headway."

Donald Soctomah, younger than these other men but a mover and shaker among his people, as well, shared some of the optimism expressed by John Stevens. There *were* positive aspects to the present day: the drop-out rate of teens in school was far better than it had been, although still well above the state average. The Creative Apparel Company the tribe had formed was still functioning, as was the blueberry farm. A nice bit of serendipity was the return to the tribe of the Island of the Bear Clan (technically Gordon's Island) in Big Lake by the Canadian Company, Domtar, which had bought out all the holdings of Georgia–Pacific. Federal funds were supporting a host of needed programs in health care, education, forestry, environmental quality, etc. Yet Don Soctomah, whose term had just ended as the Passamaquoddy representative in the Maine legislature (Indian Township and Pleasant Point alternate in holding the seat), was looking ahead and concerned about the future.

In this context, the decision by the Passamaquoddy and Penobscots to seek a casino in southern Maine became a subject of discussion. From Don's point of view, a key element was the fact the last payment on the sale of the Dragon Cement Company would be coming within four years. Unless a new source of revenue were found, nothing was slated after that. So he had been a prime mover in approaching the tribal councils about re-activating plans for a casino— plans dropped after the vote for a Calais location had been turned down.

I had been told by others that some of the Indian Township residents were unhappy with the idea of the casino being in southern Maine. They wanted it nearby, so jobs would be provided on the reservation. Since the township, itself, had 23,000 acres, there was plenty of room. This was not a subject I raised with Don, but I did ask him about the high-stakes bingo once in operation here. I remembered it well from my visit in 1990, when I was running for U.S. Senate. I had been well-received since my opponent, Senator William Cohen, had vigorously opposed the Land Claims, and I had been allowed to "call" one of the bingo games, announcing the numbers on the tokens picked automatically by a machine. The cavernous hall was packed with 1,500 people, brought to this remote corner of the state by bus and car from all over Maine and parts of Canada. But now, as Don and I passed the bingo place on Route 1, that large structure stood obviously vacant. "What happened? Why did they stop the bingo?" I asked. Don said he didn't know, exactly. There was talk of starting it up again, but evidently it hadn't been making enough money.

Which was the problem. All of their enterprises—the Creative Apparel factory, where they insulated military uniforms with chemical protection for the U.S. Army, the blueberry farm, and lumbering in their forests did not gain them much revenue. "We need to bring in income," Don said. "We can't go back to the old days."

At first, they *had* talked about having the casino in Washinton County, where there might be more impact in terms of local jobs. But a look at the numbers made it seem better to locate it "down south." Whereupon there were a few words from my companion about the "ultra-rich down south teaming up against us" and "who better represents Maine than the natives," and "double standards about gambling.... The stock market is a form of gambling."

What this quiet, soft-spoken man had as his real dream, however, was not so much a casino but a means to find funding for the goal of a tribal museum at Indian Township. There was a small museum at Pleasant Point, started years ago by my friend Joseph "Cozy" Nicholas, when he was the Passamaquoddy representative in the legislature. Don Soctomah has already published his initial book of painstakingly collected articles about the tribe from 1890 to 1920, and a sequel to it, covering the years 1920 to 1950, was now ready to go to press. The history and archaeology of his people was Don's passion, and he had begun seeking donations and grants for the $500,000 he estimated his plan would cost.

Recently, a project that had really excited him was the archaeological work he had done at Meddybemps, a lakeside town not far Indian Township in Washington County. It had been one of the Passamaquoddy's most heavily used encampments over the past 8,000 years, with estimates of an occupation going back 10,000–11,000 years. Petroglyphs had even been found there picturing the woolly mammoths and other extinct large animals of his tribe's legends.

His talk about the extent of the Passamaquoddy's range in

Donald Soctomah was a Passamaquoddy representative in Augusta when it was Indian Township's turn to hold the office. An author, forester, and historian, he hopes to build a state-of-the-art museum at Indian Township. Here, he's shown harvesting sweetgrass. COURTESY OF DONALD SOCTOMAH

prehistoric times made me think of a question I wanted to ask. Under a Passamaquoddy website on the Internet, I had seen material entitled "Quest for Qonasgamkuk," and a reference to a St. Croix Schoodic Band of Passamaquoddy. *Quonasgamkuk* was St. Andrews, New Brunswick, and in 1604 it had been the traditional capital of the Passamaquoddy, the sacred burial ground for their chiefs, and the place at which they greeted Champlain on his historic visit. St. Andrews, itself, was created in 1785 by American Loyalists, exiled from the U.S., who came to New Brunswick in droves and ousted the Passamaquoddy. The website reported the (present-day) "*Passamaquoddy* seek the immediate return of the undeveloped portions of land as *Qonasgamkuk* and the acknowledgment that our aboriginal right to our land has neither been ceded or surrendered."

In answer to my inquiry about this new (to me) land claims case, Don replied that the Maine Passamaquoddy were supporting their Schoodic band brethren, but they had been at it for years and were claiming all of Charlotte County, New Brunswick. The Canadian government didn't recognize the Passamaquoddy, considering them Maliseets, and about 300 of the tribe still lived in New Brunswick. Then he mentioned possibly seeking justice in the World Court, before telling me about a peaceful rally they'd held with their Canadian brethren that turned into a spontaneous blockade of the international bridge at Calais when they stopped, made a circle, had their spiritual people utter prayers, drummed, and sang ancient songs.

The underpinning of traditional culture is never far from the surface of Passamaquoddy life, Don made plain. He told me of his own experience when he participated in the dedication ceremony of the return of Gordon's Island to the tribe. He had been involved in the negotiations with Domtar, whose president had had good relations with the First Nations (Indian tribes) in Canada. Unlike Georgia–Pacific, "who wouldn't sell one inch" of their land to Indians, Don said, Raymond Royer, Domtar's head, *gave* the island to the tribe as a gift. Part of the dedication included ceremonies conducted by sacred pipekeepers Arnie Neptune, the Penobscot elder, and Darryl Newell of the Passamaquoddy. What most impressed Don was that as he, himself, was moderating the festivities, several eagles flew in. "The spiritual people were so impressed," he said.

Thanks to Don Soctomah, who for parts of two days drove me all around Indian Township, I had a chance to pick up a fairly broad sense of the activities there. Two concentrations of population really exist on the reservation, one centered near "The Strip" and the town of Princeton, the other, about a five-mile drive, at the exceedingly scenic setting of Peter Dana Point. The latter, located at the confluence of Long Lake and Big Lake, contains St. Ann's, the Catholic church, the elementary school, the health clinic, and a large number of houses clustered close together. As Don and I were driving, we passed a long line of school children, out for their daily exercise, jogging, and we passed a pretty little black-haired girl, Don's daughter, who, panting slightly, called out, "How fast am I going, Dad?" When he told her, "About seven miles an hour," she nodded gravely and kept on running. There are

150–180 children in the school—the size of the whole population in 1900.

At the health clinic we met with Elizabeth Neptune, the director, who administers the program funded by the federal Indian Health Service. Their "ambulatory clinic" is an outpatient service, with a full-time doctor and nurse practitioner, a retail pharmacy, twenty-four-hour ambulance, a home health agency, a WIC (nutrition for pregnant women) program, an elderly feeding center, a dental clinic, mental health services, substance abuse counseling, etc.—in other words, a pretty full range of services for this isolated rural community. Pre-natal care was available for expectant mothers, but babies were delivered at hospitals in Bangor and Calais. Those tribal members who had health insurance were billed, I was assured, and I also heard the complaint that if there were a better working relationship with the State of Maine, more program funds could be received from the federal government.

Another department of the Passamaquoddy government Don showed me was his own bailiwick—forestry. He was now the acting director of its extensive timberlands and we stopped at his small office from which he supervises ten logging crews—twenty persons—plus a staff of eight.

Possessed of a degree in Forest Management, Don originally took the job to fill in for two weeks but has been at it now for six months. The tribe's landholdings at present are 120,000 acres, with the possibility under the Land Claims Settlement of adding 30,000 acres more. They practice sustainable forestry, using tribal forest technicians to mark each tree, and keep a "reserve area"—no cutting allowed—of 10,000 acres. Recently his men had been busy after a wind storm, salvaging 300–400 cords of wood from blowdowns, some of which, not yet cleared, he could point out to me as we drove to our next stop.

This was the Creative Apparel factory. Inside, seated in rows at sewing machines—a sight familiar to me from my days campaigning in Maine textile mills and shoe-stitching plants—were ninety workers, almost all women. Charles Ray

Devoe, the Passamaquoddy manager of the operation, told me it was one of five such operations the tribe runs in Maine, with the others at Harmony, Dover–Foxcroft, Belmont, and Eastport. The uniform pants being fitted out with chemical-proof linings were either of jungle camouflage green and brown or desert-style tan and brown. Some 2,500 pairs a week were produced here by piecework, and the sewers earned from $10 to $12 an hour, depending on their skill. Devoe was straightforward in admitting only 14 percent of his workers were Passamaquoddy. Culturally, this repetitive type of labor did not suit the temperament of most native people, although those who stuck with it were among the best of his employees.

In this regard I remembered a statement I'd heard from Donna Loring, the Penobscot representative, who'd told me how Maine Governor Angus King had chided her because Maine Indians didn't seem to want to take jobs in the new "call-in" centers opening in Maine. She'd replied that she couldn't imagine "hunters" sitting down at a phone all day, a remark that drew a knowing laugh from the chief executive.

I was also mindful, as I took leave of Don Soctomah to head for my next stop at Pleasant Point, of what he'd told me about Passamaquoddy demographics. They were the largest of the Maine tribes at 3,300, growing fast, and 60 percent of their population was under the age of twenty-five. But another rather awesome statistic about the tribe was that the average age of death was forty-eight. Anyone fifty-five years or older is an "elder." And the tribe has no retirement program, as such.

That fact was brought home after visits at Pleasant Point with Joe Nicholas, the veteran state representative for the Passamaquoddy, now retired. We had served together through at least three terms, "Cozy" and I, and when I appeared at his back door out of the blue, after not seeing each other for more than a decade, it was like we had just left each other's company. "Come right in, Neil."

His house was across Route 190, the main road to and from Eastport, and opposite the main part of the Pleasant Point community. I located it easily because of the big sign outside, "Indian Baskets for Sale." And that sideline, in a sense, was his "retirement," he told me, not having social security nor even state retirement, despite his years in the legislature. It also brought home to me that no one on the reservation owns equity in property that can become an asset. This comfortable brick house, where Joe lived as a widower with his son Steve, belonged to the tribe.

Joe Nicholas is a pixyish sort of man, famed in the legislature for his sense of humor. When I asked him how he got his nickname of "Cozy," (which we never knew about in Augusta), his eyes twinkled and he coyly evaded the question. "I never told anyone. Let them think what they like," he quipped. One-liners, puns, and jokes were sprinkled through his conversation. Yes, he agreed, "The Indian population in the U.S. has increased quite a bit—especially since John Wayne died." Next, he talked of modern-day smoke signals in the West—one set of white ones, one of black; the latter were carbon copies. Even more elaborate was the story, allegedly from his childhood, of going out to repair the lighting in the outhouse near his home, which made him "*the first Indian in America to wire ahead for a reservation.*"

Yet this irrepressible gentleman in his seventies wasn't all humor. He had been a pioneer in preserving the heritage of his people, emphasizing most of all the language and how important it was to pass it on to younger generations. One of his life's works had been the creation of a Passamaquoddy dictionary, which he proudly told me was now up to 26,000 words. In one of his publications he gave me, the *Passamaquoddy/ Maliseet Reference Book,* produced with federal funds, I noted that one whole section dealt with baseball terms in his Indian tongue. He laughed and mentioned how, in his youth, they had an early form of Passamaquoddy code-talking, yelling "*Kamodin*" at teammates on third base when the enemy pitcher was distracted, meaning "Steal home!" It was not a term I found in the reference book, but there were plenty of others, like *Pasitahal* = "she/he hit it over the fence" (Passamaquoddy does not have differing gender pronouns), or

Joseph "Cozy" Nicholas, a former Passamaquoddy representative to the legislature. This genial man, now in his seventies, was renowned for his humor—still very much present. A former barber, he has been a tireless worker in preserving his people's heritage and language and was a founder of the Waponahki Museum and Resource Center at Pleasant Point.
COURTESY OF JOSEPH NICHOLAS

almost the same thing but a totally different word, *Wewciye* = "she/he hits a home run," and *Milamit* = "knuckle ball." In talking about how he taught Passamaquoddy to local school kids, Joe wrote out a long word on a piece of paper, showing it to me and saying he would ask them to translate it. KVITCHUPELYAKIN, it read. Knowing him, I looked at it hard and was able to see through the game. "Quit your bellyaching" was, of course, the correct translation.

Joe Nicholas never went to college. He says he attended high school on the G.I. Bill—i.e., after he returned from service in the navy. For his work in Passamaquoddy history and cultural development, he has been awarded two honorary degrees—from the University of Maine at Machias and St. Joseph's College. His Passamaquoddy/Maliseet bilingual program has put out various other publications, including a *Passamaquoddy Indian History* and *Nitawi Skicinuwatu—I know How to Speak Indian*. From the Waponahki Museum and Resource Center, which Joe founded, had come *Maine Indians, Brief Summary*, *The People of the Early Dawn*, and in

*Melvin Francis, governor at Pleasant Point (2003), is working
to bridge the gap between tribal elders and youth.*
DIANA GRAETTINGER PHOTO ©2002 BANGOR DAILY NEWS. USED BY PERMISSION.

conjunction with David Francis, a tribal linguist at the museum, the *Passamaquoddy Calendar*.

David Francis, unfortunately, wasn't at the museum when
I went to visit it. One of Cozy's daughters welcomed me, but
it is really geared to a self-guided tour, the "first phase of
which," according to the single-sheet guide, "is to welcome
you here today and hopefully to project some positive image
about our history by the photographs that hang on the
wall...."

Some are described in caption form, like that of Wallace
Nicholas, a porpoise hunter and fisherman, who lived at St.
Andrews on the land "being disputed today." The photo of a

384

*Emblems of the Passamaquoddy. Left, that of the Schoodic Band,
located in Canada (thus referred to as a "First Nation"), who are trying to
recover land in New Brunswick. Center, the emblem of the Passamaquoddy
at Indian Township. Right, the emblem of the Passamaquoddy at
Pleasant Point, who refer to themselves as the People of the Dawn. .*
COURTESY OF DONALD SOCTOMAH

ninety-nine-year-old man is pointed out—a man who had
fought in the Battle of Machias during the Revolution and
then had been "accommodating" enough to live to ninety-
nine "so we could take a picture of him." Then a picture of
Mary Moore who, with "Joe (Cozy) Nicholas, worked closely
in reviving the dancing which had not been done for thirty-
five years." The band instruments used "here at Sipayik" (the
native name for Pleasant Point) in 1897, purchased by Cozy
for the museum, were on display and also some of the art of
Tomah Joseph, who carved on birch bark and who had done
work for Franklin D. Roosevelt at Campobello; beautifully
decorated panels and a native canoe now hung in the visitors
center.

With politics therefore on my mind, I drove the short distance from the heart of Sipayik and beyond its road sign
boundary into the town of Perry, where the large, sprawling
tribal office facility is located. Tribal Governor Melvin Francis,
whom I was on my way to see, explained the tribe had bought
a swath of land practically all the way from Pleasant Point to
Route 1 and had built this complex there. It certainly seemed
state-of-the-art, complete with a security system just installed
so visitors now had to report at a window and identify themselves and their business before they could be buzzed inside.

Some of the tribal people in the outside lobby could be overheard griping about this newfangled loss of their old informality.

Yet I also overheard one of the workers tell someone he had been to a sweat lodge for the first time in his life the previous weekend in Presque Isle (possibly with Bernard Jerome) and what a wonderful spiritual experience it had been.

Thus tradition and modernity were clearly in co-existence here, too—that underlying sense I'd experienced everywhere I'd been in Maine "Indian Country." Melvin Francis, a burly middle-aged man, had just come from working on a backhoe. He was a construction worker by profession, trained as a journeyman, capable of doing plumbing, electrical work, heavy machine operating, "a little bit of everything." He supervised thirty-five people in the tribal office, conducting the same array of services as at Indian Township. When things got too hectic, he would just "go and jump on a bulldozer," he said. His prime goal during his four-year term as tribal governor was economic development. Currently, the tribe was in discussions with Chinese investors on a number of projects, which explained the framed Oriental prints I'd seen in the office at Indian Township and now here. Also a fuel project was under discussion where the tribe could re-sell fuel to tractor-trailers. But the real economic development engine had to be the casino, he felt, as it had been for other tribes around the country. "Yet it doesn't stop at the casino," Melvin insisted. That would only be a means to an end, to a whole series of job-producing industries that would "create something to attract young people back."

Like many others, he wasn't satisfied with the Land Claims Settlement. "It was a plus, but...." He hadn't been involved, since he'd been living out-of-state at the time. He felt the tribe should have held out for a while longer and now, in a sense, they were in the position of "having to buy their own land back." They had "settled for less" and, in his opinion, were "still settling for less." A sovereign nation, he thought, was supposed to make its own laws. He, too, regretted they were not able to go right ahead and build the casino they wanted.

My final interviews were with two of the "young" Passamaquoddy that Melvin had talked about wishing to lure back to Maine. They worked for the Sipayik Environmental Department. Dale Mitchell was a Water Quality Technician and Ed Bassett was the GIS/GPS Tech. Both seemed to be in their thirties or early forties. I'd been sent by Melvin to talk to Ed, who was an expert on birch-bark canoes and was working to revive the traditional art of making these watercraft, one of the most signal contributions of indigenous peoples to world material culture, and one that had originated among the Wabanakis. Ed called it "the automobile" of ancient days, *manufactured* wherever birch bark grew. In 1980, when he tried to find a teacher to show him how to build a canoe in the fashion of his forebears, he found that no authentically native canoe builders were left—at least not in the United States. Finally he located several in an Indian community of Quebec Province, 700–800 miles away. They were members of an Algonquin-speaking tribe, the Maniwock, and he went there and they taught him. Now he does it on his own, as a hobby more than a business, mostly making scale models that take less time than a full-fledged canoe, which will take him a whole month. But he also stresses it is more than just a hobby, but a "restoration of a significant piece of culture, the revival of a culture extinction."

This conversation was taking place in Ed's cubicle in the Environmental Office, next to a computer on which he was obviously an expert. In fact, he gave me the address of his own website on birch-bark canoes. Our discussion soon drew in Dale Mitchell from an adjoining cubicle, where he was working at a computer, and we soon were talking about another traditional Passamaquoddy activity—hunting porpoises.

The logo of the Sipayik Environmental Department shows a native on the ocean holding a trident spear poised to fling—a fit emblem—as Ed and Dale proceeded to tell me how the use of a spear in hunting porpoises, and also seals, as their ancestors did, had become for them a "spiritual experience," establishing a relationship with the animal that could never be achieved with a firearm. "It was a communication with the past," these two outwardly modern-seeming young Americans told me.

The delicate question of how they could get away with hunting protected marine mammals like porpoises and seals was adroitly sidestepped. Or rather, they seemed to indicate the authorities—particularly the Canadians—after warning them, looked the other way. They only took a few, less than a dozen a year, and contrasted that number to the thousands of porpoises killed each year in fishing nets.

They both spoke fluent Passamaquoddy and were fearful about the language's future. Ed had made an interactive CD-Rom to be used in training programs and had put his computer skills to use in making related tools, like an interactive dictionary and an audio computer capacity to create actual dialogue. One point Dale raised, after I commented on this interjection of modern methods for bringing back traditions, was the way Indian traditions were now being exploited by the New Age movement. He cited a hundred websites on which people violated Indian culture, with fake medicine men profitting from their false versions of native spirituality. The Oglala Sioux, he said, had now closed off their ceremonies to outsiders, whereas there had always been an openness before.

If I thought I had heard everything possible about the situation of Maine's tribes in my "looking around" the state, I had to think again after I left those two guys. New generations were coming, anxious to hold onto their past. Our final discussion had been on the meaning of a Passamaquoddy word that graced the T-shirt Ed Bassett was wearing. NULANKEYAS, that lone word read. When I asked its meaning, Ed said it stood for: "Taking care of each other." "Not so," quibbled Dale. "It means 'taking care of myself.'"

24

ALL HELL BREAKS LOOSE IN MAINE AGAIN

*I*t's conceivable we Mainers might have thought the Land Claims controversy the ultimate disruption the small Indian population in our state could bring to our public life. After all, its realistic threat to two-thirds of the property in the state *was* an event of seismic proportions. But the impact was stretched out over nearly a decade, and no one believed anything really dire would come of it; besides, it did end with more of a whimper than a bang, a complicated compromise, after which the whole business simmered down.

Twenty-two years went by, and only now and then a few issues erupted, like fighting over the cleanliness of the Penobscot River or the use of the word *squaw*, stuff in the newspapers that seemed far less important or immediate than the school budget in one's community.

Then a bombshell exploded suddenly in early March 2002, when the two principal Maine tribes, led once more by Tom Tureen, announced they would seek to build a large-scale gambling casino and resort hotel at the entrance to Maine in the town of Kittery!

Whereas the Land Claims dispute had been barely noticeable when it started, not really penetrating the consciousness of most Maine people until land titles became clouded, the shock of this announcement was immediate.

The legislature was in session when it happened. In fact, the discussion of an Indian casino had not been absent from its deliberations—a re-run, to a smaller extent, of the debate eight years before about a possible casino at Calais on the Washington County–Canadian border. A bill to allow the Passamaquoddy an additional nineteen years to buy a hundred acres in Calais for that purpose was enacted by both the house and senate. Governor Angus King vetoed it, however, and the measure was awaiting further action in the house when the news broke about the tribes' eyeing a piece of land at the exact opposite end of the state, an undeveloped acreage in Kittery close to the Piscataqua River, a short distance from the high-level bridge connecting Maine and New Hampshire, less than sixty miles from Boston.

Governor King was at the end of his second four-year term and could not succeed himself—a "lame duck" in the vocabulary of the political press—and a host of contenders had already lined up hoping to take his place. On March 3, 2002, the *Maine Sunday Telegram* ran a major piece on the issue and included statements from some of those who had registered with the secretary of state that they were raising money for a gubernatorial campaign.

Initially, three of the eventual top four candidates expressed an interest in the casino project. Democrat John Baldacci, then a U.S. congressman and the eventual winner of that race, said he "would look with an open mind at all proposals that could bring money or jobs into the state," while questioning casinos as economic development tools. Republican Peter Cianchette, who won his party's primary and came in a close second in the general election, said: "I'm certainly open to listening to the proposal. I have an open mind. It would receive a fair review." The former head of one of Maine's most powerful businesses, the Central Maine Power Company, David Flanagan, running as an Independent, also stated: "I'm open to considering it. I have a lot of empathy for the economic plight of the tribes." Only Jonathan Carter, the Green Party candidate, was openly negative, saying: "I don't think gambling is good for Maine. Like the lottery, people who can least afford it put most of their money into these things." However, he stopped short of promising to veto such a bill if it came to his desk.[1]

The conventional wisdom at first was that none of these candidates would ever have a chance to act upon a casino bill because one was going to be offered right then and there, before the session ended in April. The Penobscots and Passamaquoddy made it clear they would not fight to override

King's veto of the Calais legislation "out of fear it would complicate a separate proposal for a casino in southern Maine."[2]

On March 8, Governor Angus King held a news conference and said he felt the casino idea was "flat-out bad" for Maine. It would conflict with the state's "clean, outdoor, family image," would promote addictive behavior, steal workers from other employers, raise state spending, and prey on poor Mainers who cannot afford to gamble but would do so anyway.

Paul Carrier, the *Portland Press Herald* staff political writer, then commented: "His strong words effectively quashed any speculation by casino supporters that King might soften his opposition if the legislature takes up a bill this session to allow the Penobscot Nation and the Passamaquoddy Tribe to build a casino, possibly in Kittery."[3]

Even without the association of Tom Tureen's name with the project, the comparison of what was being proposed for Kittery—a $400-million to $600-million gambling complex—would have drawn comparisons with the two mega-casinos in Connecticut—Foxwoods, the world's largest, and the lesser-known but almost as big Mohegan Sun, both situated in rural settings and near a coastal resort area centered around the town of Mystic. The major newspaper closest to Kittery, the *Portsmouth Herald,* just across the river in New Hampshire, on March 10 printed a feature story based on its reporter's visit to Connecticut, and it was accompanied by a full-color night photo of the massive (and garish) Foxwoods Resort Casino buildings, along with the inquiring caption: "Coming Soon?"

The interviews with residents in the towns immediately impacted by Foxwoods—Ledyard, Preston, and North Stonington—were uniformly negative about the casino. One woman was quoted: "You've got pollution, you have garbage, your demographics are changing within the community, and that is changing the school system. There is a demand on social services we never had. We're getting lost in the dust and the quality of education is taking a nose dive."[4] The first selectman of North Stonington, Nicholas H. Mullane, declared, "I have already closed two houses of prostitution. I now have a full-fledged pornographic super-store [this undoubtedly touched a nerve in Kittery, which already had an "adult" bookstore on Route 236, the Midnight Reader, that some citizens had been trying to close for years]. I also have a smoke shop. We went from what used to be 8,800 cars a day to 27,000 cars a day. A lot of them are good, honest, straight-forward people, [but] we get a lot of riffraff with it, too."[5]

That this article had a devastating impact in the greater Kittery area seems incontrovertible, despite its writer's attempts at even-handedness by acknowledging that "the circumstances of Maine's proposal are different."

One of those differences was pointed out by Kittery's representative to the legislature, Stephen Estes, in an adjoining article, noting that the casino would be built on non-tribal land and be accountable to "state and local planning review, unlike the gambling resorts of Connecticut."

As the main article stated regarding the cited Connecticut communities: "The local townspeople make no secret of their animosity about having had no say in a land taking that led to expansion and no voice in the development of the federally recognized reservation."

That argument was soon brought to southern York County by author Jeff Benedict, who had written a book on the subject, *Without Reservation,* detailing the story of how the Mashantucket Pequots had acquired the land on which they built Foxwoods.[6] Benedict's thesis was it had been done illegally, that the Pequots were not really a legitimate Indian tribe, and, furthermore, he was running for Congress in a Democratic primary in Connecticut on a platform of taking the Mashantuckets' tribal status away from them.

Maine's connections to the Mashantucket Pequots have been touched upon already—the Penobscots' loan to them to start their first venture into gambling, Super Bingo, and Tom Tureen's handling of their land case, which followed directly from his success in getting the Non-Intercourse Act applied to the Maine tribes. Tureen and his associates developed what Tom has called "a family of law suits" representing New England tribes, with the relative handful of Mashantucket Pequots among them.

Kim Eisler, in his book *Revenge of the Pequots,* has traced the history of these people.[7] Shattered as a tribe by the Puritans during the Pequot War of 1637–38, a group of tattered survivors twenty years later were, to quote Eisler, "resettled on 2,000 acres of the worst, most snake-infested, rock-ledged, swamp-filled, uninhabitable land in the whole society of North Groton."[8] Its Indian name then was Mushantuxet. By 1936, after the acreage had been whittled down by the state to 179 acres, a mere nine resident Indians were left and only two were adults. In the early 1970s, Connecticut was ready to step in, declare these "Western Pequots" extinct, and turn the still unfruitful land into a state park. The death of the last ostensible survivor, a Mrs. Elizabeth George Plouffe, which occurred on June 6, 1973, was a signal for that to happen. The fact it didn't was due to her nephew, Richard "Skip" Hayward, who rounded up family members and induced them to move onto the reservation to keep Connecticut from declaring the tribe "extinct" and appropriating the property.

Much has been made of the accusation that Skip Hayward was only one-sixteenth Indian, had always considered himself white, and only became an Indian to gain benefits from doing so. Possibly.

Except it would have been pretty hard to predict what *benefits* might be had by taking over a commercially worthless property in a depressed area of Connecticut two years *before* the court decision in Maine gave even a glimmer of hope to any of New England's Indians.

Tureen's partners, when they came in 1975, found fifty-six persons calling themselves Mashantucket Pequots—i.e., Skip Hayward and relatives—on the land, acting in the capacity of a tribe on a reservation and now, given Judge Gignoux's ruling, in a position to bid for the land removed from them in a potentially illegal fashion.

It is a curious situation, from a historic point of view, that Connecticut did not contest Hayward, et al.'s occupation of the site in the town of Ledyard, in that: 1) The Pequot tribe had already unilaterally (and presumably legally) been declared extinct in 1638 after its destruction in the Pequot War, to the extent that the Puritans had declared its name was never officially to be uttered again; and 2) If the state wanted the land for a park, why didn't they declare Hayward and his clan not to be bonafide Pequots and evict them as squatters?

Be that as it may, by 1976 Barry Margolin of Tureen's office and Skip Hayward opened up a *southern front*, as it were, a mini-version of what was happening up north in Maine. The stakes were infinitely smaller than the 12 million acres sought by the Penobscots and Passamaquoddy; the suit against Connecticut was for only slightly less than 2,000 acres; but the principle—a violation of the Non-Intercourse Act— was the same.

The impact on local landowners was also similar. Suddenly, out of the blue, like a bad dream, their ownership rights were being questioned. Some thirty of them received a legal notice suggesting their property could be taken from them, and all on behalf of some Indians who had once lived there over a hundred years ago. Their amazement, consternation, disbelief, and anger had to be little different from those Mainers who had woken up one morning in the same fix, learning their titles were clouded and their towns unable to borrow money.

As in Maine, there eventually was a settlement. It was made easier by the fact that, as Kim Eisler wrote, "The land, itself, was among the least valuable in the state.... Most of the people who had become the current owners of the old reservation property had acquired it at tax foreclosure sales for an average price of $5 to $10 an acre."9 The majority of the proprietors had not even bothered to buy title insurance.

It took time for the Tureen folks to turn their full atten-

394

tion to Connecticut, but after 1980 and the ending of the Maine case, they were able to convince the non-Indian Mashantucket landowners' lawyer Jackson King that a smart move would be a Maine-type agreement, with the federal government picking up the tab. King's clients who wanted to sell could pocket many times the value of their land and those who decided to keep their land could have their titles cleared. By working with Connecticut's two U.S. senators, Lowell Weicker and Chris Dodd, and the region's congressman, Sam Gejdenson, a bill was entered in Congress that, in exchange for the tribe's dropping its claims, provided $900,000 to them to buy from those willing to sell. Note the figure— $900,000—identical to the payments made to the Maliseets and the Micmacs. Keeping the sum under $1 million was a specific tactical decision.

Also in the bill was a clause providing federal recognition to the Mashantucket Pequots. The exact language has been quoted by Jeff Benedict: "*Notwithstanding any other provision of law*, federal recognition is extended to the tribe."[10] The first phrase is significant because of Benedict's contention that the federal recognition process wasn't followed correctly since it violated *other laws*. In any event, that bill was first vetoed by President Ronald Reagan, then subsequently, slightly revised, signed by him. In October 1983 the Mashantucket Pequots finally had their settlement and, furthermore, it was free and clear of state restrictions, unlike that of their Penobscot and Passamaquoddy brethren in Maine, a fact that contributed greatly to their ability to build Foxwoods.

This astoundingly successful venture rose in its gigantic form in the midst of a quiet Yankee countryside, bringing with it a host of changes and problems and a seemingly undying enmity between the tribal members and many of the inhabitants and officials of the affected towns of Ledyard, Preston, and North Stonington. Not the least of the local municipalities' ire was based on the twin sore points that the casino had been thrust upon them without their say-so or input and no specific compensation was provided to them out of the many

*The casino proposed for Southern Maine was modeled on the big,
turn-of-the-century summer resorts that used to dot the coast.*
DRAWING BY WM. CUTLER OF ALBERT, RICHTER, AND TITTMAN, COURTESY OF THINK ABOUT IT

millions collected, not even to reimburse their expenses. In the
Pequots' deal with Connecticut (25 percent of the slot
machine take), the money goes straight to Hartford and none
to the casino's neighbors, except through the statewide dis-
bursement.

That resentment came full force to Kittery, Maine, and
the other concerned communities in southern York County
and the seacoast region of New Hampshire. A grass-roots
organization called Casinos No! sprang into being and effectively battled the idea. The word "firestorm" is perhaps too
tame here. The local newspapers fed the flame.

Particularly strong was the *York Independent,* a weekly in
the town of York, next-door to Kittery, which co-sponsored a
visit by anti-Foxwoods author Jeff Benedict to Kittery. The
essence of the article in the *Independent* advertising this event
was an extrapolation from Benedict's book of an attack on
Tom Tureen, saying he "committed a fraud on the U.S.
Congress to get recognition for an 'illegitimate' Indian tribe in
Connecticut, which led to the creation of the world's biggest
casino at Foxwoods...."[11] It was alleged that Tureen had hood-
winked both the U.S. Senate and House by promising to provide proof to the Department of the Interior that the

396

The largest casino in the world, the Pequot casino Foxwoods.
PHOTO BY THE AUTHOR

Mashantucket Pequots were a legitimate Indian tribe and then never providing it. The fact Skip Hayward had always called himself white "until approached by Tureen with the idea of filing a lawsuit" was also included, plus the information that Hayward was replaced by Kenneth Reels as tribal chairman and that Reels and two Pequot tribal members, who had criminal records, were "black and are not known to have any Pequot blood or any other Indian blood."[12]

So great was the emotion raised in Kittery and the surrounding communities—a region beset by extreme growth, traffic problems, school funding problems, one of the lowest unemployment rates in the country—that the mere prospect of a major industry coming to town, employing thousands, was horrific in and of itself. Add the quotient of gambling, with its images of crime and auxiliary problems, and the result was an explosion of fear and rage, exemplified by the pronouncement of one Casino No! leader that, "There can only be one opinion on this issue." Those who expressed any other view were fiercely set upon and urged to recant.

I know. I was in that position. In carrying out my research for this book, I interviewed Tom Tureen, and when the idea of a Maine casino surfaced, he asked me to be a member of the nine-person board (five Indian, four non-Indian) to help run the Indian casino, if it were ever built. My initial reason for accepting was a problem I saw with the way the proposal was structured. Unlike the situation at Foxwoods, the host community—Kittery—was to receive a direct property tax payment from the casino (estimated at $5 million a year), but nothing was proposed for the impacted surrounding towns, like my hometown of York. In any statewide disbursement, particularly if it were weighted toward school funding, York would receive little or no money due to the vagaries of our Maine laws. I was making headway on that issue with Tom when it became apparent the opposition in Kittery was too strong.

A town referendum was hastily held there, and by an overwhelming margin, the idea of a casino in Kittery was rejected. Since the Indian leaders and Tom Tureen had publicly announced they would not attempt to impose their project on an unwilling community, they ruled out Kittery as a site. Other nearby towns—York, Eliot, Wells, etc., held their own referenda, making it plain by equally large margins that they also turned down a casino—and this time the geographic range was described on the ballot as within "southern Maine."

The obvious furor against the casino in this southernmost part of the state had an effect on statewide politics. All of the gubernatorial candidates who had expressed an open mind on the issue quickly backed away and pronounced themselves opponents. The legislature, which had seemed likely to pass a bill allowing a casino, became very lukewarm. A study commission was proposed and put into effect, despite the objections of Casinos No!, which claimed it was stacked against them. The opponents particularly objected to the fact that Donna Loring was made the chair of the group. She has pointed out that this was the first time the legislative leadership had ever named an Indian representative to be the house chair on a committee or task force, and that she was scrupulously fair. In the end, however, after it finished its deliberations, the verdict of this seventeen-person body was that it could make no recommendations, particularly because it did not have a specific plan before it, since no casino site had been chosen.

This period was, to say the least, an uncomfortable time for me. My stance was not appreciated in my hometown of York—long-time friends and neighbors stopped speaking to me, and I received angry letters. Toughest of all were those from former supporters who felt I had betrayed them and pleaded with me to change my position publicly as other public figures had done. The worst moment came when I gave a talk that had been scheduled months before this controversy had arisen. I had been asked to speak in a local church about the "Seeds of Peace" program where youngsters from Israel and the Arab countries and similar warring groups, like the Greeks and Turks in Cyprus, gather at a summer camp in Maine and become friends and learn tolerance for one another. The crowd that morning listened politely to my discussion of the Middle East and the trip I had taken there with the Seeds of Peace group, how the camp worked, and the amazing techniques used to bring these enemies together, etc.

But that wasn't why an overflow audience was there. Unbeknownst to me, a flier had been circulated saying I was there to promote the casino. I had agreed at the request of the sponsor to say a few words about the project, including the news that Kittery was no longer a possible site nor, I believed, any of the surrounding towns. In the heated exchange that followed, I was, to quote the *York Independent*'s headline, "ROASTED." I've faced hostile audiences before, so, in a sense, I was more bemused by my thinking that if I were in the then-exploding Israeli-Palestinian situation at that moment, trying to express an opinion in favor of peace, I probably would have been killed. In the equivalent, maybe, of aiming a bullet at me, the tumult ended with the gesture of a young woman who owned a local bookstore returning to me two copies of my latest book which she no longer wanted to sell because she felt I no longer had the best interests of the town of York at heart.

The debate soon shifted northward in York County after

it became evident the towns down by the New Hampshire border wanted no part of an Indian casino.

Two communities—Biddeford and Sanford—both essentially working class, blue collar in nature, largely inhabited by descendants of French-Canadian immigrants, were the next focus. They both eventually decided to hold referenda, as had their more suburban, higher-income neighbors to the south.

Tom Tureen had often talked of arranging a trip to the Connecticut casinos for those of us on his proposed board, like former Governor Ken Curtis and myself, who had never seen them. The occasion presented itself when he had a request from Biddeford city officials to view the conditions in Connecticut for themselves. Thus a caravan was formed and included myself, Ken Curtis, the mayor of Biddeford Donna Dion, her city manager and police chief, and Donna Loring, the Penobscot representative to the Maine legislature.

It was a whirlwind tour, both of Foxwoods and the other casino built close by, Mohegan Sun—almost as big and glitzy, but apparently not as controversial. There were no accusations the Mohegans did not constitute a "legitimate tribe," despite James Fenimore Cooper's novel about the last of them. The mayor of the town of Montville where they were located, Russ Beatham, was pro-casino, telling us, "The two casinos have saved the economy of southeastern Connecticut," particularly following large layoffs by General Dynamics. His only gripe was the town still did not receive what he felt should be their fair share of revenue—only $500,000 a year as a separate payment from the Mohegans toward a municipal budget of $41.5 million. What about crime, we asked him. There were more OUI's and "fender-benders" than before, he said, plus concerns about Asiatic casino workers crowding too many people into local apartments, but on the whole he counted himself a strong supporter. So did his daughter, who worked for a local hotel.

Support for both casinos was voiced, as well, by tourism officials in nearby Mystic. On this coastal vacation spot's website, I already knew, were exhortations to come visit "our exciting casinos," in addition to the famed Mystic Seaport and a brand-new acquarium directed by noted underwater explorer Bob Ballard. The Mystic Chamber of Commerce bulletin strongly featured the two casinos and the "world-class" Mashantucket Pequot Museum and Research Center. "Ten years ago, we were looking down the barrel of a gun," Vivian Stanley, head of the Mystic Tourism Association told us, until the hiring of the displaced workers from Electric Boat made it possible for them to keep their homes. "Yes, there's been a transition," she said about a town that reminded me of my own York—quaint, colonial, and a magnet for tourists, "but mostly positive."

It could be argued our trip was a setup, seeing we were only brought to talk to people who were pro-casino, avoiding the antis who had been so vociferous in the Kittery–York meetings, but then again, the opposite could be claimed—that the folks we'd talked to had never been heard up north. As a veteran legislator, used to divisive debates, I had long ago learned to consider there was truth and error on both sides.

Since I could not stay overnight at Foxwoods and since we had arrived late that afternoon, I had no chance to hear from anyone official there—only to observe the scene. Like Mohegan Sun, it is a big, fancy hotel, identical in all but one respect to the luxurious Marriotts and Hyatt Regencies I've stayed in all over the world—that one respect, of course, being the spaces devoted to gambling. Otherwise, the shops, the meeting rooms, and the restaurants were no different from those other high-scale places. The crowds looked familiar, too, well-dressed, whole families on a holiday, even young couples with children.

One item that soon caught my attention was a handout card, stacks of which were placed throughout the gaming rooms. The text read: "Gambling Problem? There is help. Call the Connecticut Council on Problem Gambling." It was printed by the Foxwoods Resort and Casino, contained ten descriptions of "Signs of Problem Gambling," and an 800 number to call. I was not aware of a like program in Maine, where there is currently considerable gambling—a state lot-

tery, horse racing, off-track betting, even casino cruises origi-
nating in Portland. The pamphlet also stated: "Foxwoods provides problem gambling awareness training for its supervisors,
and financial support for the education, training, and research
efforts of the Connecticut Council on Problem Gambling."

Not being a gambler myself (it bores me), my primary
interest was to see the museum, on which millions had been
spent to recreate a Pequot village of the seventeenth century
before the devastating Puritan attack of 1637. Unfortunately,
we were there just before closing and had no time to see more
than this lifelike panorama and a few other major exhibits,
which are truly spectacular, with not a minute left to examine
the library and research collection.

Other impressions, admittedly subjective, were that on
this day, which was a Friday, we hadn't encountered the hor-
rid traffic jams I'd been led to expect. Foxwoods is in the midst
of a beautiful rural area of sylvan glades, idyllic fields, and picturesque New England farmsteads, out of which it pops up all
at once with startling incongruity as you round a curve in the
road. Yet only once on that country road was there a line of
cars, and they were stopped for a school bus, it turned out. No
doubt, the traffic problems must be real; there were plenty of
cars at the casino entrance and an admirable efficiency among
the valet-parking staff moving them to the lots.

On the way back, one of the passengers in our car, the
Biddeford police chief, added an interesting note concerning
perceptions. Knowing he'd had a private talk with the director
of security at Foxwoods, I asked him if he thought there was a
lot of crime as a result of the casinos.

"No," he answered, "but I don't think many people back
home will believe that."

He was right. When the vote was held in Biddeford,
despite the open support of Mayor Dion and her predecessor,
James Grattelo, now a member of the council, locating an
Indian casino within the city was turned down. Casinos No!
staged a vigorous campaign. Despite early polls showing support among Biddeford voters, I could tell by the lawn signs I

saw as I drove through the city close to voting day that the proposal was in trouble. A handout sheet listing "Top Ten Reasons to Oppose Gambling Casinos in Maine" was an effective piece, arguing among other things that "Casinos don't create wealth, they cannibalize local businesses...." "Casinos attract crime...." "The costs of casinos far outweigh the benefits...." and "More than anything else, gambling casinos will change the character of Maine."

Most likely the same material was distributed in Sanford, a town some fifteen miles inland from Biddeford, but the results were different. Sanford voted to proceed to explore the possibility of hosting a casino, thus keeping the idea alive in that part of the state. One reason for the opposite outcome may have been Sanford's unemployment rate—allegedly the second-highest in Maine. The planning of the pro-casino forces thus shifted direction away from the coast, but not so far away from the Maine Turnpike that a spur from it could not be built at the casino's expense, a traffic-routing solution analagous to one devised by Mohegan Sun in Connecticut.

The political strategy changed, too. Whoever became governor of Maine after the election of November 2002 was pledged to veto a casino bill. Support in the legislature would never be enough to override it. The next step, consequently—really the only recourse—was to move toward a statewide referendum.

Under a law passed in the early 1900s, Maine citizens can initiate a petition either to propose a piece of legislation or exercise a "citizen's veto" over a measure passed by the lawmakers in Augusta. The number of signatures needed is 10 percent of the previous gubernatorial vote. In recent years, this has meant 40,000–60,000 bonafide registered voters. In the case of offered legislation, the legislature can pass it as written on the petition, with no amendments, or if they turn the bill down, the measure goes to all the voters for their approval or dissent.

The requisite signatures were gathered and authenticated. Court challenges by Casinos No! of the wording to be on the ballot were rejected. Both sides then geared up for an expensive and rancorous campaign. Marnell–Corrao Associates, a Las Vegas developer of casinos, appeared to be the principal financial backer of the pro group; on the other side, there was L. L. Bean, the venerable Maine icon in the sporting goods and mail-order business, worried about the taint it felt a casino would bring to the state's outdoor, squeaky-clean image. The governor, John Baldacci, weighed in on the side of Casinos No! Meanwhile, the effect of a worsening economy on the vote, particularly in northern Maine, where a former giant industry, the Great Northern Paper Company, had just gone bankrupt, added further spice to the mix, especially with the television ads already being run by the casinoists emphasizing it would create 10,000 jobs and pay $100 million annually into the state's coffers.

Indian gaming has become big business in the United States. *Time Magazine,* in a two-part series of generally uncomplimentary articles, pegs the total take in 2001 at around $13 billion. It has kept increasing, too, while Las Vegas and Atlantic City have remained flat, according to *Time's* statistics. *Time's* muckraking approach focuses on other statistics as well, showing a great discrepancy in the amounts of money going to different tribes, with some earning huge amounts from gambling and others very little; also, large amounts are going to investors who are not Indians; but worse still, tribes who have hit it big, like the Mashantucket Pequots, the Santa Ynez in California, and the Miccosukees in Florida (where each member receives each year between a quarter of a million and $1.6 million dollars), still get federal funds on top of those earnings. It riles the *Time* writers that the Indians have entered the political arena and spend more money on lobbying than General Motors or Boeing and—pejoratively—"even Enron at its heyday."

The sense of this series is that a gigantic con game is going on, unfair to certain Indians, as well as to all other Americans, although the writers include one sidebar story on the Prairie Band, Potawatomi Nation, north of Topeka, Kansas, where 70 percent unemployment existed and 85 percent of the reservation's people were on welfare until they opened Harrah's Prairie Band Casino, "which has become the most popular tourist destination in Kansas."[13]

The tale of the Lytton Band of Pomo Indians in California is included, too—a tribe down to two families, their reservation sold to whites, but who received federal recognition, built a casino, and now, some 200 strong, represent in the *Time* writers' own words, "an American success story."

Native Peoples, an Indian publication as sleek in looks as *Time,* struck back in its May–June 2003 issue. In an editorializing "Viewpoint," the *exposé* was slammed for opening "old wounds and prejudices about Native Americans." The discrepancies between large and small tribes were attributed to "forced relocations, broken treaty obligations, illegal takings, and federal allotment and termination policies. The conditions decried by *Time's* articles, of small tribal communities with small land holdings near large population centers now realizing disproportionately large gaming revenues, is the product of these historic inequities."

Discussing tribal sovereignty the Indian writer points out that the United States has always recognized a special trust relationship with the tribes, and goes on to say: "This trust relationship is misinterpreted by the *Time* articles as an unfair commercial advantage, which enables tribal governments to conduct enterprises without being taxed or governed by state laws, except where required by federal law or mutual agreement." And as for their seeking funds from unorthodox, white, venture capitalists who have reaped large profits, another *Time* complaint, the problem was due to their inability to use federal economic assistance funds or to find a way "to pledge title to their lands held in trust by the federal government" as collateral for a loan.

Tom Tureen, had he been writing a rebuttal, would have put more succinctly his own justification for Indian gaming, which now is done by one-third of the U.S.'s 560 Native American entities. As he once said to me: "It is the property taxes on all those acres that were taken from them all those years."

The *Native Peoples* article, needless to say, did not have the circulation of the *Time* articles. That many white Americans never get a chance to hear or read an Indian point of view was brought vividly home to me in an incident that occurred at the tail end of that "roasting" I received in the church in York. After I'd finished speaking, an elderly gentleman I didn't know approached me.

"Listen," he said, "what if you went back to the Indians and pointed out to them the harm they are doing to us, the threat this would mean to us, to the value of our homes, to our way of life here."

I thought about what he'd said for a moment, then replied: "I suppose I could, but what do you think they'd say to me?"

He looked momentarily blank.

So I added: "I think they'd say: 'Well, look what you did to us.'"

After another moment, thinking this over, he nodded sadly in agreement.

NOTES

[1] *Maine Sunday Telegram,* 3 March 2002, page 8A.

[2] *Portland Press Herald,* 7 March 2002, page 1A.

[3] *Portland Press Herald,* March 8, 2002, page 1A.

[4] *Portsmouth Sunday Herald,* March 10, 2002, page A1.

[5] Ibid, page A9.

[6] Jeff Benedict, *Without Reservation: The Making of America's Most Powerful Indian Tribe and Foxwoods, the World's Largest Casino.* New York: HarperCollins, 2000.

[7] Kim Isaac Eisler, *Revenge of the Pequots.* New York: Simon and Schuster, 2001.

[8] Ibid, page 42.

[9] Ibid, page 84.

[10] Benedict, *Without Reservation,* page 128.

[11] *York Independent,* 27 March 2002, page 1.

[12] Ibid, page 7.

[13] *Time Magazine,* 16 December 2002, page 58.

25

THE REFERENDUM REJECTED

On November 4, 2003, the question of an Indian casino in Maine was definitively decided. The Down East voters answered it with a resounding NO, stunning in extent, with more than two-to-one opposed, and almost every municipality in the state defeating a project its proponents claimed would bring the state $100 million annually in tax revenue. Conventional wisdom had been that the race would be close, and that the northern areas, feeling no impact, would jump at the chance to share all that added income, most of which would be doled out in school subsidies. The bombshell of an *overwhelming* rejection was truly unexpected and has led to a good deal of conjecture as to why it happened as it did.

Maine Indians were not shy in expressing their thoughts on the matter. In the waning weeks of the campaign, casino proponents had already made public a charge of "racism." A sign in Sanford, where the controversial facility was to be located, allegedly read: "We took your land. Now get used to it." Scaremongering articles in a local York County newspaper, predicting a massive influx of presumably non-white "foreign workers," were also cited.

Implicit in the feelings of Passamaquoddy and Penobscots that more than anti-gambling sentiment was involved lay in the rather easy passage on the same November 4 ballot of a measure to allow slot machines at Maine racetracks. Barry Dana, the young Penobscot chief who was the prime Indian spokesperson for the pro-casino forces, did not use the word *racism* in a strong statement he made on television the night of the returns, but the implication was clearly there.

Ostensibly, Dana's lament was a populist one, his anger aimed at a "wealthy minority," bent on keeping "two Maines...drawn along straight economic lines"...run by an "elite" that "used all the power and influence their money could buy to keep Maine the way they want it to be." The Indian leader characterized the casino project as a *gift* of the tribes to all of Maine—good-paying jobs with health care and other benefits in a state where many work for minimum wage, alone—"...something we—as a minority—were ready to share with the 97 percent white/non-Native population of the state."

The closest these remarks came to an assertion of racism was in a reference to the tribes' history of contentious relations with the state. "There are many in Maine," Dana said, "in and out of government—who are best served if we stay quietly on our reservations, weaving baskets."

A week after the election, the *Portland Press Herald,* whose editorial policy was ferociously anti-casino, (despite its advertising policy of running ads for the "Scotia Prince Casino and Party Cruises" out of Portland), picked up on this tart phrasing of the Penobscot chief, saying it showed "well the depth of feeling that Dana and the people he leads have with respect to the casino and race."

Predictably, though, other voices in that same media outlet criticized Barry Dana for not being a *good sport* about losing. A post-campaign round-up story, assessing the political effect the campaign had on major participants of both sides, listed the Penobscot chief as *having shown personal appeal,* but that "the bitterness of his statement after the election lowered his stock."

As it turned out, other Indian leaders did not shrink from using the R word. Among a number of letters to the editor in the Portland press was one from a woman in Falmouth, complaining "I strongly resent being called a racist by Robert Newell, governor at Indian Township, when he made his comment that, 'Maine is a racist State.' I take that quite personally." Donna Loring, the Penobscots' state representative, was quoted about an incident in Bangor when tribal members protested at an anti-casino rally the Saturday before the election and were labeled with an ugly name. Said Donna, "We protest what we think are lies and, I think, racism, and we get called thugs."

A direct expression of the tribes' displeasure occurred on November 8. In what the *Bangor Daily News* called a "bitter response to the Casino vote," tribal representatives at a special meeting of the Tribal-State Commission announced they were withdrawing from the panel, which had been set up specifically under the Land Claims Settlement as a jointly funded forum for discussing issues of mutual concern. Fifteen minutes into this meeting, the Passamaquoddy representatives, Clive Dore and Wayne Newell, informed the executive director Diana Scully that they had been instructed to make a statement and then leave. Essentially, the Passamaquoddy said their tribe would be reassessing its relationship with the State of Maine in the light of the referendum outcome, stressing their belief that distortions and lies by opponents had caused the final result. As soon as the Passamaquoddy had their say, the two Penobscots present, John Banks and Mark Chavaree, declared that they would leave, too, in solidarity with their fellow Wabanakis.

Indian bitterness was further documented when, in the same *Bangor Daily News* story, Governor John Baldacci's spokesperson revealed that the chief executive's attempts to reach Indian leaders had been initially fruitless, with some refusing to accept his calls and others refusing to return them. Baldacci had taken an active role in opposing the casino.

More fuel was subsequently heaped on the blaze of Maine Indian ire in the following month by a decision of the federal government to turn over control of pollution in the state's rivers from the U.S. Environmental Protection Agency to the state's Department of Environmental Protection. Barry Dana, who earlier had been ready to go to jail over the Penobscots' predilection for maintaining federal responsibility, used this final straw, which the Indians considered a victory for the paper companies, as an occasion to deliver yet another exasperated public blast.

Maine, he stated, now had *three strikes* against it from the

Indians' point of view—and "what happens when you have three strikes?" he asked rhetorically, "You're out."

Therefore, the tribes, he announced, were calling for a repudiation and Congressional re-write of the Maine Indian Land Claims Act of 1980.

The three strikes, Dana said, were: 1) The Maine Supreme Court decision that denied Indian sovereignty in connection with tribal records, which occurred during the dispute about who would control pollution in the Penobscot River; 2) The defeat of the casino proposal, leaving the Maine tribes the only ones in the country not allowed to run a casino; 3) The final decision of the feds to turn over policing of the rivers to the state, whom the Indians saw as too cozy with the paper companies.

Inherent in all of this furor is the *never settled* question of Indian sovereignty. The concept of a separate, non-subservient governmental entity in Maine, on a par with the state, is certainly alien to most non-Indian citizens. Governors like James Longley and Joseph Brennan, inveighing against such a "state within a state" idea, forged the settlement as a compromise, and it is now seen by the Maine Indians as weighted heavily against them.

Nor are only the Passamaquoddy and Penobscots challenging the state's position. The Micmacs in Aroostook County, precisely because they were not parties to the Land Claims Settlement and consider themselves totally under federal jurisdiction, have made known their intent to sell cigarettes tax-free at two tobacco stores on land they own in Presque Isle. *No way*, state officials maintain, with Attorney-General Steven Rowe arguing that the Micmacs, indeed, are bound by the 1980 Maine Implementing Act, even though they weren't specifically involved. In Rhode Island, a similar controversy between that state and the Narragansett tribe led to a much criticized state police raid to close down a tobacco operation, with resulting violence that injured a number of people. To date, the Micmacs have not challenged the state by opening their shops, and discussions continue.

In the Monday-morning quarterbacking over the casino question's huge failure, the sovereignty factor may have been a *subliminal* cause. Expressed to me more than once was the sentiment, "Why the Indians? Why should they be the beneficiaries of all that revenue?" A barber in Augusta expressed his opinion that he—and his clients—didn't think the Indians in Maine were very good at "bootstrapping," i.e., doing things for themselves, which, inaccurate as that thought might be, showed a common underlying prejudice that Indians have failed to assimilate—*they don't want to be like the rest of us Americans.* Racism? Or just misunderstanding?

Another thought, perhaps, to explain the large anti-casino vote in the northern part of the state is the memory of the Land Claims controversy, the outrage it fomented that this small group could claim land people felt was rightly theirs (all of it in the northern two-thirds of Maine), and no appreciation for what the tribes gave up in value by agreeing to settle.

One of the key reasons for the change in the polls on the casino question was the success the Casinos No! group had in demonizing the initiated legislation on the ballot. The fact that it granted authority to the tribes for twenty years to conduct gaming and that this authority could not be amended or repealed without the tribes' consent was heavily attacked. Particularly galling to the Indians was that a clause in the bill, taken out of context and made into a devastating TV ad, charged that the legislation would allow children to gamble. This distortion was based on an exemption in the act's section entitled "Prohibition on attendance of minors" that would let kids play "*bazaar games*," a reference apparently to an arcade, which was to contain non-gambling video games, pinball machines, etc.

Other contributions to the anti-casino vote I've heard mentioned include the feeling of some voters that the amount of money going to the state—25 percent of the slot machine take—was not enough. Undoubtedly the most damning claims were that crime would flourish and Maine's pure image might be sullied. Another factor was the too-close identification of the project with the highly controversial, easily attack-able Foxwoods operation in Connecticut, to which the Maine casino was continually compared. Not much was done to showcase Indian casinos in other parts of the country that have been successful for the tribes who own them and com-patible with surrounding non-Indian communities.

Telephone interviews I had with some of the Indian lead-ers several weeks after the election showed that, although the dust had settled a bit, feelings were still raw.

By then, there *had been* a meeting with Governor Baldacci, and the Indians had been civil to him. But Donald Soctomah, the former Passamaquoddy representative , re-ported consensus among the Indians that the meeting had been a waste of time, "a show for the public." The governor had suggested they go into fish farming as a lucrative form of economic activity, while the Indians, themselves, were all aware of the tremendous problems facing that industry Down East, where disease and certain proposed federal actions on behalf of wild salmon threatened it with extinction.

Now, instead, Donald implied, the tribes' first priority would be on making changes to the Land Claims Settlement, trying to get Congress to set up an independent review of its contradictions and possibly impose the view expressed in the original U.S. Senate report that the tribes should have their full sovereignty.

Donald also described election night at Indian Township, with everyone gathered around a communal supper but unable to make the TV work and having to hear the results on the radio.

Their biggest disappointment, he said, was that their immediate neighbors in surrounding towns like Princeton had voted against them. Donald felt that the relationships they had formed locally, which the Indians felt had been growing better and better, would suffer. Asked about racism, he said he believed it might have contributed to so many people believ-ing the negative ads, and he cited a "Maine Cowboy Website" that had put out false propaganda about all of the casino money going to Las Vegas and none to Maine. There was also tribal resentment about the Maine State Police making negative public statements and leaving the impression that, despite the role of watchdog assigned to them in the legislation, no one would be able to regulate the gambling. The charge that nothing in the casino operation could be changed for twenty years seemed likewise to have been a sore point; the inclusion of the twenty-year proviso, Donald explained, was to assure investors of continuity of ownership, not to prevent any necessary modifications.

Deprived now, as Donald said, of a plan that allowed the Passamaquoddy to dream of a better future, his people were "pretty disappointed still." In fact, he conceded, they were "really dejected."

His fellow tribal member and neighbor in Indian Township, Wayne Newell, spoke of "having to go back to the drawing board" and pursue "the fundamental question of the tribe's right to determine its own future."

Gambling, to them, had been an "economic development thing," which they had seen work for other tribes throughout the country. As a major veteran of the Land Claims Settlement wars, Wayne acknowledged how "*naïve*" he'd been during that era and, knowing what he did now, he would never have compromised so easily on the settlement.

A long-time Democrat (as most of the Maine Indians have been), Wayne admitted to feeling a sense of betrayal, particularly because of the active role taken by Democratic Governor John Baldacci in opposing them. "If he hadn't been so active, things might have been different," Wayne said, "and he really didn't have to jump into it like that." Similar words were used about the governor when I spoke to another former Passamaquoddy representative, Joe Nicholas, at his home in Pleasant Point. Joe, too, had always been a strong Democrat.

Wayne Newell and I ended our talk on yet another worrisome note that he sounded about the tribe's future. He was president of their Northeastern Blueberry Company, their one

shining long-term success in "bootstrap" economic development, in which they had become the biggest blueberry growers in the state. But a lawsuit filed against the processors was
threatening to put the buyer of their millions of blueberries—
Cherryfield Farms—into bankruptcy. Thus, the frailty of what
they had achieved on their own over years of struggle was all
the more poignant to them now, when balanced against what
they felt might have been had the casino gone through—
another potential blow adding to the sense of loss sweeping all
Indian country.

Donna Loring was my final contact. The current Penobscot representative was frank in saying that she didn't think
racism was the main reason the initiative failed. As she put it,
"We unwittingly stumbled into a web of power and stepped
on toes." What the Indians were proposing was essentially an
unknown prospect for the state, a large enterprise of which
they, the tribes, were to be the owners. She felt the people of
Maine "did not know us as people" and so they believed the
real control would be by Las Vegas, by the mob, by the
criminals. Every newspaper in the state, even the earlier
favorable *Bangor Daily News*, editorialized against the casino.
Major local industries like L. L. Bean and MBNA were
aggressively opposed. Non-profit organizations like the
Audubon Society joined the fray. "Once all those boards and
companies came out against us," Donna said, "it really made
an impression."

I remembered that during the gubernatorial election,
Donna had had a Baldacci sticker on her car, one of the
first I'd seen. Now, she, too, was upset with the governor,
saying, "He didn't have to trample us into the ground."
Then, she likened her present position as a legislator
needing to go back to Augusta and work with the administration to "having to drink poison and having to smile while
you do it."

As to the future, she saw a few rays of hope. She knew that
people were calling the governor and saying it was time to do
something for the tribes. I, myself, knew that all along during

the campaign, opponents of the casino were saying the state *could* find other ways to help the Indians (albeit without offering any suggestions). Voices, post-election, were suddenly being raised editorially on that same score, and while Donna was skeptical and wary—"If you use our name, we want to benefit"—she felt her people should get what they could out of this atmosphere, including being able to increase their bingo operation, especially since smaller-than-casino-scale gambling had been approved by allowing slot machines at race tracks.

Yet her strongest feelings about future goals centered, as had those of the others I'd interviewed, on changing the settlement. Personally, she felt it should be abolished, that it was "eating away our sovereignty."

Congress, she insisted, had said, "We look at it [the settlement] as enhancing sovereignty." But the state has "used the act to hit us over the head."

So the question became: "How do we get rid of it?"

"I'm through with the friendly cooperating kind of thing," she declared and made it plain the Penobscots were hoping to cooperate with other tribes—in-state and out-of-state.

Donna saw a lot of potential there—in particular, a "real bottom line" in working with casino tribes that have lots of money.

One thing seems certain. The "tool," as Donna Loring called it, of an Indian casino serving as an engine of economic development as it has for many tribes in the United States, will be denied to the Maine tribes.

The strong feelings engendered both pro and con Indian casinos, nationwide as well as in Maine, strike me as representing a sort of cultural divide—on the one hand we have the acceptance of gaming in Indian culture as a natural and even favored activity, and on the other hand is the inheritance of America's Puritan past and gambling's association with criminality, the underworld, and other disreputable segments of society. In New England, that latter sentiment is probably deeper than elsewhere in the country; Maine, it may be remembered, was the first state in the nation to institute Prohibition (in the 1850s).

That Indians in Maine and elsewhere, as indigenous peoples, developed distinct cultures over thousands of years, ways of life that allowed them to cope harmoniously with their natural surroundings, has led them to remain relatively intact in the American melting pot. They have kept to their own ways of looking at things and doing things, despite several centuries of pressure to conform to the majority view in this country. Consequently, the unsettled future that still faces the Passamaquoddy, Penobscots, Maliseets, and Micmacs in Maine will include the fact that they will continue to insist on maintaining their heritage from the unsettled past, insisting that they are each a sovereign people with whom treaties were made and promises rendered, and they will not disown that past nor turn it into a mere ceremonious bit of color to add to the pageantry of American life. They take their claims of sovereignty very seriously and power struggles, like those we have seen in the settlement dispute and the casino fight, are bound to re-occur.

In that regard, let me travel back to the site where this foray of mine into the unfamiliar universe of *Indian country* began (Chapter 1)—not in Maine, but on Martha's Vineyard Island among the Wampanoags of Massachusetts. At the meeting I attended there to first learn about "Indian law," reference was made to a local zoning restriction preventing the Gay Head/Aquinnah tribe from building a small shed and pier at its tribal shellfish hatchery without a building permit from the town. In June 2003 a superior court judge in Massachusetts ruled that the Wampanoags could not be compelled by the town to comply with its zoning rules, despite the terms of the 1983 Settlement Act, under which they had agreed to do so. Their *"sovereign immunity,"* in the language of a local newspaper's report of Judge Richard F. Condon's opinion, "trumps the 1983 Wampanoag Settlement agreement as well as subsequent state and federal legislation that led to federal recognition of the tribe in 1987."

Local officials immediately rushed to have the judge reconsider his ruling and, failing that, were preparing to appeal to a higher court.

The potential impact, needless to say, of letting the decision stand could be immense.

And it could easily apply to the Maine Land Claims Settlement, since the Wampanoags, using the same lawyer, Tom Tureen, had followed the same pattern as the northern tribes in reaching a settlement and incorporating it in state and federal law, and achieving federal recognition.

Whatever the eventual outcome, the mere fact that a reputable judge in Massachusetts could, even in an initial ruling (which he, himself, called "unfair" but legally justified) articulate that "consent by a tribe to the laws of the state is not the equivalent of consent to a waiver of sovereign immunity" opens a door to the very goal the now-angered Maine Indians are seeking—a change, if not the nullification, of the "landmark" 1980 accord.

The beat of the war drum, as it were, if only on the legal/political front, goes on. In that same crucial year of 1980, while the Maine case was being "settled," two Native American law professors, graduates of Harvard Law School, Lawrence Barsh and James Youngblood Henderson, published a mostly forgotten book entitled *The Road*, which I found fascinating when I was introducing myself to the subject of Indian/white relations in Maine and the rest of the country. Their work, they wrote, was "addressed to a great riddle: the political relationship between these sovereign American tribes and *the other* sovereign American government, that is the government of the United States." Explaining their title, they added that "'The Road' is tribalism," and that "Tribalism has always been *the Road*, that is, the heart and spirit of the Indian people.... Tribalism is not an association of interests but a form of consciousness which faithfully reflects the spirit of Indians...."

To solve the "riddle" of this inharmonious relationship, the authors ultimately proposed an amendment to the U.S. Constitution, which would, among other provisos, resolve all previous Indian treaties "into a single constitution of undisputed authority" that would become part of the U.S. Constitution, that all Indian tribes would be deemed *states,* that tribes would have all the powers of states, that an Assembly of Tribes would choose two senators to join the U.S. Senate as voting members and two representatives for the U.S. House, that all constitutional powers would be reserved to the tribes and could not be overruled by Congress—and so on and so forth.

It is no surprise we have not heard any further word of this proposal, but the idea expressed then, which Barsh and Henderson articulated as *Tribes must have no less political liberty than the states* is still alive—at least in Indian hearts, as far as I can see.

What its next expression in Maine will be is only as far away as tomorrow's headlines.

26

INDIGENOUS PEOPLES

$\mathcal{W}$e in Maine are not alone in feeling bothered and pained, like the old gentleman in York, that a portion of our population seems to move to the beat of a different drum from that to which the vast majority march. Indigenous peoples are all over the world. Their miniscule size makes the aggravation they cause all the more exasperating. They have refused to disappear and, if anything, are getting feistier all the time.

Look on the Internet. You will find the Center for World Indigenous Studies. You will also find the Indigenous Peoples Survival Foundation. You will learn there is now a Permanent Forum on Indigenous Issues at the United Nations. The Penobscots, Passamaquoddy, Maliseets, and Micmacs are but a microcosm of a global phenomenon. The issues they have battled with in Maine—land, sovereignty, cultural renewal, resisting exploitation—are mirrored in a host of disputes and confrontations that rarely, if ever, make the news.

Another website on this score, that of the Indigenous Peoples and the Law, lists pages of activities. Many are in New Zealand, where the site originates, and involve Maori issues, but the range is worldwide whether it is the Inuit of northern Quebec claiming offshore resources, a land rights battle in Sarawak (a part of Malaysia), Brazilian Indians wanting patents on native medicine turned into pharmaceuticals, the triumphs in court of the Deni people in the Amazon and the Pintubi people of Kiwirrkuna in Western Australia, the seeking of recognition by the Anuak of Gambela (in western Ethiopia), Nicaragua's violation of the rights of the Awas Tingni community, or, closer to Maine, confrontations in Canada involving Mi'kmaq fishing rights.

This is the "Fourth World," as it has been called. The Maine Indians, modernized and sophisticated though they may be, have more than a foot in that world, which appears to be inextinguishable. It is not one that those of us who live in the "First World" find it easy to understand. *Acceptance* of it is something else, depending on where you are, and for the most part that is what this book is about: how one society—the preponderantly Anglo culture of Maine—has lived with and interacted with the aboriginal populations and their descendants on the lands we have settled.

In the Introduction I searched my memory for examples of contacts I've had, as a citizen of the United States, with our fairly ubiquitous if not often encountered Native American populations. Then the focus became the Penobscots, Passamaquoddy, Maliseets, and Micmacs—only four out of the many indigenous groups still populating North America, alone. Trying to set a context, my mind went roaming; where else on the globe had I seen or actually stepped into this "Fourth World," so surprisingly abundant and—as we have seen in Maine—dynamically alive, right on the cusp of the twenty-first century?

Just as I had first seen Passamaquoddy Indians but not known their tribal name, when I was on a fishing trip to Washington County with my dad in 1953, so, too, it was on a fishing trip with him to New Zealand in 1980 that I saw Maoris for the first time. That is, I saw them in their native setting, as opposed to the zoo-like atmosphere of the Polynesian Culture Center in Hawaii, where Pacific Island students display their individual cultures in a sort of Disneyland show-biz style. Rotorua, one of the Maori strongholds on the North Island of New Zealand, was our fishing headquarters. An unforgettable incident at our hotel one night brought home to me the Fourth World–First World dichotomy that seems to underlie native relationships, no matter how westernized the indigenous peoples become.

Our hotel was the best in town and that evening a large party of older Maori men and women, dressed in their best western clothes, were having dinner there, celebrating the birthday of an obviously much-beloved woman of their tribe who, we were told, was in her eighties. The entertainment, in keeping with the tourist draw of this heartland of Maori tradition, featured Maori dancing—lovely girls in red, white, and black skimpy plaid dresses, attractively swinging white *poi* balls on long strings in time to the music, and half-naked, sarong-wearing men, tattooed and war-painted, grimacing fiercely and sticking out their tongues as they stabbed the air with simulated spears.

Were the Maori diners offended by this hokey folk dancing? Just the opposite. Suddenly, off came the suitcoat jackets, ties were loosened, and the distinguished-looking men were soon up on the stage, whirling and making faces with the paid dancers. Not to be outdone, the dignified women with them doffed their high heels, hiked their skirts, grabbed *poi* ball strings, and flung those round white orbs around like the girls. It was an astonishing scene.

Now how could I have known these were members of the Te Arawa tribe without having gone to Rotorua, or the significance in New Zealand history of Waitangi without having been to Waitangi, a seacoast town where a treaty was signed in 1840, ending warfare as bloody as our own in Maine in the days of the French and Indian conflicts. How else would I have learned that, since there are only 3 million New Zealanders, the impact of the Maori descendants there has far more weight than that of the Native Americans in the U.S.; or that there is the Waitangi Tribunal, a special court for hearing and deciding cases of conflict between Maoris and non-Maoris, which issues orders like: "The crown should apologize and pay compensation after failing to protect Maori interests when 15,385 hectares of Maori land in the Bay of Plenty was transferred in private hands in the late 1960s." The parliament has a Maori Affairs Select Committee and Maori seats and a full panoply of legal hassles constantly before them.

Australia, I'm sure, could present a similar picture with its Aboriginal populations. My only contact with the latter was in, of all places, Taiwan. Our hotel in Taipei was featuring a display of Australian food at mealtimes and to draw attention to their public relations efforts, the entrepreneurs from Down Under had brought a group of Aboriginal drummers and dancers. The Chinese patrons gawked at these wild-haired, dark-brown, tattooed guys in loin cloths cavorting about, who afterward, dressed in street clothes, could be heard speaking the same English as their white compatriots with the same cockney-tinged accent. Also in Taiwan, I'd once flown to the opposite end of the island from Taipei, where tribal dancers of their own Oriental "aboriginal" populations, in gaudy local costumes, welcomed us.

Thus indigenous populations are not exclusively brown-, red-, or black-skinned. The Hmong refugees from Vietnam are another example of Asian indigenes among Asians. The Ainu of northern Japan have been deemed to be Caucasian—whites living not only among Asians in Japan but among other whites on Sakhalin Island and the Kuriles occupied by Russia. Some scientists claim the Ainus may not be white, but of Oceanic origin. It was not until 1997 that the Japanese Diet passed a law admitting the existence of the Ainu as an ethnic minority in Japan and took steps to protect Ainu culture. But a year later, in a statement to the U.N. Working Group on Indigenous Populations, the Ainu complained they were still being "thought of and treated as a 'barbaric' minority in Japan." They declared themselves strongly opposed to any law or agreement "which holds an assimilationist program as its basic direction."

Similar cries for help to the U.N. have come from indigenous groups far more obscure than the Ainus of Japan. In May 2002 complaints were received from the Khow and Kalash tribes, "the descendants of Alexander the Great," original Greeks from Macedonia left in the Hindu-Kush Mountains of Pakistan. Their complaint is against the Pakistanis for coming into their territory, building "large hotels and motels on sacred sites," causing pollution, cutting down their forests, and referring to the natives with the contemptuous term of "Kafirs," or non-believers. The demands of Sher Malik and Kaab Malik, their spokesmen, to the Permanent Forum on Indigenous

Issues was that: "the label of KAFIR must be removed"; "the hotels and motels of non-native civil businessmen from the mainland of Pakistan...must be removed"; "the Forest Corporation must return the remaining forests...to the indigenous people..."; "Restitutions and reparations must be paid for the damages done."

This language of anti-colonial resistance from a tiny corner of "Third World" Pakistan, posted on the Internet, turned my thoughts to a far more serious case involving the same emotions which I'd encountered on the island of New Caledonia. Technically, it is a part of France, with about a third of its population French settlers who have been there for several generations, and two-thirds Melanesians, divided into more than twenty tribes, many speaking mutually unintelligible languages. A rebellion of the natives had broken out a few years before my visit; lives were lost on both sides before an uneasy truce was signed. One beautiful spot where my wife and I stayed was on the Isles of Pines; we were in a *gite*, a rude campsite run by Melanesian women, who were perfectly wonderful to us. But the underlying tensions became clear when, in going to the beach, we wandered off a path into a native village and were chased off by a frenzied, hate-filled young man wearing Rastafarian dreadlocks, who tried to sic his dog on us.

Much more welcoming were the Indians of Panama—the San Blas on their islands on the Caribbean side and the Embera on the jungle-filled Darién Peninsula. We were on a small-ship "Eco-cruise," my wife and I, when we encounteried these two very different-looking Indian groups that have kept their way of life intact in Central America, only adapting as far as they needed in order to wring a small extra living out of the off-the-beaten-track tourists who made it to their territories. Elaborate embroideries called "*molas*" were the San Blas' specialty and delicate carvings the Emberas'. It took a four-hour ocean and river ride in a motorized dugout canoe to reach the latter. After looking at the handicrafts, we listened to their chief, a young man, American-trained, fluent in English, tell us how the jungle served as their bulwark against fears of a Colombian invasion, if not of troops then of drug peddlers, which was why they had agitated to keep the Pan American highway from being completed through the peninsula.

In the U.S., when we think of "indigenous peoples," we naturally think of Indians. Admittedly, we have a bewildering array of tribes, 560 of them, and we now are conscious they exist in almost every state. But in Alaska, I first learned about *indigenes* who do not consider themselves *Indians* and make it very plain you understand the difference.

My introduction was to the *Aleuts* (pronounced Ali-oots). I met them on St. Paul Island, one of the Pribilofs, a small archipelago in the middle of the Bering Sea. The day I arrived from Anchorage was the Fourth of July. We'd been told there was only one hotel on the island and one restaurant, run by the Native Corporation, and that the restaurant would be closed for the holiday, but not to worry—a free feast was being offered to everyone in the center of town.

This was the first I'd heard of the term *Native Corporation,* and learning more about it required a look at some interesting Alaskan–U.S. governmental history.

In Maine we have been touting our Land Claims Settlement of 1980 as *the* major breakthrough, at least for tribes in the original thirteen colonies, and a significant milestone in overall American Indian affairs. Nine years earlier, the Alaska Native Claims Settlement went through Congress, and its payout, in both money and land, dwarfed what was done in Maine. Instead of $81 million and 300,000 acres, as in the Pine Tree State, the Alaska figures were $962.5 million and 44 million acres!

However—and it's a big *however*—there were significant differences between the two accords, both in concept and intent.

First of all, unlike the Maine action, the Alaska one was not precipitated from the native side. There was no finding that a state had broken a federal law in taking over indigenous land. In fact, the prime motivation behind the Alaska legislation was—just that—to *take away* indigenous land.

The precipitating problem that motivated ANCSA, the name by which the Alaska Native Corporation Settlement Act is universally known, was expressed in the question: *Who owns the land over which the oil pipeline from Prudhoe Bay has to pass?*

The powers-that-be wanted to be sure it wasn't a bunch of natives.

Consequently, Congress acted very much like it did when it passed the Dawes Act in 1887. So much land—in this case 44 million acres—was granted to the natives, but many millions of acres more were left in federal, state, and private lands. Aboriginal title to all of Alaska was wiped out, plus their aboriginal right to hunt and fish on the 90 percent of the state they didn't receive. *Individual allotments* were not granted. The land and the money, instead, went to *native corporations*, like the one on St. Paul Island that ran the only hotel and restaurant.

Two hundred of these village corporations were created, along with twelve larger regional ones, and the idea was that they would go into business, prosper, and within twenty years be worth a fortune. The natives, all automatically owning shares in these operations, would have valuable assets they could sell.

To whom? That was the unstated kicker. As happened in Oklahoma under the Dawes Act, when Indians sold their property to non-Indians and lost it forever, here in Alaska there could be similar problems, compounded by the fact that if the corporations *lost money* and couldn't pay their debts, their creditors could take over the assets. And losing money was a real possibility. Even a layman like myself, listening to the folks on St. Paul Island tell how their corporation had just spent $10 million to fix up their harbor facilities, could wonder if that investment in their fishing fleet would pay off.

In his book *Village Journey,* a critic of ANCSA, the former Canadian judge Thomas Berger, wrote: "The Native Corporations were not formed to meet a particular need in an established market.... They had to formulate businesses after the fact," and it offered "no guarantee in perpetuity of Native ownership of land nor did it protect Native subsistence."[1]

Yet ANCSA still exists and the jury is still out, just like it is on the settlement in Maine.

In Alaska in 1991 several important "native-friendly" amendments were added that have helped avoid the worst possibilities. Amendments in Maine have not been on the same scale of change.

Besides the Aleuts, the Inuit, or as we used to call them, Eskimos, are also indigenous people in the U.S. who are not Indians. The largest group in this category, of course, are the Hawaiians.

Here in *aloha* land the word "sovereignty" has taken on a meaning far beyond its use by the Maine Indians. The fiftieth state, lest we forget, was once an independent kingdom until *annexed* to the United States in 1898. The native Hawaiian population, to a great extent, did not support this move and "sovereignty" has become the rallying cry for groups with goals that range from total independence to large land and money compensations for what they say was taken from the native Polynesians.

You have only to read Professor Haunani-Kay Trask's fiery *From a Native Daughter: Colonialism and Sovereignty in Hawaii* to gauge the depth of nativist feeling in Hawaii against the *haoles*, the whites, who have, in their eyes, illegally occupied and degraded their country. Along with her sister, Mililani Trask, the author has been a catalyst for efforts, as she defines them in her book, to achieve federal recognition of:

"Our unique status as Native People."

"The injury done by the United States at the overthrow [the deposing of the last Hawaiian monarch, Queen Lilluokalani (Lydia Kamekeha) in 1893], including the loss of land and sovereignty."

"The necessity of reparation of that injury through acknowledgment of our claim to sovereignty, recognition of some form of autonomous Native government, the return of traditional lands and waters, and a package of compensatory resources, including monies."[2]

If you talk to people in Hawaii about the sovereignty issue, they generally say it is not as red-hot as it once was since the proponents seem to have split into four different factions, each with conflicting goals and personalities. One native Hawaiian schoolteacher I met compared them to "crabs in a bucket," squabbling furiously among themselves. Another person, a resident *haole*, wisecracked that the most dangerous place to be in Hawaii nowadays was between the Trask sisters and a television camera. Ed Case, a Democratic state legislator who tried to pass a Hawaiian Autonomy bill the sovereignty people didn't like, and whom they publicly labelled a "racist," was recently elected to Congress from the state, winning in a large field of candidates.

An example of the lengths the issue has reached was related to me by Paul Cox, the director of the National Tropical Botanical Garden, headquartered on the island of Kauai. One day a Hawaiian appeared at his office, said he was the legitimate owner of the two main gardens run by NTBC in the beautiful Lawai Valley, and that the organization had thirty days to vacate the premises. Instead of arguing, Paul simply said: "Wonderful. I was wondering how I was going to meet my payroll. Now, you can take care of it." That was the last Paul heard from him.

But the issue is taken seriously. A letter to the editor in a Honolulu newspaper lauds the new governor, Linda Lingle, for calling the Hawaiian issue not a "racial issue" but "a historical issue based on a relationship between an independent government and the United States of America and what has happened since and the steps we need to take to make things right."

Governor Lingle subsequently went to Washington to lobby the Bush administration (she is a Republican) for *federal recognition of Native Hawaiians in the same manner as Indians and Alaska Natives* and to create a process for the Hawaiians to choose their own government.

The *New York Times,* after September 11, ran an article

stating that some Hawaiians had protested flying the American flag instead of the Hawaiian flag over Iolani Palace, which was described as "a historic state building downtown (in Honolulu) that had not flown the Stars and Stripes since the 1960s."[3] Among the protesters was a founder of the Hawaiian Patriotic League, a group promoting outright independence for the islands.

On the opposite side, a backlash against preferences for native Hawaiians that do exist in this heavily multi-ethnic state also seems constant. For example a longstanding program allowing Hawaiians to lease homesites for ninety-nine years for $1 has been challenged in court. A state agency—the Office of Hawaiian Affairs—was assigned to defend it.

The possibility of future such challenges in U.S. courts to Hawaiian exclusivity occasioned a much bigger uproar in the Rainbow State in 2002—one that made national headlines. The Kamehameha Schools—all-Hawaiian, free, prep schools set up by an endowment from a Hawaiian princess—accepted a student who could not prove at least one of his ancestors lived on the Hawaiian Islands in 1778, the year Captain Cook arrived. Despite the child's Hawaiian first name of Kalani, the alumni were furious that a *haole* had been admitted and let the trustees know it. Haunani-Kay Trask said: "They just got it frontally, full blast, both barrels." Their problem, the trustees rebutted, was that unlike American Indians, whom the courts hold to be political units and thus able to *discriminate*, Hawaiians are considered a race and cannot exclude others on the basis of being non-Hawaiian. Ergo, Governor Lingle's efforts to put them on the same footing with Native Americans.

The U.S. has other Fourth World, non-Indian populations under its wings—the Chamorros in Guam, the various Micronesians on the small islands of the Federated Micronesian States, and the Samoans of American Samoa. Most Americans forget we had a presence in Samoa before we had one in Hawaii, and our part is concentrated primarily on the island of Tutuila and its capital of Pago Pago (pronounced *Pango Pango*). On a January 2003 trip there and to neighboring Western Samoa, an independent country, I had a chance to see a Fourth World culture in action, operating in a modern milieu, but having kept its traditions from being attenuated. While there were some differences between the American side and the Western side, the *Samoaness* of both areas was the most striking feature of the visit.

As a territory, American Samoa sends a delegate to the U.S. Congress who functions not unlike the Penobscot and Passamaquoddy representatives to the Maine legislature. This person has no vote, except on a committee, and the long-time present delegate, the Honorable Eni Faleomavaega, has been elected so many times that he has seniority—in fact, he is the ranking Democrat on the House Foreign Relations Committee. I met him at a public meeting of the Advisory Board of the American Samoa National Park—a project which his clout in D.C. helped bring into being. It was a fascinating session whose purpose was to discuss additions to the park, which, thanks to their man in Washington, Congress and the president had just approved.

Land questions came up in the discussion and it was then I learned how this park was different from all other national parks in the U.S. The federal government did not *own* the land in it; they had *leased* the land from the natives for fifty years with options to renew. When the new lands were under discussion, a man in the audience got up and asked, "What do the *matais* think about it?" That was the first time I heard the word matai. I soon learned it meant *chief*, and that without the support of the matais in the villages—and there could be quite a few in each village—nothing could be done in Samoa. All land was communal; all decisions about it were communal; and, as an ex-legislator, I was astounded to hear from a territorial senator present at the meeting that to be eligible to be elected to the American Samoa Senate, you also had to be a *matai*.

A similar rule affected elections in Western Samoa (the country's official name is just plain Samoa). They have a parliamentary system, having been under German and New

In Falealupo, Western Samoa, we were welcomed with a feast, dances, and a traditional kava ceremony. The woman shown here is making the drink out of water and kava root, and the man will present a cupful to each of the honored guests. PHOTO BY DIETRICK VAN NEERVEEN

Zealand rule before achieving independence. Here, too, matais rule from the national government on down, but these weren't necessarily hereditary positions. You could be made a matai for outstanding service to the community. Nor did you have to be a Samoan. Our leader on the trip, Paul Cox of the National Tropical Botanical Garden, was an American, a Mormon from Utah, and he was a matai in the village of Falealupo, which he had helped greatly in working with local leaders to save their forests from logging.

Other help to them from Paul, too, contributed to the fact we were greeted like heroes when we arrived in this village. Partly through his efforts, an aerial walkway had been constructed in the nearby jungle and it had become a popular tourist attraction, bringing revenue to Falealupo that was used to help elderly people who could no longer work. The grand re-opening of the walkway after repairs was the ostensible reason for our visit. A non-visible project is the potential use of a local tree bark in its chemical composition as a drug against AIDS, a process already started in clinical trials in California. Since the idea had come from a Falealupo "healer," the vil-

Gifts to us at Falealupo included beautiful "fine mats," all part of a celebration that was clearly part of an intact culture, not a show for tourists.
PHOTO BY DIETRICK VAN NEERVEEN

lage—and the country of Western Samoa—would share in the royalties if the drug became marketable—an answer to the concern of many native people that their intellectual property was being stolen—along the lines of the complaint I heard from those young Passamaquoddy at Pleasant Point about the New Age usurpation of aspects of Indian spirituality.

In Falealupo we were treated to a spectacular *kava* ceremony (kava is a drink made from a certain tree root, very slightly intoxicating, but drunk here as a sacred offering) plus a feast and dances of welcome. Gifts were heaped upon us, including whole roasted pigs, huge, exquisitely hand-woven "fine mats," and even large tins of corned beef—all considered precious items in Samoan society (those mats sold for $1,500 American dollars in stores in the capital). For those of us from the First World, it was a vivid illustration of the Fourth World, alive and well in the twenty-first century, and in full control of its environment.

At another village on the same island of Savaii, we had another viewpoint of the interaction of these two "worlds." Again, there was a traditional kava ceremony, and the usual flowery exchange of classic Samoan rhetoric was truncated for our benefit because it can last for hours; then we had another feast, followed by our major purpose, some plain old business talk. At stake was a conservation project. If the villagers would close off their overfished lagoon for a period of years, a Berkeley, California, group, the Seacology Foundation, would pay off their school debt, a sum of $50,000.

It felt déjà-vu, but of a place I'd never been—like a Massachusetts negotiator of olden days treatying with an Indian tribe in Maine, or an equivalent First World–Fourth World interchange anywhere in the world anytime in the past—but how it had changed! This was not to take anything from them, but to give them something—an incentive that would help them, and the world at large, through resource conservation.

In the end there was no outright decision. These things could not be decided by a western clock.

I had thereby been given a glimpse—solely a glimpse—into an indigenous culture still intact to an astounding degree in this age of globalization.

Fannie Hardy Eckstorm, in writing about the Penobscots of Maine, perceptively realized that we on the outside can only see so far through the veils our Native Americans spread for us over their inner worlds.

Thousands of years in isolation brought about the skills, physical and psychological, these people use to adjust to the environments in which they find themselves. Pockets of the bearers of these antique wisdoms remain on a planet now populated by six billion humans. We, in the First World, are at last slowly learning to let them be, to accept that they will not dissolve into a generalized melting pot, and to agree that they may well have something to teach us. Our Indians in Maine have their "healers," too. I talked with Donald Soctomah about this—that maybe the same thing can be done in the Maine North Woods that was happening in far-off Falealupo, Samoa.

Dialogue, understanding, and fairness seem the keys to

such collaboration. We have much to learn from each other if we take each other seriously, respectfully, and try to help, wherever we can.

NOTES

[1] Thomas R. Berger, *Village Journey: The Report of the Alaska Native Review Commission.* New York: Hill and Wang, 1985, pages 26 and 28.

[2] Haunani-Kay Trask, *From a Native Daughter: Colonialism and Sovereignty in Hawaii.* Honolulu: University of Hawaii Press, 1999, page 27.

[3] *New York Times,* 25 November 2001.

AFTERWORD

*W*hat have the Passamaquoddy ever done for society that's noteworthy, if anything?"

The question was asked of me one evening in Eastport, at the place where I was staying while conducting my interviews at Pleasant Point. Although it might have been taken for a hostile question—the person who'd asked, a local resident, had previously remarked that the tribe had a bigger, nicer council building than the Eastport Town Hall—I didn't take it as negative, more like a genuine puzzlement. But I was momentarily stumped for an answer.

Then into my mind immediately popped the thought of two books I'd read by Jack Weatherford, *Indian Giver* and *Native Roots.* Their subtitles, even more than their titles, advertised the author's theme: *How the Indians of the Americas Transformed the World* and *How the Indians Enriched America.*

What did I remember? Foods: the potato, the tomato, corn on the cob—other stuff like chocolate, rubber, *coca* for Coca Cola, Squanto showing the Pilgrims they should stick a dead fish into mounds of loam around their plants. Woodcraft: tomahawks, toboggans, traplines, mocassins. But I had to respond to the guy quickly. It was pretty lame. "The birch-bark canoe," I managed to say, but had to add, in all honesty, I didn't know if the Passamaquoddy, alone, could take credit for its invention. It had to be much more of an overall Northeast American Indian thing.

Anyway, I tried to veer the conversation away from any vexed feeling that the local tribe didn't deserve the attention and government largesse given them and talk in broader terms, recalling Weatherford and other writers about overall contributions the Native Americans had made, including a model of federalized government some historians think we borrowed in fashioning our own United States.

Back home, I delved some more into this latter issue. One particular book I consulted was the work of a woman I knew—a professor in Texas, Judy Potts. She had given me a copy of Volume 1, *Adventure Tales of America,* the entire history of the U.S. done in cartoons for schoolchildren.

The section on the U.S. Constitution was particularly instructive. What one set of drawings described was a subgroup of the delegates to the Constitutional Convention—a five-man Committee of Detail—examining a number of documents as reference points for their work, including THE GREAT LAW OF PEACE, the Iroquois Confederacy's 200-year-old constitution. John Rutledge of South Carolina, chairman of the Committee of Detail, is pictured seated at a table, holding a sheet of paper labelled GREAT LAW OF PEACE, and stating to his fellow committee members: "Gentlemen, the Iroquois Indians' constitution has achieved peace through union for 200 years by allowing to each of the six Iroquois nations *self-government in internal affairs,* while *uniting them for external affairs.* It begins: '*We the people, to form a union,* to establish peace, equity and order....'"[1] Behind him, two Indians are peeking in a window. One says to the other: "Hey, we're being plagiarized." The other replies: "Is that bad?"

What bowled me over were those words: "We the people...." I'd had no idea the phrase could have had an Indian derivation. Some consider *"We the people,"* as inserted in our own Constitution, to be the *source of the powers* conferred by the entire document, itself. To the non-Indian world, this was an unheard of concept at the time. Previously, in English, French, Spanish, or Portuguese America, ruled by monarchies, the source of power would have been: "I, the King (or Queen), divinely ordained...." So not only was Iroquoian federalism being copied, but the very democracy implied in the term so often used by Native American tribes who describe themselves as "The People."

When I checked Jack Weatherford's books at home, here is how he describes the phenomenon: "The most consistent theme in the descriptions penned about the New World was amazement at the Indians' personal liberty, in particular their freedom from rulers and from social classes based on ownership of property. For the first time the French and the British became aware of the possibility of living in social harmony and prosperity without the rule of a king."[2] By the 1700s in the English-speaking colonies along the Atlantic Coast, new generations were beginning to speak of America as their "country," while England was referred to as "home." Nor were our forebears on these shores the only "Americans." Anyone who has traveled to Latin America knows that Spanish speakers call us *norteamericanos* and let us know in no uncertain terms that they are *Americans*, too. On my first trip to Brazil, I immediately felt an affinity to the Portuguese-speaking people there that I never felt in Portugal—how "American" they were, how open, how friendly, how informal. And there were Indian underpinnings to that society in northeast Brazil—Tupi Indians—whose language they used to borrow their nickname for themselves: *potiguares*, or "shrimpeaters"—and although the Tupis had long since vanished, assimilated if not exterminated, I met at least one person in the 1970s who described his father as "pure Indian."

That Indian names dot our languages, our landscapes, our maps, is almost too obvious to be mentioned. Weatherford has ultra-long lists of Indian derivations in English, culled from all over the Americas: "moose, caribou, raccoon, opposum, chipmunk, barracuda, manatee, cougar, puma, jaguar, terrapin, chigger, skunk, maize, manioc, succotash, tapioca, squash, mahogany, pecan, hickory, hurricane, tobacco, potato, tomato, toboggan, kayak, wampum, canoe...." Close to half of the states in the U.S. have Indian names; in Maine, the names of six of the sixteen counties, the highest mountain—Katahdin, the second largest lake—Sebago, and most of the major rivers all stem from an Indian origin, even if sometimes the names we use are anglicized versions of what the Indians said.

The sense of "personal liberty," as Jack Weatherford expressed it, which may have been the greatest gift the Native Americans gave us, does not seem, in non-Indian eyes, to coincide in them with another strong "American" value—the so-called "Protestant work ethic." That perceived lack has been a problem for Indians from the start, and still is. "Indians are lazy, they won't work their land," was an excuse used to deprive them of their hunting grounds—hunting wasn't seen as work. Nor is basket making, but pointing out that it takes hours of patient, painstaking effort to create a basket is at least a partial attempt to counterbalance the statistic that only 14 percent of Creative Apparel's workers at Indian Township are Passamaquoddy, doing repetitive, mind-numbing, non-creative, frankly boring work.

The traditionalist Penobscot woman ssipsis captures the free-spirited soul of her people well in *Molly Molasses and Me,* a series of sketches she has subtitled *A Collection of Living Adventures.* Her co-author is Georgia Mitchell, the "Molly Molasses" of the title. Although a Passamaquoddy, the latter took good-naturedly as her nickname that of the famed Penobscot consort of Old John Neptune. These two Wabanaki women love to travel and have camped all over Maine, other parts of New England, and the United States.

The piquancy of these tales, to me, lies in a sense they convey of how the protagonists maintain that "personal liberty" of their ancestors in a world "civilized" to the nth degree by development and our commercial economy.

For example, in the story called "Kaw Kaw Goose," they are in Boothbay Harbor and Molly Molasses recoils before the sign CLAMS AND LOBSTERS FOR SALE, muttering, "Paying for clams...." Although unspoken, her meaning is clear—*No way*—as they leave the fishermen's pier without buying any. After they reached a deserted beach park, they follow a kaw kaw goose—a crow—and its tapping on shells brings them to a bed of live mussels. Before long, they build a fire, cook the shellfish, gather some edible acorns, as well, and consume their feast, oblivious to the "Sunday people" just released from a nearby church who have strolled to the shore. After eating, writes ssipsis, "I felt like rolling down the sun-warmed, pine needle-covered hill and that's just what I did. Molly Molasses gave a hearty chuckle and the Sunday people just stared. Overhead, we heard the crow laugh."

Whether they are in California or the deserts of the

Southwest, the same picaresque feeling infuses their *adventures*. ssipsis has this to say about the cross-country trip they began on Mother's Day, leaving behind their families and familiar Wabanaki New England:

> From the hibernating eastern woodlands to the chaparral and sand and magic trees and cactus in bloom, we made a trip across the country to feed our curiosity and to fuel our spirit. The ordinary became mystical. Many shadows in early dawn and late night cast our imagination in legendary pursuit of ghosts and phantoms and shamans fighting with puny selves....
>
> And when the dawn came, I would have dug holes and found water, planted trees, made shade, ground corn into meal, and baked Tamales. I would have made each step, each thought, each action have meaning for I knew it had been before.
>
> But I had to hurry on.[3]

As a Maine historian, I was particularly attracted to one of their stories called "Old Bones." It was not so much the content of their adventure this time, which was the discovery of a skeleton—probably a dead dog—on the beach in a rarely visited and never manned Maine state park; it was the actual site I found of interest. For this incident occurred at Fort Point State Park and here was a bit of exquisite irony, I thought, that neither ssipsis nor Molly knew the history of the place. It was no less than the location of Fort Pownall, from which Governor Thomas Pownall set forth in 1759 on his trip up the Penobscot, laying claim to all of this land for King George II of England and establishing the precedent in subsequent negotiations with the Wabanakis that they had "submitted" to the English and forfeited their rights. Even in our modern-day Maine Land Claims dispute, an opponent like J. Russell Wiggins could cite Pownall's actions as a basis of his arguments against the Settlement and it is well known that John Adams, in winning the Peace Treaty of Paris from England in 1783 used Pownall's documents to secure Down East Maine for the U.S. Both women, Penobscot and Passamaquoddy, were standing on a headland, Cape Jellison, at the mouth of the Penobscot River, without knowing how critical that strategic spot had been to the lives of their respective tribes, and all they were seeing—and maybe appropriately so in the mystical tradition of their peoples—was the skeleton of a dead dog.

The great-grandfather of ssipsis was Joseph Nicolar, author of the 1893 *Life and Traditions of the Red Man*. She quotes him as writing: "The time of sadness covered the land with the arrival of the white man," then adds, "Perhaps in the telling of these tales [hers and Molly's] of the white man's touch another tale of happiness will be told." She is optimistic. She sees the highway of four and eight lanes on which they will be traveling "overgrown with moss and green grass and tall saplings of alder, willow, and birch." She describes herself and her companion as "scavengers from the old times, being driven in the present, and riding on hopes into the future.... We are native and allow the spirit of ourselves to drive us on to the next sunset."

A final thought of mine, like those of ssipsis and Molly, is about the future. In the course of writing this book, I have been looking at a number of modern-day American Indian publications that are now offered for subscription. They are impressive, full of color photographs and well-written articles that cover a multitude of issues and events in Indian life around the country. They show an ever-increasing sophistication among the new generations of Native Americans, much like the computer skills of Ed Bassett and Dale Mitchell at Pleasant Point. Although optimistic, these publications are also realistic and discuss openly problems that exist among various tribes. Their overall thrust, whether it be the *American Indian Report, Native Peoples Arts and Lifeways,* the quarterly publication of the *National Museum of the American Indian,* or *The Eagle's Nest* of the Native American Fish and Wildlife Society, is of an upbeat sense of forward movement, of accomplishment, and of averting threats, like the overwhelming defeat in the U.S. Senate of bill by Connecticut U.S. Senators Christopher Dodd and Joseph Lieberman for a moratorium of any further federal recognition of Indian tribes because of a situation in their state.

These publications are not pollyanna-ish. They talk openly of problems that exist among various tribes. But they show an ever-increasing sophistication among the new generations of Native Americans, much like the computer skills of Ed Bassett and Dana Mitchell at Pleasant Point.

The future in Maine of our tribes may be called unsettled, as it is in the title of this book, just as their past was anything but settled. Yet the changes I have witnessed in the conditions of the Penobscots, Passamaquoddy, Maliseets, and Micmacs since 1980 have been profound. They are infinitesimally small parts of our Maine life; population-wise, not even 1 percent. However, Maine could not be what it is without them, no more than the U.S. could be the U.S. without its Indian base. We still have much to learn *about* our Indian brethren here in the state we all inhabit, and *from* them, as well.

Stay tuned.

NOTES

[1] Judy Potts, *Adventure Tales of America: An Illustrated History of the United States: 1492–1877*, Vol. I. Dallas: Signal Media Corporation, 1994, page 154.

[2] Jack Weatherford, *Indian Givers: How the Indians of the Americas Transformed the World.* New York, Fawcett Columbione, 1988, pages 121–22.

[3] ssipsis and Georgia Mitchell, *Molly Molasses and Me: A Collection of Living Adventures.* Brooks, Maine: Little Letter Press/Robin Hood Books, 1988, page 60.

BIBLIOGRAPHY

Ahlin, John Howard. *Maine Rubicon: Downeast Settlers During the American Revolution.* Camden, Maine: Picton Press, 1966.

Allen, Paula Gunn. *Reservation: Reflections on Boundary-Busting, Border-Crossing Loose Cannons.* Lincoln, Massachusetts: Beacon Press, 1994.

American Indian Policy Review Commission. *Final Report.* Volumes 1 and 2. Washington, D.C.: U.S. Government Printing Office, 1977.

Anastas, Peter. *Glooskap's Children: Encounters with the Penobscot Indians of Maine.* Boston: Beacon Press, 1973.

Annals of the American Academy of Political and Social Science. *American Indians Today.* Philadelphia, March 1978.

Arel, Jules J. "German Prisoners of War in Maine, 1944–46," *Maine History.* Maine Historical Society Quarterly, Volume 34, Numbers 3–4, Winter–Spring, 1995.

Atlantic Geoscience Society. *The Last Billion Years.* Halifax, Nova Scotia: Nimbus Publishing, 2001.

At Loggerheads. Hallowell, Maine: Maine Indian Tribal–State Commission, 1997.

Baker, C. Alice. *True Stories of New England Captives.* Cambridge, Massachusetts: C. Alice Baker, 1897.

Banks, Ronald, et al. "Penobscot and Passamaquoddy Tribunal Claims Litigation Documents." Maine Attorney General's Office, Augusta, Maine, 1976–77. This is the research ordered by Attorney General Joseph Brennan to combat the Maine Indians' land claims, a massive effort led by a young University of Maine history professor in a losing cause.

Barry, William David. "Bogus Noses (with Apologies to André)," *Maine Life.* September 1979.

Barsh, Russell Lawrence and James Youngblood Henderson. *The Road.* Berkeley, California: University of California Press, 1980. An interesting book on national legal issues in Indian–white relations, with some imaginative proposals for changes in relevant American laws and policies.

Baxter, James Phinney. *The Baxter Manuscripts: A Documentary History of the State of Maine.* Second Series, Volume XVII. Portland, Maine: Fred L. Tower Company, 1913. Collections of the Maine Historical Society.

_____. Second Series, Volume XXII. Portland, Maine: Fred L. Tower Company, 1916.

_____. Second Series, Volume XXIV. Portland, Maine: Fred L. Tower Company, 1916.

_____. Second Series, Volume XXIII. Portland, Maine: Fred L. Tower
Company, 1916.

Beck, Horace. *The American Indian as a Sea Fighter in Colonial Times.*
Mystic, Connecticut: Marine History Association, 1959.

Benedict, Jeff. *Without Reservation: The Making of America's Most
Powerful Indian Tribe and Foxwoods, the World's Largest Casino.* New
York: HarperCollins, 2000. A muckraking attack on the Mashantucket Pequot Foxwoods Casino in Connecticut. The author has
come to Maine to fight the current Penobscot–Passamaquoddy
proposal for a casino.

Bennett, Dean. *Dirigo.* Camden, Maine: Down East Books, 1980.

Berger, Thomas R. *Village Journey: The Report of the Alaska Native Review
Commission.* New York: Hill and Wang, 1985.

Berkhofer, Robert F., Jr. *The White Man's Indian: Images of the American
Indian from Columbus to the Present.* New York: Random House,
Vintage Book, 1978.

Bordewich, Fergus M. *Killing the White Man's Indian: Reinventing Native
Americans at the End of the Twentieth Century.* New York: Random
House, 1997.

Bourque, Bruce J. *Twelve Thousand Years: American Indians in Maine.*
Lincoln, Nebraska: University of Nebraska Press, 2001.

Brain, Jeffrey P. *The Popham Colony.* Salem, Massachusetts: Peabody
Essex Museum, 2000.

Braun, Esther K. and David P. Braun. *The First Peoples of the Northeast.*
Lincoln, Massachusetts: Moccasin Hill Press, 1994.

Breyer, Justice Stephen. "The Cherokee Indians and the Supreme Court,"
Journal of Supreme Court History. Volume 25, Number 1. Boston
and Oxford, England: Blackwell Publishers, 2001.

Bridgham, Lawrence Donald. "Maine Public Lands, 1781–1795."
Dissertation, Boston University Graduate School, 1959.

Brodeur, Paul. *Restitution: The Land Claims of the Mashapee,
Passamaquoddy, and Penobscot Indians of New England.* Boston:
Northeastern University Press, 1985. The first book to detail the
Maine Indian Land Claims Settlement. Based on a series of *New
Yorker* pieces the author wrote in the 1980s.

Brown, Joseph Epes. *The Spiritual Legacy of the American Indian.* New
York: Crossroads Publishing Company, 1991.

Bruchac, Joseph. *The Waters Between: A Novel of the Dawn Land.*
Hanover, New Hampshire: University Press of New England, 1998.
A wonderful western Abenaki writer of fiction. This is one of a
series modeled on his people's legends.

Callahan, North. *Henry Knox, George Washington's General.* South
Brunswick and New York: A. S. Barnes Co., 1958.

Calloway, Colin G. *The Abenaki*. New York: Chelsea House Publishers, 1989.

_____. *Dawnland Encounters: Indians and Europeans in Northern New England*. Hanover, New Hampshire: University Press of New England, 1991.

_____. *The Western Abenaki of Vermont, 1600–1800: War, Migration, and the Survival of an Indian People*. Norman, Oklahoma: University of Oklahoma Press, 1990.

Clark, Charles E. *The Eastern Frontier: The Settlement of Northern New England, 1610–1763*. New York: Alfred A. Knopf, 1970.

Colden, Cadwallader. *The History of the Five Indian Nations of Canada*. New York: Allerton Book Company, 1922.

Coleman, Kenneth, ed. *A History of Georgia*. Athens, Georgia: University of Georgia Press, 1991.

Cook-Lynn, Elizabeth. *Anti-Indianism in Modern America: A Voice from Tatekeya's Earth*. Urbana, Illinois: University of Illinois Press, 2001. A fiery attack on white Americans and their attitudes, past and present, toward Native Americans.

Cronon, William. *Changes in the Land: Indians, Colonists, and the Ecology of New England*. New York: Hill and Wang, 1983.

Currier, Coburn Leo. "Wabanaki Ethno-History: Five Centuries of Becoming Indian." Ph.D. dissertation, Washington State University, 1978.

Davis, Stephen A. *Mi'kmaq*. Halifax, Nova Scotia: Nimbus Publishing, 1997. Part of a series, *People of the Maritimes*.

Debo, Angie. *And Still the Waters Run: The Betrayal of the Five Civilized Tribes*. Princeton, New Jersey: Princeton University Press, 1991 (reprint of 1940 book).

Delbanco, Andrew. *The Real American Dream*. Cambridge, Massachusetts: Harvard University Press, 1999.

Deloria, Vine, Jr. *Behind the Trail of Broken Treaties: An Indian Declaration of Independence*. Austin, Texas: University of Texas Press, 1985. This well-known Indian writer presents a complete picture of contemporary events in the United States involving whites and Indians.

Deloria, Vine, Jr., and David E. Wilkins. *Tribes, Treaties, and Constitutional Tribulations*. Austin, Texas: University of Texas Press, 1999.

de Tocqueville, Alexis. *Democracy in America*. New York: HarperCollins Perennial Classic, 1969.

Drinnon, Richard. *Facing West: Indian Hating and Empire Building*. New York: Schocken Books, 1980.

Dunn, Richard S. *Puritans and Yankees: The Winthrop Dynasty of New*

England. Princeton, New Jersey: Princeton University Press, 1962.

Eckstorm, Fannie Hardy. *Old John Neptune and Other Maine Indian Shamans.* Orono, Maine: University of Maine Press, Marsh Island Reprint, 1980. Maine's indispensable chronicler of the late nineteenth century—especially good for her depictions of the Penobscots.

_____. *Penobscot Man.* Somersworth, New Hampshire: New Hampshire Publishing Company, 1972.

Eisler, Kim Isaac. *Revenge of the Pequots: How a Small Native American Tribe Created the World's Most Profitable Casino.* New York: Simon and Schuster, 2001. Another version of the story of the Mashantucket Pequots, told from a much friendlier vantage than in the Jeff Benedict book.

Erickson, Vincent O. "Passamaquoddies and Protestants: Deacon Sockabason and the Reverend Kellogg of the Society for Propagating the Gospel." Dissertation, University of New Brunswick.

Farb, Peter. *Man's Rise to Civilization: As Shown by the Indians of North America from Primeval Times to the Coming of the Industrial State.* New York: Avon Books, 1968.

Fell, Barry. *America BC: Europeans Living in America 4,500 Years Before Columbus.* New York: Quadrangle, New York Times Books, 1976.

Fey, Harold E. and D'Arcy McNickle. *Indians and Other Americans: Two Ways of Life Meet.* New York: Harper and Row, 1971.

Flannery, Tim. *The Eternal Frontier: An Ecological History of North America and Its Peoples.* New York: Atlantic Monthly Press, 2001.

Forbes, Jack D. *The Indian in America's Past.* Englewood Cliffs, New Jersey: Prentice-Hall, 1964.

Foster, Benjamin Browne. *Downeast Diary.* Orono, Maine: University of Maine Press, 1975.

Gleach, Frederick W. *Powhatan's World and Colonial Virginia.* Lincoln, Nebraska: University of Nebraska Press, 1997.

Godfrey, John E. *The Ancient Penobscot.* Maine Historical Society Collections, Series 1, Volume 7.

Grumet, Robert S. *Northeastern Indian Lives, 1632–1816.* Amherst, Massachusetts: University of Massachusetts Press, 1996.

Hart, Robert Thompson. *The Nicatous History.* Privately published.

Hatzam, A. Leon. *The True Story of Hiawatha and History of the Six Nation Indians.* Toronto: McClelland and Stewart, 1925.

Hauptman, Laurence M. and James D. Wherry, eds. *The Pequots in Southern New England: The Fall and Rise of an American Indian Nation.* Norman, Oklahoma: University of Oklahoma Press, 1990.

Hearings of the Select Committee on Indian Affairs. U.S. Senate, 96th

Congress, Second Session, on S.2829. Washington, D.C.: U.S. Government Printing Office, 1980. An absolutely essential compilation of material on the Maine Indian Land Claims Settlement issue, including reams of historical material.

Historical Collections, Piscataquis County, Maine. Dover-Foxcroft, Maine: Piscataquis County Historical Society, Observer Press, 1910.

Hoxie, Frederick, ed. *Indians in American History.* Arlington Heights, Illinois: Harlan Davidson, Inc., 1988.

Hultkrantz, Ake. *The Religions of the American Indians.* Berkeley, California: University of California Press, 1979.

Jaimes, M. Annette, ed. *The State of Native America.* Boston: South End Press, 1992.

Jeffer, Susan. *Hiawatha.* New York: Puffin Pied Piper Books, 1983.

Jennings, Francis. *The Ambiguous Iroquois Empire: The Covenant Chain Confederation of Indian Tribes with English Colonies, from Its Beginning to the Lancaster Treaty of 1744.* New York: W. W. Norton and Company, 1984.

_____. *The Invasion of America: Indians, Colonialism, and the Cant of Conquest.* New York: W. W. Norton and Company, 1976.

Johansen, Bruce E. *Life and Death in Mohawk Country.* Golden, Colorado: North American Press, 1993.

Johnson, Steven F. *Ninnuock (The People): The Algonkian People of New England.* Marlborough, Massachusetts: Bliss Publishing Company, 1995.

Josephy, Alvin, Jr. "New England Indians, Then and Now," *The Pequots in Southern New England.* Norman, Oklahoma: University of Oklahoma Press, 1990.

Josselyn, John. *New England Rarities Discovered.* Boston: Massachusetts Historical Society, reprint, 1972, first printed 1672. Josselyn, a traveler to Maine in the 1600s, is always fun to read and was probably the first Englishman to write about Maine Indians.

Karr, Ronald Dale. *Indian New England, 1524–1674.* Pepperell, Massachusetts: Branch Line Press, 1999.

Kayworth, Alfred E. *Abenaki Warrior: The Life and Times of Chief Escumbuit.* Brookline, Massachusetts: Brandon Publishing Company, 1998.

Kazimiroff, Theodore L. *The Last Algonquin.* New York: Dell Publishing Company, 1982. A lovely story about a boy (the author's father) on Long Island and his friendship with a local Indian trying to live a traditional life in the shadows of New York City.

Kinney, J. P. *A Continent Lost, A Civilization Won: Indian Land Tenure in America.* Baltimore, Maryland: The Johns Hopkins Press, 1937.

Krech, Shepard, III. *The Ecological Indian: Myth and History.* New York:

W. W. Norton and Company, 1999.

Lafitau, Joseph-François. *Moeurs des Sauvages Americains*. Paris, France: François Maspero, 1983.

Laws of Maine, 1860. Augusta, Maine: Stevens and Sayward, Printers to the State.

Leach, Douglas Edward. *Flintlock and Tomahawk: New England in King Philip's War*. New York: W. W. Norton and Company, 1958.

Leader, Judith C. "An Ethno History of the Passamaquoddy of Maine." Ph.D. dissertation, Boston University Graduate School, 1995.

Leamon, James S. *Revolution Downeast: The War for American Independence in Maine*. Amherst, Massachusetts: University of Massachusetts Press, 1993.

Leland, Charles G. *The Algonquin Legends of New England*. Boston, Massachusetts: Houghton–Miflin, 1884. A classic book, known as much for its perhaps fanciful speculations about Wabanaki culture as for its pioneer retelling of their legends.

Lepore, Jill. *The Name of War*. New York: Random House, Vintage Books, 1999.

Lescarbot, Marc. *History of New France*. Volume III. New York: Green Press, 1968. Reprint of a seventeenth-century work.

Leupp, Francis E. *In Red Man's Land: A Study of the American Indian*. New York: Fleming H. Revell Company, 1914. Leupp was a director of the Bureau of Indian Affairs.

Levett, Christopher. *Christopher Levett's Voyage, 1623–24*. Portland, Maine: Maine Historical Society, 1988.

MacDougall, Pauleena M. "Indian Island, Maine, 1780–1930." Ph.D. dissertation, University of Maine Graduate School, Orono, Maine, 1995.

MacLeish, William H. *The Day Before America: Changing the Nature of the Continent*. Boston: Houghton-Mifflin, 1994.

Maine Indians, Brief Summary: The People of the Early Dawn. Perry, Maine: Pleasant Point Bilingual Program, Joseph A. Nicholas, director, text by Alberta Francis.

Maine Indian Newsletter. An important source of news and attitudes among Maine Indians from their point of view, published in the early 1970s.

Maine Law Review. Volume 31, Number 1, 1979.

Marriott, Alice and Carol K. Rachlin. *American Epic: The Story of the American Indian*. New York: New American Library, 1969.

Mather, Cotton. *Decennium Luctuosum*. Printed by B. Green and J. Allen for Samuel Phillips, 1699, at the Brick Shop near the Old Meeting House, Boston. The famed Puritan minister writes of King Philip's War and expresses his violent hatred of Indians and defenders of

Indians. A candid revelation of historical prejudice from one of the chief instigators of the Salem Witch Trials.

Maurault, J. A. *Histoire des Abenakis, Depuis 1605 Jusqu'ª Nos Jours.* Québec: Gazette de Sorel, 1866.

McBride, Bunny. *Molly Spotted Elk: A Penobscot in Paris.* Norman, Oklahoma: University of Oklahoma Press, 1995.

_____. *Women of the Dawn.* Lincoln, Nebraska: University of Nebraska Press, 1999. Both books provide valuable scholarship on the achievements of Wabanaki women.

McKenney, Thomas L. *Memoirs.* Volume I and II. New York: Paine and Burgess Company, 1846. A real find—the forgotten figure of the first director of the Bureau of Indian Affairs and his views of Indian-white relations before and after his being fired by President Andrew Jackson for being too sympathetic to the Indians.

McNickle, D'Arcy. *They Came Here First: The Epic of the American Indian.* Philadelphia and New York: J. P. Lippincott Company, 1949.

Milton, Giles. *Big Chief Elizabeth: The Adventures and Fate of the First English Colonists in America.* New York: Farrar, Straus, and Girard, 2000.

Mintz, Max M. *Seeds of Empire: The American Revolutionary Conquest of the Iroquois.* New York: New York University Press, 1999.

Moorehead, Warren K. *The American Indian in the United States, 1850–1914.* Andover, Massachusetts: Andover Press, 1914.

Nash, Captain Charles E. *The Indians of the Kennebec.* Hallowell, Maine: Valley Publishers, 1994.

Newell, Catherine. *Molly Ockett.* Bethel, Maine: Bethel Historical Society, 1981.

Nicolar, Joseph. *The Life and Traditions of the Red Man.* Bangor, Maine: C. H. Glass and Company Printers, 1893. An unsung gem of Maine historic literature; one of the first, if not the first, book by a Maine Indian, a Penobscot.

Norton, David. *Sketches of the Town of Old Town.* Bangor, Maine: S. G. Robinson Printers, 1881.

O'Brien, Sharon. *American Indian Tribal Governments.* Norman, Oklahoma: University of Oklahoma Press, 1989.

Parabola Magazine. Summer 2002. New York.

Parkman, Francis. *The Conspiracy of Pontiac,* Volume II. Boston: Little Brown and Company, 1851, reprinted 1890.

_____. *La Salle and the Discovery of the Great West.* New York: Random House, Modern Library, 1999 (original edition 1879).

Peckham, Howard H. *The Colonial Wars, 1689–1762.* Chicago: University of Chicago Press, 1964.

Perley, Henry (Chief Red Eagle). *Aboriginally Yours.* Greenville, Maine: Moosehead Communications, Inc., 1997.

Porter, Robert B. "Indian Law and Sovereignty." Seminar. Wampanoag Tribe of Gay Head/Aquinnah, Massachusetts, August 20, 2001. My initial introduction into the complicated world of Indian law in the United States.

Potts, Judy. *Adventure Tales of America: An Illustrated History of the United States, 1492–1877.* Dallas, Texas: Signal Media Corporation, 1994.

Power, Samantha. *A Problem from Hell: America and the Age of Genocide.* New York: Basic Books, 2002.

Priest, Loring Benson. *Uncle Sam's Stepchildren: The Reformation of United States Indian Policy.* Lincoln, Nebraska: University of Nebraska Press, 1975.

Pritchard, Evan T. *No Word for Time: The Way of the Algonquin People.* San Francisco/Tulsa: Council Oak Books, 1997.

Proctor, Ralph W. *Proctor Report, 1942.* Augusta, Maine.

Prucha, Francis Paul. *The Indians in American Society.* Berkeley, California: University of California Press, 1985.

Purdy, John Lloyd, ed. *The Legacy of D'Arcy McNickle: Writer, Historian, Activist.* Norman, Oklahoma: University of Oklahoma Press, 1996.

Reid, John G. *Maine, Charles II, and Massachusetts.* Portland, Maine: Maine Historical Society, 1977.

Richter, Daniel K. *Facing East from Indian Country: A Native History of Early America.* Cambridge, Massachusetts: Harvard University Press, 2001.

Roberts, Kenneth. *Arundel.* Camden, Maine: Down East Books reprint. Original published 1930.

Rolde, Neil. *The Interrupted Forest: A History of Maine's Wildlands.* Gardiner, Maine: Tilbury House, 2001.

Ross, A. C. *Mitakuye Oyasin, We Are All Related: America Before Columbus, Based on the Oral History of Thirty-Three Tribes.* Denver, Colorado: Wicóni Wasté Publishers, 1989.

Russell, Howard S. *Indian New England Before the Mayflower.* Hanover, New Hampshire: University Press of New England, 1980.

Scully, Diana. *A Summary of the Activities of the Maine Indian Tribal–State Commission.* Paper. Hallowell, Maine: Maine Indian Tribal–State Commission, 2003. .

Shay, Florence Nicola. *History of the Penobscot Tribe of Indians.* Pamphlet, no date nor publisher. An intriguing, short "protest" piece, authored by an activist Penobscot woman—one of the earliest expressions of activism on Indian Island.

Simmons, William S. *Spirit of the New England Tribes: Indian History and Folklore, 1620–1984.* Hanover, New Hampshire: University Press of New England, 1986.

Smith, David C. and Edward O. Shriver. *Maine, A History through Selected Readings.* Dubuque, Iowa: Kendall Hunt Publishing Company, 1985.

Smith, Marian Whitney. "John Neptune's Encounter with Pamola," *Down East Magazine.* Camden, Maine: February–March, 1956.

Snow, Dean R. *The Archaeology of New England.* New York: Academic Press, 1980.

Soctomah, Donald. *Passamaquoddy at the Turn of the Century, 1890–1920.* An exhaustively collected body of photographs, newspaper articles, and commentary on Passamaquoddy life, hitherto lost to public view; the first in a series, with proceeds going to the building of a museum at Indian Township.

Speck, Frank G. *Penobscot Man.* Orono, Maine: University of Maine Press, 1997.

_____. "Penobscot Shamanism." Reprinted from the minutes of the American Anthropological Association, Volume VI, Number 3, 1936.

ssipsis (Eugenia Thompson) and Georgia Mitchell. *Molly Molasses and Me: A Collection of Living Adventures.* Brooks, Maine: Little Letter Press, Robin Hood Books, 1988. A fun collection of true stories of the adventures, in Maine and elsewhere, of two Maine Indian women, one Penobscot, one Passamaquoddy.

Starbird, Charles M. *The Indians of the Androscoggin Valley.* Lewiston, Maine: Lewiston Journal Printshop, 1928.

Stevens, Susan MacCulloch. *Passamaquoddy Economic Development in Cultural and Historical Perspective.* Mt. Vernon, Maine: 1973. A serious work of analysis in the 1970s by the wife of the then Passamaquoddy governor, John Stevens.

Taylor, Aline S. *The French Baron of Pentagoet: Baron St. Castin and the Struggle for Empire in Early New England.* Camden, Maine: Picton Press, 1998.

Thayer, Mildred N. and Mrs. Edward W. Ames. *Brewer, Orrington, Holden, and Eddington: History and Families.* Brewer, Maine: 1962. Privately published.

Thoreau, Henry David. Dudley Lunt, ed. *The Maine Woods.* New York: Bramhall House, 1950 reprint.

Time Magazine. December 16, 2002.

Trask, Haunani-Kay. *From a Native Daughter: Colonialism and Sovereignty in Hawaii.* Honolulu, Hawaii: University of Hawaii Press, 1999.

Trevelyan, George Otto. *The American Revolution.* New York: David

McKay Company, 1965, reprint.

van Sertima, Ivan. *They Came Before Columbus: The African Presence in Ancient America.* New York: Random House, 1976.

Verrill, A. Hyatt. *Our Indians.* New York: G. P. Putnam's Sons, 1935.

Versluis, Arthur. *The Elements of Native American Traditions.* Shaftsbury, Dorset, England: Element Books, 1993.

Vilari, Mary Ann. "The Historical Precedents and Recent Developments of the Maine Indians' Bid for Recognition." Honors paper in History, Bowdoin College, Brunswick, Maine, 1975.

Wabanaki Collection. Huntington Free Library, Bronx, New York.

Wabanakis of Maine and the Maritimes. Bath, Maine: American Friends Service Committee, 1989.

Walker, Willard, Robert Conkling, and Gregory Buesing. "Chronological Account of the Wabanaki Confederacy," in *A Collection of Articles of Maine Indians.* Maine Indian Program, American Friends Service Committee, University Press of America, 1980.

Wallace, Paul. *White Roots of Peace: The Iroquois Book of Life.* Santa Fe, New Mexico: Clear Light Publishers, 1994.

Weatherford, Jack. *Indian Givers: How the Indians of the Americas Transformed the World.* New York: Fawcett Columbine, 1988.

_____. *Native Roots: How the Indians Enriched America.* New York: Fawcett Columbine, 1991.

Wellman, Trina. *Louis Francis Sockalexis: The Life Story of a Penobscot Indian.* Augusta, Maine: Maine Department of Indian Affairs, 1975.

Weyler, Rex. *Blood of the Land: The Government and Corporate War Against the American Indian Movement.* New York: Everett House Publishers, 1982.

Wherry, James. *The History of Maliseets and Micmacs in Aroostook County.* Association of Aroostook Indians, 1979.

Whipple, Chandler. *The Indian and the White Man in New England: First Encounter.* Stockbridge, Massachusetts: Berkshire Traveller Press, 1972.

White, Robert H. *Tribal Assets: The Rebirth of Native America.* New York: Henry Holt and Company, 1990.

Whitehead, Ruth Holmes. *Six Micmac Stories.* Halifax, Nova Scotia: Nimbus Publishing and the Nova Scotia Museum, 1992.

Wickwire, Franklin B. *British Subministers and Colonial America.* Princeton, New Jersey: Princeton University Press, 1966. An intriguing look at behind-the-scenes eighteenth-century British bureaucrats and how they affected policy toward Indians and American colonists.

Wilbur, C. Keith. *The New England Indians.* Old Saybrook, Connecticut:

Globe Pequot Press, 1996.

Williamson, William Durkee. *The History of the State of Maine.* Two volumes. Hallowell, Maine: Glazier, Masters, and Company, 1832.

Wiseman, Frederick Matthew. *The Voice of the Dawn: An Autohistory of
the Abenaki Nation.* Hanover, New Hampshire: University Press of
New England, 2001. A fine book by a western Abenaki from
Vermont, showing how his people have survived to this day.

Wood, Ethel M. "The Maine Indians and Their Relations with the
White Settlers." Series. *Sprague's Journal of Maine History.* Dover,
Maine: April 1921–March 1922.

INDEX